DARWIN
SPITFIRES

ANTHONY COOPER is a Brisbane school teacher. He is a former glider pilot instructor, has a PhD on German aviation history and is the author of *HMAS* Bataan, *1952* (UNSW Press, 2010).

This book is dedicated to that anonymous army of clerks, fitters, riggers, armourers, repairers, mechanics, drivers, orderlies, operators and controllers without whom defeat was assured.

DARWIN SPITFIRES

THE REAL BATTLE FOR AUSTRALIA

ANTHONY COOPER

Anniversary Edition

NEWSOUTH

A NewSouth book

Published by
NewSouth Publishing
University of New South Wales Press Ltd
University of New South Wales
Sydney NSW 2052
AUSTRALIA
https://unsw.press/

© Anthony Cooper 2022
First published 2011

10 9 8 7 6 5 4 3 2 1

A catalogue record for this
book is available from the
National Library of Australia

ISBN: 9781742237787 (paperback)
        9781742238616 (ebook)
        9781742239538 (ePDF)

Design Di Quick
Cover design Peter Long
Cover images (Top) Milingimbi Island, Northern Territory, 21 November 1943. A spitfire aircraft of 452 Squadron, Royal Australian Air Force flying escort duty. AWM Negative 060747; (Bottom) The 'Wingco' (in white shirt) with a mixed group of 452/457 Squadron pilots at 452 Squadron dispersals, Strauss airfield. Left to right: back row – F/O Phil Adam, F/O Ross Williams, F/Sgt 'Darky' McDowell, W/C Clive Caldwell, F/O Tim Goldsmith, F/L Ted Hall, Sgt Col Duncan; front row – Sgt Freddie White, F/O John Gould, F/Sgt Paul Tully. AWM Negative NWA0262
Printer Griffin Press

Contents

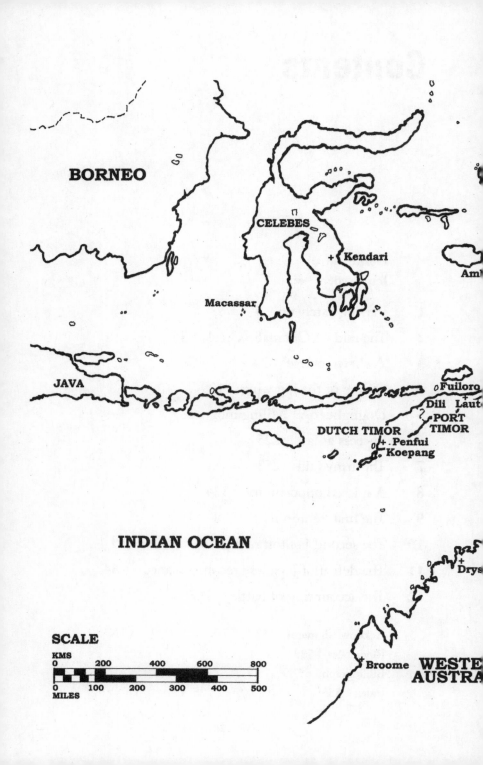

The North-Western Area
battle front, 1942–43
Trudy Cooper

PACIFIC OCEAN

Morotai

Noemfoor Is.

Hollandia

Babo

DUTCH
NEW GUINEA

We Wak

NEW
GUINEA

Kai Is.

Langoerr

Dobo

Tabertane

PAPUA

Tanimbar Is.

ARAFURA
SEA

Merauke

TORRES STRAIT

Horn Is.

Melville Is.

Millingimbi

Wessel Is.

rst Is.

Darwin
+Batchelor

ron Is.

+ Katherine

GULF
OF
CARPENTARIA

yndham

NORTHERN
TERRITORY

QUEENSLAND

Preface

Luckily for authors, war history retains a healthy readership, but as a genre it has long been distorted by both the parochialism of authors and readers and by the lingering tints of wartime propaganda and official misinformation. More than seventy years after World War Two, it is high time for both authors and readers to step back and obtain critical distance from the officially sanctioned narratives which have been told about that war (not to mention all the others!).

My second book, *Darwin Spitfires*, was an attempt to do just that. First published more than a decade ago, it offered a revisionist history of the air battles against the Japanese air raids upon Australia's Top End in 1943. Outline summaries of the raids had previously appeared in other books, and these had accepted and repeated the optimistic gloss provided by Australia's wartime propagandists, according to which Australia's Spitfire Wing shot down over 70 Japanese aircraft in air combat. It would have done wonders for book sales if I could have told *that* story, but after immersing myself in the primary sources and assessing all the evidence published by other researchers, I had instead to tell the real story, one in which the Spitfires shot down only 28 Japanese aircraft. Fearing that this more modest version of the story might upset my readers, I sought to justify my conclusions by providing a narrative sufficiently detailed and evidenced as to lay some claim to being 'authoritative' or 'definitive'. After that I sat back and waited to see if anyone objected to my conclusions or responded by publishing a revisionist account containing new evidence to correct my version of events.

Instead, the book was positively reviewed, mentioned positively in air war history blogs, used as the basis for a popular account of the campaign for the enthusiast readership,[1] and even formed the basis of an expansion set for the *Fighting Wings* series of military board games.[2] Air Vice Marshal Brian Weston used the book as the analytical basis for a monograph on the development of the wartime RAAF, aimed at a professional air force readership.[3] Then, Dr Tom Lewis's truly definitive summary of all the Japanese raids on northern Australia,[4] built upon the enviable access he had gained into Japanese wartime records, was published in 2017. I bought it at once and scanned it anxiously to see if his conclusions of the results of the fighting differed from mine. They did not: Dr Lewis's 'scorecard' closely paralleled my own.

I therefore consider that *Darwin Spitfires* has stood the test of time and am happy to present it again to the readers with only minor amendments. I hope the readers of 2022 enjoy it as much as did the readers of 2011, and that they learn something along the way about how wars are fought and how versions of history are shaped and reshaped for specific purposes.

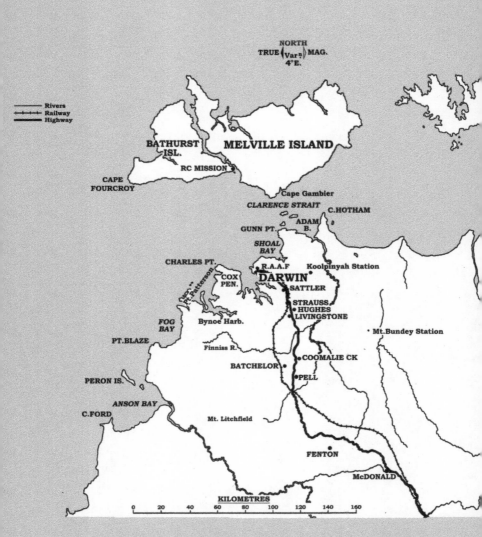

Darwin combat area
Trudy Cooper

NORTH
TRUE (Varⁿ) MAG.
4°E.

Rivers
Railway
Highway

BATHURST
ISL.

MELVILLE ISLAND

RC MISSION

CAPE
FOURCROY

Cape Gambier

CLARENCE STRAIT

C.HOTHAM

GUNN PT.

ADAM
B.

SHOAL
BAY

CHARLES PT.

R.A.A.F

Koolpinyah Station

COX
PEN.

Pt.Patterson

DARWIN

SATTLER

FOG
BAY

Bynoe Harb.

STRAUSS
HUGHES
LIVINGSTONE

PT.BLAZE

Finniss R.

Mt.Bundey Station

PERON IS.

BATCHELOR

COOMALIE CK

PELL

ANSON BAY

C.FORD

Mt. Litchfield

FENTON

McDONALD

KILOMETRES

0   20   40   60   80   100   120   140   160

Introduction

Many Australians are aware of the great bombing raid that struck Darwin on 19 February 1942, but few are aware of what followed. For almost two years, the airspace over north-west Australia was routinely penetrated by Japanese raids, a total of more than 70 being tallied against targets that included not only the area around Darwin, but places further along the coast such as Broome, Wyndham, Drysdale Mission (present-day Kalumburu) and Milingimbi Island. The Japanese air offensive extended as far west as the Pilbara region in Western Australia, as far south as Katherine and as far east as Arnhem Land, on the western edge of the Gulf of Carpentaria.

The first raid occurred in February 1942 and the last in November 1943, so the campaign was broadly of two years' duration. Within this timeframe, the Japanese waged two daylight raiding campaigns, one in each of the respective dry seasons: March–August 1942 and March–September 1943. The 1942 campaign of day raids was opposed by the 49th Fighter Group of the United States Army Air Forces (USAAF), while the 1943 campaign was opposed by the Royal Australian Air Force's (RAAF) No. 1 Fighter Wing, made up of both Australian and British units.

This book provides a detailed narrative of the 1943 season of raids, because the defence of Darwin by Commonwealth Spitfire pilots is an important and dramatic national story – but one that has been neglected in Australian history writing. The 19 February raid has been the subject of a number of books since the 1960s, whereas the ongoing raids afterwards have received little attention, with the result that the majority of Australians have no idea that they even occurred. Even the 2001 *Centenary History of the RAAF* avoided any reference to this campaign: despite one of its chapters being entitled 'The Battle for Australia', this book strangely ignored the only sustained campaign where Australians (along with Americans and Britons) fought and died in the direct defence of the Australian mainland. The original Australian Official History made the best effort to document the 1943 air battles, but has apparently been little read. Only one full-length book exclusively devoted to the topic has ever been published, by Jim Grant, a 1 Fighter Wing veteran. The depth of historical and cultural neglect of 1 Fighter Wing's story is shown by the review of Grant's book in the *RAAF News*, which unselfconsciously referred to the 1943 defensive campaign as 'little known operations over Darwin'.

Moreover, 1 Fighter Wing's combat record has been shrouded in controversy among the specialist aviation readership ever since Christopher Shores entered the field in the 1970s, for this pioneering British historian used newly accessed Japanese sources to dispute the wing's claimed victory tally. In short, the Spitfire pilots were credited at the time with more than 60 Japanese aircraft 'confirmed' shot down throughout the 1943 raids, whereas the research into Japanese records commissioned by Shores supports less than one-third this number of losses. Thus the whole combat reputation of the RAAF and Royal Air Force (RAF) Spitfire units that defended Darwin has unavoidably been brought into question. Most authors, both

British and Australian, have responded to this research by ignoring it. However, if indeed the Spitfire pilots did perform poorly in their air combat operations against the Japanese, the historian owes it to posterity to inquire into the reasons for this. This book seeks not only to provide a detailed and textured narrative of a neglected story, but also to analyse problems and to account for failures.

By telling the story of the Australian and British Spitfire pilots in 1943, I hope that Australians will recover a slice of national memory. The 1942–43 air raids on Darwin constitute the only sustained and intensive direct assault on Australian mainland territory in the whole of World War II – indeed, in the whole history of post-1788 Australia. In a war where Australians fought and died overseas, the pilots who lost their lives in this campaign met their deaths in Australian skies, on Australian soil and in the waters off the Australian coast. It is a good story: in 1943 a small band of inexperienced Australian and British fighter pilots, numbering few more than 100, fought an ongoing air battle in defence of Australia's front-line northern base, flying against a formidably skilled and proficient opponent who invariably outnumbered them. If there has ever been a chapter of Australia's military history that needs to be rediscovered, this compelling and dramatic story is it.

A note on units of measurement

In line with contemporary aviation practice, altitude references in this book are given in feet, and airspeed in knots (nautical miles per hour):

3.28 feet = 1 metre
1 knot = 1.85 km/h.

Otherwise, metric is used for distances. Longer distances are thus given in kilometres:

1 mile = 1.61 kilometres.

The sources use yards as the unit of measure for ranges and close distances, and for simplicity and roundness I have simply replaced yards with metres in this narrative. Pilots' visual estimates of range were typically inaccurate, and thus it is purely academic whether the range was 500 metres instead of 455, or 50 metres instead of 45:

1 yard = 0.91 metres.

Gun calibres are given in the original form, thus 7.7 mm for Japanese machine guns but .303 inch for British:

1 inch = 25.4 mm.

Bomb sizes are referred to in kilograms, as per the Japanese original:

1 kilogram = 2.2 pounds.

Fuel tank capacities are given in imperial gallons, as per the original sources:

1 imperial gallon = 4.55 litres or 1.2 US gallons.

1
Playing catch-up

The great raid on Darwin on 19 February 1942 needs little introduction, having assumed almost legendary status in popular Australian history. This dramatic day, when the war came so suddenly and violently to the Australian continent, understandably triggered a healthy output of historical narratives. By the 1960s, detailed accounts had been provided in the official histories of all three of Australia's services, as well as in Douglas Lockwood's definitive full-length account. Since then, this story has been regularly revived in the form of popular histories, memoirs, biographies, and even a movie: it is clear that the story of the 19 February raid has been well told, as it deserves to be. From the perspective of this book's account of the ongoing 1943 bombing campaign, that titanic first raid is noteworthy for two aspects: the massive force used by the Japanese, and the nonexistent state of the air defence.

The missing RAAF fighter force

The vast Japanese air armada on 19 February had been effectively unopposed, due to the failure of successive Australian governments to build up a defensive system in the north or to create a fighter force within the RAAF. There was not a single fighter aircraft in Australia, and this did not change between the outbreak of the war against Germany in September 1939 and the outbreak of the Pacific War in December 1941, despite clear awareness in Canberra of the very high likelihood of hostilities with Japan. Thus the home-based RAAF went through the early part of the war with no fighters, no current fighter pilots and little ongoing tradition or expertise in fighter operations.

This was because successive Australian governments had gambled that Britain's Singapore base would provide strategic protection to Australia. By this logic, if the 'Singapore Strategy' worked as advertised, there would be no need to establish a defensive fighter force on the Australian continent. If there were no fighters, there would be no need for the network of bases, radar stations and logistical systems required to support successful fighter action. According to this script, sheltered behind its Singapore shield, the home-based RAAF would merely need to patrol the sea approaches and mount air strikes against any of the small-scale seaborne forays that might temporarily slip through the defence shield further north.

In 1941, despite the steady escalation of Japan's war threats, Britain's Air Ministry was still able to make the rather patronising assertion that Australian demands for fighters were based on psychological grounds only, lacking real military justification. Working from this foundation, the RAAF's Chief of Air Staff, Air Chief Marshal Sir Charles Burnett (a British officer seconded from the RAF), had meanwhile been able to gut the home-based air force of its potential combat capability, instead turning it into a huge training machine to churn out aircrew for the RAF's expensive war against Hitler's Germany, as part of the Empire Air Training Scheme (EATS). The effect of this generous allocation of manpower and resources to the European war can be demonstrated by some simple statistics: the RAAF's entire home-based front-line strength at the outbreak of the Pacific War (ignoring the non-combat-worthy Wirraways) numbered a mere 53 Hudsons and 12 Catalinas – this for a service that in 1941 alone had trained 1367 pilots and sent almost 3000 trained aircrew to the United Kingdom.

Thus 1942 dawned without any credible means for Australia to defend itself against air attack, anywhere. Although the RAAF's failure to provide any air defence at all on 19 February was highly discreditable, it is likely that the outcome would have been little different had it actually possessed a fighter force at Darwin. It is most likely that any counterfactual Darwin-based RAAF fighters would have been accorded the same rough treatment as the Japanese handed out to the fighter garrisons at Pearl Harbor, Clark Air Base, Wake Island, Singapore, Sumatra, Ceylon and Midway. The only fighter types available in 1941 were Buffaloes or Hurricanes, and both largely failed in air combat against the Japanese. Against the great raid of 19 February, a weak force of RAAF fighters at Darwin would have merely provided more scoring opportunities for the rampant Zeros.

Air defence at last – the USAAF to the rescue

There were no further raids in February 1942, but March saw the start of an air campaign of harassment and reconnaissance against Darwin, with alternating fighter sweeps and unescorted bomber raids. Although Darwin and its airfields were attacked without hindrance, these raiding forces of fewer than ten aircraft were unlikely to have much effect.

In conjunction with this sharp downgrading of the Japanese raids, Darwin's situation improved further with the arrival of the 9th Pursuit Squadron (9th PS) of the United States Army Air Forces (USAAF) in late March. This American P-40 unit was the vanguard of its parent unit, the 49th Pursuit Group (49th PG), which was also under orders to move north. From the moment the 9th PS flew into the battered RAAF base, Darwin finally had some measure of air defence; the days of easy victories for the Japanese were coming to an end.

The Japanese responded to the American challenge by increasing the size of their raiding forces, and on 25 April for the first time since 19 February they committed an entire bomber group – after the arrival in Timor of the main body of the Takao Bomber Air Group upon the running-down of the successful Philippines campaign. After good successes earlier in April, the 49th PG found itself in a hard campaign in which the experienced Japanese, in their higher performing aircraft, held the upper hand. The loss rate of the Japanese bombers dropped from the alarming figure of 13 per cent, in the period up to the Anzac Day raid, to only 1 per cent in the six raids that followed.

Over the entire five months of this defensive campaign, the US pilots claimed 66 Japanese aircraft shot down. However, fighter pilots in the early part of World War II often overclaimed by a ratio of about three to one, and the 49th was no different. By a collation of accounts which have accessed Japanese records, it seems that, in total, the admitted Japanese loss was about 21 aircraft (13 bombers, seven fighters and one photo-reconnaissance aircraft). If these figures are accepted, and placed against the 19 P-40s that were lost in air combat, it would seem that the Americans sustained a kill-to-loss ratio of slightly more than 1:1 – a typical enough performance in defensive fighter combat using first-generation fighters in the early war period.

Even if they had not done as brilliantly as they had thought, the US pilots had done well, for they had imposed some attrition upon the Japanese, and perhaps more importantly they had completely defeated the enemy's intention to destroy the Darwin fighter force. According to Imperial Navy airpower doctrine, its land-based bomber groups were to deliver smashing blows against any Allied bases that threatened the Japanese defensive perimeter. In this context, perhaps the greatest service provided by the Darwin fighter force had been to neuter the Imperial Navy's bomber weapon. The bombers needed to drop their bombs from 10 000 feet in order to achieve the desired bombing accuracy and therefore destructive effect, yet the defence at Darwin had forced the bombers up to 25 000 feet and even higher. Japanese bomber commanders were thus caught in a catch-22: low bombing heights were needed to destroy targets, but this made the bombers too vulnerable to fighter attack. It was in this prosaic manner that the Allied fighter weapon had prevailed: it had not been decisive in 'winning the battle' for air supremacy over the Timor Sea front, but in ruining the effectiveness of Japanese bombing the fighters had provided the preconditions for the build-up of the Darwin base area into a major network of airfields, ready for the day when MacArthur's air command would permit the deployment there of an expanded and offensively configured air force.

Indeed, the 49th PG had not been committed to the defence of Darwin as an act of American charity, as deserving as the RAAF might have been. Rather, the American forces that arrived in Australia during 1942 were placed in the service of the post-Pearl Harbor US strategic agenda, which pragmatically exploited the location of Australia to turn it into a useful base from which to launch the intended American counter-offensive. From the US perspective, defending Australia was not the main concern, but the American commanders nonetheless recognised that a Japanese lodgment on the northern coast of Australia would suck in US resources and render insecure their intended Australian rear base area. In those early days of US forces in Australia, Darwin was seen as one of the two critical battle fronts, the other being Port Moresby. In early 1942, General Douglas MacArthur, the newly appointed theatre commander, had only three US fighter groups in theatre, so the deployment of one-third of this force to Darwin had signified his clear understanding that Darwin needed to be secured as the hinge for his intended right hook up through New Guinea to Rabaul.

The creation of a ground-based air defence system

In parallel with this early 1942 build-up of the Allied fighter force in the Top End, the Australians and Americans were frenetically active in laying out a substantial supporting ground network. RAAF and USAAF maintenance and logistics units arrived to back up the front-line squadrons, while engineering units improved and extended roads and airfields. An intensive program of airfield construction and site dispersal went on throughout 1942, preceding the 19 February raid and continuing in an unbroken program of civil engineering. Heavy earthmoving machinery was brought in to the Northern Territory by a broad coalition of Allied organisations, such as RAAF airfield construction squadrons, the US Army's 808th Engineering Battalion, and last but not least, road crews provided by the Main Roads Departments of the Australian state governments, operating under the umbrella of the Curtin government's Allied Works Council under the direction of Queensland ALP power-broker EG 'Red Ted' Theodore. These diverse teams of construction workers used their tip-trucks, bulldozers and graders to carve new roads and airfields out of the bush to support the Allied fightback.

Importantly, each airfield was given a ring of taxiways leading away from the airstrip into the tree cover, thus providing a network of camouflaged aircraft dispersals. This meant that by the time the Japanese raids intensified from April 1942 onwards, they had lost the ability to hit the Allied aircraft on the ground. The air force in the Top End had thus made itself virtually air raid proof, and would henceforth operate without any significant hindrance to its airfield operations. By April, the Japanese had lost the battle of the bulldozers, and this would lose them the air battle – and indeed the war.

All this activity was going on right through the supposed panic that ostensibly gripped the Australian leaders in early 1942; indeed, at the high point of the period that was associated with the purported defeatism of the 'Brisbane line' strategy. This scurrilous interpretation was popularised by the ALP politician Eddie Ward as a political attack against the previous conservative government, and then self-interestedly propagated by General Douglas MacArthur. In effect, it amounted to an allegation that Australia's political and military leaders had unpatriotically judged the northern half of the continent to be undefendable, and so had withdrawn forces from the north. The reality on the ground in the north was very different, refuting the myth.

A command organisation to direct the air forces in the Northern Territory already existed before the outbreak of the Pacific War – North-Western Area (NWA) RAAF HQ. After the great raid, officers and men were posted in to flesh out the capabilities of this organisation, and so an effective command apparatus was put in place to coordinate both the air defence and the offensive air campaign. The most impressive aspect of this new command and control capability was the progressive creation of an RAAF air defence radar network across the north-west coastline. The ability to detect and track raids was the prerequisite for effective air defence, so it was fortunate that the RAAF had belatedly made a start on this prior to the 19 February raid.

Having earlier dismissed the need for air defence radar – wedded as the service was to its 'no fighters required' doctrine – the RAAF was saved from its own intellectual complacency by a coalition of civilian scientists at the University of Sydney and in the Council for Scientific and Industrial Research (CSIR), combined within the newly established Radio Physics Laboratory (RPL). Piggybacking onto the army's earlier gun-ranging radar project, the RAAF was unwillingly cajoled into supporting the design and testing of air defence radar. As a result, even before the great raid on 19 February 1942, and even before the RAAF had any fighters to operate, No. 31 Radar Station already existed at Dripstone Caves, along the coast to the north of Darwin, set up under the personal guidance of Wing Commander Albert Pither, Director of Radar at RAAF HQ in Melbourne. Although the CSIR-designed Air Warning (AW) radar set was not erected in time to be operational on that day, it was made to work effectively by April.

Considering Australia's remoteness from the established centres of radar expertise in the United Kingdom and United States and the country's undeveloped industrial base, this was no small achievement by the country's universities and industry. To place the Australian achievement in perspective, as late as July 1942 the air defence of the west coast of the United States was still primarily based upon the visual observation of raiders: the future commander of MacArthur's 5th Air Force, General George Kenney, recorded that there were only six radar sets along that vast coastline. Moreover, once 31 Station's Australian-designed AW radar was 'de-bugged', it consistently achieved greater detection ranges than 105 Station's US-technology MAWD radar.

Further stations were added through 1942. The addition of

38 Station at Cape Fourcroy on Bathurst Island extended radar coverage an extra 120 kilometres out to sea and provided an unobstructed radar arc covering the Japanese approach route from the north-west. Additional stations included No. 105 at Point Charles and No. 307 on Perron Island, both of which extended the coverage along the coast to the west of Darwin, thickening the surveillance of likely Japanese approach paths from Timor. The RAAF supplemented its 'high-tech' radar network with 'low-tech' coastwatchers – small parties of radio-equipped observers were deployed to vantage points on the northern coast of the Cox Peninsula and on the north-west coast of Bathurst Island.

The RAAF takes over the air defence of Darwin

In August 1942, MacArthur transferred the 49th Fighter Group (49th FG) to New Guinea in order to add its strength to the Allied fightback in his South West Pacific Area (SWPA) command. The division of labour between the RAAF and USAAF within MacArthur's command was simple: the Australians would use their second-rate aircraft to look after menial defensive tasks like shipping patrols and rear area air defence, while the Americans would concentrate their better-equipped units upon the decisive battles in New Guinea. The RAAF was thus relegated to the status of a 'second eleven'. By now, however, the RAAF was not as bereft of fighter units as it had been at the start of the year. The beginnings of a home-based Australian fighter force had been made in March 1942, with the birth of No. 75 Squadron, destined for hard service in defence of Port Moresby and Milne Bay. From then on, the RAAF fighter force expanded progressively, beneficiary of the supply stream of new P-40 aircraft that were being shipped across the Pacific.

This meant that the redeployment of the 49th FG could now be covered by two RAAF Kittyhawk fighter squadrons.

Although the first of these Australian units arrived in the Northern Territory as early as July 1942, the RAAF Kittyhawk pilots were fated to miss out on the action, for their arrival in the North was concurrent with the withdrawal of the Japanese units from the Darwin front, transferred to Rabaul for operations over Guadalcanal. As a result, the RAAF's 77 and 76 Squadrons found themselves defending Darwin against an enemy that now confined its offensive operations to night raids only.

In any case, these two Australian Kittyhawk squadrons had a caretaker role only, for high-level political negotiations between the Australian and British governments had meanwhile secured agreement for a wing of Spitfires to be transferred from Britain for Australia's defence. Stung by the failure to defend against the 19 February raid and by the collapse of the Singapore 'fortress' in that same disastrous month, the Australian government had sought a countervailing act of imperial collaboration to reassure the Australian public that its defences had now been placed on a proper footing. Accordingly, when Australia's Minister for External Affairs, Dr Herbert 'Doc' Evatt, went to London for intergovernmental talks in May 1942, he secured British agreement for the dispatch of three Spitfire squadrons to Australia. RAF Fighter Command was thus politically obliged to donate three of its 60-odd Spitfire squadrons to Australia, at a time when the urgent demands of Malta and North Africa were also starting to siphon Spitfires away from the home country. Churchill saw this as the price of coexistence with Britain's demanding Dominion, but the Chief of Britain's Imperial General Staff, General Sir Alan Brooke, resented the 'strong blackmail cards' that Evatt had used in order to secure the deal – namely, the threat of withdrawal of the 9th Division from the war in North Africa. The insistence upon Spitfires was pure symbolism, exploiting the aircraft's media-manufactured image as a wonder weapon and symbol of the Allied fightback against the Axis. The composition of the wing too was heavily symbolic, with two Australian squadrons and one British. This showcased the solidarity of the fraternal ties between Australia and Britain, and between the RAAF and its parent service, the RAF.

Spitfire squadrons for Australia

It was ironic that by 1942, Britain's Royal Air Force had become so thoroughly cosmopolitan that a truly 'British' fighter unit could no longer be found. By then, British aircrew in the RAF were supplemented by men from Commonwealth nations like Canada, Australia and New Zealand, by men from occupied countries like Czechoslovakia, Belgium and Poland, and even by American volunteers. The British character of virtually every RAF squadron had become diluted by this influx of men from abroad, and this was true of the RAF squadron that was chosen to be sent to Australia – No. 54. The members of this squadron only realised that something strange was afoot when all their resident foreigners and 'colonials' were posted out, and a replacement set of purely British pilots posted in. Rumours were confirmed when the two-thirds of the squadron that was ineligible for overseas service was posted out. Filled with an ad hoc collection of newly assigned personnel, 54 Squadron thus became the only all-British unit in the British Air Force, and also became the only British unit permanently committed to the Pacific War after the collapse of Singapore. It would not be until 1945 and the arrival of the British Pacific Fleet that UK forces returned in force to the theatre.

The other two squadrons destined for Australia, No. 452 and No. 457, were the only two Australian day fighter squadrons serving with RAF Fighter Command in Britain, and were

No. 457 Squadron ground crew push a Spitfire off the taxiway into a dispersal bay at Livingstone airfield. The men model the 'tropical' working dress of the Commonwealth serviceman in the first half of the war. AWM Negative NWA0125

therefore the only possible choices. Originally built up around a core group of RAF leaders, both had rapidly assumed a strongly Australian character. Although an RAF ground staff cadre remained with these squadrons to be posted out to Australia with them, the COs, flight commanders and pilots were homogeneously Australian. All three squadrons were quite unremarkable – thoroughly average examples of RAF Fighter Command in 1942, with hastily promoted leaders, unready wartime-trained pilots and limited operational experience all round. Contrary to the media releases at the time, they were in no sense 'crack squadrons'. Moreover, they came unwillingly, loath to give up their comfortable bases in England and their high-profile role in the cross-channel war against Hitler's 'Fortress Europe'. No. 452 Squadron's former Australian CO, Squadron Leader Bob Bungey, flew into Redhill airfield to commiserate with the pilots upon hearing of their impending 'Ovidian exile'. This was an ironic reference, given that it was 54 Squadron being 'exiled' to the antipodes, rather than the two Australian squadrons.

Despite the prestige of 54 Squadron's World War I pedigree, it was effectively a new unit; indeed, it was the most inexperienced squadron of the three. Its Battle of Britain veterans had long since been posted out, and it had a far higher proportion of new graduate pilots than the other two, as shown by the fact that it was overwhelmingly peopled by sergeants and pilot officers – the lowest ranks of NCO and commissioned pilots respectively. For operations from Darwin, only three of its pilots were considered as combat experienced, while 45 per cent of them had had no combat experience at all. The CO, Squadron Leader Eric 'Bill' Gibbs, was the only prewar regular in the whole Spitfire wing, but he too had limited fighter experience, having only recently transferred from Coastal Command. He had been posted in to Fighter Command at the end of 1941, and had only joined 54 when the unit was in Scotland being rebuilt with new personnel. Having joined the squadron with the lowly rank of flying officer, his career was then fast-tracked, rapidly promoted first to flight lieutenant, to become one of the flight commanders, and then to squadron leader in April 1942 to become CO. Gibbs would be supported by two flight commanders with fighter experience from the Battle of Britain period, but only one of them, Flight Lieutenant Bob Foster, was actually a combat veteran from that campaign; the other, Flight Lieutenant Robin Norwood, had joined his first squadron only at the end of the battle, while it was resting in a rear area, and thus had missed out on the action. When Foster joined the unit prior to deployment to Australia, he found that 'there was little or no operational experience at all' among the pilots.

No. 452 was theoretically the most combat-experienced squadron of the three, having seen nine months of operations over France up to March 1942, and having gained a glittering reputation as the highest scoring unit in Fighter Command. However, its splendid reputation was misleading, for most of its victories had been scored by two star pilots, the Irishman, Brendan 'Paddy' Finucane, and the Australian, Keith 'Bluey' Truscott. Moreover, given the roughly 4:1 overclaiming ratio by RAF Fighter Command in this period, the unit's tally of 61 'confirmed victories' does not stand serious scrutiny. In gaining these claimed victories, 452 lost 23 Spitfires shot down, with 13 pilots killed in action (all these figures are very similar to those of 1 Fighter Wing as a whole in 1943).

Upon the squadron's withdrawal from combat, most of its senior pilots were posted out, greatly diluting the average experience level of those remaining. When the unit was withdrawn from offensive operations at the end of March 1942, it had 29 pilots on strength, but of these only 11 stayed with the unit when it moved to Australia – and nine of these were recent arrivals with little combat experience. The only experienced pilots from the early days of the squadron who remained were the newly appointed CO, Squadron Leader Ray Thorold-Smith DFC, and Flight Sergeant Paul Makin, whose advancement was then fast-tracked in order to permit him to be made flight commander: he was rapidly commissioned and in one day (27 April 1942) jumped two ranks from pilot officer to flight lieutenant. Thorold-Smith had been the fourth most successful pilot in 452 during its operations over northern France, being awarded the Distinguished Flying Cross (DFC) upon achieving the magic figure of five victories, but Makin was less talented – he had failed to score despite participating in dozens of operations. After arrival in Australia, the squadron's hollowed-out leadership cadre was strengthened when three further experienced combat pilots were posted in – Flight Lieutenant Ted Hall, who had seen a lot of action over France with 129 Squadron, was appointed as a flight commander; plus two Malta aces, Flying Officers Adrian 'Tim' Goldsmith DFC DFM and John Bisley DFC, who had flown together first in No. 185 Hurricane Squadron, then in No. 126 Spitfire Squadron, thus becoming known within 452 as the 'Malta Twins'. These two were appointed as deputy flight commanders, and thus the squadron reformed around five combat veterans.

By contrast, 457 had spent most of its existence as a de facto Operational Training Unit (OTU), training Australian and Canadian Spitfire pilots for service in UK-based fighter units, and living deep in the shadow of its more famous and more senior sister unit. It saw only two months of operations over France before being withdrawn from operations for transfer back to Australia. During that time, it scored only two 'confirmed kills' but suffered 11 losses to enemy fighters, with eight pilots killed and one taken prisoner – a loss of one-third of its pilot strength. These figures show that, contrary to the media-manufactured image of the time, both squadrons had in fact been involved in an unsuccessful campaign: Fighter Command's 1941–42 offensive over northern France had failed to achieve its objectives.

Despite this dubious 'blooding' in air combat, 457 arrived in Australia with a strong core group of surviving pilots – long-term squadron members of some seniority. On the one hand, this personnel stability made it the most cohesive of the three squadrons. On the other, this very stability in tandem with the unit's very brief front-line deployment meant that by the time it commenced operations in Australia only three of its pilots were considered experienced (the CO and two flight commanders), while 37 per cent of them had had no combat experience at all – not dissimilar to 54's figures. The average pilot in 457 had seen only three combats against the Luftwaffe before being posted back to Australia. No. 457 Squadron's entire leadership team – Squadron Leader Ken James and Flight Lieutenants Philip 'Pete' Watson DFC and Don Maclean – had grown up within the squadron, so from top to bottom there was only a limited pool of operational experience. Like Bill Gibbs in 54 and Makin in 452, Ken James had received fast-tracked promotion, elevated from flying officer to squadron leader in two days in order to assume the role of CO; he was by no means the most experienced man in the squadron.

It might seem odd that a big air force like the RAF was unable to provide a stronger cadre of combat-experienced pilots and leaders within these three squadrons, but this was ironically the product of its humane personnel policy. About 1500 fighter pilots had survived the Battle of Britain, but by 1942 few of these men remained in front-line fighter squadrons, which were instead now peopled by new graduates from the hugely expanded and accelerated wartime training program. Impressively, the RAF almost doubled its manpower between October 1940 and October 1941. To facilitate this expansion,

No. 54 Squadron pilots at 'B' Flight dispersals, RAAF Darwin. Left to right: Sgt P Fox, F/O Gerry Wall, F/Sgt WH Eldred, F/O Tony Hughes, F/O George Farries, Sgt Whalley. Note the camouflage net and the timber-reinforced earthen revetment around the dispersal bay. Note also the pilots' fashion of jungle knives strapped to their calves. AWM Negative 054796

tour-expired veterans had been posted away from their front-line squadrons to training jobs, staff jobs, desk jobs, even public relations jobs – although most of them would do second tours later in the war. Such an approach was alien to the air forces of the Axis powers: fighter pilots in German and Japanese service remained on operations until they were killed, or hospitalised, or the war ended. However, the downside of the RAF's forward-looking human resources management was that squadrons were deprived of that cadre of combat experience, with the result that during 1941–43 they were too often led by relatively inexperienced men who had received truncated fighter training only after the Battle of Britain had ended.

In spite of its shallow pool of experience, the new-look 452 lived under the weight of its previous reputation as a 'crack' unit, while 54 also groaned under a similar weight of history, having distinguished itself in 1940 over Dunkirk and in the Battle of Britain, likewise deriving glory from outstanding former squadron members – like the New Zealanders, Al Deere and Colin Gray. Alongside all this, 457 had nothing to boast of at all, but ironically none of this would count for anything under the unforgiving and unsentimental pressures of battle: in the 1943 Darwin campaign, 452 would fail to live up to its reputation, while the green 457 would emerge at the top of the 'league table' as the highest scoring unit.

The decision for RAF Fighter Command to donate three Spitfire squadrons to Australia had been a triumph of symbolic Commonwealth amity, bringing the most glamorous aircraft in the world to the much-neglected Pacific Dominion. It is incontestable that the Spitfire provided much better altitude performance than the P-40 and P-39 – hitherto the mainstays of Allied fighter operations in the theatre. Both US types were handicapped by the Allison V-1710 engine's undeveloped supercharger, which severely handicapped performance above

25 000 feet – precisely the height band that the Japanese raiders used, for obvious reasons.

The specific model that was assigned to Australia was the Spitfire VC (Tropical), powered by the Merlin 46 engine with an improved supercharger that boosted power above 20 000 feet. This was a highly desirable feature for Australian conditions, given that the superb flight performance of Japanese bombers permitted them to use attack altitudes that were fully 10 000 feet higher than was normal with German and Italian bombers in the Battle of Britain and the Battle for Malta. Besides the Spitfire V, no other suitable RAF type was available in mid-1942 (other than the much slower Hurricane II). As events would prove, the Spitfire VC Tropical carried serious defects and limitations, but it was actually the best British fighter aircraft available at the time.

The three squadrons were duly shipped out from the United Kingdom in June, arriving in Australia on 13 August and recommencing flying operations at Richmond RAAF base in September, after the men had returned from disembarkation leave. At first the pilots had to fly Ryan trainers and Wirraways, because their first shipment of 42 Spitfires had been hijacked mid-voyage by the RAF's Middle East Command for service in North Africa. It was not until November that sufficient Spitfires became available to permit the resumption of operational training. No. 54 Squadron's Engineering Officer, Pilot Officer RG 'Cecil' Beaton, was attached to RAAF Laverton to supervise the assembly of the crated aircraft and to give the technicians there a 'crash course' on Spitfires. Because of the belated arrival of their aircraft, the squadrons had only a short orientation and training period before packing up at the end of December for their move north. By mid-January they had settled into their Northern Territory airfields, ready for the start of the 1943 raiding campaign.

Each of the three squadrons disposed of up to 25 aircraft, about 30 pilots and more than 300 ground staff. Behind the three squadrons stood the personnel of 1 Fighter Wing HQ, of 5 Fighter Sector (5 FS) and of 7 Repair and Salvage Unit (7 RSU). Added together, the total personnel deployed in direct support of the Spitfires thus came to more than 1500 officers and men, and so each Spitfire at the 'sharp end' would be directly supported by the labours of at least 20 people.

A suitably high-profile leader

Just like the choice of aircraft, the choice of wing leader was also heavily influenced by symbolism. With 20 kills to his credit in the course of 81 air combats in North Africa, Wing Commander Clive Caldwell DFC and bar was at the time one of the most successful of all Allied fighter pilots, and he remained Australia's greatest air ace of the war. Hitherto he had built his war career flying P-40s, and so was new to Spitfires, new to wing tactics and new to defensive fighter operations. His selection for the role exploited the media's previous cultivation of him as the archetypical Australian fighter ace – dubbed by them, in rather poor taste, as 'Killer' Caldwell. Although there were officers of deeper experience in the role available, it was politically imperative for the wing leader to both be Australian and to have the broad 'brand recognition' necessary to gratify the public. Although it would turn out that Caldwell was not the ideal man in the role, the RAAF had at least opted for a meritocratic approach in choosing the EATS-trained but combat-experienced Caldwell over the many prewar officers that were also available.

Thanks to Air Chief Marshal Burnett's determination to advance RAF interests over those of the RAAF in the pre-Pearl Harbor period, very few professional RAAF officers had received relevant combat experience, having been held back to run the EATS training schools in Australia. Caldwell had only joined the RAAF in 1940 (having lied about his age), and had received his flying training as part of the very first EATS pilots' course. In the rough-and-tumble of the North African campaign, he had risen through the ranks with dizzying rapidity, moving from a newly arrived pilot officer to squadron CO after only eight months in the theatre, and thus becoming the first wartime-trained EATS graduate to command a squadron. Upon arrival back in Australia, the erstwhile pupil was given the plum job right over the heads of his former masters and teachers.

However, Caldwell's role was as 'wing commander flying' – that is, as airborne tactical leader – rather than as CO of the wing. Above him was placed a solid representative of the prewar regular RAAF, Group Captain Allan 'Wally' Walters AFC. Walters had previously taken a senior staff role within MacArthur's Allied air command, working as Director of Operations first to General George Brett and then to General George Kenney. The RAAF's appointment of such a highly placed officer to command the Spitfire wing suggests the political importance that was placed upon making the wing a success. Above Walters was Air Commodore Frank Bladin, who had commanded NWA Air HQ through the 49th Fighter Group's 1942 campaign over Darwin and therefore had good background in the role, having also been responsible for reconnoitring the air bases in the Netherlands East Indies during his previous time as RAAF Director of Intelligence. These officers would be able to keep an eye on Caldwell, but neither of them had a fighter background.

On the Japanese side of the water

While 1 Fighter Wing was making its move to the Northern Territory, on the far side of the Timor Sea the Japanese too

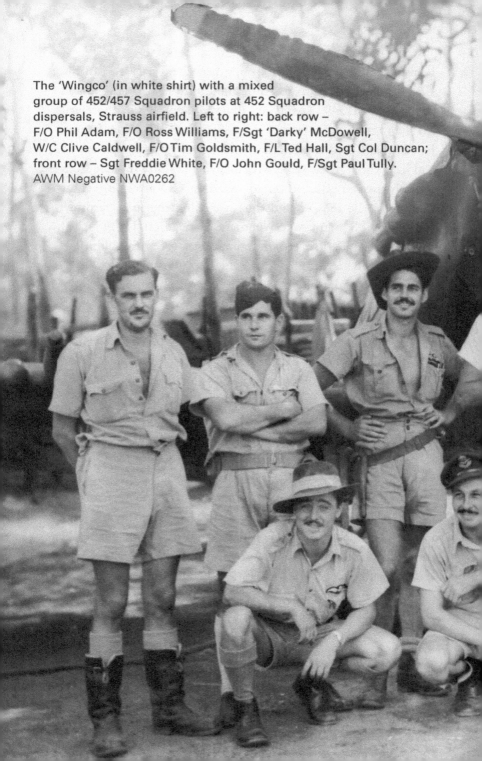

The 'Wingco' (in white shirt) with a mixed group of 452/457 Squadron pilots at 452 Squadron dispersals, Strauss airfield. Left to right: back row – F/O Phil Adam, F/O Ross Williams, F/Sgt 'Darky' McDowell, W/C Clive Caldwell, F/O Tim Goldsmith, F/L Ted Hall, Sgt Col Duncan; front row – Sgt Freddie White, F/O John Gould, F/Sgt Paul Tully. AWM Negative NWA0262

were busy with their preparations. The Imperial Navy's 23rd Air Flotilla awaited the approaching end of the 1942–43 wet season by readying itself for a resumption of the mass daylight raids that it had broken off at the end of August 1942. Headquartered at Kendari air base in the Celebes (Sulawesi), this formation was under orders from the 11th Air Fleet to make major attacks on Darwin on a monthly basis, rather than smaller attacks more often, as it had done in the early 1942 Darwin raids and as per continued Allied practice. This low operational tempo indicates a holding strategy only, designed to suppress Allied air activity against the long southern flank of the Japanese defence perimeter – which ran roughly west-to-east through Sumatra, Java, Timor and Dutch New Guinea. From the Japanese perspective, the intervening sea-air gaps of the Timor and Arafura Seas thus became buffer zones guarding the approaches to the Japanese defence line. The bombing strategy against Darwin was one of using limited force for limited objectives, maintaining only such a raiding effort as would purportedly prevent Allied air resurgence (which it emphatically did not), while at the same time avoiding excessive losses (which it largely did). Darwin operations had thus to be conducted with discretion, in a manner consistent with the maintenance of an air force 'in being' for the defence of the southern perimeter. It is clear that the Japanese were not playing a high-stakes game over Darwin – as they were, for example, over Guadalcanal.

The main Japanese flying units committed to Australian operations – the navy's 753 Bomber Air Group (753 AG, formerly known as the Takao AG) and the 3rd Fighter Air Group (3 AG, soon to be renumbered as 202 AG), had broken off their previous Darwin raids at the end of August 1942. This was because, like most other naval air units in the South West Pacific theatre, they were transferred temporarily to Rabaul to reinforce the Guadalcanal campaign. This reallocation of the

Imperial Navy's land-based air assets reflected the Solomons campaign's priority as the main Japanese push in late 1942. Air Group 753 thus flew into Rabaul on 22 September with 20 bombers, but in the course of eight raids on Guadalcanal until the end of October, lost seven aircraft and six crews in combat. Similarly, 3 AG arrived at Rabaul on 17 September with 21 Zeros and 27 pilots, but in the course of conducting 11 missions over Guadalcanal in the same five-week timeframe, the unit lost 12 aircraft in combat, with eight pilots killed. The intensity of Guadalcanal combat and the effectiveness of the US Marine and US Navy fighter opposition is shown by the heavy loss rate suffered by both units – around 10 per cent of sorties flown (twice that suffered in the Darwin campaign, either in 1942 or 1943).

However, there was a larger pool of surviving aircrew post-Guadalcanal than the above figures might suggest, as Japanese fighter units at this time 'suffered' an oversupply of pilots but a relative shortage of aircraft. Air Group 3 and 753 were able to return in November to their home base at Kendari with strong cadres of experienced airmen, and therefore with relatively high standards of operational proficiency. Meanwhile, 3 AG had confusingly been renumbered as the 202 Air Group, in another Imperial Navy reorganisation of its nomenclature – it was the selfsame unit, and thus 1 Fighter Wing's opponent in 1943 would be the same as that faced by the 49th FG in 1942.

Air Group 202 was one of the two 'most redoubtable' fighter units in the Imperial Navy (the other being the Tainan Air Group), possessed of a great depth of talent; the unit had entered the Pacific War with the majority of its pilots veterans of the China War, each with more than 1000 hours of flying time. The vastly greater experience levels of Japanese pilots relative to those of typical Allied units is shown by the fact that even Wing Commander Caldwell had only 700 flying hours

Zero over Australia: a Model 32 Zero is test-flown over south-east Queensland, 8 December 1943. Abandoned by the 2nd Air Group, it was found in unserviceable condition on Buna airfield in December 1942 and rebuilt by the Allied Technical Air Intelligence Unit at Eagle Farm airfield in Brisbane. AWM Negative P01097.007

when he took over 1 Fighter Wing, and the bulk of his pilots had only 300 or 400 hours. Moreover, because the Japanese unit's operations over Darwin in 1942 had given it an opportunity to refine its tactics and procedures for bomber escort and fighter sweeps, it had undergone an 'amazing growth in skills' during its combats against the 49th Fighter Group in 1942. Thus 202 AG was still in very good shape at the beginning of 1943, having enjoyed the advantages of spending more than a year in the same operational area; of conducting operations at a modest enough tempo to ensure 'sufficient training, rest, and recuperation'; and of retaining a 'high ratio of veteran pilots'. Following the unit's return to Kendari, intensive training was undertaken to apply the lessons learnt in combat over Guadalcanal, refining procedures for 'over-ocean navigational techniques' and improving 'formation fighting tactics'. This expert and experienced fighter unit would therefore be a very dangerous opponent for the inexperienced pilots and leaders of 1 Fighter Wing.

In the 1943 campaign, 202 AG would operate a mix of Model 21 and 32 Zeros. Like the Spitfire V, the Model 22 and 32 featured a more efficient supercharger to boost power at high altitude, but the gains were very modest, so the air combat performance of both subtypes remained very similar.

Meanwhile, throughout the period of the Guadalcanal detachment, 753 Bomber Group had maintained operations over Australia, carrying out a campaign of night raids on targets in and around Darwin from July 1942 onwards. Despite the reduced operational tempo, the night campaign through the wet season of 1942–43 still represented a considerable operational investment for 753 AG. The bomber unit launched 24 night raids, during which a total of 142 bomber sorties penetrated Australian airspace. With an average of 23 bombers crossing the coast each month, this was two-thirds of the monthly raiding commitment it had maintained during the 1942 daylight campaign.

From the end of November, the Imperial Navy reinforced its forward-based airfields on Timor in preparation for the resumption of raids. In that month, Allied reconnaissance showed 62 enemy aircraft in the Celebes and 29 on Timor, with the forward force being doubled in strength in December. There was also a new airfield under construction at Fuiloro in Portuguese Timor, 100 kilometres closer to Darwin than Dili airfield and therefore a good base location for the escorting fighters.

Before the arrival of 1 Fighter Wing, the RAAF fighter force at Darwin gained a symbolic first victory: on the night of 23–24 November, Squadron Leader Dick Cresswell, CO of the RAAF's 77 Squadron, finally achieved the impossible by shooting down a bomber at night, guided to his target by searchlights of 1/54th Anti Aircraft Searchlight Company of the Royal Australian Engineers.

In January 1943, as the wet season drew towards its water-logged and muddy close, the three Spitfire squadrons moved into their new Northern Territory bases. No. 452 and 457 Squadrons received tenure over two airfields to the south of Darwin: respectively Strauss (27-Mile) and Livingstone (34-Mile). Both had been carved out of the bush in early 1942 by the US Army's 808th Engineering Battalion, created by simply widening the north–south highway and inserting an off-strip network of taxiways and dispersals. Named after pilots of the 49th Fighter Group killed in action over Darwin, Strauss was formerly the home of the 8th Fighter Squadron USAAF, while Livingstone had hosted the 9th. The technical echelons of both Spitfire squadrons were located close to the dispersals, while the domestic camp areas were located in the bush a couple of kilometres away. The British squadron was assigned to a more exposed position at RAAF Darwin, with its dispersals in the bush at Winnellie – on the opposite side of the airfield to the

No. 1 Fighter Wing's command hierarchy

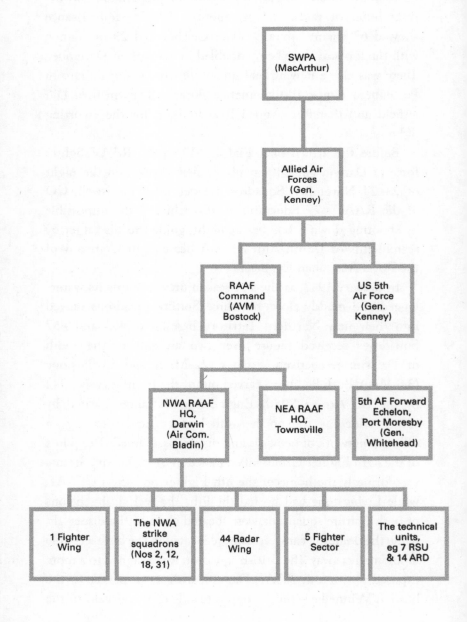

conspicuous prewar RAAF base and its bombed-out hangars. However, the squadron's domestic tent lines were at Nightcliff on the northern coast – far enough away from the much-targeted base to provide some safety from bombing.

By the end of 1942, therefore, Australia had made huge strides in overcoming the bad start at Darwin in February. The RAAF now deployed a wing of Spitfires, and these fighters were the sharp end of an integrated operational and logistical organisation. Behind the fighter squadrons stood an operational staff – NWA RAAF HQ; a network of coastal radar stations – 44 RDF Wing; a tactical fighter control organisation – 5 Fighter Sector (5 FS); a Spitfire repair organisation – No. 7 Repair and Servicing Unit (7 RSU); and, from February 1943, a deep maintenance unit – No. 14 Aircraft Repair Depot (14 ARD). Both the Spitfire squadrons and the strike squadrons that they protected were securely based upon a burgeoning network of dispersed airstrips. The NWA still lacked some significant capabilities, such as effective photo-reconnaissance aircraft and radar-equipped night fighters, but the RAAF had nonetheless done well in building-up a reasonably mature defensive apparatus in a short time, from a very low base. When 1 Fighter Wing went into action, it would have the necessary ground-based support to sustain intensive combat operations.

No. 1 Fighter Wing organisational chart 1943, showing the key personalities of this story

Wing CO	Group Captain Alan 'Wally' Walters AFC – CO until 24 Jun
	Wing Commander Clive Caldwell DFC & bar – Wing Commander Flying, then CO from 24 Jun to 25 Sep
	W/C Peter Jeffrey DSO DFC – CO from 25 Sep

Squadron no.	54		452		457	
R/T call sign	Candy		Troppo		Skeeter	
Airfield	RAAF Darwin		Strauss (27-Mile)		Livingstone (34-Mile)	
SQN CO	Squadron Leader 'Bill' Gibbs RAF		Squadron Leader Ray Thorold-Smith DFC – CO to 15 Mar		Squadron Leader Ken James	
			W/C Caldwell – Acting CO from 15 March			
			S/L Ron MacDonald – CO from 30 Mar			
			Flight Lieutenant 'Tim' Goldsmith DFC DFM – Acting CO from 10 Sep			
	A Flt	B Flt	A Flt	B Flt	A Flt	B Flt
Flight OC	F/L Rob Norwood RAF	F/L Bob Foster RAF	F/L Ted Hall – to 26 Jul	F/L Paul Makin RAF – to 28 Jul	F/L 'Pete' Watson DFC	F/L Don Maclean
			F/L Dave Evans – from 26 Jul to 10 Sep	Flying Officer John Bisley DFC – from 28 Jul		
			F/L 'Tim' Goldsmith – from 10 Sep			

2

The raid on
Coomalie Creek

As early as April 1942, the Allies' small-scale raids on Timor airfields, chiefly by the Hudson bombers of the RAAF's No. 2 and No. 13 Squadrons, had become sufficiently annoying to convince the 23rd Flotilla's commander, Rear Admiral Ryuzo Takenaka, to downgrade the Timor airfields to the status of forward operating bases only. After this withdrawal of the Japanese flying units from Timor, their main air bases on Ambon and at Kendari in the Celebes were respectively 700 kilometres and 500 kilometres further back, so Darwin operations would henceforth necessitate transit flights into Timor in the days preceding a planned raid.

Because of indiscreet Japanese signalling procedures, the resultant transit flights from Kendari to Penfui often gave RAAF

Hudson bomber A16-242 of 2 Squadron RAAF at Batchelor airfield on 28 October 1942, about to be bombed-up for a raid. Note the revetment walls in the background and the shadow of the camouflage net overhead. AWM Negative 027611

A 31 Squadron Beaufighter 'beating up' Coomalie airstrip. This is how the Japanese saw the Beaufighters – over their airfields at 50 feet. AWM Negative NWA0049

wireless eavesdroppers early warning of bombing raids. Through 1942 the RAAF developed a significant signals intelligence capability that played a role in partly overcoming NWA HQ's lack of photo-reconnaissance capability. Bomber aircraft taking off inbound for Timor announced their flight details over the W/T (Wireless Transceiver, i.e. two-way Morse radio). No. 1 Wireless Unit, based in Townsville, monitored Japanese frequencies around the clock, and was thus able to deduce the strength of the coming raid. By this means, the Allies would often have reasonable intelligence on Japanese bomber deployments.

The next raid would come from the Imperial Navy, for it was this service that ran offensive operations against Darwin. Japan's airpower was not operated by an independent air force, as per British practice. Instead, both the army and navy had their own air forces, rather like the British arrangement in World War I, when military aviation was split between the army's RFC and the navy's RNAS – both of them 'temperamentally disinclined to cross-service cooperation'. This non-unified arrangement was not dissimilar to the US system, which featured a similarly proud and autonomous US Navy air arm and US Army Air Forces.

As in 1942, the timing of Japanese raids in 1943 would come as a reaction to Allied initiatives. At the turn of the year, this came in the form of a new squadron of Bristol Beaufighter twin-engined fighters: 31 Squadron RAAF. Arriving in the NWA in November 1942, these aircraft possessed a combination of qualities unknown among the motley collection of aircraft in the NWA – range *and* firepower *and* speed (hitherto mutually exclusive characteristics). Their ability to reach out as far as 800 kilometres from base permitted 31 Squadron to strike enemy island targets on the far side of the Arafura and Timor Seas. Air Commodore Bladin exploited the Beaufighters' speed and firepower by sending them to strike enemy airfields in low-level strafing attacks, and these became the first really damaging Allied counter-blows against the Japanese air bases.

This offensive campaign had started on 2 December 1942, when 31 Squadron for the first time struck Penfui air base. The Beaufighter crews claimed to have hit more than a dozen Japanese aircraft, leaving four or five burning and setting fire to a fuel dump. Penfui was the main front-line Japanese air base for the 1942–43 campaign of bombing raids on Darwin, and so this attack represented a very direct challenge to Japanese air superiority over the Timor Sea gap. It was the 23rd Air Flotilla's strategic brief to strike Darwin with powerful raids whenever Allied air units showed signs of resurgence, and so a revenge raid was inevitable as soon as the weather cleared up sufficiently to permit high-altitude formation flying. From 26 February 1943, Japanese radio traffic indicated the movement of a large force of aircraft into Timor, and so Bladin warned the Spitfire wing to expect a raid. He also prepositioned 31 Squadron for a pre-emptive strike from Drysdale airfield – a forward bare base to the west of Darwin and hence closer to Timor. As soon as W/T intercepts revealed the bombers' arrival at Penfui, the Beaufighter strike was launched. Early in the morning of the 28th, eight aircraft swept across the Japanese airfield, finding the runways lined with aircraft. This time, they claimed to have hit more than 20 aircraft, with a dozen left burning. Even allowing for some overstating of results, this was a very damaging attack: it would take the three Spitfire squadrons half a year of hard fighting at high altitude to destroy a similar number of Japanese machines. Understandably, there was no Japanese air raid on Darwin that day, but the latest Beaufighter strike had sharpened the Japanese need for retaliation.

Reconnaissance overflights resume

The intended resumption of Japanese bombing was signalled by the reappearance of Japanese photographic reconnaissance aircraft high over Darwin from January onwards. No. 54 Squadron RAF, the most forward-based of the three Spitfire squadrons, chased these intruders regularly, but found the Mitsubishi Ki-46 army reconnaissance aircraft to be challenging prey. These were very fine machines indeed, as good as the contemporary and much-fancied de Havilland Mosquito, with the range to penetrate to the airfields south of Darwin, able to cruise easily at difficult-to-intercept heights above 25 000 feet, and on paper faster than a Spitfire VC.

No. 54 Squadron's Flight Lieutenant Bob Foster was the only Battle of Britain veteran at Darwin, and was therefore one of the most combat-experienced fighter pilots in the wing. A native of London and a fresh-faced young man of 22, he was his squadron's senior flight commander, and was lucky enough to be airborne on 6 February. Wing Commander Tony Primrose, the CO of 5 Fighter Sector and chief controller, had applied a 'standing plan' to intercept the Japanese 'reccos', placing one section of Spitfires over each of four 'stops': over the Roman Catholic Mission on Bathurst Island, Point Charles, Point Blaze and Hughes airfield. The first three stops provided a perimeter arc across Darwin's north-western approaches, while the fourth provided a 'backstop' position close to the likely photographic targets. On this day the intruder got past the Point Blaze 'stop', photographed its targets around Batchelor airfield, then headed north, going out past Darwin and over Bathurst Island.

Under the direction of the controller, Foster and his No. 2, Flight Sergeant 'Pat' Mahoney, were vectored in various directions out to sea before they finally sighted the recco machine ahead at 17 000 feet. The Japanese crew saw the Spitfire when it was only 1000 metres off, and tried to evade by climbing away. This would have worked if Darwin's defenders had still been equipped with the slow-climbing Curtiss P-40. However, they were not; Foster was in a Spitfire, and even the Mark VC climbed well. Thus he was able to slowly gain on the Japanese aircraft in a climb to 22 000 feet. When the Japanese saw the Spitfire drawing closer, they gave up climbing, and the pilot put his aircraft's nose down in a run for home. Foster found that his Spitfire gained slowly on the Japanese machine in the dive, and he finally opened fire in a relatively easy shot from dead astern at the good firing range of 300 metres. After several bursts, the unarmed aircraft caught fire and spiralled down into the water, leaving a pool of blazing petrol on the surface of the sea.

Having scored the wing's first 'recco' kill on 6 February, F/L Bob Foster (left) is debriefed by 54 Squadron's intelligence officer, P/O Jimmy Councer (right), observed by the CO, S/L Bill Gibbs. Note the 'Mae West' life preservers. AWM Negative 014482

A Japanese reconnaissance photo taken on 4 March 1942. Note the crossed runways of RAAF Darwin at bottom, Darwin town at top with the harbour top left, Darwin Civil airport (Parap) appearing between the two clouds, and the highway running into town past the southern fringes of the RAAF base.
AWM Negative 100886

Mahoney had not been able to get past Foster to open fire, but was able to confirm his No. 1's kill.

The Imperial Army's 70th Independent Reconnaissance Squadron would henceforth have to contend with the unwelcome attentions of high-altitude interceptors as it went about its intelligence-gathering duties over northern Australia. RAAF radar capability was improving: this interception had only been achieved through the use of new ground-controlled interception (GCI) radar that provided the fine signal discrimination, height-finding mode and PPI (Plan Position Indicator) display necessary to achieve an interception of a single aircraft. Despite this, the Japanese spy-planes would remain elusive targets, as shown by what happened the next day: 54 Squadron's readiness section was scrambled too late, when the Ki-46 was already high overhead at 20 000 feet, because of the failure of the air warning radars to detect it. Because the aerial arrays of the air warning radar sets were rotated and threw a narrow beam, it was possible for an intruder to slip past outside the search arc without being identified as a 'blip' on the screen.

Reconnaissance flights or not, the unleashing of the first Japanese raid of 1943 depended on the weather, and the weather was bad throughout February. The end of the wet season produced tropical thunderstorms and torrential rain – conditions that made impracticable the massed formation raids which were the Japanese specialty. A Ki-46 came over on 28 February but probably went home without any photos, because it was so wet that 54 Squadron's intercepting Spitfires flew the whole mission in continuous rain. However, after the arrival of the Japanese force at Penfui on 27 February, it was only a matter of time before they came. These Japanese movements into Timor caused a 'big flap' of anticipation at 54 Squadron, but the 'filthy weather' at Darwin cooled expectations, and solid rain persisted for a couple of days thereafter.

The wet season weather was a hazard in itself, as shown by what happened to Flying Officer Bill Ford on 27 February, during a transit flight to Wyndham by six aircraft from 452 in company with a 13 Squadron Hudson. Encountering a wide front of severe thunderstorms with 10/10th cloud, the Spitfires closed up on the Hudson, their pilots concentrating on holding position in the murky turbulence while the Hudson pilot flew on instruments. Flight Lieutenant Ted Hall, the flight commander, saw Ford suddenly break away from the formation and climb steeply, disappearing into the blanketing mass of dark cloud that was piled up above. When the formation emerged into clear air on the other side of the weather, Ford's Spitfire was nowhere to be seen, and neither did he respond over the R/T.

The wreckage of his aircraft was discovered the next day by air search, its twisted debris strewn all over the precipitous rocky slopes of Table Top Range. A ground party led by Flying Officer Hal Whillans, one of Ford's squadron mates, undertook an expedition to the crash site – forced by flooded roads to leave their vehicles, and by necessity to swim a 'crocodile infested' river before reaching the wreck on 12 March. Disorientated by the cloud, Ford had spun in descending vertically, his aircraft exploding against the hard ground and shattering into small pieces. His body was incinerated in the fire, so Whillans and his men had 'great difficulty' in 'dissecting the charred mass'. All they got were a few big bones, and these they buried under a stone cairn surmounted by the twisted propeller of Spitfire BS175, with its seat armour propped up as a headstone.

Having landed at Wyndham, the others were tasked with providing cover for a detachment of Beaufighters using that base for operations across the Timor Sea. On 28 February (the day after Ford died), four returning Beaufighters were followed in by a Zero which made two runs over the airfield at 10 000 feet. The Spitfires were scrambled after it and visually controlled from the

No. 54 Squadron dispersals at Winnellie on 24 March. While waiting for an alert under the leaden sky of the wet season, the men play football on the water-logged airfield. AWM Negative 014494

ground by Flying Officer Jack Lamerton, but the Zero escaped into cloud before they could get to height.

The 2 March raid

Meanwhile, 2 March had dawned clear, and the Japanese came over for Raid No. 52 on Darwin. They took advantage of the fine morning to send over a pre-strike weather-reconnaissance that penetrated as far south as Cape Fourcroy, from where the crew had clear observation over Darwin. No. 452 Squadron scrambled two Spitfires, but it retired out to sea before it could be approached by the fighters – having already transmitted its report that the weather over the target was fine.

Later, at 1.57 pm, radar detected an incoming formation at 190 kilometres north-west of Darwin. The controller straight-away ordered two squadrons of Spitfires to rendezvous over Port Patterson. 'Winco Section', the wing's airborne command element consisting of Wing Commander Clive Caldwell and Group Captain 'Wally' Walters, took off with 54 Squadron – the British unit based at RAAF Darwin. No. 54 headed south-west to the rendezvous, while the Australian 457 Squadron – based at Livingstone 40 kilometres south – headed due west. The two squadrons started far apart and were destined never to meet in the air that day.

The incoming formation of Zeros had proceeded independ-ently and from a more northerly bearing than the bombers. Lautem airfield in Portuguese Timor was only 650 kilometres away and was therefore the preferable take-off point for the fighters, while the long-legged G4M bombers could easily operate from Penfui, 850 kilometres distant from Darwin. Having achieved an underway rendezvous with the bombers at a point 100 kilometres out to sea, the combined raid formation proceeded inbound on a south-east course and crossed the coast to the west of Darwin. The Japanese had sent nine bombers, 21 fighters and at least one Ki-46 reconnaissance plane. Their target was Coomalie Creek airfield, 70 kilometres south of Darwin, the home base of the offending Beaufighter squadron that had recently visited so much trouble upon them. It was to be retribution for 28 February.

The organisation responsible for using the radar data to plot the enemy's movements and to control the interception was No. 5 Fighter Sector (5 FS), under the command of Wing Commander Primrose. The operations staff had been brought together at RAAF Richmond in October 1942, and then moved forward to Darwin with the fighter wing in January. No. 5 FS replaced the USAAF's 49th Fighter Group Interception Control Squadron, which had controlled the 49th Fighter Group's operations largely independently of the RAAF organisation, and which had departed with its parent unit to New Guinea. The new personnel staffed the filter room – where they took the calls from the radar stations, anti-aircraft (AA) batteries and visual observers, assessed these reports for redundancies and inaccuracies, and then provided the distilled positional data to the plotters in the operations room; and the ops room itself – where they tracked the raids' movements on a plotting board, presenting the relative positions of 'bandits' and 'friendlies' for the controllers. The system was a facsimile of that developed by RAF Fighter Command, as used with great effect in the Battle of Britain. Although the processes and systems were battle-proven, the functioning of the whole was dependent upon many newly trained personnel. They would learn very fast and would soon be performing excellently, but it was hardly surprising that the whole apparatus found itself on a steep learning curve on this, the first raid of the season.

The pattern of the 1942 daylight raids had been to bomb Darwin itself – generally either the port or the RAAF base.

Therefore on this day, control vectored the two Spitfire squadrons westward to Bynoe Harbour – on the coast 35 kilometres south-west of Darwin. This was a good point from which to intercept the raid as it went past inbound to Darwin. However, today the Japanese headed further south, giving Darwin a wide berth and thereby unintentionally throwing the controller's neat intercept geometry into disarray. As the Japanese approached the coast, the plot was seen to be heading south-east rather than east, going inbound towards the group of airfields around Batchelor. By turning onto this more southerly course, the Japanese were now heading straight at the Spitfires' rendezvous point. Because the latter were still climbing, the Japanese would get there first and with an altitude advantage. Worried that the Spitfires would be bounced, control turned the wing 180 degrees to continue its climb to the eastward away from the incoming raid.

To further confuse the plot, one Japanese formation stayed as top-cover above 20000 feet while another descended to low-level. As the Japanese moved inland at different heights, the Operations Room 'lost the plot'. Although the radars performed well in fulfilling their basic function of detecting aircraft approaching over the sea, difficulty was often experienced in tracking targets once they were over land, and therefore maintaining a reliable plot often depended upon supplementary reports from ground observations and from airborne aircraft. Similar limitations in radar performance had applied in the Battle of Britain, but in that campaign the raids were tracked reasonably effectively by a dense network of observer posts as they moved overland. There was no such network in the remote, roadless and unpopulated bush to the west of Darwin, and thus there were few visual position reports to enable 5 Fighter Sector to maintain the raid's position on the plotting board.

At 457's base at Livingstone, the squadron's 12 aircraft

had just headed to the north-west and disappeared from sight behind low-lying stratocumulus cloud. Soon after, the ground staff saw seven Zeros going past in the opposite direction. The incoming Zeros and the outbound Spitfires had evidently passed each other on near reciprocal courses, separated by the bank of cloud. Soon after, 30 kilometres to the south, Flying Officer Ken McDonald, a Beaufighter pilot with 31 Squadron, was standing outside his tent in the squadron's Coomalie Creek camp area when the yellow alert sounded at 2.34 pm. He suddenly heard cannon fire, and then a Zero whistled past overhead, diving down the gully towards the airstrip which nestled in the hollow at the foot of the hill. McDonald counted five more go past after it, and only then did the station ops room ring the red alert: control had been completely misled as to the speed and direction of the Japanese thrust. The Zero pilots' achievement of surprise was a little ironic given that, as the perpetrators of the 28 February strike, 31 Squadron had fully expected to cop a 'special hate' on the day of the first raid. The 225th LAA Battery salvaged some honour by firing 30 rounds of 40 mm at the now retiring low-level Zeros before they disappeared from sight, claiming to have hit one of them.

However, thanks to the Allied air forces' bulldozer-led recovery, Coomalie airfield had proved hard to hit. Because of the extensive taxiways and dispersals winding through the trees, the unit's parked Beaufighters were not visible to the Japanese pilots as they roared low over the treetops at speed. Lacking obvious targets, the Japanese pilots instead sprayed gunfire indiscriminately over the 3 Brigade camp near the airfield, wounding two soldiers. Frank Gregory was relaxing in his tent in the army tent lines, lying on a camp stretcher, when his post-lunch reverie was suddenly disturbed by the thunderclap of the Zeros hurtling past overhead. With a start he rolled out of his stretcher on to the floor, and looked out under the tent flap

Beaufighter A19-31 destroyed by strafing Zeros at Coomalie airfield on 2 March. AWM Negative P01164.006

in time to see a Zero go past: 'All I could see was the bloody big red circles on the wings'.

Only Beaufighter A19-31 stood visible out in the open, and it was accordingly hammered with 20 mm fire, burning itself away to molten metal. Another Beaufighter was caught low and slow, perilously airborne in the circuit area: Sergeant Neville Armstrong was returning from a routine cross-country exercise at the same time as the Zeros arrived. He was about to turn onto final approach with wheels and flaps down, when his observer, Sergeant Stan Robertson, warned that three Zeros were coming in behind. Armstrong retracted his undercarriage and flaps, opened his throttles and intelligently headed south, putting further distance between the chasing Zeros and their base. Not for the last time, a speeding, jinking, low-level Beaufighter proved to be a difficult target for fuel-sensitive Zeros a long way from home, and so the Japanese pilots got off a few bursts, then gave up and turned about. Their big revenge attack had succeeded in destroying just one aircraft.

Once control had apprised itself of the attack on Coomalie, 457 was too far north to interfere with the strafers. Baffled by the Zeros' swift movements, control was forced to go 'low tech', falling back upon the 'Mark 1 eye ball' to put the raid back onto the plotting board. The Spitfires of 457 were vectored southward, split up into flights and sent along various search headings. As these blundered about the sky looking around them for Zeros, the confused plot and multiple Japanese tracks inevitably caused false alarms. Wing Commander Caldwell, by now leading the main section of 54 Squadron southward towards Coomalie, was told by control that the enemy were straight ahead 7 kilometres away. An anonymous pilot even announced 'Tally-ho' ('Enemy in sight'), but there were plenty of small formations of fighters in the air, both Allied and Japanese, and none of these leads led anywhere.

There was one more sighting of the Zeros, this time from 452's airfield at Strauss, when three of them were spotted at 5000 feet heading back north, outbound after strafing Coomalie. Two four-aircraft sections were scrambled after them, one led by the CO, Squadron Leader Ray Thorold-Smith, and the other by Flight Lieutenant Paul Makin, the 'B' Flight commander, but they pursued into an empty sky.

As the plot faded in the south, Caldwell's 54 Squadron formation was turned around and vectored northward again. Control detached yet another section to orbit overhead the three-airfield cluster of Strauss, Hughes and Livingstone. As a result of such diversions, by the time Caldwell arrived back over Darwin, he found that the wing had suffered great attrition; it had been reduced from its initial strength of 26 Spitfires to a mere six, consisting merely of his own Winco Section and 54 Squadron's Red Section. Control's splitting-up of the fighter force shows that it remained in the dark about the enemy's movements and intentions – would the Japanese bomb Batchelor, or Hughes, or Coomalie, or Darwin?

To add to the confusion, the Japanese bomber squadron had been merely a decoy, there being no evidence of it crossing the coast, let alone bombing. This was a standard Japanese tactic, designed to draw the defending fighters into the air (to be shot down) without exposing the precious bombers to any risk. Cleverly, the Japanese also exploited the evasive bomber plot as cover to send one Ki-46 recco over Darwin. This too was a standard tactic, and an effective one too – control and the Spitfires were too busy with the raid to bother about the recco, permitting it to get in and out without being intercepted. This Ki-46 was seen from the ground only after it had taken its photos, already heading out west at 19 000 feet. The newly arrived 19th AA Battery greeted the intruder with three rounds of 3.7 inch before it disappeared behind some cloud.

The dogfight out to sea

As the Zeros headed back across the coast, the GCI radar reacquired the target, enabling control to vector Caldwell's small formation of Spitfires to the west. However, now that the Japanese were heading back out to sea, the interception geometry had become unfavourable: the enemy's retirement meant that the Spitfires were now committed to a cut-off intercept from the Zeros' starboard rear quarter. Caldwell's force, in a gradual descent from their earlier altitude of 26 000 feet, were gaining on the Zeros, but only slowly – the Japanese were doing an economical 175 knots indicated airspeed (IAS), while the Spitfires approached from their starboard rear quarter at a similarly fuel-conscious 200 knots.

The Spitfires had been airborne for fully 90 minutes – approaching the upper limit of the Spitfire's endurance – when they finally sighted the Japanese at 3.30 pm. Caldwell saw them ahead and slightly to port. With less than 30 gallons of petrol left in his own tank, his Spitfires' fuel state was so critical that Caldwell no longer had time for any 'fancy tactics'. Instead, he just led his small formation in under the enemy top-cover for a single firing pass at the lowest group of Japanese. By then, they were 30 kilometres offshore, west-north-west of Point Charles.

As the Spitfires made their approach at 12 500 feet, Caldwell saw that the Japanese formation consisted of 15 aircraft, with three single-engined bombers and three Zeros at 10 000, plus two further groups of Zeros, one on each flank: on the left were four Zeros at the Spitfires' height, while on the right were another five, higher up at 15 000. Caldwell identified the three centre aircraft as Nakajima B5N carrier torpedo bombers – but in fact they were Zeros like the rest. Having misidentified them, and without enough fuel to climb, he went straight in at the 'bombers', leading his small force of Spitfires right underneath the high-cover Zeros that were positioned out on the enemy's right flank.

Six Spitfires thus engaged 15 Zeros in spite of an altitude disadvantage – not a good way to start a fight. Caldwell had accepted these inauspicious terms because, having spent so long blundering about under control's direction looking for the Japanese, and having finally found them at the eleventh hour, he was hardly likely to let the opportunity slip by; he was moreover the Spitfire wing leader; this was the first raid of the season and the very first encounter between Spitfires and Zeros; and the day had gone quite badly up to this point. Honour demanded that he make a challenge to the Japanese, and his whole credibility as a fighter leader rested upon his readiness to take bold and aggressive action and to live up to the RAF fighter tradition of attacking the enemy no matter what the odds.

This time, the enemy did not see his low rearward approach and so there was no response from any of the high-cover Zeros as Caldwell's small formation approached them from behind, probably obscured by the 'scattered' cloud around the Spitfires' approach altitude (estimated as either 6/10ths or 8/10ths). Thus they got right into the heart of the Japanese force unchallenged. Thinking that his chosen targets were multi-seat bombers with rear gunners, Caldwell set his formation up for a diving beam attack, in order to avoid the rear gunners' defensive fire – correct practice if they had in fact been bombers. Shaking themselves out into line astern, the Spitfires thus went down in a long string on the leading vee of Zeros. The first three places in the queue were taken by senior officers: Wing Commander Caldwell, Group Captain Walters and Squadron Leader Gibbs.

The four Zeros out on the left flank had now seen the attack, for Caldwell had seen them turning in to cut him off, but he assessed that they were too far off to harm him yet, and so pressed on regardless. However, the main formation of six Zeros was caught completely unawares, holding their steady course and their economical cruising speed as the Spitfires dived upon them. Lacking R/T, the Japanese high-cover pilots were unable to warn the others that they were being attacked.

Caldwell had committed all his pilots to a 90 degree deflection shot at a high closing speed – very difficult for anyone but a top shot. As the leading Allied air ace in the North African campaign, Caldwell had a reputation for impressive deflection shooting, and so alone of the six Spitfire pilots he was skilled enough to make this challenging gunnery pass successful. He pressed the gun button on the joystick, his guns roared and his aircraft vibrated with the recoil. He saw hits on the fuselage of his target, and then broke off, for the Zeros coming down on him from the left were already too close for comfort. Among the three 'bombers' that had been bounced, only the pilot of the targeted aircraft on the right noticed anything, for he belatedly broke into a turn while his two colleagues sailed on undisturbed. Caldwell pulled out of the dive into a climbing turn to port and zoomed up to regain his altitude, scanning the sky as he turned.

Finding himself in clear air up above the dogfight that was developing behind him to his left, Caldwell saw an aircraft hit the water, believing it to be the 'bomber' he had fired upon. His attempt to reposition for another attack was disrupted when two or three of the high-cover Zeros started to dive at him one by one in successive head-on passes from different directions. In each instance he would turn into the attack, and then the enemy pilot would break away downwards before he came into firing range. As each Zero came down to make its run, he would try to dive after it as it broke away downwards, only to see another one coming in at him. Each time he was forced thereby to break off and meet the new attack. Caldwell was fighting alone, whereas the Zeros were coordinating their firing passes to cover each other's tails and to discomfit his attempts to close in on them.

Group Captain Walters had meanwhile followed Caldwell in at the 'bombers', but his own firing pass was interrupted when he saw tracers shooting past from behind. This was his very first air combat, so in his inexperience he thought the tracers were from a Spitfire behind firing past him at the 'bombers' up ahead (in fact, the Spitfires did not use tracer ammunition). However, when the tracers started flicking closer over the top of his canopy, he realised he was under attack. Walters broke left at once, and as he turned he saw a second Zero coming in from that side – his sudden turn had spoiled its attack. Still moving fast from its dive, the Zero overshot him then pulled up and over into a loop. As Walters rolled to dive away, it came back down inverted and firing. However, the aerobatic enemy pilot missed his high-deflection shot from right overhead, permitting Walters to dive away unscathed, trying to follow after Caldwell in order to fulfil his duties as a wingman.

After Walters, 54 Squadron's CO, Squadron Leader Bill Gibbs, was next to dive in. Like the 'Groupie' he fired without success at one of the 'bombers', pulled up into a breaking turn to the left, and was straightaway attacked by the next aerobatic Zero coming down from above. As he turned, he saw yet another Zero pulling up into a loop at the end of its dive, and so pulled up after it. As he did so, there came a volley of bangs all around him: his aircraft had been hit by a further, unseen, assailant firing at him from the side in a high-deflection shot. To evade this unseen attacker, Gibbs pulled harder into a nose-high vertically banked turn, retaining enough coolness under fire to keep aiming at the other Zero in front of him while it was still going up into its loop. As it hung there he fired a relatively low-deflection, low-closure shot, and saw hits around its cockpit; but his own aircraft, now too nose-high to keep flying, stalled out. Recovering at once into a diving turn, he followed the Zero down to 6000 feet and watched it dive into the water.

Behind his CO, Pilot Officer Bob Ashby dived quite steeply at the two 'bombers' that remained in formation after Caldwell's attack. He attacked the starboard aircraft (the leader) and saw strikes along the top of its engine cowling. Pulling away into a steep climbing turn to starboard, he then dived for home, conscious of his aircraft's parlous fuel state, landing to claim one Japanese 'bomber' damaged.

Sergeant WH Eldred also followed Gibbs in, but by the time he arrived the counter-attacking Zeros had cut him off, and the formation of 'bombers' had broken up to join the dogfight. He fired a high-deflection shot at a Zero that was pulling up into a climbing turn after its firing pass at Gibbs. Having pulled up after it, he was then faced by three successive head-on passes from further diving Zeros. Eldred fired at each one as they came at him in turn and saw the Zeros' tracers shooting past him in reply. As each Zero flashed past him after firing, he would turn to go after it, only to find another one boring in at him from another direction – the Zeros were working together, fighting as a team. This combat ended when Eldred turned hard to meet the final attack, but saw that he was not turning fast enough to get his guns on target. He rolled inverted and dived away, but upon looking behind saw the Zero rolling over to come after him.

Caldwell had meanwhile been continuing his solo combat against several Zeros, and had allowed himself to be drawn into a turning fight in pursuit of his intention to assess the relative performance of the Spitfire and Zero in this, the first-ever combat between these two types. Thus he found himself banked over in a near-vertical turn, pulling so hard that his aircraft was juddering on the edge of a stall. The Zero was on the opposite side of his turn, and he met the gaze of the Japanese pilot as both of them looked up at each other through the top of their canopies. Caldwell was getting overconfident, however, for he let his aircraft slow in the turn to 140 knots IAS, thereby putting himself into the Zero pilots' favoured end of the performance envelope. By the end of the second complete 360 degree turn, his Spitfire was slowing further, and by then the Zero was confirming its reputation for flying more slowly and turning more tightly than the Spitfire: it was now getting in behind him. Caldwell knew where this was going, so he bunted violently out of the turn and ended the contest.

To enter the bunt, he 'parked everything in the left hand corner' – in other words, pushed the stick forward and to the left while also kicking the left rudder pedal. He used full control deflections, simultaneously moving the throttle through the emergency gate to obtain maximum revs – 3000 rpm. The aircraft's nose tucked violently under and skidded left into the beginnings of a messy, lopsided outside loop. Pushed violently against his straps as the aircraft nosed over under full power, his vision 'redded out', the result of extreme negative G produced by blood rushing into the head (rather than away from it, as in a normal positive G manoeuvre). As the aircraft pitched, he rolled and pulled into a positive G turn, hard enough to induce a blackout. After a couple of seconds, he eased the stick pressure, recovered his vision and looked behind to verify that he had shaken off the enemy.

This extreme evasive manoeuvre had been used by Spitfire pilots in the Battle of Britain (and not invented by Caldwell in the desert, as is often stated), and was just as effective at evading Zeros as Me109s. Because of their float carburettors, the engines of Battle of Britain-era Spitfires had cut out under negative G. Judging by 1 Fighter Wing pilots' habitual use of full-power bunts as evasive manoeuvres, the SU anti-G carburettor functioned well enough to maintain power for the few seconds necessary to push through this manoeuvre and then roll out.

Banked over in his clearing turn, Caldwell saw a Spitfire diving away in front of him with a Zero on its tail – Eldred.

Caldwell saw that the faster Spitfire was drawing away, but too slowly for comfort, so he dived after the pursuing Zero. Approaching unseen, he fired a low-deflection shot from nearly dead astern, and debris fell away from the Zero as his rounds struck the airframe. Caldwell followed it down to 5000 feet, then pulled out, but reported seeing the enemy fighter dive into the sea. Meanwhile, Gibbs was also down low, recovering from his own dive and turning to check his tail; as he did so, he saw this second aircraft dive into the water. Eldred also pulled out and broke into a turn to clear his tail; finding that he had 'lost contact' with his pursuer, he flew home.

Flying Officer John Lenagen, in the 'arse-end Charlie' position, had meanwhile dived into a hornet's nest of manoeuvring Zeros. He failed to get his guns on target and ended up diving away without firing – like the others, very mindful of his fuel situation. Gibbs meanwhile took stock of the state of his aircraft, noticing that the top of the engine cowling had been pierced by gunfire and that glycol coolant was escaping in a stream of white vapour – three rounds of enemy 7.7 mm had struck the aircraft from the side, perforating his radiator and striking his headrest (only centimetres from his head). Fortunately for Gibbs, only the higher velocity and flatter trajectory 7.7 mm had hit, while the slower but more deadly 20 mm cannon shells had flown harmlessly past behind him. In view of the condition of his aircraft, he throttled back to 1800 rpm and dived away heading for land. Seeing Lenagen's Spitfire nearby, Gibbs ordered him to join up and escort him home, knowing that 'independence courts death'. They both got back safely and Gibbs landed with only 5 gallons of fuel left. Gibbs's Spitfire was the only one hit in this action, and was easily repaired on the squadron. The Spitfires had fought a dogfight of nearly ten minutes' duration, and were now at a critical fuel state, but fortunately Darwin was only a 12-minute flight away. One by one, they dived away and headed home, with Caldwell one of the last to leave the scene.

As the defending fighters were landing safely between 3.35 and 3.50 pm, another intruder was detected by radar coming in over the coast from Fog Bay, on an easterly course for Coomalie Creek. It arrived overhead the airfield at 3.47 and was greeted with 29 rounds of 3 inch (76 mm) gunfire from 233 LAA Battery. Identified in the gunners' range-finding optics as a Ki-46, the reconnaissance machine circled overhead to get its post-strike photos and then headed back out to the north-west undisturbed.

Results

In spite of the unpromising tactical situation, the Spitfires had succeeded in bouncing the Japanese formation. Moreover, they had suffered no casualties themselves but had claimed three Japanese shot down: Caldwell claimed the 'bomber' he had seen to crash after his initial attack as well as the fighter he had shot off Eldred's tail into the water; Gibbs also claimed a fighter, which he had likewise observed to hit the water. Gibbs's and Caldwell's Zeros had been seen to go into the sea in close succession, with both victorious pilots following their victims down and observing their crashes from a low altitude, undisturbed by Zeros. Walters confirmed these observations, seeing two large splashes 'almost simultaneously', as per Gibbs's observation of the second Zero hitting the sea straight after his own kill. The evidence was thus very strong in support of these two Zero claims, with three eyewitnesses and with positive evidence in each case of the Japanese aircraft's destruction.

Caldwell's 'bomber' claim, however, is not so well attested. He himself had a relatively poor view of the crash, for he had not followed it down nor seen it going down; he had merely been able to glance down from about 11 000 feet, in the midst of his constant scanning for Zero threats, in time to see a splash. In the absence of third-party corroboration, Caldwell's bomber claim seems poorly supported by evidence, and would be adequately explained by the splash of a drop tank rather than of an aircraft. The Zeros' long drop tanks were tumbling into the sea before and during the early part of the action, and these tanks certainly kicked up big splashes after such a long drop: during the raids on Rabaul later in the year, 'geysers of water' were visible from a great distance as Zero belly tanks hit the water after falling from 10 000 feet. The observed evidence therefore suggests that two Japanese fighters were shot down, but no 'bombers'.

However, Japanese records do not in fact support a single loss. No. 1 Fighter Wing certainly became guilty of overclaiming as the campaign progressed, its 'kills' typically characterised by a lack of positive evidence, but the crash observations on this day were both credible and corroborated, and so call for further research into Japanese records. Irrespective of factual niceties, the RAAF announced to the press that six Japanese machines had been shot down, simultaneously revealing to the public the presence of the hitherto top-secret Spitfire wing in Australia. The pilots had certainly not claimed six, so somewhere between NWA HQ and RAAF Command the figure had been doubled. This set a bad precedent for reporting integrity, as noted sardonically by the pilots when they read the papers.

The misidentification of the 'light bombers'

The identification of the main Japanese formation as Nakajima B5N light bombers was recognised as odd at the time. Gibbs had got a good look at them on the approach, seeing them as, compared with the Zeros, 'rather larger single radial engined machines'. Ashby had dived from such a steep angle that he had

had a good view of them from above, becoming 'fairly certain' that they were B5Ns. This difference in perceived size and wing plan-form would be explained if the three centre aircraft were Model 21 Zeros, which featured longer span wings and rounded wingtips – thus providing a visual contrast with those on the flanks if these had been Model 32 Zeros, with their shorter, squared-off wings. Such a mixture of models was normal in Japanese naval fighter units in 1943.

The failure of the 'bombers' to bomb gave rise to a bizarre theory, originating with the wing intelligence officer, Flying Officer Alister McLean, and supported by Caldwell. They concluded that the non-bombing Nakajima 'light bombers' had been carrying expert observers and photographers, sent over to gather intelligence on the Spitfires and their tactics. This was an absurd suggestion, suggesting a superiority complex that would very quickly be disabused by reality. In fact, the Japanese had been identifying P-40s and P-39s as 'Spitfires' since the start of the war, and were thus unaware that these British aircraft had in fact only just entered the theatre. In spite of its access to photo-reconnaissance photos from the Imperial Army's 70th Reconnaissance Squadron, the 23rd Air Flotilla had such poor intelligence on their opponents that the Zero pilots on this day identified the slender Spitfires as P-39 Airacobras and, in a travesty of aircraft recognition, even as corpulent radial-engined Brewster Buffalos! Even had they got it right, the Japanese would not have cared anyway, for they had seen off opponents of all types in the war so far, and were entirely unlikely to accord any especial respect to this new Spitfire outfit.

Overconfidence

Contrary to this Japanese complacency, the wing had discovered that the Spitfire was a very handy fighter against the Zero.

Caldwell correctly concluded that it was faster than the Zero and climbed just as well, although it was less manoeuvrable. Of similar size and power to the contemporary Model 32 Zero, it was half a tonne heavier because of greater structural weight. Although this extra weight meant that the Spitfire could not manoeuvre as slowly and tightly as the Zero, the resultant structural strength meant that the Spitfire pilots could dive their aircraft to great speeds with great confidence – unlike Japanese pilots. They could also roll their aircraft faster and manoeuvre more aggressively at speed. Thanks to the superior power output of its Merlin engine, the Spitfire generated a much better climb rate at high IAS and was 20 knots faster at height. In practice, however, this speed margin was rarely tactically decisive, for the advantage of speed would go to whichever side was diving from a position of superior height.

There were signs of future trouble, however, in the Spitfire's armament system: of the four pilots who had fired their guns, two experienced cannon failures. Eldred's starboard cannon had jammed after only eight rounds, while Ashby's port cannon jammed after 30. Cannon trouble would indeed dog 1 Fighter Wing's 1943 campaign and seriously retard its results.

There was another problem that, although intangible, was just as serious – the overconfidence of inexperience. Squadron Leader Gibbs was quite inexperienced in air combat, yet he had very confidently ignored fighter attacks upon himself to close with his first-identified target and carry through with his firing. Not every pilot would get away with this cool disregard for danger and enemy gunnery, as the next raid would so lamentably show. Gibbs's aircraft was hit around the cockpit area, suggesting that he could easily have failed to survive his first dogfight. This officer had been posted in to 54 Squadron from Coastal Command, having previously flown Hudson patrol bombers – an unlikely career jump, assisted according to Bob Foster by some string-pulling via his personal contacts with the AOC Fighter Command, Air Marshal Sir William Sholto Douglas. Although Gibbs would indeed earn his squadron command by aggressive and effective flying, he was very inexperienced on 2 March.

Wally Walters was also extremely inexperienced in air combat, likewise being an ex-Hudson bomber pilot and new to fighter aviation. Indeed, he had only started his 'crash course' on Spitfires on 31 October 1942, once he had been appointed to command the wing. At 37, he liked to boast that he was the air force's oldest fighter pilot. Flying as Caldwell's No. 2 was certainly a suitable position from which to 'learn the ropes', and reflected well upon Walters's character as both willing to lead from the front and willing to delegate. However, having been bounced from behind, he too was lucky to survive his first combat. Had the Japanese gunnery been as good as it was on some other days, the wing would have finished its first combat with two COs shot down.

Caldwell had had the coolness in combat to survey what was happening around him, retaining the detachment to critique the Japanese performance even in the middle of the dogfight. However, he showed little awareness of the situation of his own pilots, who were meanwhile battling their way out of the swarm of diving Zeros behind him. He might have been sufficiently skilled and situation-aware to fight his own way out of trouble, but this could not be assumed of all the Spitfire pilots in the wing, most of whom were pretty green. He was setting these pilots a hard act to follow in so confidently attacking a large Japanese formation from such a positional disadvantage, and then in persisting with the engagement by dogfighting with them alone and outnumbered.

Moreover, his use of the raw Group Captain Walters as his No. 2 represented a public devaluing of the discipline of flying in pairs for mutual support. Walters, in his first combat, would always have been hard-pressed to keep up with his talented No. 1, and Caldwell seemed to accept this, flying off quite happily to fight by himself and leaving the wing CO to fend for himself in a sky filled with Zeros. Caldwell had ended up protecting Eldred by shooting the Zero off his tail, but this had been the result of a serendipitous encounter rather than the product of any combat drill or tactical procedure. Bobby Gibbes, a leading RAAF fighter pilot who had flown with Caldwell in the desert, had found him to be unsympathetic towards junior pilots and their problems, and there was more than a touch of this Olympian attitude on 2 March. In spite of Walters's excellent qualities, he had been placed in an awkward position as Caldwell's CO. Until he himself 'learnt the ropes', he would be in a poor position to counsel or guide his ace-pilot wing leader.

No. 1 Fighter Wing had come into the Australian theatre of war overestimating itself and underestimating the Japanese enemy. As Caldwell's biographer, Kristen Alexander, explains, the Spitfire pilots had been told that the 49th FG had flown successfully against the 1942 Darwin raids by fighting on the 'dive and zoom' and by strictly avoiding 'dogfighting'. However, the Australian and British fighter leaders had 'treated the American assessments as suspect'; indeed, Caldwell himself had disrespectfully attributed some of the US combat reports to 'imagination'. In short, the US pilots' victory claims were simply not believed within the wing leadership, even though, as events would prove, their overclaiming was no worse than the Spitfire pilots' would be (and no worse than that of Caldwell himself).

A similarly dismissive overconfidence was shown in the response to Group Captain Patrick Heffernan's report from a visit to Port Moresby. 'Paddy' Heffernan was the Officer Commanding RAAF Richmond – where the Spitfire wing had been headquartered prior to its move to Darwin. Newly briefed on intelligence gleaned from a captured Zero, he had warned the Spitfire pilots that the Zero was dangerous, better in manoeuvre than the Spitfire, but this report too was disregarded.

The wing's dismissal of Heffernan's message is related to the unnecessary offence the latter had caused during the work-up at Richmond. Having been forced to host this large group of 'blow-ins' from Britain at 'his' base, he resented the inconvenience of it all, and lectured them on how they needed to behave now they were in Australia; he sarcastically taunted the assembled pilots with the question, 'who has 5000 hours?' – knowing full well that no wartime-trained fighter pilot could have even 1000. His point was sound, a reminder to the Spitfire pilots that they had less to be confident about than they thought they did. However, the point was made most undiplomatically, and could only have caused offence. Heffernan had proven that he himself had a lot to learn – about leadership.

The unhappy result was that the Spitfire pilots, all freshly transferred from the UK-based RAF, developed an animus against the Australia-based regular RAAF. Henceforth, regular RAAF officers and everything they stood for would be sarcastically referred to within the wing as the 'Real Air Force', the imputation being that the home-RAAF considered the wartime-trained EATS men to be amateurs. Predictably, the Spitfire pilots wore this as a badge of honour, considering themselves to be the real fighting airmen, while the home-RAAF officers were tarred as rear area 'Colonel Blimp' types with no understanding of war flying. Interestingly, the 49th Fighter Group had formed much the same impression of the regular RAAF during its work-up in southern Australia prior to its move to Darwin, and had responded in much the same contemptuous way. Nonetheless, the local deities had to be outwardly appeased: while stuck at Richmond under the watchful glare of Group Captain Heffernan, 54 Squadron's flying program was held up twice a day for squadron parades; and even worse, officers were dismayed to discover that they were expected to attend as well! Even on its remote bush airfields, the wing was not safe from sniping by the starchy home-based air force: immediately upon moving into its bush base at Strauss, 452 was picked at by senior officers from NWA HQ for its allegedly poor disciplinary standards. Many RAAF men had been shocked when posted to units in the United Kingdom to see how scruffy the wartime RAF had become; clearly, front-line squadrons gave a lot more attention to aircraft serviceability than to 'spit and polish'. From the perspective of prewar officers who had never left Australia, 452 and 457 had 'gone native' during their service in England, and had brought these poor standards back to Australia to pollute the rest of the air force. The Spitfire units responded to all this by drawing closer together within their individual squadron communities and by doing it their own way.

Even after the early combats over Darwin exposed the limitations of this knowledge, the same resistance to learning from other parts of the RAAF continued: when Bladin visited No. 9 Operational Group in May 1943, under orders from Air Marshal George Jones to 'learn how things were done in New Guinea', its AOC, Air Commodore Joe Hewitt, found him 'correct' but 'cool', with an attitude of 'We have nothing to learn from you'.

2 March pilot table

Sqn	Section	No.	Pilots engaging	Pilots not engaging	Remarks
Pilots engaged:					
		1	W/C Caldwell		
Wing	Winco	2	G/C Walters		
		1	S/L Gibbs RAF		Spitfire BR164 damaged, repaired on unit
		2	Sgt Eldred RAF		1 cannon failed
	Red	4	P/O Ashby RAF		1 cannon failed
54	White	2	F/O Lenagen RAF		
Vectored to orbit over likely targets:					
				F/L Norwood RAF	
				F/Sgt Millar RAF	
				P/O Leonard RAF	
				Sgt Cooper RAF	
				F/L Foster RAF	
				P/O Brook RAF	
				P/O Farries RAF	
54				F/Sgt Mahoney RAF	
Vectored in pursuit of retreating Zeros:					
		1		S/L Thorold-Smith	
		2		F/O Colyer	
		3		F/O Goldsmith	
	Red	4		F/O J Gould	
		1		F/L Makin	
		2		F/O Watkin	
		3		F/O Downes	
452	White	4		F/Sgt Stagg	
Vectored on visual searches, pilots unknown:					
				12 aircraft	main formation
457				1 aircraft	base defence patrol
Totals: Scrambled: 35 Engaged: 6 Damaged: 1					

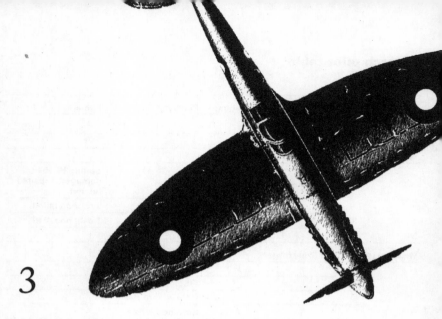

3

'A sharp reverse'

The radar and control problems that had been exposed on the 2 March raid greatly concerned NWA RAAF HQ, for the Japanese had penetrated relatively far inland without being intercepted, and the ultimate engagement had been achieved very late, at a tactical disadvantage, in small numbers and at the very limit of the Spitfires' endurance. As a result, it had been indecisive. There would be pressure to achieve an early interception next time, and this pressure would be fateful.

More specifically, the last raid had revealed the vulnerability of the NWA's air defence system to low-level raiders. In the previous year, Air Commodore Bladin had advised Colonel Wurtsmith to commit his whole fighter force against the first incoming plot, because he judged that the Japanese were unlikely to make simultaneous or sequential raids. This assessment had proved correct for the 1942 raids, but the first raid of 1943 had punctured this certainty. Caldwell, Walters and Primrose decided upon the use of 'Yellow Sections', by which each squadron would provide one element to patrol the likely low-level approach lanes to the airfields further south – such as Coomalie and Batchelor. These 'Jim Crow' patrols were intended to find and report the raid in the event of the failure of radar plotting, and thus get it onto 5 FS's plotting board in order to effect an interception. Besides giving verbal position reports over the R/T, the shadowing Yellow Section pilots would also switch on their HF/DF sets to indicate the raid's position to ground-based radio direction-finders.

The continuance of the photo-reconnaissance overflights suggested that a further raid would follow up the inconclusive 2 March foray. On 3 March, a high-flying intruder appeared overhead without having been plotted on radar, and so Darwin's AA guns opened fire while 54's pilots were still sitting at lunch in their Nightcliff mess. However, on 7 March luck ran out again for the Imperial Army's 70th Reconnaissance Squadron, when 457's Red Section was vectored to a successful interception. The intruder came in across country from the west, photographing Batchelor, Coomalie and Hughes airfields without being detected, and then turned left to head out past Darwin to the north.

Flight Lieutenant Don Maclean and Flight Sergeant FRJ 'Darky' McDowell were orbiting overhead Hughes airfield when it went past, but they only spotted the Ki-46 when it was already 25 kilometres away and 2000 feet higher than they were. Fortunately for them, the Spitfires' performance again proved sufficient to catch it, for in a shallow climb at 182 knots IAS (276 knots true airspeed – TAS), they got so rapidly to the enemy aircraft's height of 26 000 feet that they had to zoom up above it to avoid overshooting. Maclean and McDowell then took turns firing from the intruder's rear quarter. At first, the Japanese aircraft confined its evasion to moderate alterations of course and nose attitude, in order to put off the Spitfires' aim. Giving up on this, the pilot then put the nose down and tried to run for it, but going at 217 knots IAS the Spitfires had no difficulty keeping up.

One of the enemy aircraft's engines was already smoking when Maclean fired a long burst from dead astern right in to 25 metres range. The Ki-46 jerked up into a wingover and then spun down in flames. Both Spitfires followed as it plummeted down to disintegrate at 5000 feet and fall into the sea in pieces. The whole thing was watched enviously by 452's Flight Lieutenant Ted Hall and Flight Sergeant Keith Cross, neither of whom had been close enough to make an attack. This fiery event was also played out in clear view of an envious 54 Squadron down below, for the assembled British pilots were standing awestruck in front of their mess tent, watching as the stricken machine fell in flames into the sea off Lee Point. Circling overhead the impact point, Maclean and McDowell saw the crushed tail and rear fuselage floating near the main wreckage, which lay as a flaming mass on the water.

The Japanese had started their 1943 air campaign unaware that they faced a new opponent. This seems strange, given their photo-reconnaissance activity, but intelligence and the interpretation of intelligence was a weak point for the Japanese, resulting in a persistent tendency to be surprised by developments. Once they belatedly identified the Spitfires, the Japanese commanders mistakenly took the arrival of the new force as evidence of an Allied air build-up in the Darwin area. This was believed to signal an imminent air offensive against their own air bases along their southern defended perimeter, and this fear prompted a reinforcement of the 23rd Air Flotilla's units in order to 'crush the enemy's intent to retaliate'.

The Imperial Navy would be sending over a bomber group in tight formation at high altitude, with a full fighter group as close escort. This was a continuation of the tactics it had used in the previous year's Darwin raids from 25 April onwards: the navy was playing to its strengths, for this was exactly the operational employment for which it had equipped and trained its air arm since 1937, and in which it was highly practised as a result of continuous combat experience over China. Indeed, it had been Japan's war in China that had opened up the strategic bombing mission for the navy's land-based bomber units, and pioneered for the navy's fighter units the revolutionary role of the long-range strategic fighter. The navy airmen would therefore be playing to a well-rehearsed script when they arrived over Darwin. According to the script, the bombers would 'crush' the Darwin base through bombing while the fighters would 'annihilate' the defending fighter force (as can be seen, the use of grandiloquent rhetoric was mandatory within the Japanese command chain).

The 15 March raid

March 15 dawned as a hot and sunny morning, a sign of the fine weather that had come with the beginning of the long dry season. At 10.39 am, both No. 109 and No. 132 Radar Stations detected an incoming formation at 190 kilometres to the north-west, but control initially assumed it to be a reconnaissance flight. Just before 11.00 it was spotted by RAAF coastwatchers positioned on the south-west tip of Bathurst Island, who confirmed it as a raid – the 53rd on the Darwin area since 19 February 1942.

This time, wireless eavesdropping had failed to interpret the signals, with the result that the wing was caught unprepared – as shown by the fact that Caldwell was getting medical treatment at Berrimah when the alert was broadcast. Because of the initial uncertainty about the plot, control scrambled the wing late, so 457 and 54 did not get airborne until about 10.45. However, part of 452 Squadron had taken off at 10.30, and these pilots would form the kernel of the main intercepting formation. The unit's CO, Squadron Leader Ray Thorold-Smith, had overnighted at Darwin with his four most senior pilots for night-flying practice. Having departed Darwin in the morning for the transit flight back to their home base at Strauss, they found themselves scrambled in midair and vectored to Hughes for a rendezvous with the rest of the wing. Unfortunately, the five pilots were tired after completing their program of night flying, and their aircraft's oxygen bottles had not been refilled – a significant deficiency if the day turned into a high-altitude interception. In Caldwell's absence, Thorold-Smith assumed the role of wing leader. Although he was the most experienced of the squadron COs, it was nonetheless the first time he had led even a squadron into action, let alone a wing.

No. 54 Squadron got off the ground in two waves: Flight Lieutenant Rob Norwood's flight of five aircraft got away promptly, while Flight Lieutenant Bob Foster's flight of five Spitfires got off a few minutes afterwards, chasing the others and eventually succeeding in joining on behind them. The CO, Squadron Leader Gibbs, took off five minutes later still, alone, but failed to catch the others and so missed the action. No. 452 Squadron was likewise split up, for three sections got off at two different times from two different bases. No. 457 was little better, sending its aircraft off in three waves. Thus not one of the squadrons had managed to concentrate itself properly, let alone the full wing. Worried about follow-up raids and unplotted low-level penetrations, control also detached half of 457 to patrol independently over the southern airfields around Fenton.

The British squadron, based at Darwin, had furthest to come to the rendezvous, while the two Australian squadrons were conveniently based side by side further south, nearer to Hughes. However, the plot was developing too fast for a proper wing rendezvous, so when control advised that the raid was now approaching Darwin, Thorold-Smith set course at once to intercept with the small force he actually had with him, ordering the other sections to follow. No. 54 Squadron had still not caught up with 452, while 457's Blue and Yellow Sections set off independently. Each of the three squadrons was therefore separate as they set course to intercept.

After the aborted wing rendezvous, Norwood found himself at the head of 54, chasing Thorold-Smith in a 'balls out' stern chase as the wing headed back north towards Darwin. The Spitfires were flying at maximum revs and boost in a 'buster' climb, trying to get height over the escorting Zeros before the raid arrived. Unfortunately, this sense of haste meant that the formation straggled badly, as each individual Spitfire performed differently, each flying at slightly different airspeeds and climb rates. As a result, formation was lost and the machines spread out 'all over the sky'. The pace of the chase was so high that by the time Norwood succeeded in joining on behind Thorold-Smith's formation, the initial ten aircraft of his squadron had been whittled down to seven, the others failing to join on or dropping behind and losing contact.

The raiders were flying a south-east course towards Darwin, while the Spitfire wing was flying north-west on a reciprocal heading which placed the approaching Japanese to its left front. The controllers had done a good job with their intercept geometry, as the Spitfires would merely have to turn left 90 degrees to make their firing runs. However, as the wing approached visual contact with the raid, its sections were in ragged formation, spread out in a rough column. No. 457 Squadron's sections and 452's Red Section had proceeded independently of Thorold-Smith's 452/54 group, but they were heading to the same point, and so their courses converged with the others' as they got closer to the Japanese. Yellow Section of 457, the 'Jim Crow' patrol, was much lower and out in front, on the far side (to the south) of the Japanese track.

Thorold-Smith's small 452 section was in the van of the wing column, with 54 behind; 457 was behind but further out to the left, while 452's straggling Red Section was lowest and last. Despite the failure to concentrate these sections, all of them were approaching the Japanese from the same direction, thereby foregoing the element of surprise or uncertainty, and permitting all the Japanese fighters to concentrate on the bombers' threatened left flank. No. 1 Fighter Wing had 'telegraphed its punches', and was now queuing up to be hit.

No. 54 Squadron was still strung out in the chase when Thorold-Smith ordered them to take position above 452 as top-cover. Because the British squadron was already chasing at full revs, this was impossible, but in obedience to orders, Norwood continued his climb after 452, but he never got his formation into its assigned position above the Australians. Moreover, 54 inevitably lost ground as it climbed, with the unfortunate effect that Thorold-Smith moved further out ahead, thereby isolating his section from its supposed top-cover. Meanwhile, two of his own pilots had dropped out due to oxygen shortage, leaving only three Spitfires in the CO's group.

This dreadful straggling was particularly ironic considering that Thorold-Smith had earlier complained to Caldwell about precisely this problem: after wing formation practices at Richmond, prior to the deployment to Darwin, he had told the wing leader, 'we think you fly very fast'. Bobby Gibbes had made a similar complaint about Caldwell earlier on in the North African campaign. They both meant that Caldwell, when flying at the head of the formation, tended to set too fast a pace for the pilots trying to keep formation behind him. If the leader was flying at a high throttle setting, the junior pilots behind lost the ability to adjust their power, because their throttle was already set at or close to its maximum setting. They therefore fell behind every time they used their controls, and as they did so they started cutting corners, drifting back to the centre of the formation. In this way, an intended broad line abreast battle formation turned into a ragged cluster of machines around the leader at the front, followed by a straggling line of aircraft behind and below. This was no way for a fighter unit to go into battle.

Strangely, in spite of Thorold-Smith's awareness of the problem, he imposed the same thing on his pilots on this day. His main force of 17 Spitfires was spread out in an untidy column as it climbed past 20 000 feet over Lee Point, in time to collide with the Japanese formation as it came in towards Darwin Harbour. By contrast, the enemy pilots were flying in the Imperial Navy's trademark impeccable formation. At 23 000 feet, the bombers were still higher than the Spitfires, and to compound the wing's tactical disarray, 54 was still in line astern, having never had a chance in their 'balls out chase' to get into battle formation; and although 452 and 457 had adopted line abreast battle formation, the same hard climbing had spread them out into a ragged zigzag.

The first air battle, over Darwin Harbour

The first pilot to see and report the raid was Flight Sergeant Evan Batchelor, who reported the position of the Japanese formation as 25 kilometres north-west of Point Charles, inbound. He was flying as No. 2 to Flight Lieutenant Pete Watson in 457 Squadron's Yellow Section. They were below the wing at 9000 feet, craning their heads upwards to peer through their canopies into the yawning sun-blazing brightness above. In their role as an airborne scouting element, they had set out independently of the wing to find and follow the enemy and to send position reports back to control over the R/T. This they now did, and they would continue to operate independently in this role throughout the action.

Blue Section of 457 was off the port rear quarter of Thorold-Smith's group – but closest to the incoming Japanese, who would soon be visible out to that side. The section leader, Flying Officer FD 'Bush' Hamilton, was thus the next to see and report the enemy, out beyond his port wingtip. He led his section closer in a gentle turn to port, only then noticing the swarm of enemy fighters 'surrounding' the bombers. He counted 20–25 bombers in a tight line abreast formation, still climbing, and saw that the Zeros were grouped in threes; about 2000 feet above the bombers and about a kilometre out on the side and out in front.

Ahead and to starboard of Hamilton, Thorold-Smith was next to spot the enemy. By then the bombers were about 15 kilometres north-west of Darwin, just west of Point Charles, and now at the same height as Thorold-Smith. The latter continued the climb until he had bare height superiority over the bombers, and then he led his tiny 452 formation in a left turn towards the enemy, calling 'attack' on the R/T and making a shallow dive at their port rear quarter. Although the Spitfires had gained about 500 feet over the bombers, the escorting Zeros were higher still. Due to their very small height advantage, the Spitfires were committed to a shallow dive only. Moreover, as they were coming in from the bombers' rear quarter, they had only a modest overtaking speed. Thorold-Smith's attack was thus played out in excruciatingly slow motion, giving the Japanese fighter pilots poised overhead plenty of time to react and manoeuvre.

As the 452 and 457 elements turned left towards the bombers, they found themselves flying either side of the group of escorting Zeros on the enemy's left flank – Hamilton was trying to dive past in front of them while Thorold-Smith was trying to sneak past behind. By now, 54 was too far behind and too low to provide top-cover to anyone. Moreover, Thorold-Smith was now also separated from Hamilton by the intervening Zeros. To put it mildly, it was not a good tactical position. None of the three elements of the wing had enough height to get through the escort without being intercepted, and they were too far away from each other to provide any mutual support. The action therefore took the form of three separate fights by three isolated sections of Spitfires.

Instead of keeping the fighters off Thorold-Smith's form-ation, 54 was bounced by Zeros coming down out of the sun. The British pilots' punishing stern chase on 452, and their acute difficulty in fulfilling Thorold-Smith's orders, had left them anxious and preoccupied, looking to their front as they continued the climb, fixated upon getting into position above him. As the day had developed, layers of cloud had built up at around 20000 and 30000 feet, shielding from view the approach of the highest Zeros. The sky otherwise was blazingly bright, and so those Zeros were able to remain hidden up in the sun, unseen until too late. Bob Foster now saw them, but they were already on the way down. He shouted a warning over the R/T and 54 Squadron's Spitfires split up to evade the attack.

Sergeant Bert Cooper was not quick enough in breaking; his aircraft was hit, and smoke and flame streamed out of the engine. He was in such a hurry to abandon his aircraft before being burnt that he just jettisoned the canopy, stood up, and jumped over the cockpit side. The prescribed technique was to roll the aircraft onto its back and drop out of the cockpit, but this was easier said than done in an emergency. As he tumbled untidily out of the cockpit, his head hit the tailplane; his neck was broken by the impact and his body fell 20000 feet into Darwin Harbour. Cooper was a mature married man from Worcestershire; he had joined the RAF after the outbreak of war, and now he died, at 28 years of age, in the yawning blue sky over Darwin. He had only arrived in Australia to join 54 in December, and now he was dead – even before his service papers arrived from England. His pilotless Spitfire plunged vertically into the waters of the harbour, marking the sky with a thin column of smoke. Cooper had been unlucky in the NWA, having already been involved in a runway collision with another Spitfire on 5 February, in which Sergeant Peter McCarthy had been killed.

After the break, Norwood found himself in a target-rich environment and fired four times at Zeros; he got visible hits on three, and saw a stream of smoke from one, optimistically making claims afterwards for all four. His No. 2, Flight Sergeant Ken Biggs, saw Norwood hit the first Zero, and saw smoke and flames coming from its engine, fuselage and wing root. With further Zeros coming down from above, Norwood broke away into an evasive rolling dive. Biggs now did his job as Norwood's No. 2: when he saw these Zeros coming down after his leader, he fired at the first one and saw strikes on it; then flames came out from under its belly. This Zero went down in a spiral dive, but Biggs could no longer give it his attention, for two more Zeros now came in at him. Breaking downwards, he followed Norwood in a tight spiral dive to 15 000 feet. Pulling out, he saw a smoking 'Zero' dive past and go straight into the sea. In fact, this was probably Cooper's pilotless Spitfire – an easy misidentification to make in the quick glances of an air battle.

Bob Foster, further back in the 54 Squadron straggle, saw Norwood and Biggs under attack by Zeros, but went past them at the bombers. Seeing three Zeros coming in behind him, he nonetheless continued with his attack, and got off a quick burst at the bombers before continuing straight on, in an evasive dive down to 14 000 feet. Foster's No. 2, Flying Officer Ian Taylor, followed his leader in towards the bombers, but a Zero attacked him from behind before he could open fire. Tracers shot past underneath him, and then the Zero that had fired them went by as well, still going fast at the end of its dive. Taylor turned and fired at it, but his cannons jammed immediately. He and Foster dived away from the fight in different directions.

Flying Officer Al Mawer (one of five Australian pilots attached to 54 during March to make up the numbers) had been positioned above and behind the 54 Squadron aircraft just before the bounce. As 'weaver' at the rear of 54's strung-out line astern formation, he was ostensibly on lookout duty, but like most others that day he failed to see the Zeros coming down from out of the sun. Tracers suddenly came from behind, flicking past his port wing, and then they flashed right over his head. He broke into a hard turn, thereby forcing the Zero that had fired at him to overshoot. As it passed in front, Mawer reversed his bank, turned inside it, got onto its tail, and fired from 50 metres with only one ring of deflection (that is, a comparatively simple shot with a fair probability of hitting). The Zero rolled onto its back and dived, with Mawer following. It then pulled out too early with Mawer still behind it, and so he was able to fire again from dead astern at 200 metres. Intense flames shot from the underside of the Zero; it rolled again onto its back and went straight down. Mawer followed it all the way down to 1000 feet and saw it hit the water. All this had been a commendably rapid and cool-headed counter-attack under the alarming circumstances of the initial bounce, reflecting both this pilot's talent as a fighter pilot and his previous combat experience: he had flown Hurricanes and Spitfires with RAF Fighter Command from October 1941, had completed 80 operational hours, and had previously claimed two German aircraft.

While 54 was getting bounced, Thorold-Smith continued his attack on the bombers – a bold move under the circumstances. His No. 2, Flight Lieutenant Ted Hall, warned him that there were fighters above, but the CO continued his shallow dive at the outside end of the bomber formation, even as Hall saw that a section of Zeros were now diving in behind. The leader kept on going, and was last seen firing at a Zero but under attack by three more coming at him from different directions – as usual, the Zeros were working together.

Ted Hall and Tim Goldsmith, Thorold-Smith's wingmen, were experienced combat pilots. Goldsmith was the wing's second ace after Caldwell (indeed, he finished the war as Australia's second-ranked ace, with 16 'kills'), having done a tour in the 'target rich environment' of Malta during the 1942 'blitz'. Both these pilots tried to follow their leader in towards the bombers, but both were cut off by the escorting fighters. Goldsmith was diverted from his attack on the bombers by two Zeros coming in at him from his right. Turning in to face this attack, he took his eyes off Thorold-Smith's machine ahead of him, and never saw it again. The first Zero dived out in front acting as a decoy for the second, which hung back waiting to pounce once Goldsmith committed himself. Surprisingly, he did so, turning after the first Zero and firing from 300 metres. He saw strikes on his target and the Zero turned sharply left, trailing black smoke – he later claimed it as damaged. By now, the second Zero was behind him, closing inside 200 metres – a dangerous firing range. Red tracer flicked past as Goldsmith rolled over, pulled and dived away. As he went, he saw a smoking Spitfire going down in a vertical dive – probably Cooper's machine. Goldsmith had acted aggressively, but he had perhaps been a little cavalier in ignoring the Zero behind him and permitting himself to be fired upon; he would try something similar on 2 May and be shot down for it.

Ted Hall meanwhile had approached one Zero unseen and got a shot from dead astern at the killing distance of 100 yards. It smoked badly and spun away – he later claimed it as probably destroyed, but his claim was later downgraded to 'damaged'. Like

Goldsmith, Hall was in turn attacked by a further Zero that had hung back. Red tracers suddenly shot past, so he bunted to break out of its line of fire. About 30 seconds after the fight began, Hall saw a smoking Spitfire turning from west to north in a slight dive. This was probably Thorold-Smith, trying to get his damaged aircraft back to safety. Pulling up into a climbing turn, Hall saw another Zero racing in above him, inverted. It pulled through to come down vertically, firing at him from directly overhead. Hall held his height, held his aircraft in its tight turn, and presented the aggressive Japanese aerobat with a difficult full deflection shot. The Zero duly missed and plunged past him below. Hall found that as he kept turning, the Zeros were losing height to him, and were now continually climbing up steeply in attempts to get on his tail. Hall successfully turned in to each attack from this pack of Zeros, but meanwhile the bombers were steadily drawing away.

To the rear, Bush Hamilton's Blue Section from 457 also tried to dive at the bombers. Hamilton saw 54's dogfight behind and to his right, and heard it on the R/T, and now found his way to the bombers blocked by the front group of Zeros. He took the easiest course and instead went after the nearest group of three enemy fighters 1000 feet below. The Zeros broke just in time, but Hamilton made a good attack on one of them, chasing it in a tight turn, firing twice, and seeing strikes on its wing. A second Zero came in behind him, so he was forced to break off by half-rolling and exiting the fight in a rolling dive. Sensibly anxious about being pursued, he continued the dive to 1000 feet.

Hamilton's No. 2, Flight Sergeant Rex Watson (the reader should distinguish between the flight commander, Pete Watson, and his unrelated subordinate, Rex Watson), followed Hamilton into the fight, likewise chasing a Zero round in a turn, likewise getting off two bursts at it from the rear quarter, and likewise breaking when another Zero dived at him. This was one of the high-cover Zeros, and as it came within gun range, Watson throttled back, broke left and pulled his stick coarsely backward to pitch his aircraft into a high-speed stall. The Spitfire flicked to the right, forcing the Zero into an overshoot. As the Japanese fighter overshot, Watson exploited the Spitfire's excellent handling characteristics, easing the stick to recover normal flight at once, now in a good position to chase. He half-rolled after the Zero and chased it in a steep dive, losing 8000 feet. As the Zero pulled out of its dive ahead of him, Watson was doing nearly 350 knots IAS. Pulling so hard that he started to black out, he held the G, lined up and fired, closing right in to 25 metres. Both cannons jammed, but he saw strikes on the Zero's wing root and cowling. As he broke away, he saw smoke coming from its engine, and then it spun away with its forward fuselage aflame, so he justifiably claimed it as destroyed.

Pilot Officer Norm Robinson, Hamilton's No. 3, saw the Zero diving onto his leader's tail, so he got behind it and fired a good burst from 200 metres, but missed his shot – the Zero pulled straight upwards, violently and suddenly. Displaying the Japanese pilots' liking for aerobatics in combat, it performed a 'hammerhead' stall-turn to come back down onto him from above. Robinson pulled up after it but could not get his gunsight on, so broke off and dived away.

Meanwhile, Flight Sergeant Frank Varney from 54 Squadron had descended from the combat area and attempted a forced landing on the beach next to Kahlin Hospital in Darwin. Evidently suffering physical impairment, he undershot the aiming point and hit the shelf of large boulders in front of Myilly Point. His aircraft was 'smashed to pieces' in the crash-landing and caught fire. He was removed from the wreckage by hospital staff, but was critically injured in the crash.

No. 54 Squadron's engineering officer, Pilot Officer 'Cecil' Beaton, later examined the wreckage but could find no bullet holes, so the cause of Varney's fate remains inconclusive. However, his squadron concluded that the cause of the attempted forced landing had been a glycol leak into the cockpit. This was more than plausible, as this technical fault would cause the loss of many of 1 Fighter Wing's aircraft, and would result in several other pilot fatalities. Moreover, the squadron attributed the glycol leak to an overrevving engine caused by propeller overspeeding, an oft-repeated failure that was all too prevalent during sudden dives at high revs from high altitude – precisely the condition in which Varney found himself. He had not been injured by enemy gunfire, yet he had deliberately landed next to the hospital in order to obtain urgent medical assistance, so glycol poisoning seems the only explanation for his haste in trying to get to help. Certainly this would explain Varney's desperate hurry to put his aircraft on the ground, as well as his poorly executed forced landing.

. Frank Varney died the next afternoon in the intensive care ward, aged 20, a long way from his home and his young wife in Crawley, Middlesex, and two months away from his 21st birthday. Although so young, he had been the most senior NCO pilot on the squadron, having joined 54 fresh from OTU back in December 1941. Sadly, while Varney lay dying, Bert Cooper's body was brought in, having been recovered from the harbour by the Royal Australian Navy (RAN), leaving the bodies of two young Englishmen lying side by side in the hospital morgue.

While the Spitfires of Cooper, Thorold-Smith and Varney dived away out of the fight, along came the three aircraft of 452's Red Section, led by Flying Officer Clive 'Bill' Lloyd. They had initially been assigned the task of orbiting Hughes airfield at 10 000 feet, but control had relented and vectored the three Spitfires towards the approaching raid: they climbed northward, trying to intercept the wing, but never quite managing to catch up. It was not until he was approaching Darwin that Lloyd spotted

The wreckage of Bill Lloyd's Spitfire BS293 QY-E at Picnic Cove, Cox Peninsula, shot down on 15 March. AWM Negative 014565

the rest of the wing up ahead, and he had almost attached his section to the bottom rear end of the ragged Spitfire formation when the action started. Unfortunately, Lloyd had become too preoccupied with the task of chasing the wing and getting into position, and so he failed to spot the vast bomber formation until it was only a kilometre away, ahead and on his left.

Although Lloyd had not seen any fighters, they had seen him. To make matters worse, in a pattern that was characteristic of 1 Fighter Wing's performance on this day, he had been climbing so fast in his attempt to catch up that he had left his No. 2 and No. 3 behind, thus inadvertently isolating himself in a patch of sky full of high-flying Zeros. Lloyd turned left to go in at the bombers, and was only 300 metres out about to open fire, when he suddenly spotted three Zeros coming in at him from the front. Distracted by them, he failed to see the fourth Zero, which had worked its way in behind him.

Bomb damage to the RAN's harbour-side oil tanks in the 15 March raid. Fire crews shelter from the heat behind an asbestos shield while directing a hose onto the fire. AWM Negative 157291

Suddenly his aircraft was thumped and hammered from behind, struck in the engine and wing; and at once oil and glycol came back all over his windscreen. Lloyd bunted his aircraft violently out of the Zero's gunsight, but too late, for smoke and choking glycol fumes already filled the cockpit. Fortunately, the Zeros did not follow him down, having presumably already chalked up his smoking aircraft as a confirmed kill. Lloyd therefore had enough time to switch off the engine, trim the aircraft into a glide, descend to 5000 feet, assess the forced-landing options, reject them, and then bail out. Trimming the aircraft nose-heavy, he undid his harness, unplugged the oxygen and R/T leads, rolled the aircraft onto its back, and then shoved forward on the stick to propel himself out of the cockpit. He detached cleanly, pulled the parachute D-ring, and then floated down in the sudden peace and quiet under his parachute canopy, to watch his aircraft catch fire and fly into the ground south of Point Charles. He landed about 3 kilometres south of the burning wreckage. Lloyd was considered one of 457's most experienced pilots, but he had been shot down in his first combat with the Japanese.

Lloyd's No. 3, Flying Officer Ross Williams, saw his leader get bounced in front of him, and so he gained a moment of warning. Looking up at once, he saw Zeros coming down at him too, and evaded them by diving steeply away. As he went down, he plunged right through the middle of another formation of six Zeros, but was going too fast to fire. As he pulled out, two Zeros then came in at him head-on. He fired, saw no hits, and again broke away downwards. Control vectored him back to Darwin, as it was still concerned about additional raids and unplotted low-level formations. Lloyd's No. 2, Flying Officer John Gould, had also received enough warning to evade the bounce, disengaging at once by diving away out of contact.

The bomber formation, which had so far been unmolested by fighter attack, now went in to the target and bombed. Air Group 753's lead bombardier dropped accurately from 22 000 feet, helped not only by the clear sky that was so typical of the Darwin dry season, but also by the absence of either fighter attack or AA fire. Control had wrongly thought that the Spitfires were attacking the bombers, and had issued a 'do not fire' order to the guns. Standing in their gun pits, the gunners watched in frustration as the great crescent of bombers went overhead on its bombing run, but the men retained the objectivity to admire the enemy's 'very tight' formation. The Japanese dropped a pattern of around 100 bombs, which burst in a destructive swath across the waterfront. The bombs, of 60 and 100 kg, both high explosive (HE) and incendiaries, fell in the town area, in among the harbour-side oil tanks, and into the harbour near the floating dock. The US Army HQ building was destroyed by a direct hit, while further bombs fell across the Public Works Department's compound, damaging workshops and buildings. More seriously, two of the great oil tanks by the harbour were set ablaze; two empty tanks received direct hits and two others were damaged. The Japanese had done a good job in striking at the RAN's naval base, for 2300 tons of oil were lost as well as 7100 tons of diesel. As Bob Foster re-climbed after his first attack, he watched the oil tanks burn, sending up huge columns of black smoke. Luckily there had been no fatalities, but 14 men were injured – six army, three RAN and five civilians. Taking advantage of 202 AG's defeat of the Spitfires in the initial engagement, one Zero added insult to injury by descending to strafe the oil tanks; gunners from the 2/11th Australian Field Regiment engaged it with their machine guns as it went past.

Wing Commander Caldwell had been caught at Berrimah when the alert sounded, and had raced back to RAAF Darwin to belatedly take off alone, just in time to see the bombers drop their loads. He kept them in sight as he climbed to the west at full throttle, chasing until he was 110 kilometres out to sea. By then the Japanese had passed out of sight, and so he missed the battle.

The second engagement, out to sea

Once the Zeros had beaten off the Spitfires' first attack, the Japanese air armada flew further inland to the south-east and then made a wide turn back for the coast, with the bombers still impeccably arranged in their majestic crescent formation. Their steady progress to the west at 175 knots left the dogfighting Spitfires and Zeros behind. Having disengaged from the initial fight, individual Spitfire pilots now started following the bombers out to sea to reattack, climbing from lower levels as they did so. Meanwhile, the Japanese fighter pilots applied a well-practised battle drill, flying back in twos and threes and rejoining the bombers at predesignated rallying positions above and to the flanks. This meant that the Zeros would be back in their places above the bombers by the time the Spitfires arrived, ready for round two of the day's air battle.

Ian Taylor from 54 had heard an R/T message advising that the bombers were heading outbound for Port Patterson. Spotting them in the distance, he slowly overhauled them in a climbing stern chase, but three Zeros flew out ahead of him in line abreast and so he decided to bounce these instead. Taylor was just lining his sights up on the right-hand one when all three turned about suddenly in unison. One pulled straight up into a loop and came back at him, firing while inverted; its tracers flashed past just underneath him. As this Zero roared right overhead, another came curving in towards him from the side. Taylor broke into this one, turned inside it, fired from its rear quarter, and saw thick white smoke coming from its engine cowling. However, whatever the source of the smoke, this Zero was still very much in business, for it tightened up and started to gain on him in the turn. Recognising imminent defeat, Taylor spun his aircraft out of the fight and dived away a second time.

Both Bush Hamilton's Blue Section and Pete Watson's Yellow Section from 457 emerged from the initial combat in relatively good order, but Hamilton's men had split in all directions in escaping from the Zeros, and so followed the bombers out independently. All four pilots of Hamilton's Blue Section re-engaged, but the fighter escort would keep three of the four away from the bombers.

Norm Robinson caught the bombers south-west of Port Patterson and was about to dive in at the right-most bomber when he saw two Zeros coming in behind him. He broke left to dive away from them – in towards the concave rear of the bombers' crescent formation. As he dived, he noticed two other Zeros in line astern 1 kilometre behind the bombers. Deciding that these would be an easier target, Robinson turned in behind them and lined up on the trailing one. Firing from astern and above, he saw strikes on its wing and then broke into a turn to check his tail. The two Zeros were still there behind him, so he pushed over into a 380 knot IAS spiral dive and kept going all the way down to 600 feet, landing with only 10 gallons left and claiming the Zero as a 'probable'.

Rex Watson reacquired the bombers as they headed outbound for Port Patterson, reporting their position to control and continuing his climb until he was 1000 feet above and 1000 metres behind them. However, this put him into a straight stern chase, and so he was now a conspicuous target as he slowly overhauled the formation. A Zero came in from out of the sun, spoiling his hopes of attacking the bombers unmolested. Watson half-rolled and dived away; upon pulling out, he could no longer see the bombers, so he returned to base too.

Having dived out of the initial fight, Bush Hamilton set course for Cape Fourcroy on the south-west tip of Bathurst Island. It was only as he climbed past 20 000 feet that he reacquired the bombers, now flying north-west, still in the same broad and flat crescent formation seen earlier. Encouragingly, there were no fighters visible, so he advised control of the enemy position and climbed up sun at maximum revs. Getting 3000 feet above, he now belatedly noticed nine Zeros slightly above the bombers, but as he was still in a perfect position to attack, he announced 'Tally-ho' over the R/T and dived in. Although Hamilton did not see any other Spitfires, there were in fact several Spitfires in visual distance behind him. As he dived towards the bombers, he was cut off by a Zero coming in across his front. He turned and fired at it in a deflection shot from 100 metres – and afterwards claimed it as damaged. He then saw other Zeros converging on him, so broke away into a rolling dive and disengaged. As he returned to base, he saw a large patch of oil on the sea 30 kilometres from Port Patterson on a bearing of 280 degrees. No Spitfire crashed out to sea, so this may have marked the position of a shot-down Japanese aircraft.

John Gould from Lloyd's 452 Red Section came along behind the strung-out aircraft of Hamilton's section, following them to join the fight with the Zeros. Gould turned steeply behind one enemy fighter, got a shot at it and then broke off to clear his own tail. Another Zero immediately shot straight up in front of him into a stall turn. Gould pulled his nose up and fired at it as it hung there suspended at the top of its zoom, but his starboard cannon jammed and he saw no strikes. The Zero stalled and plunged away vertically out of sight under his nose. While he was pulling up after this Zero, the first one had turned around after him, zooming up behind and firing. Tracers flashed past his wing, and machine-gun bullets hit his engine: oil leaked back over the windscreen and smoke streamed from the engine exhaust stubs. He bunted violently out of the Zero pilot's line of fire, dived down into the safety of a cloud layer, throttled back, and set course for Strauss, monitoring his engine instruments. His engine kept going, so he made a normal landing.

Pete Watson, leader of 457's Yellow Section, took a constructive role in the re-engagement by discharging his duties as the 'Jim Crow' Yellow Section. Having lost contact with the raid over Darwin because of an intervening layer of cloud, he was re-vectored onto the bombers by control as they retired out to sea. Accompanied by his No. 2, Evan Batchelor, he found the bombers again and shadowed them from underneath, climbing as he went and periodically reporting their position over the R/T. He counted them as 21 bombers in three line abreast vees, and observed eight to ten Zeros weaving about above them. Watson was going 25 knots faster than the Japanese, and was thus overtaking them as he emerged on their starboard side, climbing up sun. As the two Spitfires went past, the Japanese pilots spotted them and went after them, but the Spitfires were climbing at too great an IAS, and so the Zeros were unable to catch up.

Batchelor was nonetheless concerned about Zeros and kept scanning the sky behind. Looking back to the front, he found that Watson's aircraft had become obscured by the glare of the sun, and thereby lost sight of his No. 1. Thus isolated, Batchelor then found himself sandwiched between three groups of Zeros, with the closest group of four already diving in at him from the side. He pulled up into a steep climbing turn to get above these, but three more then came in from behind. Seeing the bombers ahead to his left and 4000 feet lower, he tried to dive away after them, but a third group of Zeros moved in from his right to block this. He evaded these in a steep climbing turn, and found himself above and behind yet another two. He dived and fired on the second one, but the leader pulled up into a loop to come back at him. Batchelor pulled hard and followed this Zero up, and it filled his gunsight as it pulled slowly over the top of the loop. He fired a good burst from 50 metres, and the Zero stalled out of the loop and plunged away vertically. Batchelor watched it fall through 4000 feet without recovering, so he claimed it as a probable. Meanwhile, he too had run out of airspeed, and so he also stalled out and spun away. Recovering from the spin, he leaned forward and checked the reading on his fuel gauge. It was low, so he decided to continue the dive and head back to base, where he landed with only 5 gallons left. In this single-handed combat against an entire squadron of Zeros, Batchelor had been a target for several Zeros' gunnery, returning with 7.7 mm bullet holes in oil feeder pipes, fuel lines, engine mounting, and in the petrol tank – all had hit in the engine area, so they were dangerously close to doing vital damage. Batchelor had been very lucky to get away with this boldly flown engagement, but he had done very well for a first tour pilot with the very low figure of 258 hours in his logbook.

While the escorting Zeros were busy trying to kill Batchelor, Pete Watson had moved over to the opposite side of the bombers, and was thus able to get a free run at the left-hand end of their formation. However, he used poor gunnery technique, spraying the whole formation rather than aiming at a single aircraft. Nonetheless, as he broke away he saw white smoke coming from the port engine of the outermost bomber – probably escaping fuel from a punctured wing tank. By then the Zeros had seen him and were coming in, so he peeled off into a rolling dive. Recovering at 13 000 feet, he checked his tail to confirm that there were no Zeros with him and then re-climbed at full revs and boost. He overtook the bombers again in ten minutes; by then they were in a shallow dive, descending through 20 000 feet, and heading for an obscuring layer of cloud up ahead.

Watson got above them and dived in again, but was diverted from the bombers by the proximity of two Zeros off to the right of the formation. He dived in behind these and fired a two-second burst at one of them, right in to 50 metres. The Zero zoomed straight up into the air, standing on its tail with smoke coming from the fuselage. Watson chose not to stick around to watch, instead half-rolling and diving away. He put the pursuit off by diving through two obscuring layers of cloud, continuing down to 2000 feet. Checking his fuel, he found he had only 25 gallons left, so broke off, landing with near-empty tanks.

Flight Sergeant 'Darky' McDowell followed after the bombers, with other Spitfires in sight ahead. However, his engine started running roughly, and so after throttling back he turned about to go home. However, at reduced revs the engine started firing properly again, so he reversed his course and continued after the bombers. At reduced revs and boost he inevitably lagged behind the others, and thus he watched from behind as his colleagues were engaged by the fighter escort and chased away. He estimated the position of this engagement as 60 kilometres off Port Patterson at a bearing of 300 degrees, and heard one Spitfire report trouble and dive away through the clouds – either Batchelor or Gould. McDowell continued his climb, nursing his engine temperatures at reduced revs, and finally caught up when the bombers were 100 kilometres off the coast. He then dived in from their left flank, and although his engine had again started to run 'erratically', he completed his firing run. Unfortunately, he used poor gunnery technique, firing 'across the formation' rather than at a single target bomber. Smoke came from one bomber on the port side, but he could not say that it was his target, so ambiguously claimed one bomber as 'possibly damaged'.

McDowell was then jumped by three Zeros, but he saw them coming in time and spoiled their gunnery by kicking his rudder pedals to skid his aircraft violently to one side and the other. Breaking away into a hard left turn, two other Zeros came at him in a head-on pass, their tracers passing very close. As he pulled around after them, he saw that the original three Zeros were coming in behind him again, so he half-rolled and dived away, again yawing his aircraft violently from side to side to evade their gunfire.

Bob Foster had also re-climbed, re-spotting the bombers on their outbound track. As he drew closer, he counted 20 of them, and also noticed the Zeros that hovered around and above. By the time the bombers were out to sea 80 kilometres north-west of Darwin, he was above them at 25 000 feet, and then he dived in at their starboard flank. Like Pete Watson and McDowell, however, he used incorrect gunnery technique, raking the whole formation from its starboard end. However, as he only broke off firing when he was 50 metres away from the middle bomber, he got close enough to get hits. Pulling up, Foster saw two Zeros coming in behind him, so he broke and dived away. As he went down he saw one bomber towards the starboard end of the line drop out of formation, descending with thick smoke streaming from the port engine. Another bomber was similarly emitting thick black smoke from one engine, but still held its place in the formation. This was the opposite end to that attacked by Pete Watson, so both men had got results in spite of their poor gunnery technique.

Tim Goldsmith had likewise been left behind by the outbound passage of the bombers, but was guided back in by Pete Watson's R/T reports. He re-climbed and only caught up with the bombers when they were 120 kilometres offshore. As he approached, a Zero flew up beside him, watching him, but then it turned and flew away. Goldsmith took his opportunity, diving at once upon the right flank of the bombers. However, he was deflected by a Zero that dived at him in a head-on pass.

Pulling his nose up, he fired at it and saw the Zero roll over as it went past. Turning after it, Goldsmith watched it going down spinning and smoking as far as 8000 feet. Needing to maintain visual scanning around him, he had to take his eyes off his victim, but he saw a large splash in the sea soon after. Ted Hall, following along behind at a greater distance, saw Goldsmith's Zero spin right into the water.

Having disposed of the escort, Goldsmith re-climbed to resume his attack on the bombers, which were still tightly arranged in a great crescent. He then attacked in a shallow dive from 24000 feet, but found that he was going too fast for easy gunnery. As he fired from 300 metres range from the rear quarter of the right-most bomber, red tracer came arching back at him from the bomber's side gunners, while the bright muzzle flashes from the tail gunner's 20 mm cannon were also visible. He saw his bullets striking its wing and fuselage just before he bunted underneath. Pulling around into a steep climbing turn, he came back in from behind and below to reattack the same bomber, which by now had dropped out of formation, evidently damaged. He fired another burst, and a spray of incendiary flashes raked the underside of the Japanese aircraft. As Goldsmith broke away, he saw that the bomber had drifted further behind, and was now two wing-spans out to one side, gliding down towards the sea. He could not stay to watch, however, as he now saw Zeros coming in behind him, so rolled over and dived away.

Thorold-Smith did not land after the action. A Spitfire had been observed to crash into the sea 13 kilometres offshore on a bearing of 230 degrees from Flagstaff Hill (which is on the northern tip of the Middle Arm of Darwin Harbour). Air searches were begun that afternoon, but they failed to find anything, and so 452's popular CO had disappeared without trace. It was not until 1986 that the wreck of Spitfire BS231 was finally found in that position, resting more or less intact and on an even keel in the mud on the bottom of the West Arm of Darwin Harbour. This shows that Thorold-Smith had been alive, retaining enough control to attempt to ditch his aircraft wings-level in the water; but he had not survived the ditching. The Spitfire was a very dangerous aircraft to ditch, as it did not so much land on the water as dive into it upon first impact. This is reflected in the advice given to 'Bluey' Truscott by his flight commander, 'Paddy' Finucane, upon his joining 452 early in 1941:

> Don't ditch her, Truscott. If you are over water and in trouble, bail out ... get out of her fast. She doesn't take to water like a duck; she takes to it like a fish and goes straight down.

Thorold-Smith had joined the squadron the same time as Truscott, and was as well aware of this advice as the others. His decision to ditch suggests that he was wounded or incapacitated, and thus unable to bail out. That he was partly incapacitated when he ditched is shown by the fact that he left his propeller in coarse pitch – the incorrect setting; this experienced pilot with 510 hours on Spitfires had not completed his landing checks properly.

Playing the blame game

The deaths of three pilots in this one action was a great shock, driving home to the men the uncomfortable reality that they faced an enemy every bit as good as their previous opponents from the Luftwaffe. Air combat was inherently a dangerous business, but these losses were salutary. To put it in context, the 49th Fighter Group lost only four pilots in combat during the course of their entire 1942 defensive campaign. There had obviously been something wrong on 15 March, and 1 Fighter Wing would need to identify its failings and rectify them.

Caldwell's post-mortem of the operation reflected very badly upon both the professionalism and moral fibre of his subordinates. He condemned 54 Squadron for its failure to adopt the ordered 'high-cover' position over Thorold-Smith, thereby holding the British unit responsible for the Zeros' bounce on 452. This was unfair to his British colleagues, because by flying so fast, Thorold-Smith had made it impossible for the already-trailing 54 to both catch up *and* to get above him. Caldwell also condemned 54 for failing to get out of line astern and into line abreast battle formation, but the same circumstances had rendered this equally impracticable, for moving out from a straggling line astern to the desired broad line abreast was impossible to achieve if 54 was simultaneously required to both keep up with 452 *and* to climb overhead.

Line astern	Line abreast		
±			
±	±		
	±	±	
±			±
±			

One of Caldwell's more substantive criticisms was that 54 had maintained poor lookout and thus failed in its duty as the wing's 'high-cover' squadron. Indeed, the British pilots admitted afterwards that they were looking ahead rather than up and behind. This was indeed blameworthy, but the same thing had happened to Lloyd's Red Section of 452; likewise looking ahead in the anxiety to catch up. The imperative of getting into position had degraded airmanship, and the obsessive chase after Thorold-Smith had pre-empted the demands of lookout.

Moving on from 54's specific faults to those of the wing in general, Caldwell alleged that after the wing's 'initial reverse' over Point Charles, the pilots 'appeared to have made no serious attempt at reforming', and that in Thorold-Smith's absence, no 'deputy' had assumed the initiative in leading further attacks. This was an invidious criticism, for 1 Fighter Wing's entire 1943 combat record demonstrates that the squadrons *never* reformed after first contact, even when under Caldwell's direction. Moreover, the section leaders had indeed shown leadership: Pete Watson had continued to fulfil his Yellow Section duties by reporting the raid's position; Goldsmith had found the bombers again because Watson had guided him in over the R/T; Watson had set a good example by leading his No. 2 in engaging the enemy; Hamilton had led his section into the chase and given them the 'Tally-ho'; Gould from 452 had joined on behind 457.

Caldwell's most morally damaging allegation was that after the bounce 'all of our aircraft acted independently from here on and there does not seem to have been the expected number of these still engaging'. The highly critical and condemnatory subtext of this is unfair and untrue. Only 19 pilots had been involved in the initial contact, and by the time the Japanese headed back out to sea, only 14 of these were still airborne in serviceable aircraft, for four Spitfires had been destroyed and one (Gould's) had been damaged and had returned to base. Of these 14, at least ten proceeded out to sea in pursuit – a good proportion. One pilot, McDowell, had persisted with the chase in spite of ongoing engine problems, which was a meritoriously courageous action in view of his distance from land. The number of reattacking aircraft would have been higher except that control started *ordering* pilots back to patrol the air bases in case of further attacks.

In the course of this second round of attacks, Watson, Foster, Goldsmith and McDowell had got hits on bombers, which was the object of the whole exercise. The reattacking pilots had moreover escaped without loss to themselves, in spite of being outnumbered throughout. Contrary to Caldwell's condemnations, the arithmetic suggests that these scattered pilots had in fact done a lot better in taking the fight to the Japanese than the whole wing had done in the initial attack.

Thorold-Smith's tragic error

Ray Thorold-Smith had previously been a good fighter pilot, but he had made some terrible misjudgments on this day. Unhappily, Caldwell was thus forced to critique the performance of his dead friend as well. He criticised him for setting off on the interception before the wing had been rendezvoused, and for climbing too fast, thus causing the bad straggling. Moreover, Caldwell considered that 452's CO should not have taken his wing in underneath the Japanese fighters, but should rather have continued the climb off to one side, waiting to attain the advantage of height before going in to the attack.

These last two points are incontestably true, and three men had died because of these errors. Indeed, for an experienced fighter pilot who enjoyed the confidence of his pilots, Thorold-Smith had made strangely poor decisions this day. He had straggled the wing, ordered 54 Squadron to do the impossible and remained strangely oblivious to the chaos that was descending upon the pilots behind him. He had thereby inadvertently ensured that his pilots entered the battle distracted, worried, frustrated and in formational disarray.

Clearly, Thorold-Smith had felt the need to attack with the greatest urgency; in his perception, there had been no time to form up, no time to manoeuvre for advantage, no time for 'fancy tactics'. Under the weight of this perception, he had accepted the risks and taken his wing in at a great disadvantage – of height, of sun and of position. He had evidently been desperate to get into the bombers *before* they bombed. Other pilots explained afterwards that his intention had been to 'break them up' – in other words, to attack the bombers so fiercely that they would abandon their formation, jettison their bombs and head for home prematurely. Although this was a worthy aim, it was virtually impossible to achieve, for bomber crews very rarely abandoned their formations; instead, they rode out fighter attacks in the relative security of the 'herd' – for them the only way out was ahead, alongside everybody else.

Although Ray Thorold-Smith died with the relatively large total of 747 hours in his logbook, he did not in fact possess vast experience. After joining the RAAF in May 1940, he went so quickly through the accelerated wartime training syllabus that he joined his first squadron in the United Kingdom less than a year later. Hurriedly promoted to flight lieutenant, he flew in only six combats as 452 Squadron's 'A' Flight commander before being precipitately promoted (somewhat unwillingly) to Squadron CO in March 1942 – after less than a year of operational flying. This sort of rushed advancement was inconceivable in a veteran Japanese outfit like the 202 AG, where the flight leaders remained airmen of great experience and seniority. In Allied air forces the talent was spread deeply throughout the organisation, thanks to the practice of rotating personnel back to training units after the completion of defined tours of duty. Although this permitted an exponential expansion of training output, it was hard to avoid a major dilution of experience levels in Allied

Squadron Leader Ray Thorold-Smith at Darwin, standing with his back to the contested Arafura Sea, circa February 1943. Note the DFC ribbon under his pilot's wings. He looks very tired.
AWM Negative 044242

front-line flying units. However, in the longer term this process provided the trained manpower necessary to win air supremacy for the Allies on all fronts.

In the middle part of the war, this expansion process had left men like Thorold-Smith ascending a learning curve too rapidly for comfort. His pre-NWA experience had been exclusively in offensive fighter sweeps with Fighter Command; he had never previously led a squadron into action, let alone a wing; 15 March was his very first defensive fighter operation against an escorted bomber formation; and he had also missed the 2 March combat.

S/L Ron MacDonald with the Wingco at Strauss airfield, circa June 1943. Contrary to RAAF regulations, Caldwell wore a beard to ease a troublesome sweat-related skin condition. The wool-lined RAF flying boots were a prized fashion item despite the climate, admired and much used by the Americans as well. AWM Negative NWA0403

Moreover, since 452's arrival in Australia, he had been bogged down with paperwork, and this had detracted from his currency and retarded his ability to lead the squadron in the air.

On top of these adverse contextual factors, oxygen starvation was probably the immediate reason for Thorold-Smith's poor judgment, as has been suggested by Jim Grant – an ex-457 Squadron fitter and a significant historian of 1 Fighter Wing. The oxygen bottles of the five 452 Squadron aircraft that had overnighted at RAAF Darwin had evidently not been refilled after the night flying, as the intention had been merely to ferry them back to Strauss. The five pilots had been scrambled in-transit and thereby committed to an extended flight above 10 000 feet with only partly filled oxygen tanks.

If Thorold-Smith was indeed suffering from oxygen starvation by the time he went into the fight, this would at least explain his remarkably bad decision-making on this day. His disastrous tactics went totally against his previous combat record as a capable and intelligent air leader with five kills. Indeed, his DFC citation had commended his 'skilful and capable leadership of his flight'; as confirmed by Ted Sly, who remembered from his time with 452 that Thorold-Smith was a 'wonderful operator who looked after his men very well'. His bereaved squadron gave tribute to his 'acute intellect', his 'inspiring' leadership, and his 'grasp' of the 'essentials of fighter combat'. Clearly, something had marred his judgment on this day. There are other examples of senior 1 Fighter Wing pilots continuing to fly and fight in a hypoxic state after exhausting their oxygen: Clive Caldwell and Bill Gibbs would do this in the 30 June and 6 July combats respectively. In spite of some imprudent decision-making, they would get away with it, but Thorold-Smith did not.

Two of the five pilots in Thorold-Smith's night-flying section did indeed abort before the battle due to oxygen shortage. These were Flight Lieutenant Paul Makin and Flying Officer John

Bisley DFC – experienced men making good decisions. If he was likewise low on oxygen, Thorold-Smith should have aborted too, but Caldwell was absent, Bill Gibbs had failed to join up in the botched rendezvous, and 457's CO Ken James had been kept out of battle, leading the force of Spitfires patrolling over the rear air bases. Thus it had been incumbent upon 452's CO to accept the delegated wing command and to do his duty.

The unfortunate Thorold-Smith had thus fallen victim to RAF Fighter Command's 'big wing' doctrine. This went back to the well-known Battle of Britain controversy between Air Vice Marshals Keith Park and Trafford Leigh-Mallory. Park, as AOC 11 Group during 1940, had sent his fighter force into battle against the German raids in small packets of one or at most two squadrons. On the other side of the argument, Leigh-Mallory, AOC 12 Group, championed Squadron Leader Douglas Bader's preference for going into battle in massed formations or 'Balbos' of three or more squadrons. At the conclusion of the battle, when Air Marshal Sholto Douglas was elevated to the position of AOC Fighter Command, he sided with Leigh-Mallory, adopting the big wing as Fighter Command's standard deployment for its offensive operations over France in 1941–42. Thorold-Smith had thus received his entire operational experience in a context where the big wing was normative.

This doctrine had been transplanted whole to the NWA as part of the Spitfire wing's baggage. The 1943 Darwin raids would thus be a rerun of the Battle of Britain, but this time with the spirit of Leigh-Mallory in charge rather than Keith Park. No. 1 Fighter Wing's leadership team thus adhered to the doctrine that raids needed to be met with a full wing attack, with the assembled 'Balbo' of squadrons commanded centrally by a wing leader. Individual squadron attacks were only to be countenanced as a last resort or forced expedient. The weight of this doctrine bore down upon Thorold-Smith on this day, obliging him to lead the whole wing into action more or less no matter what.

The fixity of this big wing doctrine was unfortunate, for if Hamilton, Lloyd, Watson, Norwood and Foster had been allowed to set up their own attacks, they would all have been freed from the pernicious effects of this day's 'big wing' straggling, permitting their sections to maintain functional battle formation as they entered the fight. The result would certainly have been better lookout and thus fewer bounces. Individual aircraft sections would also have been able to climb faster than the whole Balbo, and as a result would have been higher when the action started, and thus out of the Zeros' killing zone. In any case, these junior leaders could hardly have done worse than Thorold-Smith did on this day.

Yet another contributing factor to Thorold-Smith's apparently reckless tactics on 15 March was the precedent set in the 2 March combat. On that day, Caldwell had acted similarly, leading an outnumbered force of Spitfires straight in at the enemy, right underneath the higher-flying escort. Once again, he had gotten away with it, but Thorold-Smith had not.

No. 452 was understandably left shattered by the loss of its CO, leaving Paul Makin in a lonely position as the sole surviving foundation member of the squadron. Thorold-Smith was remembered as a truly great man, as an inspiration and a role model: 'His loss is a great one to the Squadron, to the RAAF, to Australia and to the British Commonwealth of Nations'. Caldwell moved in to Strauss and took over as acting CO until a new officer was appointed, and then handed over to the new appointee at the end of the month: Squadron Leader Ron MacDonald, formerly CO of No. 12 dive-bomber squadron at nearby Batchelor airfield. MacDonald was an EATS graduate who had clocked up hundreds of hours as an instructor on

Wirraways, but he had very limited fighter experience, having flown only 17 hours in Brewster Buffalos during a brief attachment to 67 Squadron RAF in Malaya during 1941; he had never attended a fighter course at an OTU, and had seen no action. His promotion and advancement had been fast-tracked, but he was certainly an odd choice as a CO of a front-line fighter squadron. Even at the end of MacDonald's time with 452 in February 1944, Wing Commander Peter Jeffrey reported that 'his operational experience and knowledge of the employment of fighter aeroplanes is limited'. MacDonald's appointment in spite of this weak background shows that both Frank Bladin and 'Wally' Walters valued him, and he was to largely justify their confidence by proving to be an aggressive combat leader. However, with his very modest fighter CV, MacDonald must have wondered what he was doing in that role, very much put in the shade by the star pilots who had previously led the squadron.

Gunnery failings

Of the four surviving 452 aircraft that had fired their guns, two had suffered cannon failures, as had every single one of 54's surviving aircraft; Taylor's port cannon had jammed after firing only two rounds, while Foster's and Goldsmith's attacks on the bombers had likewise been conducted with only one cannon firing. The pilots learnt to compensate for the resultant asymmetrical gun recoil by applying opposite rudder as they fired, but this was certainly not conducive to good gunnery results. No. 1 Fighter Wing's cannon failures would never be cured in 1943, and thus the pilots' gun-aiming would be bedevilled by this problem right to the end of the campaign.

The gunnery results on this day suggest the seriousness of the problem: Japanese records indicate that eight bombers returned to Timor damaged, but that none were shot down.

Getting hits on eight bombers seems a good result, considering that only four pilots – Pete Watson and McDowell from 457, Goldsmith from 452, and Foster from 54 – had actually attacked them. On the other hand, it is clear that although these Spitfires had got many hits, they had not hit accurately enough to shoot their targets down.

This failure is not only attributable to the yawing produced by the malfunctioning cannons' asymmetrical recoil, but also to the pilots' poor technique – three of the four pilots who fired at the bombers had used 'spraying' fire, rather than aiming in a concentrated fashion at one targeted aircraft, as they had trained to do in air-to-air practice firings. Pilots were later to be pointedly rebuked for this by NWA RAAF HQ, after these disappointing gunnery results continued in the 2 May and 28 May actions. Squadron Leader Adolph 'Sailor' Malan's 'Ten Rules', which enjoyed canonical status in UK-based OTUs during 1941–42 (the very period when 1 Fighter Wing's pilots were trained), emphasised deliberate aiming as well as closing to short range before firing. Watson, Foster and McDowell had neglected these rules in the heat of combat, for by using 'spraying fire' against the bombers they had necessarily opened fire at longer ranges, in order to sight upon the whole formation. As a result, their fire had distributed hits broadly around the bomber airframes rather than concentrating upon vital areas like engines and fuel tanks. Significantly, the only pilot with recent experience of attacking bombers, Tim Goldsmith, had aimed correctly and obtained the best results.

Four bombers were reported as emitting white or black smoke, perhaps indicating punctured fuel tanks and engine fires respectively. From the Spitfire pilots' point of view, the failure of the fuel-venting bombers to burn was most vexing, given the Mitsubishi bombers' lack of self-sealing fuel tanks and the justified reputation for flammability that the type acquired elsewhere in the Pacific theatre. This is doubly puzzling considering the high proportion of incendiary ammunition loaded into both the 20 mm and .303 inch (7.7 mm) guns of the Spitfires: the cannon were loaded with both HEI (high explosive incendiary) and SAPI (semi armour piercing incendiary), and the .303 with AP (armour piercing) and incendiary. Given that the cannon ammunition was proven in RAF tests to both penetrate armour *and* ignite fuel, to scatter shrapnel through the airframe up to 5 metres from the impact point, and to blow big holes in fuel tanks, it must be assumed that the problem lay with the inability of the pilots to concentrate their fire, rather than in any faults in the ammunition.

Nonetheless, in spite of the frustrating inability of the Spitfires to actually shoot down the bombers, 753 AG had certainly not had an easy day: 40 per cent of its aircraft returned to Timor damaged. The ground crews were then confronted with the task of patching up damage, repairing tanks and changing engines, in order to get the aircraft airworthy again for the similarly long overwater flight back to Kendari. The bomber crews had had good luck in getting home, but this had certainly been no 'milk run'.

The results from the day's fighter versus fighter combats are more ambiguous: in the initial fight over Darwin Harbour, Norwood, Biggs, Rex Watson and Mawer all made claims on the basis of observed crashes, while Goldsmith made a similarly well-justified claim in the fight out to sea – and thus five Zeros were claimed as 'confirmed'. In all cases but Goldsmith's, flames were observed coming from the Zero as it went down: Biggs was able to corroborate Norwood's claim, attesting to the flames issuing from the Zero's engine, fuselage and wing; Rex Watson likewise reported his 'kill' spinning down with the fuselage afire. Furthermore, there were sightings of Zeros crashing into the water; the strongest instance being Mawer's

No. 54 Squadron's scoreboard (the wingtip of the Zero shot down on 15 March) displayed outside the readiness hut at Winnellie on 10 May, showing a very optimistic tally of eight kills. Left to right: Sgt WH Eldred, F/O F Quinn (Wing intelligence officer), F/O JB Yerby (an American in the RAF), F/O Ian Taylor, F/O George Farries. A West Australian unit (probably 25 Squadron) has 'zapped' the British unit's scoreboard with a black swan motif. AWM Negative NWA0323

'kill', for he followed it down to 1000 feet and from there observed it to go into the sea. Goldsmith's splashing of a Zero into the water out beyond Port Patterson was corroborated by Hall. Since there were no Spitfires shot down in this later action out to sea, if Goldsmith and Hall saw an aircraft hit the sea, it must have been a Zero.

The trouble with all this is that 202 AG records indicate that only one Zero failed to return – that of Petty Officer Seiji Tajiri. The RAN in Darwin Harbour witnessed a Zero falling in flames at high speed and breaking up into pieces before it hit the water 300 metres south of West Point and 200 metres offshore. A motor patrol vessel, HMAS *Coongoola*, buoyed the crash position and then afterwards HMAS *Malanda* arrived with a diving party, which found and recovered a 2 metre section of wing and the starboard tailplane – everything else had been swept away into deep water by the rushing tides. Because of its base location close to the harbour, 54 Squadron was presented with the Zero wingtip, and this became a war trophy and the unit's scoreboard in time-honoured fighter squadron fashion. This Zero crash proves that at least one of the Spitfire pilots had been successful in the initial combat over the harbour. Several pilots probably saw the same burning Zero going down in the same area of sky as their own engagements, and some also saw Cooper's Spitfire splashing in – both could have been taken as mistaken proof of their own 'kill'. However, such double or triple claiming does not explain everything: Tajiri's loss does not explain Goldsmith's Zero hitting the sea 130 kilometres and 20 minutes away, as corroborated by Hall. The evidence thus suggests that more than one Zero went into the water on this day – all existing accounts that have used Japanese sources are sketchy in the extreme, so only the publication of detailed research into Japanese records can resolve this conundrum.

Putting aside such reservations, it is clear that the wing had greatly overstated its results. As later combats would prove, the overclaiming problem was related to the fact that the COs and intelligence officers routinely confirmed claims in spite of lack of actually observed crashes. The claimants' reports of enemy aircraft descending and smoking were too often accepted as indicating destruction, whereas this type of evidence should at most have justified claims for 'probably destroyed'. Indeed, the supposed criteria for 'confirmed destroyed' were eyewitness testimony to either the aircraft crashing, breaking up in the air or descending on fire (not just smoking). Foster's bomber claim shows that these standards had not been applied: he had observed it descending leaving a thick trail of black smoke, and appropriately claimed it as probably destroyed. The intelligence officers afterwards upgraded this to 'confirmed destroyed', yet without any eyewitness testimony to its actually crashing. This lack of rigour in applying the stipulated criteria would be a feature of 1 Fighter Wing's 1943 campaign, and would result in an apparent 3:1 overclaiming ratio.

Although overclaiming would become endemic within 1 Fighter Wing, it was neither unique nor unusual among comparable Allied formations. Certainly the RAF's self-righteous reputation for meticulous conservatism in confirming claims was greatly exaggerated.

Tactics

If Tajiri was indeed the only Japanese loss, then 1 Fighter Wing had suffered a severe reverse in the initial action, with an adverse 1:4 kill ratio. However, this was only to be expected given the dreadful tactical position into which they had been led at the start – bounced by Zeros that enjoyed the advantages of sun, height, surprise, position, speed and numbers.

Reporting on the 15 March combat, 54 Squadron's war diary

gave tribute to the Zero pilots' skill in keeping the Spitfires away from the bombers, noting that their bomber escort tactics were now regarded by the pilots 'with considerable respect'. Ambiguously, such compliments were confusingly juxtaposed with the complacent observation that 'although there are brilliant exceptions the Jap pilot is not as formidable as he has been painted in some quarters'. Some of the old Spitfire hubris remained: after inspecting the Zero wingtip, 'Cecil' Beaton, the squadron engineering officer, reassured the pilots by declaring that its construction was 'much inferior to that of our Spitfires'.

While this might have mollified the pilots' concerns, it was entirely inaccurate: the Zero was constructed with 'Super Ultra Duralumin', a new zinc-based alloy developed by Sumitomo Metals that was stronger than conventional aluminium alloys and therefore permitted lighter construction; moreover, the Zero's skinning was flush-riveted all over, thereby producing a cleaner external finish and lower surface drag than the Spitfire. In addition, considering that Mitsubishi had pioneered the bubble canopy for rearward visibility and the large drop tank for long range, it is clear that the Zero airframe could scarcely be considered technically inferior to that of the Spitfire.

Despite the advanced technology of the Zero's airframe, the superior power output of the Spitfire's Rolls Royce engine meant that the latter were well able to hold their own in air combat. In fact, although the Zero pilots' manoeuvring had often been spectacular, it was of questionable effectiveness, as shown by the number of times they themselves were engaged by Spitfire gunnery – 11 Zeros found themselves under fire within effective range, usually from the rear quarter, with the Spitfire pilot believing that he had observed bullet strikes. Given the Zeros' initially overwhelming tactical advantage, the Spitfires had therefore done remarkably well in counter-attacking and reversing the roles in the subsequent dogfighting. The Zero pilots had proved that they could shoot down Spitfires in the bounce, but not in the dogfight. In the actual dogfighting phase of the action, two Spitfires – Gould's and Batchelor's – were hit but returned to base safely, while at least one Zero was shot down, and several others damaged. The Spitfires therefore did well here: contrary to the myth that they could not and should not dogfight with Zeros, they had in fact won the dogfight phase of the engagement.

The vertical pull-up that had been so noticeable a part of the Japanese dogfighting technique was a trademark manoeuvre of the Imperial Navy. Called the 'Turning-in' manoeuvre, it involved pulling up into a loop, then slide-slipping out of the top of the loop to cut across the radius of the vertical turn and drop down onto the tail of the enemy fighter. This manoeuvre was beyond the skill level of Allied fighter pilots, who anyway eschewed aerobatic manoeuvres in combat as inefficient self-indulgence. Indeed, the Spitfire pilots did not even recognise it for what it was, describing the observed Japanese vertical manoeuvres as loops or stall turns. As it turned out, the prejudices of the Allied fighter pilots were well justified, for in spite of the impressive aerobatic one-upmanship of the Japanese, they scored few if any Spitfire kills by using this manoeuvre. Rather, they got their kills like everyone else: by very conventionally bouncing their unwary opponents from behind.

The outcomes of World War II fighter combats in all theatres of war in all air forces were determined by the same fundamentals of height, speed, position and surprise as pioneered by Max Immelmann and Oswald Boelcke in 1915. What would go on killing Spitfire pilots above Northern Australia was not obsessively practised Japanese aerobatics, but rather the persistent failures in their own lookout and their unintentional preference for fighting alone. Conversely, the true source of Japanese air combat superiority lay not in bravura aerobatics, but in the enemy pilots' ability to apply team drills to manoeuvre cooperatively – as shown by the repeated observations of Zeros operating in twos and threes throughout the dogfight.

The relative primitiveness of RAF/RAAF air combat technique is shown by the fact that even when Spitfires were in the same area of sky, the pilots did not join up into proper battle formation. Hamilton's men were close enough to each other to watch others attack, while Hall was close enough behind Goldsmith to see his victim splash. However, neither had thought it important to join up properly as line abreast pairs to fight together and cover each other against fighter attack – this is odd, considering that they had R/T intercommunication and were moreover section mates. Batchelor accompanied Pete Watson in to the fight, but the latter flew away from his wingman at first contact, leaving the latter to his lone fight at odds, and then carrying out his own attack without anyone covering his tail. Caldwell criticised his pilots for this, but he was no different, having done the same thing to Walters on 2 March.

The basis of any combat coordination was the pair, often referred to in the RAF as 'line abreast' – an arrangement whereby each pilot flew up beside his colleague, about 100–200 metres out to the side, and far enough forward to permit each pilot to see the patch of sky behind the other's tail. Such pairs were added to one another to form a four – which was also known as the 'finger four', as the resultant relative positions of each aircraft resembled the positions of the four fingertips of the human hand. A number of such fours were added together to form an eight or 12, similarly broadly spread across the sky in a wide line abreast. Theoretically, a fighter formation flying line abreast was impossible to bounce because of the mutual observation provided by each element over its neighbour's tail. Squadron Leader Stan Turner, the Canadian CO of 249 Squadron on Malta in early 1942, explained it thus to one of his new flight commanders:

We can't have any more of these goddam VIC [vee] formations otherwise we'll get bumped, that's for sure. I want you to learn this line-abreast stuff with me ... This way ... a couple of guys will never get bounced: attacked maybe, yes; but never surprised ...

The American ace, Major Gerald Johnson of the UK-based 56th Fighter Group, agreed with this assessment of the rearward view provided by this formation, considering that there could be no excuse for not seeing an attack coming.

Unfortunately, although these principles formed part of RAF doctrine, they were often poorly understood at the squadron level. This is shown by the fact that throughout 1941–42, RAF fighter squadrons in all theatres flew a bewildering variety of non-standard formations, consisting of variations of line astern, vee and line abreast, with or without 'weavers'. On 15 March, 1 Fighter Wing typified this by going into the combat in line astern formation, the most common RAF fighter formation up to 1943. Using this formation, sections could keep an eye on other sections' tails, but a single section was blind to the rear: the 'arse-end Charlie' was inevitably and necessarily left behind out of everyone else's vision, as shown by what happened to Bert Cooper. The employment of Al Mawer as a 'weaver' at the rear of 54 shows that the RAF squadron's battle formation was mired in the inadequate practices of 1940–41. Line astern combat formation should theoretically have been deleted from the RAF tactical repertoire long before 1943, but 1 Fighter Wing went into the campaign needing to 'unlearn' this dysfunctional procedure.

This skill deficiency is related to the pilots' previous service with RAF Fighter Command during 1941–42. Both 452 and 457 Squadrons had in turn served as part of the Kenley Wing, but unfortunately this wing was very unprogressive in its use of fighter formation. Evan Mackie, who became the top RNZAF ace of the war, found that the Kenley Wing flew the obsolete line astern combat formation through to the end of 1942. 'Johnnie' Johnson – the RAF's top ace pilot of the war – was surprised to find the same thing when he joined the wing. Squadron Leader 'Bluey' Truscott had trialled the 'fluid four' formation during his brief period as 452's CO, but once he was posted out of the squadron it was not persisted with and had to be reintroduced in 1943 after the wing arrived in the NWA. Under the force of continuous combat experience, the RAF continued to develop its fighter tactics and combat formations through 1942–43, but 1 Fighter Wing arrived in Australia almost frozen in time, a relic of the undeveloped tactics of 1941–42.

Having grown up operationally in a retrograde tactical environment, none of the squadron COs were versed in modern combat formation, and nor was Caldwell in any position to progress the wing's tactical understanding: he had suffered from the same deficient instruction as his pilots, having been attached to the same Kenley Wing for operational experience before being posted off to Australia. Having previously flown the dysfunctional line astern in North Africa with 250 and 112 Squadrons, the Wingco arrived in Australia with a deficient tactical education. Although 54 Squadron had had no contact with the Kenley Wing, it was similarly non-progressive, likewise a late adopter of line abreast combat formation: Bob Foster recalls that as late as September 1943, the unit was still flying in the archaic vee formation. In an unfortunate coincidence, therefore, all three of 1 Fighter Wing's squadrons and its wing leader entered the 1943 campaign with a deficient understanding of modern combat formation, and with inadequate appreciation of the cross-cover benefits that this would have provided. Poor lookout and poor combat coordination were the inevitable results. Group Captain Walters was no help here, being a raw beginner in fighters.

Although the units of the Japanese navy did not fly in line abreast pairs, as per 'world best practice' (the Luftwaffe and the US Navy), they had reinvented the three aircraft vee to make it a highly functional combat formation, spreading it out to a loose and broad line abreast. In so doing they had turned this seemingly archaic formation into a flexible tactical system, by which each three-aircraft section entered an engagement with one or two aircraft ahead and with the other one or two held back to pounce on any enemy fighter that committed itself. Imperial Navy fighter training emphasised 'keeping formation *during* aerial combat', and practised standard sets of three-plane team manoeuvres that could cope with any scenario, from a simple three versus one engagement, through to counter-attacking a bounce, and up to the extreme-case scenario of a single Zero pilot attacking six adversaries. The Spitfire wing never came close to this sophisticated understanding of concerted battle drill; indeed, never even aspired to it. Among all the post-operation analysis conducted within 1 Fighter Wing, NWA RAAF HQ, and RAAF Command, no one pointed out the vast superiority in team fighting skills demonstrated by the Japanese, and no one highlighted the need to drill the wing's pilots more intensely in order to make up the deficiency. No one noticed, and so the Spitfire pilots would go on fighting as individuals.

Instead, Caldwell blamed the adverse outcome of 15 March on two things: the failure to concentrate the wing, and the failure to get a favourable position before attacking. The second point is absolutely correct and self-evident, but in pressing for wing concentration he misread the combat as it actually happened on this day. In the fight out over the sea, small sections of Spitfires and even individual aircraft were able not only to survive against the Zeros but to seriously discomfit both the escort and the bombers. They were able to do this by attacking with the advantage of height at different times, from different directions. This is the way the 49th FG had fought in 1942, with considerable success: by feeding one section after another into the fight, they retained surprise and initiative, and often put the escort off balance. No. 1 Fighter Wing would have benefited greatly from following this precedent, but instead it would inflexibly employ centralised control over an unwieldy three-squadron Balbo.

A further pointer to future problems lay in the fact that fuel shortage was a big problem for all aircraft that had chased the Japanese out to sea: all of the 457 aircraft returned 'dangerously short of fuel'. The squadron noted the problem carefully in its diary, and included it in its report to wing. This was in addition to the fuel shortage experienced in the 2 March action, thus clearly emphasising the Spitfire's inherently limited fuel load. Designed for short-range interception duties over England, the type was insufficiently long-legged for the more extensive operations in Northern Australia: Darwin's Spitfires could fly up to 160 kilometres from base, fight, and get back to base with fuel in their tanks – but only just. By contrast, the Zeros were flying 600 kilometres, fighting, and flying home again without apparent trouble. The Spitfire's range limitation was not substantively addressed at wing HQ or area HQ, and so everyone would have to wait for the next raid to brutally expose the problem.

While the higher echelons responded to the 15 March reverse by rigidly re-emphasising existing doctrine, 54 Squadron was left personally bereft by the loss of two pilots who had come a long way to be killed in Australian skies. More prosaically, they were also left grappling with the embarrassment of having disappointed their new-found chums at the nearby RAN base. As the unit diarist recorded, the British pilots' naval friends had spent 15 March fighting fires in the dock area, and had been near-missed by bomb bursts during the actual raid, for 'the bombs fell in scattered clumps among them. This of course, was after we had boasted and assured them that now the Spitfires were here to defend the place, all would be well. They were a bit cool to say the least, especially as the bombers had dropped their bombs before we even got close to them, and they were on their way out'. There would therefore be great self-imposed moral pressure upon the pilots to do better next time.

15 March pilot table

Sqn	Section	No.	Pilot	Remarks
Pilots engaged, in the order in which they approached the battle:				
		1	F/L P Watson	
457	Yellow	2	F/Sgt Batchelor	Spitfire damaged, repaired on unit
		1	S/L Thorold-Smith	shot down & killed; BS231 QY-D lost, West Arm Darwin Harbour
		2	F/L Hall	
452	White	3	F/O Goldsmith	1 cannon failed
		1	F/L Norwood RAF	1 cannon failed
		2	F/Sgt Biggs RAF	1 cannon failed
	White	3	Sgt Cooper RAF	shot down & killed; AR620 lost, Darwin Harbour
		1	F/L Foster RAF	1 cannon failed
	Blue	2	F/O Taylor RAF	both cannons failed
		3	F/Sgt Varney RAF	killed in crash-landing; AR619 destroyed, Myilly Point
54	Red	4	F/O Mawer RAAF	1 cannon failed
		1	F/O Hamilton	
		2	F/Sgt R Watson	both cannons failed
		3	P/O Robinson	
457	Blue	4	F/Sgt McDowell	

		1	F/O Lloyd		shot down & bailed out at Picnic Cove, Cox Peninsula; BS293 QY-E destroyed, crashed 5 km W Picnic Point, 16 km S Point Charles
		2	F/O J Gould		1 cannon jammed; BS162 QY-F damaged; repaired by unit
452	Red	3	F/O Williams		

Pilots airborne but who did not engage:

	Winco			W/C Caldwell	took off late, never caught up
54	Red	1		S/L Gibbs RAF	
				F/O Bassett	
	Blue			F/Sgt Tully	base patrol
452	Yellow			Sgt Stagg	low-level early warning patrol
				S/L James	
				F/O Munro	
				P/O Barker	
	Red			F/O Turner	
				F/L Maclean	
				P/O Clark	
				F/O Edwards	base patrols over southern airfields
457	White			F/Sgt Hardwick	
		19		13	

Totals:
Aircraft scrambled: 32
Aircraft engaged: 19
Aircraft lost: 4
Aircraft damaged: 2
Pilots killed: 3

4
Failure of the big wing

The month of April brought an awkward hiatus to the Japanese raiding schedule after the completion of only one full-scale bombing raid on 15 March. This was related to the Imperial Navy's concentration of its land-based air force for a short-lived but maximum-effort air offensive against both Port Moresby and Milne Bay – Admiral Yamamoto's Operation *I-Go*. The Kendari-based units were not committed to these raids, but were necessarily redeployed in support of these operations further east.

Although starved of action during this lull, the Spitfire pilots were meanwhile kept busy maintaining a full flying program seven days a week, consisting of both practice flights and operational flying. The training flights included practice scrambles, with aircraft launched into the air from opposite directions alternately from both ends of the runway – in order to cut down response times, to avoid long taxiing and consequent engine overheating, and to ameliorate the dust pall at either end of the strip. Also included in the program were night flying, gunnery practice, formation practice, squadron and wing combat climbs, and one-versus-one dogfighting. Flying discipline under Group Captain Walters and Wing Commander Clive Caldwell DFC's leadership was tight – unlike so many World War II fighter units, 1 Fighter Wing did not lose a single pilot to stupid low-level aerobatics. As an illustration, when 452's Flying Officers Tim Goldsmith and Ross Williams 'beat up' Coomalie Creek airstrip after the 2 March raid, they were placed on a charge by Air Commodore Bladin.

Although this 'nil tolerance' policy must have avoided several fatal accidents, flight operations from the narrow bush runways of Strauss and Livingstone nonetheless produced a rich crop of damaged aircraft. The pilots on the two Australian squadrons had to get used to landing and taking off from these constricted spaces, which were a poor swap for the wide grass expanses they were used to on airfields in Britain and New South Wales. This was reflected in their higher accident rate during taxiing, taking off and landing: whereas 7 RSU had only six 'call-outs' to pick up damaged aircraft from 54 Squadron's base at Darwin from February to September, the same repair unit recovered 16 crashed Spitfires from 452 at Strauss, and 13 from 457 at Livingstone. On those strips, any loss of direction in landing meant a collision with the roadside water pipe on one side of the strip, or tipping over into the drainage ditch on the other. Similarly, any inattention or distraction while taxiing along the winding tree-lined taxiways would easily bring a wingtip into contact with trees, vehicles or parked aircraft. The accident rate was very high in February and March, before the pilots got used to these challenging conditions.

The waiting game

In addition to the training schedule, the squadrons would be kept busy dispatching sections of Spitfires to the satellite airfields of Drysdale and Milingimbi, 500 kilometres east and west of Darwin respectively, as well as rotations of night readiness sections at RAAF Darwin during every month's moon period. These commitments meant that the equivalent of one squadron was often unavailable for operations at Darwin. There were often almost daily scrambles against reconnaissance intrusions, plus an irritating succession of full wing scrambles against 'false alarms' – either Beaufighters or B-24s returning from their raids but not keeping to the designated friendly-aircraft approach routes, or offshore enemy shipping or weather reconnaissance patrols that stayed out of range. Therefore only a very small proportion of operational scrambles resulted in contact with the enemy – when they did, it came as quite a surprise to the pilots. Further operational tasking included rotations of airborne patrols over coastal shipping, and even close support exercises with the army. All this meant that available aircraft flying hours were heavily committed to routine tasks, with little time left over for tactically relevant training, such as improving air combat skills by trialling new formations, drills and procedures. There was also little training time left over for gunnery practice or bomber attacks.

Besides the rotation of machines through the routine tasks mentioned above, each squadron had to maintain a nominated number of aircraft at readiness until they were stood down in the afternoon (once it was too late for any raiders to make it back to Timor in daylight). The pilots reported for duty each day at the readiness tent near the dispersals. If their names appeared on the squadron readiness board underneath the marquee, they spent the day at readiness waiting for an alarm. Squadron readiness was connected to the fighter ops room at Berrimah by radio link, via

The two Australian squadrons were based close enough together to visit one another's messes at night. Here a mixed group of 452/457 pilots enjoys the luxury of a chilled beer. Left to right along the bar: F/L 'Snapper' Newton, F/L Ted Hall, S/L Ken James, F/O Ian Mackenzie, F/L Don Maclean and barman, LAC Fred Storey. AWM Negative 015510 a radio tender. Alarms were broadcast by a loudspeaker system that extended through all camp areas. Caldwell and Walters kept their fingers on the pulse by rostering themselves onto the squadrons' readiness boards, giving both of them opportunity to spend time with the pilots and to be seen and heard by the ground crew. Bladin too was often present to discuss issues with the men, particularly after actions. All three of these higher officers were unpretentious men who earned respect and loyalty: Caldwell was given to openly talking 'shop' among his brother pilots (contrary to RAF culture), while the avuncular Bladin was known as 'Pop' or 'Dad' throughout the air force.

Meanwhile, across the Timor Sea, 753 Bomber Group had to spread itself very thinly in order to perform its primary defensive function of maritime patrol along the broad southern front of the Japanese forward perimeter. This required it to disperse itself into small detachments operating from a swath of airfields from Sumatra to Dutch New Guinea. However, the Japanese command organisation, 23rd Air Flotilla, was under instructions to reconcentrate it on a monthly basis in order to carry out its secondary duty of suppressing Allied air activity from Darwin. By 15 April therefore, the crews of Allied strike aircraft operating over Timor were bringing back reports of a concentration of Japanese aircraft on the island's airfields. These were estimated as numbering 38 machines in total, so the Japanese were evidently building up for another raid; and this was confirmed by the resumption of Japanese photo-reconnaissance flights.

The 2 May raid

However, after the triumphant shoot-downs of February and March, these recco overflights were now proving irritatingly hard to intercept: on 20 April, aircraft from both 452 and 457 failed to contact a high-flying intruder, while on the 29th three sections of 54 similarly failed to make an interception despite the Ki-46 being clearly visible from the ground as it overflew Batchelor airfield. Frustratingly, another recco on 1 May evaded interception by four 457 Squadron aircraft. Having completed their pre-strike reconnaissance program, the Japanese launched the second bombing raid of the season early on 2 May. It was a maximum effort, with a full bomber group of 25 G4Ms from 753 AG escorted by a full fighter group of 27 Zeros. This would be Raid No. 54 on Darwin.

As 1 Fighter Wing's diarist put it, 2 May was a 'beautiful day ... interrupted by the sounding of sirens'. In spite of the warnings and the intelligence, this raid once again caught the wing a little flat-footed; as shown by the fact that a large contingent of the squadrons' experienced flight leaders were away on leave 'down south'. Both of 457's flight commanders, Don Maclean and Pete Watson, were away, as were both those of 54 – Bob Foster and Rob Norwood. No. 452 Squadron was better placed, with both flight commanders on duty; however, it lacked the services of three senior pilots who were away on leave: Flying Officers Ross Williams, Bill Lloyd and Dave Downs.

At 9.35 am, 38 Radar Station at Cape Fourcroy on Bathurst Island picked up the first plot at 220 kilometres from Darwin, approaching from the north-west. It was at first believed to be only a single reconnaissance aircraft, but once the radar signal became stronger, it was recognised as a raid, and at 9.40 the wing was scrambled, with 33 Spitfires getting airborne. Ordered to rendezvous at 10 000 feet over Hughes airfield, Caldwell managed to get the three squadrons formed up by 10 am. Advised that the enemy was approaching from the west-north-west at 20 000 feet, he was vectored to the north at the head of the wing, climbing for an up sun position 15 kilometres north-east of the presumed target, Darwin. Caldwell deployed his squadrons into a wide and flat line abreast, with 452 in the centre, 54 to port and 457 to starboard. He was leading 452 personally, still solicitous of the pilots after the loss of their CO in the previous combat, and also seeking to give the new CO, Ron MacDonald, an easier orientation to fighter combat than would have been the case had he flung him in straightaway as 452's leader. As part of his rushed apprenticeship, MacDonald was placed on Caldwell's wing as his No. 2.

When the wing was passing east of Darwin, still climbing through 16 000 feet, Caldwell was advised that the Japanese were already nearing Point Charles on the far side of Darwin but 9000 feet higher. He sighted them 20 kilometres away, heading inbound on a course of 120 degrees. Control was intending to turn the wing onto a westerly course, placing the Spitfires more or less on a reciprocal heading to the bombers but displaced to the north, and with the sun advantageously behind them – similar to the arrangement on 15 March, this would become the controllers' standard intercept solution.

The enemy formation complicated things, however, by continuing its climb as it crossed the coast, thereby retaining height superiority over the Spitfires. Caldwell was at 26 000 feet when the bomber formation crossed over West Point at the start of its run across Darwin Harbour. He saw that the enemy fighters were still 1000 feet higher than his Spitfires, so advised control that 'we would not attack under any circumstances until our aircraft were in position'; and that the wing would only do so when the bombers retired out to sea after bombing. After the reverse suffered over Darwin Harbour on 15 March, caused by Thorold-Smith taking the wing in below the Japanese fighters, Caldwell was not going to suffer any repetition, and so he continued the climb and bided his time. The Spitfire pilots therefore had to watch impotently as the Japanese bombers went over the target at the impressive bombing altitude of 26 000 feet, with the top-cover Zeros even higher at 31 000 feet.

The bombers' target today was once again RAAF Darwin – 54 Squadron's base – which they bombed at 10.15. Dug in within the 'Darwin fortress', 2nd and 19th HAA batteries pockmarked the clear sky behind the bombers with bursts from their 3.7 inch (94 mm) guns, firing 219 rounds in total but without observable result. Following standard Japanese practice, one Ki-46 reconnaissance machine detached itself from the formation and headed south to photograph Hughes and Batchelor, exploiting the confusion to get away unscathed and almost unnoticed. The bombers dropped more than 100 bombs on the RAAF base, consisting in similar proportions of 60 kg 'daisy-cutters' and 250 kg HE. They fell in a line along the southern edge of the airfield and across the adjoining road and railway; some of the overshoots sent up tall columns of water in Frances Bay, near the floating dock, but most of the bombs wasted their explosions in the bush. Of the bombs that fell on the RAAF side of the railway line, none made direct hits on any of the buildings; two 60 kg 'daisy-cutter' bombs hit the southern end of the north–south runway but failed to damage it, and one 250 kg bomb cratered the highway; other detonations inflicted shrapnel and blast damage to huts, damaged electrical installations and pipelines and injured one man.

The bombs detonated with searing red flashes, bursts of black smoke and columns of dust. Although visually spectacular, as an attempt to impede the operation of the airfield and to suppress flying activity there, it was spectacularly unsuccessful. During the bombing, the pilots overhead watched the bombs kicking up columns of dust in the bush, permitting Caldwell to reassure himself that the bombing had failed, and therefore that there had been little consequence to his failure to launch the wing attack prior to the bomb run.

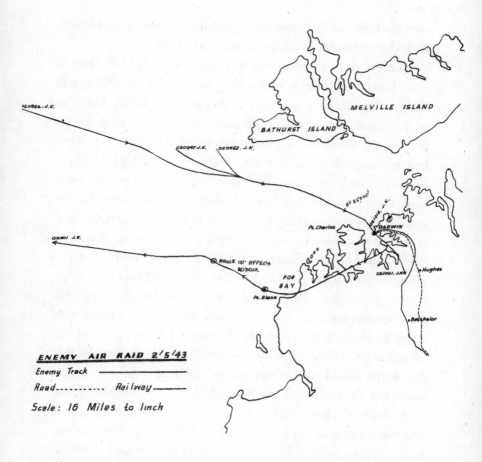

ENEMY AIR RAID 2'5'43
Enemy Track ————————
Road............ Railway————
Scale: 16 Miles to 1inch

Plot of the 2 May raid on Darwin. This flight path was similar to that on 2 March and 28 June: the bombers and fighters would rendezvous off Bathurst Island, then the bombers would turn right after bombing and retire south-west initially before a final turn onto west-north-west. Note the pencilled locations of Caldwell's first sighting and of the subsequent engagement on the way out; note too the recco that separated from the raid, heading south to photograph the southern airfields.
NAA: A11231, 5/72/INT

The bombing had nonetheless been a galling experience for all the RAF and RAAF men caught underneath the bombs, who claimed that throughout the whole bomb run they had not seen a single Spitfire from the ground. Although this was not strictly correct, the gist of it was true. Control retained some uncertainty about supplementary low-level penetrations, so had scrambled another eight aircraft from 54 Squadron under Flight Lieutenant Rob Norwood to patrol over Gunn Point, 30 kilometres north-east of Darwin, and these aircraft had circled the airfield and climbed away just before the bomb run, but too low to engage. There was also a single Spitfire tailing the bombers: Flying Officer Ian Mackenzie from 457 had suffered an R/T failure ten minutes after the rendezvous and abandoned formation, but remained airborne, watching the bombers go through the AA bursts over the target and following them out. Apprehensively scanning the sky for fighters, he declined to attack alone, and so returned to base.

After bombing, the big Japanese formation wheeled about in a wide starboard turn. This wrong-footed Caldwell, who had been expecting them to turn left instead, and had set the wing up for this. It is not clear why he assumed this, given that the raid had also turned right on 15 March. Placed to the rear by the bombers' turn, he led the wing west after them, continuing his climb to get above the high-cover Zeros. Initially retiring towards the south-west, the enemy then turned right over Bynoe Harbour to head west across the coast at Fog Bay. Leading the wing at the head of 452, Caldwell reached 33 000 feet after a hard climb at 105 knots IAS (174 knots TAS). Levelling off at that height, he now chased after the bombers on a parallel westward course, positioned up sun to the north-east. During the extended full-power climb, four Spitfires had aborted due to technical problems, and thus the Balbo had been whittled down to 31 aircraft – ten from 54, 11 from 452 and ten from 457.

Having thrown out the Spitfires' interception by climbing so high prior to bombing, then by turning right instead of left, the Japanese now for the third time threw out the interception by descending rapidly after bombing. This was a standard bomber tactic in all theatres: once free of the weight of their bombs and away from the AA guns around the target, bombers would typically put their noses down in a shallow dive, trading height for speed, and forcing the defending fighters to expend fuel, time and distance in chasing them. With their noses pointed only a few degrees below the horizon, the big Mitsubishis now sped away at a respectable 220 knots.

The tactical effect of this evasive technique was amplified because Caldwell maintained the wing's height above 30 000 feet. Therefore the Spitfires were denied the extra speed from a similar dive. As Caldwell stalwartly held 32 500 feet, the bombers increased the vertical distance from the Spitfires as they ran out to sea, also increasing the horizontal distance made over the ground (helped by a light tailwind). The fuel-conscious Caldwell pursued the escaping bombers at a moderate 160 knots IAS (about 260 knots TAS), giving only a modest overtaking margin, overhauling the bombers at the rate of less than a mile a minute. The Spitfires were still 10 000 feet or more above the bombers when they finally caught up to them. Because of this slow stern chase, a full 18 minutes elapsed between the initial sighting and the eventual engagement. By then, all aircraft had moved far out to sea, consuming the Spitfires' limited fuel and imperilling their ability to get back to base.

As they chased the Japanese formation, the previously neat line abreast arrangement of the three squadrons was lost. The Spitfires closed upon the bombers by moving towards their left front, resulting in an untidy echelon of squadrons and sections. The sustained high revs at high altitude was too much for the aircraft of 54's Sergeant J Cavanagh, which now suffered a failure of its propeller constant speed unit (CSU), causing the engine to overrev to 4000 rpm (3000 was the limit). He executed the prescribed corrective drill by pulling back both the boost and propeller levers, selecting coarse pitch with the propeller lever, then half-opening the throttle. This reduced the revs, but his engine's seals had already failed under the heat and pressure of the overrevving: the oil pressure dropped 'off the clock', and the exhausts streamed white smoke from an internal coolant leak. Cavanagh switched off the ignition before anything worse happened, and glided down for a forced landing at Point Charles. His aircraft was written off and converted to salvageable spare parts.

Caldwell assigned 54 the job of attacking the nine 'top-cover' Zeros about 3 kilometres behind the bombers. Although 452 and 457 were already in what Tim Goldsmith considered a perfect position from which to attack – up sun and above with a large height advantage – Caldwell delayed their attacks because he considered that 54 had lagged so far behind that it was no longer in a position to make its attack as ordered. However, this judgment was a matter of opinion, for 54's CO, Bill Gibbs, simultaneously thought he had got his squadron into a perfect position from which to deliver his attack on the fighters. When assigned the trailing group of Zeros as his squadron's target, Gibbs had dropped back behind the other two squadrons by moving further to the right, out on the up sun side, thereby keeping the Zeros in sight down to the left and holding his squadron in a good position to make its attack. However, after five minutes, Caldwell saw this and ordered Gibbs to close up on the other squadrons.

Irked by his leader's micro-managing, Gibbs complied, but it took three to four minutes to close the gap and in the process he lost his squadron's previously good attacking position. No. 54's move in compliance with Caldwell's order now placed the Zeros right underneath, in the blind spot under their wings, and in an awkward place to attack: when the attack order finally came, 54 would have to peel off into an almost vertical dive. This would have been hard for a single section to execute, let alone a full squadron, as the pilots would lose their formation in the dive and lose contact with their wingmen.

Caldwell adhered to his predetermined plan, holding 452 and 457 back in order for 54 to get into his preferred position to commence its attack. The extra delay meant that the action, when it finally came, was another 40 kilometres further out to sea. Put another way, this delay meant 80 extra kilometres for the Spitfires to cover, thus consuming about 15 gallons of valuable fuel – the equivalent of almost 30 minutes' endurance when trying to get back to base afterwards. There had now been three cumulative sources of delay that had imposed extra distance, extra minutes, and extra fuel: the slow climb of the wing before the bombing; the failure to conform to the Japanese dive; and the micro-managing of 54's attack.

54's attack

In the final approach to combat, 452 was in front, 457 close behind and lower, and 54 further back. Once 54 caught back up, the attack was finally started; it was just before 10.45, nearly an hour after take-off. By then the bombers were out to sea, almost 100 kilometres west of Darwin. Caldwell's plan was for 457 to dive at the bombers, covered by 54's engagement of the top-cover Zeros, while 452 followed up this attack and 'covered the withdrawal'. Unfortunately, this plan was far too complex and interdependent, and proved unworkable.

Following its instructions, 54 dived out of the sun at its designated targets – the nine Zeros that were flying 3 kilometres behind the bombers. The British squadron's mission was to engage the escort and thus prevent them from interfering with 452 and 457's attacks on the bombers. Oddly, however, this plan ignored the other 18 fighters, most of which Caldwell himself had seen. In particular, the plan ignored the eight fighters that he had seen off the bombers' port bow – in a good position to bounce any Spitfires diving upon the bombers. Other Japanese fighters had been reported at 30 000 feet only ten minutes before the attack, so it is clear that the nine Zeros which became the subject of 54's attack were the least threatening part of the escort. Being so far behind, they were in an exceedingly poor position to prevent attacks upon the bombers, and were moreover at an altitude not much greater than that of their charges. In spite of these flaws in the plan, it was these Zeros that 54 attacked, thereby unwittingly permitting 452 and 457 to be attacked by the other Zeros that were more advantageously positioned higher up on the flanks of the bomber formation.

Caldwell would later criticise 54 for failing to neutralise all the fighters, but Gibbs was under especial pressure to start his attack without any further delay, as the two Australian squadrons had already been waiting on him to start his attack – and moreover everyone's petrol tanks were rapidly emptying. Having been previously rebuked by Caldwell for its alleged faults on 15 March, and having now been goaded over the R/T to get back into position and hurry up, 54 was now hardly likely to do anything but go straight down upon the Japanese – indeed, it is hardly credible that the already impatient Caldwell would have permitted them to take an excursion out to the flank and thus delay the attack further. Caught in this web of frustration, impatience and anxiety, Gibbs chose to 'just get on with it' and took the most direct route directly downwards.

The British pilots dived from out of the sun, but found themselves diving at a ridiculous angle, starting from 30 000 feet and descending almost vertically upon the enemy fighters far below. Gibbs was greatly frustrated having to make this impractical attack after having previously set his men up for a more manageable attack from the Zeros' starboard rear quarter. No. 1 Fighter Wing practised diving rear-quarter attacks during their 'shadow shooting' training sorties, but the pilots did not practise full deflection shots from directly overhead – yet this is what they found themselves doing now. Bad shooting would be the inevitable result.

Propeller constant speed unit failures

A steep dive from above 30 000 feet provided ideal conditions for failures of the Spitfire's unreliable propeller CSU. This mechanism automatically adjusted the angle of the propeller blades in order to optimise thrust under all flight regimes; rpm was controllable by the propeller pitch lever next to the throttle, with the CSU holding the propeller at any given rpm value irrespective of aircraft attitude, speed or height. Unfortunately, the CSU mechanism was faulty, and therefore as the nine machines from 54 pushed over into their dives, another aircraft suffered a propeller failure. Sergeant P Fox failed to correct his overrevving propeller, and as it went past 4000 rpm the engine unsurprisingly ruptured its internal seals and gaskets. Overheated glycol coolant forced its way into the combustion chambers and plumed its white smoke thickly out of the engine exhausts. Explosive disassembly of the engine would be next and perhaps in-flight airframe disassembly. Fox was forced to make a snap decision.

Throughout the 1943 Darwin raids, the RAAF's Spitfire VC aircraft would be plagued by failures of the Hamilton Hydromatic propeller (manufactured under licence by de Havilland). Alex Henshaw, the chief test pilot at the Castle Bromwich Spitfire factory, explained the problem as a valve failure within the

LAC JL Langford of 54 Squadron inspecting a Spitfire's propeller constant speed unit. Note the Vokes carburettor air filter under the nose, and the battery trolley visible under the starboard wing. AWM Negative NWA0513B

pitch-change mechanism, which jammed the propeller blades in fully fine pitch, caused by the pilots' overvigorous opening of their throttles in dives. However, 457's Flight Sergeant Bill Hardwick, who was almost killed as a result of such a failure (as we shall see), saw it less as a product of pilot error than as a 'basic design fault' in the propeller CSU:

> At ... sub-zero temperatures at high altitudes the ... oil would congeal, and with the bleed-back ports between the front ... and rear chambers ... being too small, the unit would not operate properly. On nosing over into a dive, the airscrew would act like any fixed-pitch airscrew and override the preset maximum setting of 3,000 rpm.

Squadron Leader Ron MacDonald pinned the fault down to an oil pressure spring within the CSU mechanism, explaining that the resultant uncontrollable overrevving had a destructive effect upon the engine: 'You would get up to round about 4,200 revolutions and then boom!'

Air Vice Marshal George Jones, the RAAF Chief of Air Staff, investigated the power plant failures following the 2 May combat, reporting to the Advisory War Council that it was the pilots' poor engine management that was to blame. Although pilot inexperience may indeed have been a factor, the Pilot's Notes provided for the Spitfire VC's Merlin 46 engine point to the extreme delicacy of the mechanism, and show the labour-intensive piloting demands of operating this engine/propeller combination. When diving, the pilot was advised to throttle back first, and then once settled into the dive to gradually open up to the required boost to safeguard against 'overrevving'. This seems an onerous requirement in the circumstances of a combat, when overstimulated pilots were manoeuvring aggressively to attack the enemy, or when they were throwing their aircraft into violent evasive manoeuvres while under enemy attack. It seems inescapable that a pressured pilot manoeuvring his aircraft in combat might fail to handle his engine controls with the required delicacy and forethought.

A crucial factor that exacerbated 1 Fighter Wing's propeller problems was the typically extreme altitude of the engagements in the NWA. By penetrating Australian airspace in the top height band of the Spitfire VC's performance, the Japanese inadvertently put the Spitfires into precisely those flight conditions most likely to produce CSU failures. It is noticeable that Spitfire VC aircraft operating from Malta (fitted with identical de Havilland propellers) had few failures, helped by the much lower combat heights in that theatre – bombers came over at 15 000 feet in the raids on Malta, 10 000 feet lower than 1 Fighter Wing had to contend with at Darwin. Moreover, Spitfire V aircraft assigned to squadrons in the United Kingdom and North Africa were mostly fitted with Rotol propellers, which were not subject to such failures. The conjunction of defective DH propellers and the NWA's extreme altitude engagements spelled disaster for 1 Fighter Wing, but it was not until July that a contingent of de Havilland technical representatives arrived in the NWA to investigate the issues and provide solutions. Upon arrival, they had an 'exchange of views' with the pilots of 54 Squadron, but by then it was too late – the daylight raiding campaign was over.

It was thus an uncured design defect that caused Sergeant Fox to pull out of position with his aircraft streaming white smoke. He rolled his aircraft onto its back, unplugged his leads, unpinned his harness and dropped out. The Spitfire, with its engine still roaring, plunged vertically earthwards in a spectacular final descent, in full view of the men crouching in their slit trenches within the Darwin fortress. It missed the army camps and detonated against the ground in a roiling ball of black smoke and red flame.

54's dogfight

As his Spitfires descended upon the nine Zeros at the rear, Squadron Leader Gibbs's Red Section lined up on the centre vee, Flying Officer John Lenagen's Blue Section took the right vee, and Flying Officer Tony Tuckson's White Section took the port vee. However, the gunnery demands of this attack were always going to be challenging, given not only the high-deflection as the Spitfires dropped down nearly vertically upon the Zeros, but also the high closure rate from the high-speed dive. Gibbs admitted that 'the only snag was excess speed', in spite of having dived with his own engine throttled right back.

Aided by this precipitous dive angle, Red Section in the middle succeeded in bouncing its target Zeros, and so Gibbs, at the head of the queue, was able to open fire while the Japanese still flew unsuspectingly straight and level. He thereby followed up his success on 2 March by claiming a Zero shot down: he fired upon one of the outside aircraft and saw an incendiary round strike behind its cockpit. The Japanese aircraft turned to the right after being hit and then 'went straight down smoking'.

Sergeant Eldred followed Gibbs in and attacked the Zero to the right; he fired but saw no result, then unavoidably overshot his target, carried forward by his excessive speed. Despite pulling as tight as he could, he was going too fast from the dive and so his turn was too wide, and the Zero was therefore able to swap roles by turning in behind him. Seeing this, Eldred disengaged by rolling over into a diving turn which the Zero could not follow: at high speed the Spitfire's ailerons were still effective enough to keep manoeuvring, although the pilot had to apply a lot of force with both hands to move the stick sideways; whereas the much larger ailerons of the Zeros stiffened-up much earlier and rapidly became immovable – this weakness at high speed meant that all Allied fighter types could reliably escape pursuit by rolling into turns as they dived, first one way and then the other.

Flying Officer Gerry Wall saw his CO hit the Zero in the left-hand position within the vee, and so he lined himself up to attack the centre Zero. However, he was already too late, for Gibbs's initial pass had alerted the other Zeros. The enemy pilot performed the standard Japanese counter-attack manoeuvre by pulling up into a half-loop, then executed the aerobatic variation of a chandelle, pulling around out of the top of the loop into a horizontal combat turn. Wall zoomed up after him, simultaneously banking and pulling up so hard that his vision greyed out; but he held the G pressure as he turned after his quarry. He recovered his sight by laying his head on his shoulder and shifting his feet onto the upper rudder pedals; this produced a more reclined posture, which helped resist the flow of blood away from his head. With his vision returning, he saw that the Zero was still there, turning in front of him, and he fired a very optimistic burst from extreme range and with a very challenging 70 degrees of deflection.

Wall pursued the Zero as it descended off the top of its zoom into a diving turn. As the speed increased, Wall found that he could now turn inside the Zero, and he started to get onto its tail. The Japanese pilot evidently thought he had shaken his pursuer off, for he straightened up and pulled up into a climb. This mistake permitted Wall to close from astern with a 50 knot overtaking speed and then to recommence firing. To avoid colliding, he broke off at only 50 metres range by stamping on one rudder pedal and skidding out to one side. Here he found himself in the strange position of flying in formation off the Zero's rear quarter, only 40 metres away – oddly, the Zero had not attempted to evade, evidently still unaware of his presence. Wall's gunnery had been poor; he had not seen any hits in spite of the very favourable gunnery parameters that he had been presented with by the inattentive Japanese pilot.

Flying closely side by side, the Zero and the Spitfire pulled up into steep climbs, with Wall's aircraft decelerating rapidly despite his 2850 revs and +9 pounds of boost. He turned left to initiate another firing pass, but by now his IAS had sunk to only 85 knots, and as he turned his aircraft stalled and spun. Wall recovered immediately into a diving turn, but the sudden descent at full throttle caused a propeller CSU failure and an engine overspeed. He applied the prescribed corrective action, succeeding thereby in reducing the engine's revs to under 3000 rpm. Meanwhile, he had dived away so rapidly that he only pulled out at 1500 feet. Gerry Wall had had a most stimulating combat, but in the excitement he had neglected to monitor his fuel state.

The other two sections of 54 also entered the fight, diving behind Gibbs's Red Section, but by the time they arrived the Zeros had broken up to dogfight. As was usual with attacks in line astern, only the very first aircraft in the line had been able to exploit the bounce. In combination with the high-speed descent and consequent gunnery challenges, the results of 54's attack were therefore very disappointing.

Behind Gibbs came Flying Officer John Lenagen and Pilot Officer George Farries (Blue Section had been reduced to only two aircraft when Cavanagh aborted), both pilots arriving in what had now become a 'general melee' at 18 000 feet. As he dived in, Lenagen saw three Spitfires already engaged in a dogfight with four Zeros, and saw a Spitfire dive away with a Zero on its tail; then it got hit and went down smoking (this must have been 'Joe' Gifford's aircraft from 457, as 452 had not yet attacked). After pulling out, Lenagen turned to clear his own tail, in time to see a Zero coming in from his right rear quarter. Farries at once performed his wingman duty for Lenagen, turning in behind this Zero and firing a five-second burst in to 100 metres. There were incendiary flashes all over the Zero, then it turned over onto its back and dived away trailing thick smoke.

Farries broke hard left to clear his own tail, and as he turned through a full 360 degrees he observed that the Zero was now going down in flames. Seeing another Zero coming in at him, he rolled out of his turn, lined up on it for a head-on pass, and fired a two-second burst in to 50 metres. As this Zero broke left, also trailing black smoke, Farries saw yet another Zero approaching at a lower altitude, so he dived nearly head-on at it and fired, seeing strikes on its wing and fuselage. As soon as this Zero roared past, he pulled up into a steep climbing turn after it, getting around quickly enough to dive back in and reattack the same Zero from its rear quarter. He fired another short burst and saw more strikes, but the Zero broke away into a hard turn, disappointingly still flying and self-evidently under its pilot's control.

Farries pulled up again into another steeply banked turn to clear his tail, but too late – he had fixated too long upon his last target. Just as he pulled into the turn, his aircraft was hit from behind by both 20 mm and 7.7 mm fire. The radiator was hit, the coolant escaped, and the engine ran dry. Bellowing at 2850 rpm, it seized up within half a minute. Farries dived steeply away with a windmilling propeller and set course for the coast, but it was too far away to glide. Recognising the unavoidable and sensibly declining to ditch, he bailed out. This hyperactively aggressive and confident fighter pilot from Lancashire had fired four times, aiming at three different Zeros – claiming one Zero shot down and one damaged – but he should have disengaged earlier. He spent five hours in his dinghy before being rescued in mid-afternoon (the RAF K-type inflatable dinghy was folded into a canvas bag and clipped to the parachute harness; having splashed into the water and inflated his Mae West, the pilot had to extract the dinghy, unfold it, and inflate it with a compressed air canister).

After Sergeant Fox's CSU failure, White Section had also been reduced to two pilots only – Tony Tuckson and Sergeant

George Spencer – and these dived in on the other side of the fight. Spencer was a new graduate, but flew confidently and aggressively. He dived behind a Zero and fired at it, but was at once jumped from behind. Seeing tracers shooting past underneath his wing, he broke into a hard turn and dived away, then zoomed back up to rejoin the dogfight. He, Tuckson and Flying Officer Ian Taylor engaged in a running fight, going through a succession of turns and dives and zooms, getting shots at fleeting targets but without result. All the hard turning took the fight downwards to around 7000 feet, where the Spitfires continued to pursue the dogfight at this lower altitude.

Meanwhile, having spiralled away from the initial fight, Eldred's momentum had taken him far below the Zeros' altitude. Re-climbing to 13 000 feet, he observed this same dogfight, so came over to help. Eldred saw that the Spitfires were maintaining a high airspeed by fighting in a series of dives and zooms, that the Zero pilots were firing a lot of tracer, and that the Japanese pilots spent a lot of time 'flying on their backs'. He came in head-on at one Zero, fired and saw strikes on it. The Zero broke off by pulling to its right; Eldred turned after it and found himself scissoring with the enemy fighter as it turned back at him for another head-on pass. He fired again and the Zero bunted steeply under him as they passed each other. Believing that he could see bullet holes in its fuselage as it went past, he claimed it as a probable.

457's attack

Meanwhile, 3 kilometres further ahead, 457 had been holding its position 11 000 feet above the bombers; the Australian pilots would also have to dive at a 70 degree angle to make their attacks. Over the R/T, Ken James heard 54 dive in, and then heard Bill Gibbs give him the word: 'Righto, Skeeter squadron'. Like Gibbs, and for similar reasons, he simply took his squadron straight down, directly at the enemy. Due to all the delays, the intercept position was already far offshore, and his own petrol gauge told James that he had no time for any further fuel-consuming manoeuvring. As with 54, the wing's retention of height as the Japanese dived for home meant that the Spitfire's height advantage had now become an embarrassment. Caldwell would later criticise both 54 and 457 for diving in so steeply, but he himself would choose the same steep diving attack when he led 452 down a little later. He had set up the three-dimensional geometry for a steep diving attack, and that is what all three squadrons made.

While 457 was waiting to attack, Ken James's No. 4, Warrant Officer Clive Briggs, had dropped out due to mechanical problems. First his engine's oil temperature rose, and then the engine cut out. He pushed the nose down to glide back to base, but was able to restart the engine and so reversed his course, following after the squadron but now lagging behind and below it, all by himself. He followed the R/T chatter, gamely intent on launching his own attack upon the rear of the Japanese formation while the rest of the squadron attacked from further ahead.

Once the order was given and they commenced their dive at the bombers, the 457 Squadron pilots found that they were doing 330 knots IAS – this equates to about 460 knots TAS, which is a good speed by which to escape attack, but too fast for gun aiming or any other useful offensive purpose. Like other World War II fighters, Spitfires' controls became harder and harder to move as speed increased. At speeds like this, both hands and considerable force were needed to move the stick a small distance in order to adjust bank angle and therefore to control direction.

As Ken James led the squadron down upon the bombers, he saw three Zeros on the bombers' port rear quarter turning towards him, climbing up and already firing. James broke away to avoid their gunfire, leading his section around in a 360 degree turn to the left, but this hard turn at high speed split his pilots up, and they never reformed. A small force of escorting fighters had thereby deflected Red Section from the bombers and broken up its formation. In breaking to avoid the Zeros' counter-attacks, 457 had ceded its erstwhile advantages of speed and height, while the 360 degree turn had now placed the bombers too far ahead to be attacked without a re-climb.

The only pilot who pressed on and attacked the bombers was James's No. 2, Flight Sergeant Bruce Little. He passed straight through the fighters and made a rear-quarter attack on the bombers, firing from 800 metres out – far too great a range, particularly as he used machine guns only. At that speed, at that closure rate, at that deflection angle, and at that range, it was unsurprising that he saw no strikes. Looking up from his gunsight just in time, Little saw a Zero diving at him, already firing. At once he broke downwards and dived away, going all the way to 1000 feet before pulling out. Typically for 1 Fighter Wing, Little's lone gunnery pass meant that 457's CO was now separated from his wingman.

Having rolled out of his 360 degree turn, Ken James was all alone as he saw four Zeros up ahead and slightly higher. Climbing after them, he got into range and fired from 300 yards, but the Zeros broke at once, and one of them whipped around in a hard turn to come at him from the side. James prudently half-rolled and dived away. This evasion took him far below the bombers' height, and down in this lower altitude band he saw a Spitfire diving away leaving a trail of white smoke, with a parachute descending (this was Bill Hardwick from his own squadron). After pulling out at 3000 feet, James then saw a Zero circling with a Spitfire, down close to the water (this aircraft was probably from 54 Squadron, forced down low at the end of the turning fight described above). This was a dangerous place for a Spitfire to be, as the pilot lacked height in which to dive away, and was therefore unable to disengage; moreover, the Zero could fly more slowly in a turn and would thus inevitably get on the Spitfire's tail. James intervened before the Spitfire was dispatched into the sea: he dived in behind the Zero, but the Japanese pilot saw him coming and pulled up into a half-loop, firing at him head-on and inverted. James fired back at the Zero as it loomed up at him, keeping his finger on the trigger as it 'filled and overflowed' his gunsight. He saw pieces come off it, then it roared past. Both aircraft kept going their separate ways, their respective pilots agreeing that discretion was the better part of valour at such low altitude. James claimed his opponent as a probable, but irrespective of the actual result of his fire, he had likely saved the other Spitfire from being shot down.

Clive Briggs, lagging behind the rest of the squadron all alone because of his earlier engine trouble, was still intending a solo attack on the bombers' rear quarter. He saw three Spitfires behind him and to his left and thankfully moved over to join them; as he did so, however, he looked again – they were Zeros! They had seen him too, and he found himself in a head-on pass with one of them; Briggs fired and saw it flash past underneath with strips of debris peeling off its wing. As soon as it went by, he broke downwards and dived away, claiming his target as damaged.

The three aircraft of Flying Officer Harry Blake's Blue Section followed Ken James's Red Section down in a spiral dive from right overhead the bombers. Blake's R/T had failed just prior to the attack, so he had lost his ability to control his section's engagement, but his choice of a flatter spiralling approach was an attempt to prevent too great a speed on the descent. The Spitfires nonetheless attained more than 310 knots IAS as they turned in behind the bombers. As they did so, Blake was suddenly distracted by a single Zero flying out in front of him, its pilot oblivious to the Spitfires approaching from behind – evidently intent on overhauling the bombers to get back into escorting position. Accidentally presented with a perfect opportunity for a bounce, Blake lined up for an ideal shot from dead astern at close range. He got right in to 100 metres before opening fire, keeping his finger on the button until he broke away at 30 metres. The Zero jerked and snapped upward into a 20 degree climb – as though the pilot had been hit and had pulled back on the stick involuntarily. Blake zoomed up after it, pulling so hard that he passed right over the top of the Zero with his margin of speed. As the Zero disappeared underneath him, he heard an explosion, which raised his hopes of its destruction, but his own aircraft was now so nose-high that it stalled and spun away. Blake had unknowingly almost fallen victim to a further Zero behind him, which had fired at him but missed. His No. 2, Flying Officer Bill Gregory, had followed him in at a distance and seen a second Zero come in behind his No. 1 and open fire. Gregory got a good burst at his leader's assailant and saw incendiary strikes on its wing, claiming it as damaged. Blake thus survived, returning safely to base to claim his own Zero as a probable.

While Blake and Gregory attacked, the last man in Blue Section had become isolated behind them: Alex MacPherson had been blinded by the sun while turning onto attack heading and had thereby lost the others. MacPherson then dived at the bombers by himself, but he saw a Zero in front of him and decided it would be safer to attack it instead, rather than continuing down to the bombers' level all alone. He pulled out of his dive, zoomed up underneath the Zero, and opened fire from behind, but missed his shot. Having missed his chance, he broke downwards and away, heading for base. This had been an understandably tentative first combat for this very green pilot.

Like Blake, Flying Officer Gordon 'Joe' Gifford led 457's White Section down in a spiral dive, descending at 300 knots IAS for a run through the bombers. Flying Officer Ken Barker, Gifford's No. 2, sprayed one of the bomber vees ineffectually from 1000 metres away – much too far – but had to stop firing when he lost forward vision: his windscreen, canopy and instruments frosted over because of the sudden descent through a warmer layer of air. The bombers became blurred shapes as he closed the range, but he fired again – very hopefully – as they loomed up opaquely in his windscreen. Looking behind, he could see the vague shape of an unidentified aircraft behind him. He assumed it was a Zero, so rolled onto his back at once and broke away into an evasive spiral dive. While descending, he rubbed a small area of the canopy with his glove in order to regain some rear vision; and by the time he had dived down to nearly sea level, had succeeded in making a small clear patch in the frost. Looking up through this clear patch, he saw a Zero diving away, leaving a trail of white smoke that got thicker and heavier as he watched. Barker headed back to base, the frosted windscreen rapidly clearing in the warm air down low.

Flight Sergeant Ian Morse, leading the second pair in Gifford's White Section, followed the others down in the spiral dive from right overhead the bombers, but 'at a speed which I consider too fast at which to manoeuvre'. On the way down, he saw a group of six Zeros out on each side of the bomber formation, and decided to attack the left-hand group. The Zeros saw him coming and broke in good time, forcing Morse to take a difficult full deflection shot, and then only one cannon fired. He hit the Zero's slipstream as he passed through, his aircraft jolting violently in the disturbed air before he overshot his target and dived below. Morse pulled out so forcefully that he blacked out; coming to in a climbing turn, he noticed a Spitfire going down smoking – probably Joe Gifford, his own section leader.

Gifford himself was not seen again, nor was any trace ever found of his aircraft. John Lenagen's sighting of a Spitfire being shot down, as related above, shows that Gifford was hit while manoeuvring against the Zeros after pulling out of his initial diving pass. Given Ken Barker's experience just behind him, it is likely that Gifford's canopy had also frosted up, as they must both have passed through the same layers of air. He might have been hit as he turned blindly, lacking situation awareness because of a fogged-up canopy.

As the squadron dived in, Flight Sergeant Bill Hardwick was no longer present: like 54's Fox and Cavanagh, he fell victim to propeller CSU failure. Just as he peeled off after the others into the dive, the aircraft began vibrating violently. Looking down at the engine instruments, he saw that the engine was already running at 4000 rpm – his CSU had failed and the propeller had gone into fully fine pitch. He abandoned the dive immediately and pulled up into a climb to reduce his speed, meanwhile pulling back the throttle and propeller levers to coarsen the pitch, but this had no effect. Running at these revs, the engine was already overheating and boiling its coolant, and white glycol vapour was already starting to stream out of the exhausts. With his oil pressure needle dropping off the dial and his coolant temperature needle jammed in the red, Hardwick gave up trying to correct the fault. Instead, he switched the engine off and rolled his aircraft over into a dive – he would make a dead-stick attack all alone. He plunged vertically straight through the melee, looking out for targets on the way through. Seeing a Spitfire under attack by a Zero, he fired at the enemy fighter, but saw no strikes before he flashed close over the top of it. Another Zero appeared in his windscreen, banked right over in a turn, then he was past and it was gone. Hardwick saw a further Zero taking a long-range high-deflection shot at him as he went past, but by now his aircraft was already doomed, pouring out black smoke from the engine.

Once clear of the fight, Hardwick started pulling out of the dive, to slow the aircraft down so that he could bail out. Because of his great speed, he only regained level flight at 2000 feet. He no longer had the height to roll the aircraft safely onto its back to bail out, so he trimmed it nose-heavy, pulled both his feet up onto the seat, then kicked the stick forward with one boot. His body shot out of the cockpit under the resultant negative G, but the parachute bag snagged the radio mast as he exited. Torn open, the parachute canopy spilled out prematurely into the 300 knot slipstream. He was yanked violently away from the aircraft, but the streaming parachute entangled itself around his thighs and neck, pinning his head down against his chest in a tight tangle of hammering shroud lines. With his head pinioned he plummeted through the void, wrapped in a knot of silk and cordage. Feeling blindly behind his head with both hands, he found the tangle of parachute shrouds, separated them, pulled them away from his neck, and tore his head free at last. With the entanglement loosened, the canopy snapped open properly and his body fell into its proper place beneath; and so he found himself floating down peacefully to flop into the water. The taut cords that had entangled him had burned the exposed skin on his neck and lacerated his bare legs. With his wounds stinging in the salt water, he clung to the side of his inflated dinghy and waited to get his breath back.

As Clive Briggs dived away from combat, about 100 kilometres west of Point Blaze, he saw a Spitfire going down pouring smoke, and then saw a parachute float down as the Spitfire splashed into the sea. In company with Ian Morse, Briggs circled overhead, and saw that it was Bill Hardwick from his own squadron. Both pilots wound back their canopies and waved, watching Hardwick get into his dinghy, which floated only a short distance away from the aircraft's swelling oil patch on the surface of the sea. Setting course for home, Briggs radioed Hardwick's position to control.

After his initial attack, Bruce Little re-climbed, chasing after the bombers and getting to 22 000 feet. Still 8 kilometres behind them, he saw two Zeros closer than that at his own height, so climbed further up sun to get behind them. As he dived to attack the right-hand Zero, another Spitfire got in the way, so he moved over to attack the other one instead. Despite firing a long burst from both cannons and machine guns, right in to 50 metres, he saw no strikes. Instead, the Zero flicked onto its back and pulled through into a split S to come back at him. Little broke into a hard turn; looking down, he saw that the aerobatic Zero was 500 feet below, pulling up at him and already inside his turn. Despite pulling as hard as he could, Little could not turn inside it, and the Zero shot past only 2 metres underneath him at the end of its zoom. Thankfully, the Japanese pilot had also missed his shot, and by the time Little had reversed his turn to go after it, the enemy fighter was already heading away at long range. Having survived the Zero's aggressive counter-attack, Little looked around in time to see another Zero coming in at him, so he broke downwards and headed back to base.

452's attack

The third squadron attack was led by Caldwell personally. He was positioned in the centre of 452's line abreast, with Squadron Leader Ron MacDonald and Pilot Officer Ken Fox as his wingmen. White Section was out on the left, led by Flight Lieutenant Ted Hall, whose second element was led by Flying Officer Tim Goldsmith. Both of these veteran pilots had as their wingmen very inexperienced men in their first combat: Sergeant Bill Nichterlein and Flying Officer Sandy McNab respectively. Moreover, because Goldsmith's aircraft could not keep up, he and McNab had dropped out and lagged behind lower down. That left only Hall and Nichterlein out on the left in Caldwell's formation, closest to the bombers as 452 advanced on the enemy. The enemy fighters were 8000 feet below, in a blocking position between the Spitfires and the bombers. As they got ready to attack, Nichterlein also dropped behind, having trouble keeping up and unable to hold his assigned position as Hall's wingman. White Section of 452 had thus unravelled itself just before the action started.

Caldwell now gave the order, and 452 went down straight through the fighter cover, diving very steeply as the others had done. First in were Tim Goldsmith and Sandy McNab, who were now flying by themselves a couple of thousand feet lower, having lost contact with the squadron because of Goldsmith's underperforming engine. These two pilots thus dived into the fight from lower down and from further to the rear, but they still had sufficient height to go straight past the fighter escort to attack the outermost bomber on the far side of the formation. Goldsmith flattened out the dive as he approached in a left-hand turn, firing a long burst from the rear quarter. Despite one cannon failing, he fired right in to 50 metres, observing so many strikes around the cockpit and wing-root that he claimed it as probably destroyed. He got so close that he could read the bomber's tail number, then broke away by steepening his turn and pulling hard to the left. With his wings vertical, he looked straight up through the top of his canopy to see a Zero diving in from his port beam, but could not bunt out of its way as the bombers were still immediately below.

Surprised by how close the Zeros already were, as soon as he passed beyond the bombers he rolled over into a steep diving turn to evade them. He dived away to below 10 000 feet, but the Zero followed him down, able to stay with him by flying straight while Goldsmith yawed and rolled and thus failed to accelerate. Doing 350 knots, Goldsmith saw the Zero and broke again to shake it off, but his aircraft was hit in the turn:

the Japanese pilot had pulled off a brilliant deflection shot on the fast-moving, manoeuvring Spitfire. A bullet punched a hole through his canopy, narrowly missing his head, then the stick moved freely in his hand – the controls had been severed. In the fraction of a second that followed, the aircraft bunted violently and uncontrollably, breaking up under the strain and ejecting Goldsmith out of his seat harness and straight through the cockpit hood in a shower of splintering perspex. Suddenly finding himself outside his aircraft, he pulled the parachute D-ring. Blinded by blood running down from his forehead into his eyes, he heard the Zero making runs at him as he floated down beneath the parachute, and believed he had been fired upon. If so, the Japanese pilot missed, for Goldsmith splashed into the water unscathed. He was nonetheless left in a state of some distress and exhaustion, for it was only with difficulty that he was able to get up over the side of his dinghy. There he flopped down and waited, a lucky man to have survived.

Goldsmith had come to combat in the NWA as Australia's second greatest ace – with 12 victories, he was a veteran of 26 air combats against the Axis air forces over Malta – but he had just been shot down in only his second air combat against the Japanese. He had been similarly chased by fighters many times over Malta, and had been applying a proven evasive technique when he was hit. Steep downwards turns would otherwise prove to be just as effective in escaping Zeros over Darwin as Me109s over Malta, and would become the recommended evasive manoeuvre, so Goldsmith was unlucky to have been chased by a persistent and patient Zero pilot who was also a master of deflection shooting. Goldsmith was also exceedingly lucky to have survived the catastrophic break-up of his aircraft.

Goldsmith's attack prefaced that of the rest of his squadron, and during that interval, his squadron mates saw his bomber descending out of the formation. Several of them then observed it going into the sea. Having already lost his section through mechanical failings, Hall now peeled off to the left to lead 452's main attack. As the sole member of White Section still in position, he went down all by himself, but like Goldsmith was going too fast to be stopped or even challenged by the Zeros. Leading the squadron attack, he made an attack upon the fighters and then zoomed back up above the combat. Bill Nichterlein, lagging behind, followed Hall down at a distance but found himself diving through a swarm of enemy fighters, and as a result he was unable to get anywhere near the bombers. He opened fire at a Zero from the unrealistic range of 600 metres, then broke off to clear his tail, finding he had lost contact with his squadron. Acutely aware of his own inexperience, he looked around to find Hall or one of the others to join up with. However, they had disappeared, and so he dived away for home by himself.

Behind Hall, Caldwell dived in from a perfect position against a group of enemy fighters. Ron MacDonald, Caldwell's No. 2, was in his very first combat. He lined up on one of the Zeros and pressed his gun button, but nothing happened: his aircraft had suffered a total armament failure. So he kept going down, sensibly diving away out of the fight. Upon landing at base, he found that all six of his aircraft's guns had frozen up in the high-altitude cold, caused by the lack of gun heating tubes in the wings.

Spotting the gap in the line left by the CO's sudden departure, Pilot Officer Ken Fox moved into position as the Wingco's No. 2 and 'almost immediately' saw a Zero getting onto Caldwell's tail: three of the enemy fighters had come in to attack the wing leader. Caldwell turned underneath the first one, but the second one got behind him. Conscientiously fulfilling his wingman duties, Fox fired on this Zero and saw it break away, and then he pulled into a hard clearing turn. However, there was no one watching his own tail, and thus he was in turn fired upon by a further unseen assailant behind him. The 202 AG pilots had followed the standard Japanese tactical procedure of leaving the third man hanging behind, ready to jump whoever manoeuvred against the other two.

As in Goldsmith's case, Fox's attacker pulled off a brilliant shot, getting hits with a full deflection shot at a turning Spitfire. Fox's engine was hit, glycol poured out in a streamer of white vapour, and the coolant temperature climbed up the gauge. Within a minute, the engine seized completely and the propeller stopped. He pulled the stick back to slow the aircraft down, rolled it upside down, undid his straps and leads, and dropped out. By then the aircraft was on the point of pitching down into an inverted stall, so as he tumbled out of his seat the aircraft fell back on top of him; he hit one of the stationary propeller blades on the way past, and then the Spitfire fell away past him and he was free. Floating down beneath his parachute, Ken Fox saw his Spitfire splash into the sea beneath him.

Hall had stayed up above, using his altitude advantage to repeatedly dive into the fight then zoom back up out of trouble; he used these 'German' tactics to keep intervening in the dogfight, diving upon Zeros to distract them from Spitfires lower down. Caldwell also zoomed back up above the developing dogfight, maintaining his airspeed thereafter by fighting judiciously on the dive and zoom, and claiming two Zeros shot down. Although the evidence for these claims is unclear on the basis of the extant combat records, Hall reported seeing one of Caldwell's victims going down in flames.

Blue Section of 452, led by Flight Lieutenant Paul Makin, meanwhile dived in behind Caldwell's section in two separated pairs. Makin's engine had been giving trouble and so he had been lagging behind the Wingco. When he tried increasing revs to catch up, his CSU failed, causing him to drop even further behind. His No. 2, Flight Sergeant Ross Stagg, stayed with him, but the other two – Flying Officers Al Mawer and Dave Evans – went straight past, unwilling to be held up. Once they got up ahead of their leader, these two pilots were deflected from the bombers by some Zeros that appeared in front of them. Evans was moving at great speed as he dived past one Zero, but was able to line up on another one as he closed rapidly from behind it. He fired without visible result and then zoomed up and away. Mawer too was initially going too fast to get a bead on his first target, but as his aircraft slowed down, he got a shot at one Zero as he turned in behind it, claiming it as a probable. Makin meanwhile commenced his own attack dive, but he too was diverted from the bombers by an intervening group of fighters. He fired at one of these Zeros but then saw others coming in behind him, so he broke violently away to clear them off his tail.

Makin's wingman, Ross Stagg, was no longer there, for like Fox, Cavanagh and Hardwick, his propeller CSU failed as he dived. Stagg's engine overrevved, and the prescribed corrective actions had no effect. There was nothing that an engine that kept running at 4000 rpm could do but burst its seals, lose its oil and vent its coolant into the combustion chambers. Keen to pre-empt the inevitable engine fire or explosion, Stagg announced his intention to bail out over the R/T, then did so. He floated down into the wide waters of Fog Bay, 15 kilometres offshore.

As Makin dived away from the combat, he saw Stagg beneath his parachute descending through 5000 feet. Stagg splashed into the water, detached his parachute and waved to Makin, who circled overhead, climbing to get better radio reception and to provide control with a fix on the position. However, the frequency was jammed with transmissions, so Makin triangulated Stagg's position by orbiting overhead and taking bearings along his nose at Cape Fourcroy, Point Charles and Point Blaze. Jotting down the figures, he left Stagg lying in his dinghy and headed back to base, intending to initiate the search and rescue by telephone if necessary.

Bill Gibbs, 54's CO, after his first attack on the fighters, had meanwhile climbed by himself up sun, adding 20 000 feet to his height and getting up above the right-hand side of the bomber formation. When he saw a formation of Spitfires below him diving in to attack (probably 452), he dived in too, attacking the starboard flank of the formation and firing a long burst at one of the bombers from its rear quarter. Despite one of his cannons stopping, he saw strikes on his target's fuselage and tail before he peeled off to the rear, claiming the bomber as damaged. Checking his fuel, he saw that he had only 22 gallons left, so turned for home, landing back at Darwin with only 2 gallons. As Gibbs headed back, he saw seven distinct disturbances in the sea, which he presumed had been made by crashing aircraft (all Spitfires, as it turned out). He also saw one Spitfire spinning down (Farries's aircraft).

In all of this, it is striking to see how the Spitfire wing's vast height and great speed had been wasted. If there was ever a time to engage in dive-and-zoom tactics, then this was it, for the 400+ knot TAS diving speeds represented both safety from enemy fighter attack and the kinetic energy to zoom back up several thousand feet to regroup and reattack. Unfortunately, the Spitfire pilots consistently chose to pull out of their dives and start dogfighting, abandoning their advantages in one stroke and playing to the Zeros' strengths. The Japanese fighter escort did their job so effectively that only five pilots fired at the bombers – Gibbs from 54, Little from 457, and Hall, Goldsmith and McNab from 452. Tim Goldsmith attributed the poor result 'entirely to individual pilots' lack of initiative and armament failures'; the latter point might have been true, but whatever faults the pilots might have had it was not lack of initiative (for they had certainly done something).

Spitfires 'falling into the sea'

Sandy McNab had followed Goldsmith in to attack the bombers, but was not seen again by his squadron colleagues. He reappeared after the action, joining up with 457's Bruce Little and Ken Barker as they flew home. They found him to be 'flying alright and not damaged in any way'. However, there was something wrong, for McNab was trying to get their attention, pointing downwards inside his cockpit. He also called them up twice on the R/T to tell them something, but the transmission was garbled. Neither of the other pilots understood either message, and both had to watch non-comprehendingly as McNab broke abruptly downwards into a spiral dive, finally flattening out in an attempt to make a controlled ditching on the sea. He clearly faced a serious technical failure, which may well have been the result of an unlucky 7.7 mm hit in some vital spot. Like so many other Spitfire pilots in this campaign, he had chosen to ditch instead of bailing out. Upon hitting the water, however, the aircraft turned over and went straight down. McNab did not re-emerge, carried down in his cockpit as Thorold-Smith had been on 15 March. Whatever the problem, he should not have attempted to ditch a Spitfire if he had any choice at all.

The reluctance of some pilots to bail out was well justified, because it was indeed risky trying to get out of a Spitfire cockpit in flight. No. 452 Squadron's pilots had taken the death of their squadron mate, Sergeant Eric Moore, on 6 March, as a salutary warning: having suffered a glycol leak, Moore had made a late decision to bail out and his parachute harness had snagged the cockpit on the way out, preventing a clean separation. His No. 1, Flying Officer Ross Williams, had to watch as Moore's aircraft dived into the ground vertically; sickeningly, Moore landed right next to his aircraft and was killed instantly. When his squadron mates buried him at Adelaide River cemetery on the 10th, they reflected sadly on the fact that he had been with them only four days before he was killed.

While McNab was ditching, other pilots had perfectly serviceable aircraft to fly home in, but they had used up too much fuel to make the distance. At 10.36 am, 16 minutes after the action started, Caldwell came on the air and advised everyone to check their fuel and go home on a heading of 110 degrees, and this instruction was repeated at 10.40 by control. Pilots checked their fuel gauges and broke off one by one, but several had left it too late: pilots had severely underestimated how far they were from shore, thinking they were only 60 kilometres from Darwin when the actual position of the combat was twice that distance – more than 60 kilometres west of Port Patterson and thus almost 130 kilometres from Darwin. Some had evidently mistaken the headland west of Port Patterson for Point Charles, producing a position error of about 30 kilometres. Such errors were perhaps understandable, for while they were flying westward in pursuit of the enemy, the receding coastline had been placed behind them in their blind spot. Clearly, the pilots' navigation had suffered as they fixated on the enemy to their front, and too many pilots had left this to their formation leaders rather than keeping track of their own positions.

The inexperienced pilots of 54 had cut it particularly fine, for the squadron lost three aircraft to fuel starvation. Gerry Wall had pulled out of his escape dive at 1500 feet to find that he was lost; his aircraft compass had been toppled by all the manoeuvring, and at such low altitude he had no visual indication of the direction of land, with the coastline sunk beneath the horizon. He circled over the blank sea and climbed to get his bearings, then finally set course after wasting ten valuable minutes and the fuel that that time represented. Finally heading back at a very economical 140 knots, he nervously checked and rechecked his fuel gauge until it indicated ½ gallon, and then his engine stopped from fuel starvation, forcing him into a dead-stick descent from 4500 feet.

He trimmed his aircraft into a glide at 115 knots, and watched the sea come closer, the propeller slowly windmilling in front of him from the aircraft's forward motion. Wall could see an exposed sandbank in the water ahead of him, about 8 kilometres west of Point Charles, so he set himself up for a gliding approach to land on it. However, as he descended nearer, he saw that it was in fact a coral reef – too rough to land on, so he adjusted his approach to land in deep water about 40 metres short. Wall tightened his harness, locked back the canopy, undid his helmet leads and chin strap, lifted his feet up onto the top pedals, and braced his left hand against the gunsight. The propeller stopped rotating on final approach at 85 knots, and he applied backward pressure on the stick to hold off, skimming his aircraft just above the waves. First the tail wheel dragged in the water with a 'slight bump', and then the nose pitched forward into the water with a 'terrific jerk'. The aircraft stopped almost immediately and floated momentarily nose down. It took no more than two seconds for the cockpit to fill with water, and then it sank, going down too fast for Wall to consciously take a breath before he disappeared beneath the water. The Spitfire came to rest on the bottom at a depth of 5 metres, lying with the nose buried in the mud and the tail pointing up at a 45 degree angle.

Trapped below the sunlit shimmer of the water surface above, Wall found that his fingers could not feel the seat harness securing pin. Hastily ripping his gloves off, he found the pin and unlatched it, but he was still stuck fast to the seat, so punched the parachute harness release to get clear. His buoyant body floated above the seat, but his right foot was now tangled in the bundle of harness that was swaying about in the cockpit. He tore at his shoe, pulled it off, and shot to the surface at once, heaving the air in to his lungs. Wall had come very close to becoming a statistic. He had to stay off the sharp coral of the nearby reef, so he got into his dinghy and spent the afternoon drifting about in the current, observing a number of rescues in the sea about him. Sick of waiting, he attracted the attention of an RAN launch by the use of an improvised heliograph – reflecting the sun's bright rays off the polished chrome of the whistle on his Mae West life preserver.

George Spencer was able to stretch his glide a little further than Wall, and force-landed with his wheels up on the beach off West Point in Darwin Harbour. He made a good belly landing on the sand, but this availed little as the tide came in and swamped his aircraft before it could be removed from the beach. Ian Taylor got even further, arriving back in the Darwin circuit area before his engine cut on final approach – a terrifying situation with trees below. Suddenly engineless, he undershot the aiming point badly and landed in the bush – and was a very lucky man to walk away uninjured. Wall's aircraft was lost at sea, but both Spencer's and Taylor's were sent off to 7 RSU at Pell to be repaired.

The inexperienced Sergeant Bill Nichterlein had spent 15 minutes in the fight with his engine at full throttle. Belatedly realising that his fuel state was critical, he turned for home all alone, steering for safety towards the nearest land to the south – and thus off his direct track back to Strauss. Fifteen kilometres short of the airfield fuel starvation stopped his engine dead, and he had to glide in to make a forced landing with his wheels up in an open field, 10 kilometres west-south-west of Tumbling Waters. Unfortunately, he overshot the clearing and went into the trees, with considerable damage to his aircraft; and so 452's BS226 was disassembled for spare parts. He had only 364 hours in his logbook; this was his first operational posting and his first combat.

The same could not be said of the other one of 452's pilots who failed to make an airfield; embarrassingly, it was none other than one of the flight commanders – Paul Makin. He afterwards reported that his fuel gauge was still indicating 22 gallons when he broke off orbiting overhead Ross Stagg. Despite progressively reducing his revs to 1600 rpm and descending to 10 000 feet to save fuel, his gauge rapidly dropped to 10 gallons, and then six minutes later his engine cut out – this was only 70 kilometres from Stagg's splash-down point. He glided in for a forced landing on the beach, 500 metres along the coast to the south-west of Point Charles, noting that another Spitfire had already landed further along the beach (Cavanagh from 54). Seeing that the tide was coming in, Makin tried to remove valuable accessories and instruments from the cockpit before the aircraft was inundated, but he had no tools, so was forced to try to use a threepenny piece as a screwdriver. The water came higher and higher up the fuselage side as he wrestled with the screws on the instrument panel, and he finally gave up with very little to show for his efforts. He waded ashore through the muddy water and walked inland to the track, where he was picked up by a patrol of the 2/8 Independent Company and delivered to the nearby 105 Radar Station.

Caldwell and the RAAF hierarchy were happy to blame the day's setbacks upon the inexperience of the pilots, but Makin's inclusion in the rollcall of fuel-starved pilots suggests that there was something systemic to these losses, rather than merely the product of some species of youthful enthusiasm, as Caldwell's biographer suggests. Makin later complained that his fuel gauge had led him astray as he circled over a pilot in the water 'within sight of Darwin', and that the gauge was indicating 10 gallons even as the engine quit. However, this is inconsistent with the details in his combat report: Makin had headed north-east for RAAF Darwin rather than straight east to his home base at

Strauss, showing that he realised his desperate need to reduce his airborne time and to retain safe forced-landing options along the coastline. Ten gallons was too little and he came down 30 kilometres short.

None of 457's pilots ran out of fuel, although Clive Briggs, the most senior of the squadron's NCO pilots, came closest to disaster when his engine cut out just as he landed. Those pilots who made good decisions to break off and head home, such as Caldwell, Hall and Evans from 452, and Gibbs, Lenagen and Tuckson from 54, landed back at base between 11.10 and 11.25 am with near-empty tanks. Within that same timeframe, their more navigationally astray colleagues were making their forced landings with empty fuel tanks up to 50 kilometres to the west, showing that some pilots had stayed in the combat area 15 minutes longer than the others; all surviving aircraft landed within the same time window, whether on an airfield or not. Four of the fuel-starved aircraft came down in a loose cluster centred around the northern end of the Cox Peninsula, while two others went down when they were almost home. This pattern supports the conclusion that the fuel-starved aircraft came down not because of Japanese gunfire draining their tanks prematurely, but because of self-inflicted fuel exhaustion – as stated in all unit records. No. 7 RSU inspected the aircraft upon salvaging them and drew the same conclusion.

As the pilots disengaged and dived for home, they saw dinghies floating on the surface of the sea – there were seven wet Spitfire pilots on the water awaiting rescue. Ken James and others had been low enough to circle over each dinghy to establish the identity of its occupant, and had also radioed each dinghy's position to the Air Sea Rescue organisation. Unfortunately, 457's missing man, Joe Gifford, was not among the wet men who waved back.

Gifford had been one of the old hands in the squadron

from its early days in England, and was touchingly described by the unit diarist as a 'swarthy, tough young man' with a 'grim exterior' and a hidden inner gentleness. He had been dubbed 'Joe for Wing' by his fellow pilots; this was a play on the popular RAF expression, 'Joe for King' – a naive tribute to Stalin. The epithet was bestowed as a tribute to Gifford's evident ambition to get on in the service: he spent hours polishing his Spitfire to obtain greater speed, and was heavily involved in squadron life, for he 'initiated all the sporting activities on the Squadron, and followed them actively'; and he also served both as squadron transport officer and as officer in charge of the airmen's mess. With this sort of active involvement with the non-commissioned men, it is no wonder that the diarist recorded that 'all pilots, and particularly the airmen, miss him'.

The wing learnt from the fuel starvation losses of 2 May, having unfortunately ignored earlier warning signs of the same problem on 2 March and 15 March. Drop tanks would henceforth be used to extend the Spitfires' range – this extra 30 gallons of fuel gave almost an hour's extra endurance at a 175 knot IAS economical cruising speed. These tanks were already available, forming part of the suite of support equipment and spare parts that was shipped from Britain to support the RAAF's Spitfire fleet, at the rate of three tanks per aircraft. If the warnings of 2 March and 15 March had been heeded, and if these tanks had been fitted on 2 May, no aircraft would have been lost because of fuel.

Nearly four hours after Bill Hardwick went into the water, a Supermarine Walrus amphibian of 6 CU landed on the water and taxied over to pick him up. After getting airborne again and heading home, the pilot, Pilot Officer Levine, spotted 54's George Farries in his dinghy and landed on the water to pick him up too. Having got the second wet pilot aboard, Levine saw an RAN corvette approaching, and waited for one of the ship's

A Walrus amphibian. A couple of these aircraft were operated by 6 Communications Unit, proving useful on 2 May in fishing downed Spitfire pilots out of the sea. AWM Negative 029521

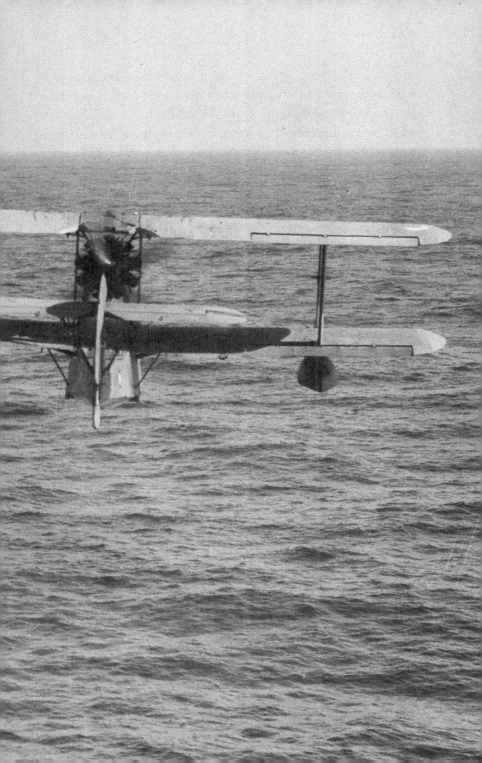

boats to come near, hoping the navy would take at least one of the bedraggled Spitfire pilots off his hands – reducing the load would help the poorly performing Walrus to successfully take off again from the open water. However, the navy coxswain accidentally tore the fabric of the lower wing with the boat's prow, triggering an angry outburst from Levine: 'I'm forced to land on the ocean and who prangs me but the bloody Navy!' Once Levine had applied adhesive tape to the aircraft's wounds, all three air force men elected to refuse the navy's hospitality; resolved to hazard another take-off from the open sea in order to facilitate the most rapid possible return to their units. Having achieved the feat of getting his overloaded Walrus to unstick from the water, Levine delivered the pilots back to RAAF Darwin. Hardwick was then chauffeured in Bladin's staff car back to Livingstone, where he arrived at 7.20 pm, stiff from bruises and lacerations, sporting a nasty friction burn from ear to ear across his neck, but very much a survivor of his ordeal. He only had 305 hours in his logbook, and this had been his first combat.

Tim Goldsmith spent the afternoon, that night, and much of the next day floating in his dinghy, forced to spend the time in uncomfortable contemplation of his close escape, before he was finally picked up by a naval ASR launch. Besides dehydration and sunburn, he had cut his face as he went through the perspex canopy, visitors from the squadron finding him in the Naval Base Hospital with 'ugly' lacerations on his face. Unfortunately, he had had his goggles up when the aircraft broke apart, and so had suffered eye damage when ejected through the shards of perspex; although he returned to operations, his vision was still defective as late as August.

2 May Spitfire losses

Pilot	Sqn	Fate	Location	Aircraft
Lost before entering combat by propeller CSU failure: 4				
Cavanagh	54	force-landed	on beach 6 km SW Point Charles	BR480 written off
P Fox	54	bailed out	crashed at Knightscliffe, Darwin	BS221 DL-N destroyed
Stagg	452	bailed out	into Fog Bay, 15 km offshore, paddled ashore	BR547 QY-S lost
Hardwick	457	bailed out	into Anson Bay	BS171 ZP-B lost
Shot down by Zeros: 4				
Farries	54	bailed out	into sea 30 km SW Peron Is.	BR239 lost
K Fox	452	bailed out	into sea	BS162 lost
Goldsmith	452	bailed out	into sea	BR526 QY-J lost
Gifford	457	killed	130 km W Darwin	BS173 ZP-G lost
Lost due to fuel starvation after the action: 5				
Wall	54	ditched	into sea 8 km W Point Charles, 11.10 am	BR572 lost
Spencer	54	force-landed	on beach West Point, Darwin Harbour, 11.20 am	BR536 DL-H repaired by 7RSU & 14 ARD, reissued to 54 Sqn 28 Oct
Taylor	54	force-landed	in the bush in RAAF Darwin circuit area, 11.20 am	BS220 DL-U salvaged for repair but never repaired
Makin	452	force-landed	on beach, 500 metres SW Point Charles, 11.15 am	BS191 QY-X repaired, reissued to 452 Sqn
Nichterlein	452	force-landed	16 km W Strauss, near Tumbling Waters, 11.15 am	BS226 QY-A written off
Lost, unknown defect, cause unknown: 1				
McNab	452	ditched, cause unknown, killed	into sea 100 km WNW Darwin	BS225 QY-B lost

Total aircraft lost or written off: 12
Total aircraft damaged and repaired: 2
Pilots killed: 2

Losses and claims

To put it mildly, having suffered a 50 per cent loss rate, the day had not gone well for 1 Fighter Wing, and thus it was unsurprising when a high-powered post-mortem followed. The unit diarist of 54 recorded that a conference was held at wing headquarters that night 'to discuss the action, the result of which is not regarded as satisfactory'. The pilots seemed bemused by the 'general flap all round', as though it were a storm in a teacup. No. 452 was a little more realistic, for the best that the unit diarist could find to say of the action was that it had fought a 'series of dog-fights', 'some successful and others not so fruitful'.

On the other side of the Timor Sea, the Japanese were very pleased with the operation. They claimed 21 Spitfires shot down – a figure that must have greatly encouraged the belief that their air raids were grinding down the Spitfires in a successful war of attrition. In fact 202 AG had shot down only four or five Spitfires, but on this day the Japanese pilots could be excused their overclaiming – understandably thinking that all the smoking and crashing Spitfires were the result of their own gunfire.

The Spitfire pilots claimed one bomber probably destroyed, four fighters 'confirmed' shot down and five fighters probably shot down. However, of the 22 Spitfire gunnery attacks recorded, only one cited evidence of the destruction of the Japanese aircraft – Farries's burning Zero. In addition, 452 pilots reported one bomber from the starboard end of the formation going down and hitting the sea after Tim Goldsmith's attack. For the rest, the evidence was equivocal. Gibbs's observation of seven splash rings on the sea surface and of an additional aircraft spinning down correlates closely with the number of Spitfires known to have gone into the sea, suggesting that few, if any, Japanese aircraft had in fact been shot down. Caldwell reported that he had observed

12 aircraft crash into the sea, and made the dubious assertion that only two of these were Spitfires. In support of the wing's claims, the best evidence he could adduce was that he had seen two enemy aircraft burning – but had not seen them crash – plus an additional machine 'smoking badly'. As usual, the intelligence officers at all three levels – at the squadrons, at wing and at Area HQ – confirmed the pilots' claims in spite of the circumstantial evidence; very few of the claims awarded on this day came close to meeting the criteria for 'confirmed destroyed'.

One of the reasons for this systemic overclaiming was a type of political pressure from the RAAF Area HQ, evidently for the purpose of producing a more favourable balance sheet from operations. None of the intelligence officers were immune to this type of thinking, but Flying Officer FH Quinn RAF, 1 Fighter Wing's intelligence officer, retained the clarity of mind to critique the Area HQ's role in undermining RAF claiming standards. After HQ circulated inflated claims for the 2 May combat, Quinn rebutted his superiors, telling them that their summary of claims was 'very much at variance with established fact', and warning of the 'evil repercussions' of such dissemination of 'erroneous intelligence'. He argued that the pilots themselves were losing trust in the claim assessment process: although he had found them to be 'meticulously truthful and conservative' in making their own claims, it was 'not encouraging to those pilots who have had the good fortune to have been genuinely successful, to know that the mere firing of another pilot's guns, has been accepted as sufficient evidence' for a claim. Quinn cited the example of 54's Gerry Wall, who had admitted he missed his shot and had therefore made no claim, but had been awarded a 'damaged' by Area HQ. Quinn called for the intelligence community to adhere strictly to RAF Air Ministry orders regarding the confirmation of claims, 'irrespective of whether the picture painted is a colourful one or not'.

Quinn had a point, for Japanese records show only a single fighter lost, indicating also that seven fighters had been damaged and that 'only' six bombers had been 'hit by shells'. Considering that only five Spitfires had fired at the bombers, this number of damaged bombers seems highly creditable, but just like on 15 March, none had actually been shot down. Nonetheless, it does seem extraordinary that so many damaged Japanese aircraft could make it back to Timor without adverse incident, particularly when so many of them were single-engined fighters. Wartime research on combat damage to US Navy aircraft showed that 62 per cent of engine hits caused the loss of the engine, and that more than 80 per cent of single-engined aircraft that were hit in the fuel or oil system failed to survive. In this context, the ability of damaged Japanese aircraft to complete the 650 kilometre overwater trip back to Lautem suggests a happy combination of very great luck and very fine airmanship indeed. Judging by the usually quoted Japanese loss figures, the airmen of the 23rd Air Flotilla were able to enjoy this happy conjunction on virtually every raid.

The Spitfire pilots knew they had not performed well, but it was perhaps a mercy that they did not know how poorly. Instead, the wing tallied its results and put the result of the combat as a draw, with four Spitfires shot down against four 'confirmed kills'. The Spitfire pilots' gunnery results had been hindered by the steep dives and high-deflection attacks, not to mention the debilitating spate of gun stoppages: of 54 Squadron's four surviving aircraft, three had had 20 mm cannon failures. The guns of 452's CO, Squadron Leader MacDonald, had refused to fire at all. A total of 16 aircraft experienced armament failures of some sort. Out of the 11 pilots who fired and made claims, in only two cases had the guns fired as advertised (these were Farries from 54 and Blake from 457).

The Spitfire V relied for its hitting power primarily upon its

Armourers from 54 Squadron reload a Spitfire's port ammunition bays. The men above the wing are loading 20 mm cannon ammunition, while those underneath reload the 303 machine guns. AWM Negative NWA0308

two 20 mm Hispano cannon, each of which had ten times the destructive effect of a .303 inch Browning machine gun. However, four of the latter had been included in the Spitfire V's gun battery as a compromise, indicative of the RAF's lack of confidence in the reliability of the new cannon. Despite redesigning the gun to cure known problems, the RAF remained concerned about the gun's propensity to jam at low temperatures – precisely the operating regime in which 1 Fighter Wing operated, with most combats commencing above 25 000 feet. Although the aircraft featured a gun heating system that took hot air from the exhaust manifolds out to the wings, many aircraft had unaccountably been dispatched to Australia without the ducting! Under normal operating conditions, RAF tests showed that the gun averaged one stoppage every 1500 rounds, but this stoppage rate doubled in dusty conditions (like those in the Northern Territory's long dry season). Moreover, many stoppages occurred outside the gun itself: Jim Grant records that the Hispano 20 mm's Austin Belt Feed Mechanism was officially a failure as a weapon system, because of the propensity for the ammunition belt to jam. Despite claims that the Hispano's unreliability problems had been solved in 1941, 1 Fighter Wing's experience throughout 1943 suggests that a solution was still far away.

No. 1 Fighter Wing thus fought its war with a triply dysfunctional armament system: one unable to cope either with the cold of altitude or with the ingestion of dust from bush airfields, and with an unsuccessful ammunition feed mechanism. Evidently the RAF had backed the wrong horse when selecting a 20 mm cannon for service in all conditions. By contrast, the Japanese had chosen the competing Oerlikon FF, which although technically inferior in ballistics and hitting power, was at least reliable. The Spitfire and the Zero were fitted with similar mixed batteries of 20 mm cannons and 7.7 mm machine guns, but there was a great disparity in the functionality of both armament systems.

The difference between the two types' armament is that when a Japanese pilot pressed his gun button, his cannons fired until they ran out of ammunition, whereas when a Spitfire pilot pressed the button, one gun jammed immediately, and the other soon after. As with the propeller CSU failures, the extreme altitude of NWA engagements exacerbated cannon failures, producing a rate of gun failure far in excess of that experienced by Spitfire squadrons in Britain or Malta.

Tactical debates

Crucially, the big wing tactic was unsuited to the range limitations of Spitfire aircraft, contributing not only to the loss of five aircraft to fuel starvation, but also to the hasty and ineffective attacks that all three squadrons finally delivered. The enemy had been sighted on approach to Darwin a full 18 minutes before the eventual interception, and this delay proved to be decisive in the day's ungratifying result.

Nonetheless, Caldwell stalwartly defended the elaborate wing rendezvous, arguing that it had been smoothly executed without any extra delay – as indeed it had, in comparison with the untidy affair on 15 March under Thorold-Smith's leadership. In practice, however, his insistence upon a full wing of Spitfires climbing together had meant a painfully slow formation climb. The Spitfire VC was a fast-climbing aircraft, needing less than 15 minutes to get to 30 000 feet if it was flown individually. However, an entire wing of them climbing together was anything but sprightly, slowed down by the demands of station-keeping. Indeed, 1 Fighter Wing experiments proved that it took up to 37 minutes to climb a wing of Spitfires to 30 000 feet. This was less than half the climb rate attainable by a single aircraft, and was no better than that achieved by the Americans' notoriously slow-climbing Grumman F4F Wildcat in defensive missions above Guadalcanal. The laborious wing climb on this day explains why the Spitfires were still so far below the enemy at first sighting, and why the climb to superior altitude thereafter took a further eight minutes.

It is significant that neither the US Army Air Forces nor the US Navy – both of them highly effective air combat organisations – used big wings in defensive fighter operations. Nor did the Germans, who scored very well against RAF fighter units by fighting flexibly in small groups (twos, fours and eights); and now the Japanese were also scoring well by using similar decentralised German-style tactics. Despite plentiful RAF fighter combat experience in the war so far, a sort of doctrinal paralysis seems to have precluded the possibility of learning from and adapting enemy tactics.

Given the Spitfire's well-understood limitations in fuel capacity, 1 Fighter Wing's tactics should have been shaped to permit rapid climbs and early engagement, thereby permitting the Spitfire to fight on its own terms: namely using its rapid climb and good speed to 'get in and get out', and fighting as close to base as possible to compensate for the aircraft's short range. Instead, Caldwell's interception tactics were shaped to conform to a predetermined tactical dogma – to operate all three squadrons together within a single Balbo, no matter what.

To his credit, Bladin took a more doctrinally open-minded view, for he was aware of the successful use of the 'American' tactics by 49th Fighter Group during the 1942 Darwin raids. This historical insight permitted his NWA HQ to critique Caldwell's overly rigid control of the wing – for the waste of time and petrol that this entailed, as well as for its curtailment of initiative by the squadron COs. However, Caldwell's tactical appreciation of the combat did not retreat an inch from his position as an advocate of the big wing, and in his refusal to apply the 49th's proven tactics:

It is appreciated that American Squadrons frequently made a practice of independent or 'piece-meal' interception during their tour of duty in this Area. It is not considered desirable to sacrifice the obvious advantages of a full Wing interception for the saving of the few minutes involved attaining rendezvous and organised battle formation for co-ordinated attack.

The prickly defensiveness of the wing's response to the day's disastrous outcome was also seen in Squadron Leader Ron MacDonald's posture of outright denial: he asserted that, 'under no circumstances could it be said that the Japanese tactics were superior'; and dismissed the wing's casualties by saying that 'we lost only two pilots and most of the aircraft were salvaged'. Tim Goldsmith was similarly trenchant in denying that the wing's tactics had been in any way deficient; he backed up Caldwell by insisting that the wing's tactical position of height and sun had been so 'perfect' that the combat should have been a 'smashing success'. Somehow it had not been. Even the shock of two defeats in a row would have little effect in challenging entrenched doctrinal positions within the wing leadership.

The Beaufighter counter-raid

After the action, the ever-aggressive Bladin saw an opportunity to attack the Japanese bomber fleet at Penfui air base after it landed. Knowing that the Japanese withdrew their aircraft to Kendari as quickly as they could be refuelled, a fast response was essential in order to strike them on the airfield that afternoon. No. 31 Squadron could only make five aircraft available, and one aborted after take-off, but Wing Commander Charles Read, the CO, led the four remaining aircraft across the Timor Sea and arrived over Penfui after the usual low-level penetration of

Japanese airspace. The contrast between the four-aircraft RAAF attack and the 52-aircraft Japanese bombing raid sums up the gulf in strike capability between the two sides at this time. However, the contrasting tactics used by both sides attest to the defending fighters' continuing air superiority over their respective base areas: over Timor, the airspace above 500 feet belonged to the defending Zeros and AA guns, while over Darwin, the airspace below 25 000 feet and above 30 000 feet belonged to Australian Army AA batteries and the Spitfires. Both sides were reduced to operating within very narrow height bands because of enemy air defence capability; neither side dared to penetrate hostile airspace at medium altitudes.

Thus the Beaufighters ran in across the airfield at 'zero feet', but found that most of the bombers had landed elsewhere – the long-legged G4Ms had the range to make more northerly airfields, and so could bypass the vulnerable Penfui on their return. There were only two fighters and two bombers visible on the field, but the Australian pilots strafed all four of these and left them burning. Only two Beaufighters had been able to fire, as the others suffered gun failures – the Spitfire wing was not alone in having problems with its Hispano cannon. Nonetheless, the gunnery of two pilots, Wing Commander Read and Flying Officer Ken McDonald, had apparently produced a better result than the whole Spitfire wing had achieved over the three major raids of 2 March, 15 March and 2 May.

Air Sea Rescue

On the Australian side of the Timor Sea, meanwhile, an even more immediate response to the day's combat was the program of air searches for survivors: 452 alone had six missing men. It was fortunate that the Air Sea Rescue system had been upgraded since 1942, for on 2 May seven pilots had ended up floating on the sea in their dinghies. Five of these were rescued that day, one paddled ashore 'under his own steam', and the final one was found and recovered from the water the next day.

Aircraft were sent out for days afterwards, searching out to sea and along the coastline. Ken Fox was spotted by a patrolling Hudson, and picked up that afternoon by ML815 – an RAN Fairmile patrol boat. The missing man still alive was Ross Stagg, who paddled his dinghy more than 15 kilometres to come ashore near Point Jenny, and then undertook a 16-day odyssey in the swamp flats, crossing creeks, wading thigh-deep in mud and struggling through mangroves. He finally made it to the Finniss River, 60 kilometres from the coast, where he was found and rescued by a prospector, Bill Essex, and taken to a miners' camp, whence he was finally sent off to 1 MRS in emaciated condition for an extended convalescence. He was lucky to survive his ordeal in the wilderness, and the squadron was very glad to hear on 17 May that he had been found alive.

2 May pilot table

Sqn	Section	No.	Pilots engaging	Pilots not engaging	Remarks (see table of 2 May Spitfire losses for details)
		1	S/L Gibbs RAF		1 cannon failed
		2	Sgt Eldred RAF		1 cannon failed, plus 3 .303
		3	F/O Wall RAF		fuel starvation, ditched
	Red	4	F/O Taylor RAF		fuel starvation, force-landed on airfield
		1	F/O Lenagen RAF		
		2		Sgt Cavanagh RAF	CSU failure, crash-landed
	Blue	3	P/O Farries RAF		shot down, bailed out
		1	F/O Tuckson RAF		1 cannon failed
		2	Sgt Spencer RAF		fuel starvation, force-landed, aircraft damaged
54	White	3		Sgt P Fox RAF	CSU failure, bailed out

		1	W/C Caldwell		1 cannon failed
		2	S/L MacDonald		all guns failed
	Red	3	P/O K Fox		shot down, bailed out
		1	F/L Hall		1 cannon failed
		2	Sgt Nichterlein		fuel starvation, force-landed, aircraft written-off
		3	F/O Goldsmith		1 cannon failed, shot down, bailed out
	White	4	F/O McNab		ditched, cause unknown, killed
		1	F/L Makin		fuel starvation, force-landed, aircraft damaged
		2		F/Sgt Stagg	CSU failure, bailed out
		3	F/O Mawer		both cannons failed
452	Blue	4	F/O Evans		1 cannon failed
		1	S/L James		
		2	F/Sgt Little		
		3		F/O Mackenzie	R/T failure, aborted
	Red	4	W/O Briggs		
		1	F/O Gifford		shot down, killed
		2	F/O Barker		
		3	F/Sgt Morse		1 cannon jammed
	White	4	F/Sgt Hardwick		CSU failure, bailed out
		1	F/O Blake		
		2	F/O Gregory		
		3		P/O Robinson	Oxygen failure, aborted
457	Blue	4	Sgt MacPherson		
		28		5	

Totals:
Scrambled: 47
In wing formation: 33
Engaged: 28
Shot down: 5
Written-off (non combat causes): 7
Damaged in forced landings due to fuel starvation & repaired: 3
Pilots killed: 2

5

Dogfights over Milingimbi

Only one week later (a short interval by NWA standards) but 500 kilometres east of Darwin, seven Japanese twin-engined bombers reappeared in Australian skies high overhead the Aboriginal Mission on Milingimbi island. At 11.10 am on 9 May, they dropped a stick of bombs out of a baking blue sky, and thus the war came uninvited to this isolated community of Yolngu people. It was this community's misfortune to have built a prewar airfield for the needs of the Methodist Overseas Mission, an act that had now brought these bombs.

Milingimbi was a low-lying island of clay, sand and mud, lying among the convoluted mangrove waterways of the northern Arnhem Land coast. Only 8 kilometres across, the island's mission settlement lay along its eastern shore between two large swampy clay-pans, so undeveloped that it lacked so

The Milingimbi waterfront: 44 gallon drums are dumped on the beach and dragged up the sand by caterpillar tractor, with Yolngu men providing the manual labour. AWM Negative 060524

much as a jetty or wharf to assist offloading of supplies from ships in the channel. As soon as the wet season finished, the RAAF's 1 Mobile Works Squadron had started upgrading the small prewar airstrip from the status of an 'Emergency Landing Ground' (ELG) to an 'Advanced Operational Base' (AOB) by extending and widening the runways. Bladin was desperate to extend the reach of his air operations eastward over the Arafura Sea, and pressed Milingimbi into service despite its grossly unsuitable port facilities.

The operation of this rudimentary logistical base became an integrated inter-service affair: there was a tented RAAF HQ ashore, and an RAN supply ship (HMAS *Chinampa*) moored at the mouth of the creek inlet just to the north of the mission settlement; while it was the army's 2/5 Australian Docks Operations Company that used an army landing barge and a couple of unpowered lighters to transfer stores from ship to shore. The heavy 44 gallon fuel drums were floated in to the beach, gathered along the waterline and lashed together, whence Caterpillar tractors dragged them up the sand to the beachside fuel dump, there to be transferred to the airfield by truck. These arduous chores, so necessary to the maintenance of flight operations, were very manpower-intensive, and so the local missionary coordinated the services of Yolngu men to help with the heavy lifting.

The airfield itself was an X-shaped straight-edged expanse of red sand and gravel, hacked out of the timber about 3 kilometres west of the mission. The main runway was 1200 metres long, running roughly east–west, while the shorter cross-strip ran north–south. Other than the cleared earth of the runways themselves, there was no permanent infrastructure on the airfield, with only a rutted dirt road running east to the mission and the equally vestigial waterfront. Milingimbi was too remote and its port facilities too poor to easily accommodate major works, so the dirt runway was only usable in the dry season. The RAAF's 1 Mobile Works Squadron had only recently managed to make Milingimbi ready for operations as an AOB, and the first shipment of 2567 drums of 100 octane fuel was still being brought ashore and dispersed into the bush as war operations commenced.

As rough as it was, Milingimbi airfield served the RAAF's purposes, having been pressed into wartime service as 59 Operational Base Unit (59 OBU). This was one airfield in the chain of bare bases that were used to give the air force's small force of Hudson patrol bombers greater reach to the east and west of Darwin in their coastal patrols along the Top End shipping lanes. This was inoffensive enough, and would hardly have attracted Japanese attention. However, the airfield was put to more aggressive use in early 1943, which changed the rules of the game and brought the bombers.

Provocation and escalation

It was the marauding Beaufighters of 31 Squadron that challenged Japanese dominance over the Arafura Sea. This sea gap had become the sphere of operations of the Imperial Navy's 934 Air Group, an Ambon-based floatplane unit tasked with reconnoitring and attacking the Australian coastal shipping that plied the supply route from Queensland to Darwin. This unit had announced its presence in the area on 22 January 1943 through sinking the 300 tonne wooden supply vessel HMAS *Patricia Cam* when she was heading from Milingimbi to Wessel Island carrying stores and personnel on a routine run. A Japanese floatplane (almost certainly an Aichi E13A three-seater) surprised her and shattered her hull with a direct bomb hit on the cargo hatch. Having bombed and strafed the survivors, the pilot landed his aircraft alongside them, and Reverend Len Kentish, chairman of the Methodist Northern Australian Mission District, was forced at revolver point to climb up into the cockpit and conveyed for interrogation to the unit's base at Dobo in the Aru Islands. Eighteen other survivors were ultimately rescued, while six other men were lost.

Reverend Kentish was beheaded at Dobo on 5 May 1943 under the orders of naval Lieutenant Sagejima Mangan as an act of symbolic revenge for the stinging Beaufighter raids on 934 AG's forward base.

In this contest for dominance over the Arafura Sea, 934 AG upped the ante by moving into its new beachside operating base at Taberfane – also in the Aru Islands, but closer to the Australian coast. This base's forward location provided the Japanese navy floatplanes with extra reach over the waters to the eastward, right up to the edge of the Gulf of Carpentaria. However, the new Japanese base was quickly discovered by patrolling Hudson crews, and so in a cycle of tit-for-tat escalation, Bladin deployed a flight of Beaufighters to Milingimbi in order to give them the necessary radius of action for a surprise early-morning raid on Taberfane on 6 May. They caught the floatplanes drawn up on the beach and moored offshore, and nine Japanese aircraft were claimed destroyed by the crews of the six strafing aircraft.

No. 31 Squadron's aggressive operations in the eastern sector could not go unchallenged. The Imperial Japanese Navy's 23rd Air Flotilla responded by rapidly deploying a squadron of 753 AG to Babo airfield in Dutch New Guinea. This was a prewar airfield that, ironically, had been upgraded by the RAAF as a forward base for 13 Squadron's Hudsons in the last months before Pearl Harbor. By the morning of 9 May the Japanese bombers were in situ at Babo, fuelled up, bombed up, and briefed for their first 2200 kilometre round trip to Milingimbi. The Mitsubishi G4M1 naval attack bombers of 753 AG possessed the performance to fly this long-range mission comfortably with a bomb load. The Japanese had concluded that there were no fighters stationed at Milingimbi, so they risked sending their big bombers over without fighter escort.

The 9 May raid

It was at 10.40 am on 9 May that Milingimbi's No. 308 Radar Station detected an incoming formation at 110 kilometres to the north – about 20 minutes' flight-time away. The airfield had no AA guns, so there was little that could be done except to wait and watch the tight formation of seven bombers cruise overhead and drop their load of twenty 100 kg bombs. The Japanese lead bombardier's aim was good, for ten of these bombs exploded in the airfield area.

However, the undeveloped airfield contained little of value and so most of these bombs exploded in the bush, the damage limited to the splintering of trees and the scattering of clouds of bark and sand. Only one bomb burst on the runway itself, but the effect of this was negligible, as the Japanese had dropped anti-personnel bombs – nicknamed 'daisy-cutters' by the troops as they were fused to scatter shrapnel far and wide at ground level, rather than to shift a great mass of earth as high explosive bombs did. As a result, only a tiny crater was left in the runway, which was therefore effectively undamaged. When 31 Squadron's Flying Officer Dave Delaporte landed his Beaufighter after the raid, the crater was so small he was able to straddle it with his aircraft's wheels upon landing.

The *Islander*, a 70 tonne coastal vessel under charter to the RAAF, had picked a bad time to call in to Milingimbi en route to Wessel Island further east. It was carrying Flying Officer Richardson and 20 men of the RAAF's No. 1 Mobile Works Squadron (1 MWS) in order to build a new radar station there – in response to the Japanese floatplanes' recent strikes against

Allied coastal shipping. Unloading was interrupted by the raid, and the air force men onboard were forced to watch the airfield bombing, and counted all 20 bombs falling there. Then they got to witness the action closer up, because the bombers repositioned themselves for a second run, this time on the *Islander* moored in the channel. The bombs straddled the ship in a wall of white water bomb bursts, catching the men of the 2/5 Docks Company on the water. Sapper Vic Paget was killed and two other sappers wounded.

The Japanese bombers, having completed their double orbit, droned back out to sea still in perfect formation. However, they were not to depart without a challenge, appropriately enough from 31 Squadron. Since 4 May, the unit had been shuttling Beaufighters in and out of Milingimbi in order to provide fighter cover against floatplane attack for the *Islander* and its naval escort, the corvette HMAS *Latrobe*.

Today it was Dave Delaporte's turn on the roster. When the alarm was phoned through to the airfield from the radar station, he and his observer, Sergeant Albert Patterson, boarded the oven-like interior of their sun-cooked aircraft, started engines, taxied and took off, relieved to have air flowing at last through their sweatbox fuselage. The heavy Beaufighter climbed for height, but by the time they reached the cold air of 17 000 feet, the Japanese had bombed and were heading outbound.

While the Japanese formation was still only a few kilometres offshore, Delaporte used his height advantage to dive from the beam at the left-most bomber, but got off only a short burst before all four of his cannons jammed. Some debris was observed to fly off the target bomber's fuselage, but it flew on undisturbed in its formation as Delaporte dived underneath and then zoomed up on the opposite side out of machine-gun range. He recocked the cannons and made a second pass at the bombers, but the guns jammed again.

The Beaufighter crew claimed one bomber damaged, but all seven of the enemy machines got back to Babo safely. Nonetheless, this inconclusive combat served warning to the Japanese that Milingimbi was not entirely undefended after all – as usual, Japanese intelligence was defective. Delaporte had successfully achieved an interception, but his good work had been wasted by the failure of his aircraft's armament system. If the guns had worked as advertised, 753 AG would have emerged from this first Milingimbi raid with some loss. Instead, the Japanese got away with it, a sign of the bad luck that would dog the RAAF's defensive effort throughout the 1943 raiding season.

The intention behind the raid had been to degrade Milingimbi's base facilities and to suppress Allied air operations from there. However, despite the technical accuracy of the Japanese bombing, the base itself remained unharmed, and the RAAF's use of the airfield continued without the slightest check. No. 31 Squadron deployed another six aircraft to Milingimbi that very afternoon for a previously planned second strike on the Taberfane seaplane base the next day: business as usual would reign at 59 OBU.

Indeed, far from having his activities 'suppressed' by the bombing, Air Commodore Bladin's reply to the 9 May raid was to escalate the RAAF's Milingimbi operations. Not only would he continue unaltered the program of coastal patrols and Beaufighter strikes, but he would now provide a fighter force for air defence as well: that very afternoon he ordered to Milingimbi a detachment of six Spitfires from 457 Squadron, supported by a small staff of about a dozen ground crew, ferried in with their gear aboard a Hudson bomber from 2 Squadron. With the newly arrived Beaufighters, that made 12 aircraft overnighting at Milingimbi on the very evening of the raid – a testimony to the utter failure of the Japanese operation.

The 18 pilots and observers slept under the wings of their

aircraft and suffered the mosquito-plagued discomfort that was normal at this low-lying, swamp-surrounded airfield.

10 May – the first scramble

The Spitfire detachment had been directed to have its aircraft ready for operations in time for any follow-up raid from the Japanese the next day, tasked to remain at five-minute warning during the bombing window from 10 am to 4 pm (calculated on bomber flight times from their known bases). The pilots were briefed to expect a similarly sized force of bombers, but this time with a small fighter escort of two Zeros.

At Milingimbi, a routine airfield operation like refuelling was not as easy as it might seem, as flight operations there were not supported by fuel tankers, relying instead upon prepositioned 44 imperial gallon (50 US gallons) fuel drums that had been dispersed in the bush surrounding the strip. The intention behind this was to make it impossible for the Japanese to destroy the base's fuel dump – because there was in fact no single dump. The fuel tanks of each Spitfire (including the 30 gallon belly tank) took almost three drums, while a Beaufighter took 12. This meant back-breaking labour retrieving and repositioning these heavy drums, rolling them out of the bush onto the runway perimeter one at a time. Once retrieved, each drum had to be loaded (by brute strength) onto a trailer, which was then towed along the edge of the airfield behind the antique airfield tractor (a relic of the prewar days). Then the contents were laboriously emptied into each aircraft's tanks by a hand pump. In practice, it took two to three hours to refuel just two Spitfires. It must be remembered that the Japanese faced similar difficulties at all their forward bases – hence the three-day delay between the 6 May Beaufighter provocation and the 9 May Japanese response. They too had been wearing themselves out unloading

F/L Pete Watson DFC with LAC L Reneke, operating the radio at
457's Readiness hut, Livingstone airfield – showing the bulkiness
of World War II-era valve radios. AWM Negative NWA0115

fuel drums from coastal vessels, manhandling drums around airfields and endlessly hand-pumping fuel into the cavernous fuel cells of the big Mitsubishis.

The Beaufighter detachment had refuelled the day before in preparation for its pre-planned strike, permitting it to launch its aircraft while the 457 men were still sweating away completing refuelling. Although the Spitfire detachment was organised to achieve the 10 am readiness deadline as briefed, and although the Spitfires were formally placed at readiness at 8 am, not all of their tanks had in fact been topped up – with all the rigmarole that that involved with drums and tractors and hand pumps.

It was therefore bad timing when at 9 am the radar station detected an inbound formation only 19 kilometres to the north – an hour earlier than the briefed alert time. This gave precious little warning, as the enemy were only a few minutes' flight time away. When the radar operators phoned the news through to the airfield operations tent, it produced instant action. Flight Lieutenant Pete Watson, 457's 'A' Flight commander, was in the operations tent when the news came through, and he ran out at once, shouting to the ground crew to start the engines and for the pilots to steer 078 degrees magnetic once airborne. The ops tent was sited at the intersection of the two airstrips, and the Spitfires were parked nearby along the edge of the main runway, so he sprinted the short distance along the dusty strip to his own aircraft. The resulting scramble was a truly 'scrambling' and improvised affair at this ill-equipped field, as the understaffed ground crew rushed to finish topping up the last of the aircraft and to drag the single starter trolley to each of the Spitfires in turn. Therefore it took 12 minutes before the last aircraft was finally airborne – caught too early, they had not achieved their five-minute readiness standard.

Flying Officer 'Bush' Hamilton's aircraft would not start at all; the magnetos were producing a good spark, but the engine could not get enough fuel pressure to sustain ignition because of a cracked primer line. He was left standing by his inert aircraft at the side of the runway while the fitters pulled off the cowling panels to get at the problem. Milingimbi had no ground control, not even a ground-based radio set capable of communicating with the aircraft. Hamilton made the best of the situation by now assuming the role of 'Spitfire Control', using the radio of his broken-down aircraft to provide ground-to-air communication. He tried to push his aircraft off the runway and into the cover of the tree line 50 metres away, but even with the help of four squadron ground crew, the clumpy grass off the edge of the strip was too tall, and the sandy soil too soft to make any headway. He shouted for more help but the other men stayed where they were in the slit trenches, so his Spitfire would have to stay put. Hamilton climbed up on the wing of the exposed aircraft, put his pilot's headphones on and used the R/T set to update the airborne Spitfires with the enemy's position. As the radar operators phoned the plot through to the ops tent, he organised a line of six men to stand between there and his stranded aircraft to verbally relay the information. Hamilton was a mature man of 27 who in civilian life had served as a volunteer lifesaver at Woonona on the south coast of New South Wales, and so the role of taking responsibility and looking out for others came naturally.

Soon after taking off, the Spitfires saw the raiding aircraft – two of the Beaufighters were returning early from the Taberfane strike. It was a false alarm. The Beaufighters lacked VHF radio, and thus were unable to achieve communication with the Spitfires or with 'Spitfire Control'. This potential 'friendly fire' incident was averted by the Spitfire pilots' recognition of the distinctive snub nose shape of the Beaufighter. Having reported them as Beaufighters over the R/T, Pete Watson continued the climb. When he reached 14 000 feet, Hamilton (improvising in the role of fighter controller) cancelled the scramble and ordered the Spitfires to land (for further refuelling!).

The two returning Beaufighters, flown respectively by Flight Lieutenant Phil Biven and Pilot Officer Evan Frith, landed and taxied around onto the cross-strip to the 31 Squadron flight line. The five Spitfires were following them in, at that stage descending through 1500–3000 feet to join the circuit. The first Spitfire, that of the newly commissioned Pilot Officer Bruce Little, already had its wheels down on final approach to land when a second plot was identified on the radar, 50 kilometres out at 340 degrees magnetic from Milingimbi. This information was phoned through to the ops hut, and Hamilton relayed this to the pilots over the R/T. No one yet knew it, but nine Zero fighters were following the Beaufighters in.

The second scramble

By now Little was already on the ground, rolling along the runway with the string of Spitfires circling around the circuit area above him. When Hamilton transmitted his warning, Pete Watson responded by ordering a scramble to 20 000 feet, and so the four Spitfires still airborne aborted their approaches, retracted their undercarriages, and climbed away at maximum climb power, followed by Little who took off again and hurried after them.

Thus five Spitfires climbed away from the airfield towards the incoming raid, all on a course of 340 degrees but at different heights and positions, having been scrambled direct from the circuit. They were dispersed, strung out in no formation at all, with each pilot unaware of the others' positions. Meanwhile, the enemy were only a few minutes' flying time away, inbound. Because of the time pressure, and the need to get height for safety, Watson accepted that he wouldn't be unable to reform his flight until they were at the top of their climb. This proved to be a bad decision, for which his pilots would hazard their lives.

In Watson's defence, however, no one yet understood that the intruders were fighters rather than bombers, as everyone had been briefed to expect a repeat of the previous day's bombing raid. The Japanese therefore achieved complete surprise when they appeared as a full squadron of fighters. This feat was made possible by their use of the airfield at Langgoer in the Kai Islands, 350 kilometres closer to Milingimbi than the previous day's bomber airfield at Babo – hence their arrival earlier in the morning, catching 457 unprepared. The 1500 kilometre round trip from Langgoer airfield was a very considerable flight for a fighter unit in 1943. It must be remembered that the maximum operating radius that was practically possible with the Spitfire V was 260 kilometres, as Wing Commander Caldwell had regretfully emphasised to an offensively minded Bladin at the beginning of the year. The 750 kilometre radius demonstrated by 202 AG on this day was an uncomfortable reminder of the technical superiority of the Zero across the extended battle fronts of the Timor and Arafura Seas.

The high-level dogfight

So the five Spitfires climbed separately, in a terrible hurry to get height before the Japanese arrived. At least this separation meant that each pilot generated a good climb rate – forming up and keeping formation greatly slowed down climb rates, as 2 May had shown. The scattered Spitfires took less than four minutes to get to 11 000 feet, which was good going and a confirmation of the Spitfire's qualities as a fast-climbing interceptor. However, a maximum climb rate like this was achieved at a slow airspeed of just 120 knots IAS, and it was in this slow and vulnerable climbing condition that the Zeros found them.

By then the Spitfires were starting to close in on one another to form up; Rex Watson was banking his aircraft, trying to see Bruce Little, his No. 2, behind him. He could not see him there, but as he climbed through 11 000 feet he formed up on Pilot Officer Ian Morse's aircraft instead. Morse saw Rex Watson's aircraft approach and misidentified it, thinking it was that of his flight commander, Pete Watson. By now they were more than 20 kilometres north-west of the airfield, out over the sea. Having spent the whole flight so far at lower altitudes and having conducted two full-power climbs away from the airfield, the pilots were uncomfortable and sweaty in their confined cockpits, the interiors of which were heated up by the sun glaring down through the perspex.

Of course, the Japanese were out there too, out there to the north-east, up sun. As he climbed through 10 000 feet, peering into the sky's oppressive brightness, Flight Sergeant Evan Batchelor made the first sighting, reporting Zeros at 3 o'clock. The Japanese were at 12 000 feet, flying on a south-east course inbound towards Milingimbi – more or less on a reciprocal course to the Spitfires, but displaced to their right. Soon after, Morse called his first sighting too: he saw the group of three Zeros initially sighted, and then a separate group of six Zeros, 1500–2000 feet further above.

The flight leader, Pete Watson, had still not found his No. 2, Ian Morse. Therefore, as the latter gave his sighting reports, Watson was misled into looking along a false bearing – for the enemy bore differently from each of the scattered Spitfires. Morse had thought that his leader was beside him and did not understand why Pete Watson could not see what he was seeing. Thus the Spitfire flight went into the fight with its leader unable to see the enemy and therefore unable to lead. The Spitfire pilots' poor lookout was caused by their preoccupation with looking for each other, rather than scanning the sky for the enemy. Pete

Watson's decision to 'climb now and form up later' had brought his flight into action in a state of disorder. Ironically, he himself was in the greatest disarray, being remote from the others, looking in the wrong direction, and troublingly unable to see the Japanese lurking above in the glare of the sun.

By now, three Spitfires (Morse, Batchelor and Rex Watson's) had managed to reform in a rough vee formation, while Little had almost caught up and was only a kilometre behind. Now Little saw the enemy, observing three widely spaced vees, each of three Zeros, with the lead vee lower than those following. At this stage, therefore, three of the Spitfire pilots had seen the enemy, while two (both of the Watsons) had not. It was about 9.30 am.

'Vee' formation

±

±   ±

Having made the first sighting, and with his leader still failing to see the enemy, Morse tried to take control of the engagement by leading a climbing turn into the sun towards the main group of six enemy fighters. However, the other three Zeros had meanwhile detached themselves from the six and were even now curving around behind the Spitfires in a diving right-hand turn. While looking at the group of six, Morse was suddenly jumped by 'another' Zero diving in from his starboard beam. He saw it at the last second and broke downwards in a violent bunt. As he did so, he saw another Zero getting on Rex Watson's tail, and called on him to break. Rex Watson saw tracers going over his starboard wing in the same moment as he heard Morse's warning; he too broke downwards in a violent skidding bunt, pushing his engine levers forward as he did so for maximum boost and revs. Zooming back up into a steep climbing turn to the right, he looked behind to see that he had shaken the Zero off his tail.

Pete Watson only now spotted the three Zeros as they pulled around onto Rex Watson's and Morse's tails, and saw the Spitfires break away downwards. As Watson's DFC would suggest, he was an experienced fighter pilot, well able to recognise a bad bounce when he saw one. He took his cue from the others, half-rolling at once and disengaging in a high-speed spiral dive. Pulling out at 4000 feet, he looked behind to confirm that there was no one on his tail, and then re-climbed up sun to rejoin the combat, which was now about 20 kilometres away. Thus the flight commander missed the combat. His initial disengagement was a good decision under the circumstances, for to persist in an engagement under every disadvantage was indeed bad tactics. However, Watson's flock of junior pilots were perhaps too unsophisticated to recognise the situation for what it was, for they had meanwhile stayed where they were and fought back.

Ian Morse thus found himself in a dogfight. Rolling out of his initial break and then reversing his turn, he saw a Zero directly above him, so pulled up hard after it. His aircraft hung on its propeller, decelerating in a near-vertical climb, and he fired and saw strikes on the Zero's wing. His Spitfire then ran out of airspeed and stalled; the heavy nose pitched into a spin and the aircraft went straight down, rotating about the vertical axis. As he spun towards the sea, Morse found that the engine was overspeeding to 4000 revs – his propeller CSU had failed. The oil seals had already burst: hot engine oil ran back from the engine, leaking into the cockpit, running up over the interior perspex of the windscreen, and spurting painfully onto his bare legs. Morse held the aircraft in the spin by holding the stick back and keeping his foot pressed on the rudder pedal – he was exploiting the inadvertent spin as an evasive manoeuvre – trying to correct the engine overspeeding as his aircraft gyrated down. He pulled back the rpm lever and then cycled it back and forth to clear the fault. Fortunately, this succeeded in reducing the revs, but the spin had produced a formidable rate of descent, and thus he did not recover until very low, pulling out at only 600 feet and wisely deciding to take his misbehaving aircraft home.

Evan Batchelor had followed Morse into the initial break, and then fired at a Zero that came at him head-on and inverted. As he turned steeply left to go after it, he too stalled and spun out – like the others, Batchelor had begun his fight at climbing speed, and the extra drag of his hard turn had lost him his last bit of flying speed. As his aircraft flicked into the spin, he saw that the inverted Zero was now looping down onto his tail, but his accidental spin ruined the Zero's gunnery pass: it overshot and dived harmlessly past. Like Morse, Batchelor held the Spitfire in the spin as an evasive manoeuvre, and then pulled out at 8000 feet. Turning to clear his tail, he saw another Spitfire still spinning down, pursued by a Zero – this was Morse; the two Spitfires had spun down side by side, each unaware of the other. However, the distraction of this neighbouring combat almost proved fatal for Batchelor: only five seconds after recovering from his own spin, his aircraft was hit from behind by an unseen Zero; his opponent, like Morse's, had followed him down. For the second time, Batchelor broke violently downwards, rolling into a series of evasive turns. The gunfire damage consisted of only a couple of 7.7 mm bullet holes through his port wing, but the consequent hasty descent at high revs caused his propeller CSU to fail as well, overspeeding his engine to 4000 rpm. Like Morse, he succeeded in getting his revs under control, then levelled out at 2000 feet over the sea and headed back to the field.

Rex Watson had seen Batchelor under attack, and came in to join him. He was at once greeted by a fast-moving Zero that came at him head-on. It passed underneath, too fast for either of them to fire. Watson did a wingover to the right and dived after the Zero, firing a two-second burst from 150 metres at the enemy machine's starboard rear quarter. The Zero fell out of control, spinning from 10 000 feet with black smoke coming from its engine cowling, so Watson claimed it as destroyed (corroborated by Morse, who had seen this spinning and smoking Zero).

However, like Batchelor, Watson was almost killed for looking too long. As he watched his victim plunging away below, he was bounced a second time: tracer flashed over his port wing; his pursuer had followed him down. He broke right and downwards in a violent skidding bunt at emergency power, rolling out 5000 feet lower and heading away in the opposite direction.

Bruce Little meanwhile had joined the dogfight, attacking a Zero that was on the tail of a Spitfire (probably Rex Watson's). He had climbed at 175 knots IAS towards it from its port side, then dived and pulled up under its tail for an unseen shot from behind. He fired from 300 metres, but with machine guns only as his cannons did not fire (his gloved thumb must have slipped off the cannon button). He missed, for the Zero broke into a climbing turn. Little pulled up after it, cutting across the radius of its turn so that he was able to look right along the top of its fuselage. He fired again from 200 metres with a five-second burst of both cannon and machine gun, and this time saw the bright splashes of bullet strikes on its wing.

Just then an explosion shook the fuselage of his Spitfire and the stick jumped in his hand: a 20 mm shell had exploded against the tail of his aircraft. He had spent too long on his own attack, too long looking ahead; and the Japanese were working together. Little broke violently left, looking behind to see a Zero 200 metres away, firing from his port rear quarter. He pushed the stick hard over, rolled inverted and pulled hard.

Accelerating into the dive, he noticed that his aircraft's elevator trim had been damaged by the shell explosion, for the aircraft was now flying very nose-heavy. He found he had to hold strong backward pressure on the stick as the aircraft dived, otherwise the nose would tuck under past the vertical, threatening to push the Spitfire through a wing-snapping high-speed bunt. The airflow howled past the canopy in the vertical dive; the Spitfire had light elevators, but he was now going so fast that he had to pull firmly on the stick to make it move at all. Aware of the danger of pulling his wings off by overstressing the airframe, he throttled back and gingerly held the backwards pressure on the stick, hoping that the damaged elevator control would hold together while using the elevator trimmer to assist with the pull out. As the G built up, he leaned his body forward and held his feet up on the upper rudder pedals to ease the strain. The elevator held, he recovered to normal flight, and like Morse and Batchelor, sensibly decided to take his damaged aircraft back to Milingimbi for some mechanical attention. Little turned back over the sea, heading south-east for the 25 kilometre run back to the airfield – but it would not be as simple as that.

Rex Watson, having survived being bounced a second time, and having pulled out from his evasive dive, re-climbed five separate times to rejoin the fight. Each time he found himself in close combat with a Zero, and got shots at three of them. In spite of manoeuvring so aggressively that he twice spun out of his turns, he had to content himself with speculative high-deflection shots. At the end he found Batchelor, joined up with him and headed for home. Both pilots were lucky to be still alive: this was the first time that two Spitfires had operated as a pair in the whole engagement. Rex Watson had lied about his age to get into the air force, and was by far the oldest line pilot in the wing (Gibbs and Caldwell were of a similar age, Caldwell having similarly lied about his birth year in order to get into the air force). In a fighter wing where pilots' ages varied from the early twenties to mid-twenties, Watson was an 'old man' of 33, but he had fought with all the vigour expected of a far younger man.

The low-level fight over the airfield

Five minutes after the Spitfires climbed away in the second scramble, Bush Hamilton was still standing by his exposed aircraft when he heard 'strange motors'. As 'Spitfire Control', he was aware of the general plotting picture, so he knew what the noise must be: at once he abandoned his Spitfire and ran for cover in trenches, 70 metres away in the bush by the runway intersection. He was beaten to the spot by his six attendant airmen.

While six of the Zeros stayed to engage the Spitfires up above, three others descended for a strafing attack. They first approached the island from the east, using up most of their 20 mm cannon ammunition on a firing run upon the anchored cutter HMAS *Maroubra*, a coastal supply vessel. The 20 mm high explosive rounds hammered into the hull and ignited its POL (petrol, oil and lubricant) cargo; and so the vessel burned with the loss of 30 tons of RAAF stores. Although this was certainly a successful attack, it was a questionable priority, as it reduced the Zeros' armament to only two 7.7 mm machine guns for the airfield attack. This certainly saved several Beaufighters from destruction, for the Zeros arrived overhead right in the middle of busy runway operations by 31 Squadron.

On the ground, Biven and Frith had just taxied their Beaufighters around onto the cross-strip, parking them along the edge of the runway. Shutting down the engines, the four men climbed down their aircraft ladders to ritually urinate on their rudders, relieving themselves thankfully after the five-hour flight. Just then the Zeros appeared above the tree line, arrogantly flying in a neat vee at the provocatively slow speed of 175 knots. As they flew east to west along the main runway, they saw the three parked Beaufighters to their left and at once turned to position themselves for a run along the north–south cross-strip. Both aircrew and ground crew scattered from the 31 Squadron flight line, heading for the trenches or as far as they could go away from the airstrip into the cover of the bush. The Zeros completed their methodical orbit and then lined up to unhurriedly commence their strafing run on the Beaufighters, using machine guns only. The 7.7 mm gunfire perforated the wing fuel tanks of Biven's machine, A19-72, and the leaking petrol caught alight. Biven and his observer, Sergeant John Newton, were obliged to watch as their aircraft burnt itself to an incinerated mess of molten aluminium – Milingimbi lacked the fire truck and the foam fire extinguishers necessary to contain a petrol-fed fire. Frith's recently landed A19-16 was also holed by machine-gun bullets but did not burn – it was fortunate that the Zeros had used up their 20 mm ammunition on the *Maroubra*.

Two other Beaufighters were caught at the worst possible moment – on take-off. Unable to hear anything over their own engine noise, and unable to receive warnings because of their aircraft's lack of VHF radio, both Pilot Officer Kev McDavitt's aircraft and that of Sergeant Don Ferguson were taxiing and lining up for take-off on a routine shipping patrol – the show must go on, irrespective of air raids. McDavitt was first in line, and got his aircraft off the ground just before the strafers arrived. One Zero detached itself from the others to chase him, but McDavitt did not see it, too busy in the cockpit retracting the undercarriage and flaps, watching his cylinder head temperatures, resetting boost and revs for the climb, and watching his ASI for the single-engine safety speed of 140 knots. His navigator,

HMAS *Maroubra* on fire in the Milingimbi anchorage, strafed by Zeros on 10 May. AWM Negative 300992

Sergeant Neville McNamara, was also head down, too intent on getting his nav log in order to look out behind.

The crew thus remained unaware of anything amiss until they saw tracers shooting past the wing. McDavitt did the only thing a Beaufighter pilot could do in such a circumstance: he opened his throttles to emergency boost and revs and made his aircraft a difficult gunnery target by coarse use of the controls, turning, skidding and rolling as he accelerated away. The Japanese pilot was mindful of the fuel he needed for the long overwater flight to Langgoer, so he gave up the fuel-wasting high-speed chase and went back to strafing. McDavitt's A19-51 thus escaped with 7.7 mm bullet holes through its wing. Meanwhile, Ferguson was turning his aircraft to line up on the runway when he saw the Zeros coming in. He shut down and, together with his observer, Pilot Officer Ron Blades, exited the aircraft in a hurry and scuttled into the bush. Their A19-29 was likewise perforated by machine-gun bullets but did not burn. In what was thankfully a consistent pattern on this day, the Japanese gunnery was usually just wide of the mark. This could not be assumed to last forever.

While the Zeros were making their runs up and down the runways, an unsuspecting Bruce Little was approaching in his damaged Spitfire, joining the circuit area at 1000 feet for a landing on the east–west runway. From his trench near the runway intersection, Hamilton saw a Spitfire approaching with undercarriage down, so he ran back to his stranded aircraft, intending to warn the pilot over the R/T. He turned the radio on, but infuriatingly found that the set had gone cold – it would remain unusable until the valves warmed up again. Hamilton therefore could only stand and watch as Little came in and landed unsuspectingly. Hamilton stayed on the wing of his Spitfire with his earphones on, waiting for his R/T set to become usable.

Bruce Little would now have to make his third rushed take-off of the day. As his aircraft was rolling along the runway towards

Hamilton, Little suddenly spotted the three Zeros, still flying in a neat vee, still with their drop tanks on. The primary flight controls of Little's Spitfire had been seriously damaged, and the aircraft was difficult to fly. It was obviously unserviceable, but Little had to make a snap decision: he opened the throttle at once and took off, still with his hood slid open. He would never have time to shut it, not knowing that his aircraft had just made its last take-off. He got to 2000 feet, jettisoned the belly tank, and dived in behind the Zeros. They had not seen him as they were now in line astern, turning in for another strafing run on the parked aircraft; Little turned in behind them and set himself up to pick off the last one in line.

Hamilton saw that this time the Zeros were lining up on his own grounded Spitfire. He also saw Little's Spitfire further back, lining up on the Zeros. Hamilton ran for the trenches a second time. The Zeros fired, but the Japanese pilots were still having difficulty with their gunnery; they succeeded only in putting four 7.7 mm bullet holes in Hamilton's Spitfire to add to its broken primer line.

Behind them, Little's attack achieved complete surprise: as he took aim, the Zeros were still conserving fuel for the return flight, still flying at an economical 175 knots, following one another around in an orderly procession as they came off their firing runs. Little fired on the third Zero from 500 metres, closing in to 200 metres as he fired. Unfortunately for him, he missed, and so his opportunity was gone: all three Zeros suddenly broke left, while Little flew straight on – because of his low altitude, he had no other means of disengaging than by using his speed superiority. His erstwhile target demonstrated the Zero's ability to perform startlingly rapid changes of direction when flying at slow speed: it pulled up and around onto his tail in a moment. The roles were now neatly reversed, and Little lacked the height to dive away – the Spitfire pilot's standard evasive manoeuvre.

He would now have to fight for his life in an aircraft with defective elevator control.

Little fought the Zero in a ten-minute dogfight above the airfield, never getting above 500 feet. He executed a sequence of steep climbing turns followed by dives down to as low as 100 feet. Because he could not trade height for speed, it was a low-speed fight; he pulled his aircraft through its turns at 100 knots and accelerated briefly to no more than 175 knots at the bottom of the dives. Repeatedly, Little would break into the Zero's attack, and then the Zero would pull up into a steep climbing turn. It would reach 300–500 feet at the top of the zoom before turning and diving down on him again. Little was forced to break into each attack, time after time. Although his left hand jammed the engine controls fully forward to maintain 3000 rpm and maximum boost, the aircraft nonetheless shuddered in stall warning as it staggered through the turns, now struggling to hold even 85 knots. Little was getting lower and slower. There was now only one way for this fight to finish.

Ground observers at the airfield saw that the Japanese pilot was getting onto Little's tail. Hamilton could see that the Zero was easily outmanoeuvring the Spitfire, the pull-ups and turns of which were obviously getting lower and lower. Viewed from the airstrip, the fight descended in height until both aircraft disappeared from view below the tree line. Thereafter only the Zero reappeared, circling the place of combat and then calmly returning across the airfield, northbound for Timor, already throttled back to 130 knots – economical cruise speed for the long overwater journey.

Running out of height and speed, Little had been turning below the tree line; the airframe shuddering and quivering in an incipient stall as he forced it around in yet another steep turn, the engine bellowing at maximum revs. Still the lower wingtip slipped towards the grass; the ground was getting too close.

Flight Sergeant Bruce Little of 457 Squadron. Note the oxygen mask and dangling oxygen and R/T leads. It is a staged shot, for he is not wearing his Mae West, and it is actually F/L Jack Newton's aircraft, BR543. Note the rear-vision mirror above the windscreen and the reflector gunsight. AWM Negative NWA0130

Abruptly rolling out of the turn to arrest the descent rate, he eased backward pressure on the stick to unload the wing and regain flying speed. However, it was too late, he was too low. Still descending, the underside of the nose struck the ground at 130 knots. Luckily, he came down in the open grassy expanse of a dried-up swamp, rather than in the trees; it was doubly lucky that he got the wings level before his aircraft hit the dirt.

The aircraft's nose drove itself into the clumpy grass of the paddock, ripping off the propeller. As the nose dug in, the Spitfire flicked into a violent somersault. Little sat strapped tightly to his seat, but his head, arms and legs flailed about within the cockpit's confined spaces as the aircraft cartwheeled sideways in a tumbling procession of dust and debris. It rolled three or four times, snapping its wings and tail unit clean off. The dismembered fuselage came to rest about 100 metres away from the severed wings, tail and propeller, lying on its side in a mess of dirt and sand.

In another great stroke of luck, the petrol tank in front of Little's knees did not catch fire: the wings had absorbed the crash impact, fortunately leaving the fuselage intact and the fuel tank unruptured. Once everything had stopped moving, Little reached forward and switched off the electrics. He had survived the combat, and now he had survived the crash. Lying there on his side, regarding the coarse red sand only inches from his face, with blood flowing into his eyes, he listened to the ominous hisses and clicks of the hot engine exhausts, and heard the smooth growling of the Zero's engine as it circled close overhead. In spite of the fire danger, Little did not move from the cockpit, afraid that the Japanese pilot would strafe him if he was spotted trying to get out. Then at last the Zero's engine sound faded away. Little now tried to get out, struggling with the canopy, which had jammed in the half-open position. Finally succeeding in pushing it back, he unpinned his harness, slid out, surveyed the wreck, regathered his wits, and then started out on his 5 kilometre walk back to the airfield. He had suffered nothing worse than lacerations and bruises on his forehead, elbows and knees from his violent tumbling within the cockpit.

Unsurprisingly, Spitfire BS199 ZP-S was a write-off. For a pilot on his first operational posting with only 385 flying hours in his logbook, Bruce Little had displayed the most remarkable self-confidence throughout. Despite making some rash decisions, he had backed himself and remained cool-headed and aggressive irrespective of the situation. Little obviously had 'the right stuff' to be a fighter pilot – indeed, he was so self-confident as to consider that he had held his own in the dogfight, and even to claim the Zero as destroyed. However, this may have been self-protective bravado, for he would be noticeably more cautious with enemy fighters in all his future combats.

Little made his claim because the ground crew had very loyally reported that the Zero's engine had 'sounded rough' as it passed overhead, and that it had then crashed out of sight 'with an explosion'. His returning pilot colleagues added to this by reporting an oil slick offshore – heedless of the consideration that, for two days running, ships' hulls had been holed by gunfire in those same waters. The credibility of these reports was dubious in the extreme, not only in the indefiniteness of the evidence, but also in its inconsistency – the Zero was simultaneously reported as having crashed on land at the northern end of the airfield. The fact that there was no actual wreckage there, in clear view within the circuit area, had apparently not entered into the decision to make the claim.

To his credit, however, 457 Squadron's intelligence officer, Flying Officer PE Goldin RAF, recognised this, rebutting that the Zero's engine had merely been throttled back and concluding that there was 'no basis for any claim whatever'. Given the overclaiming that was to be characteristic of 1 Fighter Wing's war in the NWA, it is gratifying to recognise this evidence of intellectual integrity in the squadron's claim-screening process.

Ian Morse's fight out to sea

'Grumpy' Morse meanwhile, having nursed his overspeeding and oil-leaking engine back to recovery, had reconsidered his decision to return to base, and instead he had climbed flat out up sun to 17000 feet, to a position north-east of Milingimbi Island. There he saw Pete Watson's aircraft at 21000 feet, but by then there were no Zeros in sight. It is interesting to note that although he flew close enough to read the other machine's code letter, he made no attempt to join up with Watson in order to fight as a pair. The squadron culture of aggressive airborne individualism would prove hard to break.

Pete Watson orbited for a while and then returned to base, while Morse turned down sun by himself, intent upon resuming the fight. He entered a shallow dive at 260 knots IAS, searching the sky out to the north-west for the retiring Japanese fighters, and positioning himself to bounce them from out of the sun. As he did so, he did not neglect to weave, to uncover the blind spot below and behind in order to clear his tail. The corvette HMAS *Latrobe* was below, serving as the convoy escort – the protection of such vessels had been the original purpose of the RAAF's Milingimbi detachments. Morse now noticed that the ship was firing at enemy aircraft, and looking in the direction of the gunfire, he saw two Zeros crossing the ship's stern, flying at sea level, going north – these were two of the airfield strafers.

Morse dived after them, pushing his engine levers forward to get 12½ lb boost and 3000 rpm. He passed overhead the corvette at 1500 feet, but having descended, he could now see only one Zero ahead, weaving slightly and climbing. Morse had lost his height advantage in his rush to catch up with it, and so was now committed to re-climbing in pursuit, setting himself up on an intercepting course from the Zero's starboard rear quarter.

Because of his much shorter distance to base, Morse was less fuel-sensitive than the Zero, so he could afford to maintain his engine's high revs. He thus found that he was overtaking his quarry by 50 knots in the climb. Upon reaching 8000 feet, he came up on its starboard side to set himself up for a diving beam attack from a 700 feet altitude advantage. This was a standard attack profile when attacking bombers in order to avoid their return fire, but this was a fighter, so it would have been preferable to attack it from the rear. Nonetheless, Morse turned steeply left into a front-quarter attack, dived in and fired a snap burst from 200 metres: it was a rushed shot because of the high closing speed, and a difficult shot because of the high-deflection angle. He had achieved a bounce, but had chosen too difficult a shot, and so he missed. No. 1 Fighter Wing would fight its entire 1943 campaign exhibiting this sort of gunnery overconfidence, and would too often get similarly disappointing results from otherwise well set-up bounces upon enemy fighters.

As he flashed past 100 feet underneath the Zero, Morse saw that the Japanese pilot had now noticed the attack and was breaking left. Morse also broke violently left, the continuation of his dive taking him below the Zero, which meanwhile had pulled up vertically into an Immelmann turn: this involved pulling up into the first half of a loop, then rolling out, right way up – thereby simultaneously gaining height and reversing direction. Once again, entering such manoeuvres straight from low-speed level flight showed the Zero's ability to perform like a high-powered sports plane. Having gained 700 feet, the Zero then dived from above, firing. Morse pulled his nose up to meet the Zero in a head-on pass. He fired a burst from 200 metres, seeing the Zero's tracers go past 20 metres to port, but saw no strikes from his own firing.

After this head-on pass, Morse broke violently to the right and downwards in a yawing bunt to stop the tight-turning Zero from getting around behind him. Looking back, he saw that the Zero was also turning right and descending. Morse was now at 6000 feet, having lost 2000 feet in three hard turns. The Zero was now 500 feet below him and still diving. It flew on, descending steeply until it went straight into the water with a big splash, with no attempt on the part of the pilot to ditch. Morse returned to base to claim one Zero destroyed.

10 May considered

No. 457 Squadron emerged with some credit from this engagement, having lost only one Spitfire and having certainly shot down one Zero. Most importantly, none of its pilots had been killed. This was very lucky, considering that Rex Watson, Batchelor, Morse and Little had all been bounced in a very dangerous fashion, some of them more than once. The bounces on this day had provided the Japanese with the best shots of the whole engagement, but they had failed to hit. With better Japanese gunnery in their initial bounce, when everything was stacked against the Spitfires, 457 could easily have lost two or more pilots, as happened on other days of the campaign. It was only the wayward Japanese shooting that enabled the Spitfire pilots to get back to base with their aircraft intact and their lives preserved. They would clearly not be able to rely upon such luck forever.

However, the Japanese had not had it all their own way, for they had suffered two losses themselves in spite of holding all the initial advantages. Japanese records are quoted as confirming that one Zero was shot down (Morse's), while the engine of one other Zero (presumably Rex Watson's spinning and smoking victim) was sufficiently damaged to necessitate a crash-landing on the way home. Thus the Spitfire pilots' gunnery was about as good as that of the much-fancied 202 Air Group pilots on this day.

The Spitfires and Zeros therefore emerged from 10 May with honours about even: taking the destroyed Beaufighter into consideration, the Japanese had destroyed two Allied aircraft, while losing two themselves. Two other Spitfires had been holed but remained serviceable – Hamilton's ZP-X on the ground and Batchelor's ZP-M in the air. The pilots' observations of incendiary bullet flashes on Zeros' wings suggest that a couple of enemy fighters likewise returned to their airfield with some bullet holes in them. The Spitfires had fought back so fiercely that only one 202 AG pilot returned home to lodge a claim; this single Japanese victory was poor reward indeed for such a well set-up bounce.

Indeed, for the Japanese, their 10 May raid was a failure, with no effect whatsoever upon the RAAF's occupancy and use of the Milingimbi base. Like the previous day's bombing raid, it failed to suppress Allied air operations in the eastern sector in any way. Bladin ordered 457 to fly in replacement Spitfires that afternoon for those destroyed and damaged, and so the detachment was up to full strength again the next day. No. 31 Squadron continued to use Milingimbi for strikes against the Japanese bases at Langgoer, and the coastal convoy patrols continued unabated.

As if to underline the RAAF's newfound Milingimbi-based dominance of the Arnhem Land coastline, the very next day a Beaufighter on a shipping protection patrol shot down one of three 934 AG floatplanes that attacked shipping at Wessel Island, more than 200 kilometres to the east of Milingimbi. Flight Lieutenant John Madden spotted an Aichi E13A that had made a bombing run over a convoy entering the harbour and narrowly missed HMAS *Latrobe*. Madden dived after it and caught it before it reached the sanctuary of a storm cloud, and this time the Beaufighter's cannon worked: the Japanese aircraft flamed and fell into the sea between two of the ships of the convoy it had sought to bomb. Three Japanese naval airmen were added to the death toll of Australia's northern air war.

10 May pilot table

457 Sqn pilot	Remarks	
F/L P Watson	did not fire	
F/Sgt Batchelor	CSU failure; ZP-M damaged in air combat	
P/O Morse	CSU failure	
P/O Little	BS199 ZP-S driven into ground during air combat, destroyed	
F/Sgt R Watson		
F/O Hamilton	ZP-X unserviceable, remained on ground, damaged by 7.7 mm during strafing	
Beaufighters hit:		
A19-72	strafed, burnt & destroyed	F/L PE Biven & Sgt JW Newton
A19-16	strafed & hit by 7.7 mm	P/O EJ Frith & P/O HI McLennon
A19-29	strafed & hit by 7.7 mm	Sgt DW Ferguson & P/O RA Blades
A19-51	attacked while airborne, hit by 7.7 mm	P/O K McDavitt & Sgt McNamara

6

Success
at last

After the 2 May disaster, the lucky result of 457 Squadron's
10 May skirmish over Milingimbi came as reassuring evidence
of the combat efficacy of the Spitfire squadrons. Nonetheless, in
reality the Spitfires had hitherto failed to shoot down a single
bomber in the two major interceptions of 15 March and 2 May,
because in both combats only a handful of Spitfires had fought
through the escort to get at the bombers. It would be important
to hit the bombers hard next time.

On 13 May, the Imperial Navy signalled its continued
interest in the task of subduing the Milingimbi base by laying
on a second fighter sweep: six Zeros went over Milingimbi
airfield at 15 000 feet, but this time they did not come down to
strafe. The detachment from 54 Squadron did not achieve an

interception as the Japanese were overhead before the Spitfires were even scrambled, due to a failure of the radar early warning system. In the two weeks that followed, the Japanese built up the capacity to launch a combined raid on the troublesome airfield, with the result that on 28 May they returned with a force of eight bombers escorted by five fighters. The modest size of this raid suggests the sheer logistical difficulty of supporting intensive operations from their remote bare bases in the eastern area of operations.

Although the 23rd Air Flotilla seems to have regarded Milingimbi as the Japanese equivalent of a 'milk run', Air Commodore Bladin had not only maintained a Spitfire detachment at Milingimbi, but upgraded it slightly to eight aircraft. After its honourable defence of Milingimbi on 10 May, 457 Squadron had done the lion's share of the detachment duty there, as a form of 'hard labour' – punishment for Squadron Leader Ken James's rather cavalier disregard for administrative niceties. The CO had incurred Bladin's displeasure for poaching other units' men and equipment to support his squadron's Milingimbi detachment. The use of Milingimbi as a punishment detail shows that service at this isolated and primitive base was unpopular with the squadrons. The men cherished the relative comfort of their own airfields and considered that service at Darwin offered better chances of seeing action. How wrong they were.

Thus it came about that the third Milingimbi raid was once again defended by 457, with Pete Watson again the flight commander in charge of the detachment. RAAF Command had considered his performance on 10 May so poor as to consider him unfit for command. However, his superiors within the wing and NWA HQ had successfully defended him against these harsh criticisms, and so here he was in charge again, his case no doubt helped by a consideration of his creditable performance in the 15 March combat. On the other hand, given Milingimbi's status as a punishment duty, Watson may have been exiled there deliberately!

The 28 May raid

On the 28th, Milingimbi radar detected an incoming plot at 100 kilometres to the north-west, and the Spitfires were scrambled at 1.25 pm. By then, the defending force had been reduced to seven aircraft only as Pilot Officer Stuart 'Bill' Reilly had damaged his aircraft earlier that morning, rendering it unserviceable. The ground staff got to work on this machine as the bombers approached, getting it into a flyable state sufficient to enable Reilly to take off and to get it away from the airfield and out of danger.

Watson's Red Section got off the ground first, but as the Spitfires climbed away from the airfield they promptly lost one another. The confusion and delay in forming up after take-off was not helped by the thick layer of haze which seriously degraded visibility below 10000 feet. Also, Watson did not help the situation by repeating his error of 10 May – he set off for the interception without waiting for the others. The flight leader normally circled the field after take-off to let the others cut across the circle and join on, but Watson was again in too great a hurry to do this. Having failed to concentrate his force, he would again leave his pilots to fight their individual battles.

Watson's No. 2, Flying Officer Warwick Turner, was the only one who managed to stay with him, while Flying Officer Harry Blake managed to keep only two of his three aircraft from Blue Section together. Three lost pilots, Flying Officers Tommy Clark and Bruce Beale and Flight Sergeant Rod Jenkins, weaved about in the murk trying to find their respective sections, but upon failing to see anyone else, they then climbed independently, hoping to join up as they went. While Beale was looking about through the haze for Red Section, he saw Blue Section go past and so joined up with them instead, taking Jenkins's place as Blue 2. This would prove to be a fateful reassignment. Watson tried to sort out the mess over the R/T, but neither Jenkins nor Clark succeeded in finding anyone else, and so both would go into the fight alone.

After failing to form up above the airfield, the Spitfires also failed to get to height before the Japanese bombed – in spite of having received 18 minutes' radar warning. The Japanese were therefore able to bomb unopposed, running in to the target from the north-west before going back out to sea to the east. They bombed the airfield from about 23 000 feet, completely unmolested either by AA fire or by fighters. Despite these favourable conditions, the bombs once again went uselessly into the bush around the runways. As was typical in the NWA, the known presence of fighters had raised the bombing height and so ruined the bombing.

When Watson and Turner popped up out of the murk into the clearer air above, they got the first sighting of the bomber formation as it cruised past them 2000 feet higher, still inbound to the target. Watson climbed after the bombers as they retired out to sea, but he lost his No. 2 as he did so – just as he had lost Evan Batchelor on 15 March. Turner failed to follow his leader's turns while his No. 1 was climbing through the glare of the sun, to suddenly find himself alone. From this point on, Red Section was now completely atomised into four individual Spitfires all operating out of visual contact from one another. Pete Watson had lost his section.

The fight begins

Four of Watson's pilots had never before seen action, but they retrieved the situation nonetheless: each of his isolated junior pilots focused on the task autonomously, manoeuvring themselves to launch repeated attacking runs on the bombers. Tommy Clark emerged by himself through the murk and spotted the Japanese formation as it flew out to sea after bombing. He climbed up in front of it and off to the side, getting into position to make a front-quarter attack. As he did so, however, four Zeros emerged from behind the bombers, accelerating to fighting speed and coming after him. Clark decided to wait for a better moment and so used his Spitfire's speed to disengage. This was observed by Watson, who saw him dive away with two Zeros on his tail.

Warwick Turner meanwhile, having lost Watson, similarly overtook the bombers out to one side, but when he turned in towards them, the remaining two Zeros climbed up to head him off as well, and a short two-versus-one dogfight ensued. He fired at each one in turn from head-on, but in turning hard to avoid the third attack he stalled out and spun away. Upon recovering from the spin thousands of feet below to start re-climbing, he was glad to find that the Zeros were gone. Clark and Turner had been chased right out of the bombers' altitude band, but they had inadvertently achieved something useful: dangerously for the 753 AG crews, there were now no Zeros left with the bombers, which had meanwhile turned around and started reapproaching Milingimbi from the east. As the bombers' squadron commander stalwartly lined his men up for their second bomb run, Watson decided to wait for them where he was, continuing his climb to 27 000 feet to be ready for them as they came past.

Further behind the scattered Spitfires of Watson's Red Section, Harry Blake was climbing through 18 000 feet at the head of Blue Section, leading them up at 120 knots IAS to wring the best climb rate out of their aircraft. He spotted the bombers about 10 kilometres ahead as they reapproached from the east at about 20 000 feet, and so continued climbing. There were no fighters visible, so it looked like Blake's three Spitfires would be making an unopposed attack upon unescorted bombers.

As the bombers came past, inbound on their second bomb run on the airfield, Watson made his attack. Unfortunately, as he had done on 15 March, he employed spraying fire against the whole formation rather than focusing upon killing an individual bomber. Observing no result, he dived away to reposition himself, having been observed by Rod Jenkins, who was still climbing up by himself further out to the north. Seeing the bombers go past 25 kilometres away, off his starboard wingtip, Jenkins turned in and continued climbing, witnessing a single Spitfire making its attack (Watson). His long-distance observations show that visibility was good around 20 000 feet, in sharp contrast to the poor visibility lower down within the inversion layer.

As Jenkins neared the bombers, approaching them from the north, he saw a single Zero climbing up at him – this was the fifth and last Zero in the escorting force, hitherto totally unmarked by any of the Spitfires. Intent upon carrying through his predetermined attack upon the bombers, Jenkins avoided it easily by exploiting his height advantage and climbing away. Once he had left the Zero behind, he repositioned himself and dived at the bombers. However, on the way down his propeller CSU failed and his engine overrevved; forced to deal with an in-flight emergency, he aborted the attack and pulled up to slow the propeller down. Juggling with the rpm and pitch controls, it was only when he got his engine revs below 3000 that he could belatedly resume his attack. By then, he had slipped further behind the bombers and so he was now forced to approach them from the rear. In a low-closure overtake he fired right in to 20 metres range before bunting underneath. This attack had given him a relatively easy low-deflection shot from astern, but it also put him right in the firing arc of the bombers' 20 mm tail guns. Jenkins's own fire failed to have any noticeable effect, but the Japanese tail gunner did not miss: a 20 mm shell exploded with a blinding white flash against the Spitfire's nose, the shrapnel nicking the propeller and damaging the propeller reduction gear. Some 7.7 mm machine-gun bullets also penetrated one of his wings and punctured one of the tyres.

Jenkins shoved on the stick and bunted violently out of the gunners' sights. As he dived away underneath the bombers, he did an anxious stocktake of his engine instrument readings, but his aircraft still responded normally to its controls, the propeller reassuringly still maintained its 2850 rpm, and the coolant temperature and oil pressure stayed steady. He climbed back out in front and then rolled in for a head-on attack. This time, he fired a snap shot – all that was possible with the 450 knot closing speed – and as he flashed past, was rewarded with the sight of the bomber he had fired at dropping out of formation and diving vertically, pouring black smoke from a fuel fire within the fuselage. Flight Sergeant Freddie White, at that moment getting ready to attack as part of Harry Blake's Blue Section, saw it plunge away from the formation in a vertical spiral dive before disappearing into the layer of haze below. Bill Reilly, who was flying out to sea below them, trying to get his unairworthy Spitfire out of harm's way, also saw the bomber dive out of formation. Jenkins himself, pulling up after his attack and turning to clear his tail, looked straight down through the murk and saw the bomber splash into the sea, about 8 kilometres east of the island. It had been a very good combat debut for an inexperienced pilot.

Now reduced to seven aircraft, the Japanese bomber formation closed ranks and completed its second bomb run, then turned right and moved away to the north-east to position itself for a third run. Multiple bombing runs like this were suitable only for attacks on undefended targets, which as 10 May had demonstrated was very clearly not the case at Milingimbi. This tactic exposed the bomber crews to repeated fighter attacks for minimal, if any, benefit to bombing results. For the unfortunate Japanese crews over Milingimbi, however, orders were orders, and thus the formation shuttled back and forth over the island, making itself available for ongoing firing runs from the disorganised but still aggressive Spitfires. In the course of these bomb runs, they dropped about fifty 60 kg bombs but succeeded only in burning some fuel drums and wrecking a shed.

Assisted by the rhythm of the bombers' regular and predictable re-arrivals, Watson was able to re-climb and position himself to cut the bombers off as they came back in the next time. Diving into another attack from the front quarter, he again sprayed the whole formation by skidding across it as he came in from above. Once more there was no visible result.

Harry Blake's Blue Section made their attack soon after Watson, diving in line astern and at a shallow angle and moderate speed in order to assist gun-aiming. The three Spitfires made a concerted section attack – the only such attack made by 457 in the whole engagement. Harry Blake and Bruce Beale, the first two pilots through, attacked from the bombers' beam, but as arse-end Charlie in the string of three diving and turning Spitfires, Freddie White found the others getting in his way. He swung out wider to give himself some clear air, and was thereby forced further to the rear for a stern attack. As Jenkins had discovered, this was an attack profile from which he would be vulnerable to return fire, so White changed his mind again, breaking off to reposition for a safer solo attack from the beam. White's fussy manoeuvring shows him behaving as though there was no fighter escort, in spite of the R/T chatter which must have confirmed that they had recently been in evidence.

Coming after Blake and Beale's firing runs, Freddie White's belated attack proved to be worth the wait. He attacked from the starboard beam, firing in to 150 metres range with strikes on the bomber's wing root. As he broke left and to the rear of the bombers, he looked back to see that his target bomber was dropping out of formation, descending. It then fell away into a spiral dive, plunging away almost vertically to disappear into the haze about 8000 feet below. One of the bomber gunners had also been on target, as White's Spitfire was hit through the wing by one round of 7.7 mm. At about the same time, Blake and Beale made a second firing run, and Blake saw the same bomber going down and attributed it to his own fire, announcing over the R/T that he had made an attack and that his target was dropping out of formation. He and White had probably fired upon the same bomber without seeing one another. Pete Watson was up above getting ready for his third attack when he saw White make his lone attack, and witnessed the bomber crash into the sea 16 kilometres north of the island. White had done well to shoot so straight in his first combat.

He zoomed back up and started re-climbing after the bombers, but his engine started to overheat, so he had to reduce his power setting to 2400 rpm and +4 pounds boost, and thus could not catch up. This probably indicates that his engine had been hit: two of the surviving Spitfires received engine changes at Milingimbi starting 1 June: one of these was Jenkins's, so the second damaged engine must have been White's.

Turner now made his reappearance, very soon after Blue Section but without seeing them attack; focusing their attention on the bombers, the Spitfire pilots were simply not seeing one another. Turner had earlier escaped his pursuers and had climbed back to height quicker than the Zeros, so now he was free to make his run at the bombers. He saw that the bomber formation had wide gaps in it once the two stricken aircraft had dropped out. Turner dived from the beam, fired, then pulled up underneath to fire again from below and behind. As he fired, tracers from the Japanese gunners arced towards him, and he saw the bright flashes of the tail 20 mm cannons firing at him. In spite of the favourable gunnery conditions on both sides, neither he nor the Japanese rear gunners saw any effect from their fire.

As Turner broke away he heard someone say, 'a Spit has gone in' over the R/T. This was the voice of either Blake or Beale, but probably Blake: one of the two had been bounced soon after coming off the bombers. The Zeros were back, having climbed up through the murk unnoticed by anyone. Tragically, that was not the end of it, for as he looked down at the splash, the speaker was himself shot down, also surprised from behind by an unseen enemy fighter. After so often failing to hit in the previous Milingimbi combat, this time the Japanese cannon shells hit hard, and a second Spitfire followed its partner into a watery grave, unnoticed among the hissing static in the other pilots' earphones. The Zeros had been tardy in protecting their bombers, but they were still working together, and soon after this they arrived back in the fight as a coherent four-aircraft unit flying in a neat diamond box formation.

By now the six remaining bombers had turned off the target for the last time and were heading back home, out to sea to the north-west. The final turn must have come as a great relief to the long-suffering crews, but it was not the end of it for them either. Both Watson and White reattacked, separately, again without seeing each other, but without result. Fresh from their silent killing of Blake and Beale, the Zeros now made their public reappearance: White was repositioning for his third attack when he noticed four Zeros flying past him, above and to the side. Although in a perfect position to attack, they ignored him, evidently hurrying back to belatedly provide some cover for the harassed bombers. Watson was positioning himself for a fourth attack when he noticed two Zeros above him, so he dived away at once and headed home.

Tommy Clark, having been chased away by these same Zeros at the start of the action, had made a long climb back to height, and only now did he arrive back in the fight as the bombers headed for home out to sea. He could see six bombers ahead of him in two tight vees, with the Zeros back in their places, spread out around and above them. Clark now had so much height that this did not matter: he dived at the left-hand side of the bomber formation, firing at a Zero on the way down, although at the very long range of 800 metres – too great a distance at too high a closing speed and with too much deflection for any hope of a hit. As he dived past the unharmed enemy fighter, he was chased by two further Zeros, but was going fast enough to leave them behind and continue his dive at the bombers further below. By now the bomber pilots had rallied after their losses and restored their tight formation, with wingtips tucked right in. Clark picked out the left-most bomber and opened fire at it from the beam, but his closing speed from the dive was too great for an accurate shot. He pushed his right rudder pedal and skidded across the top, spraying the whole formation as Watson had done, and from too great a firing range.

Seeing no result, Clark then turned hard underneath the bombers to come back at the right-most Mitsubishi. Slowing down in the climbing turn, this time he came in from below and astern, firing a long burst right in to 30 metres. This time, he fired with only a moderate closure rate, and with little deflection, so now he got hits, but he himself was also a much easier target for the bombers' gunners: a web of tracers reached out to touch his Spitfire, and one of them was right on-target. An armour-piercing 7.7 mm bullet came in from the front, penetrated through the side of his aircraft's fuel tank and finally stopped just in front of his knees, burying itself into the back of the gyro horizon on the instrument panel. Other bullets went through the starboard wing and through the radiator. However, the fuel tank did not burn, and nor did his engine lose its coolant – Spitfire pilots could enjoy some luck too, sometimes.

This time, Clark's own shooting was good, for the bomber he had fired at went down in a vertical dive, disappearing into the haze layer like the others had done before it. Clark now dived away a second time and headed home, having been a very troublesome opponent for the Japanese raiders. All three of the successful pilots had been beginners in their first combat. Freddie White, reapproaching after his close shave with the four returning Zeros, was close enough to see Clark's attacks and to see the last bomber go down 55 kilometres north-west of the island. He did not catch up, but watched the Japanese disappear into the distant haze, the formation now composed of only five bombers and four fighters.

The missing men

The Spitfires returned to the airfield one by one. Having heard the radioed distress call, the pilots knew that one of their number would not be landing, and then two of them failed to respond to Watson's radio check. In the sudden silence after switching off, each pilot draped his sweat-dampened leather helmet over the joystick, climbed out onto the wing, and peeled off his Mae West to air his sweat-drenched torso. The men swapped combat impressions in the sudden quiet left behind after the cessation of the engine noise, scanning the sky for the missing men. Neither of the overdue aircraft reappeared. With four of the remaining aircraft damaged, the ground crew refuelled the two good machines, and these took off again to search the sea and coastline for signs of life. Next day, the search was upgraded by the arrival of four Hudsons from No. 2 Squadron. However, both men were gone forever, disappeared into the muddy brown waters around the mangrove coasts of the Crocodile

Islands. Neither wreckage nor human remains were ever found.

At his death, Bruce Beale had 333 hours in his logbook, a thoroughly average 1 Fighter Wing pilot. He had been with the squadron for an entire year, but this had been his first and last combat. He had been on operational flying since October 1941, so his low flying hours emphasise the brevity of the wartime training received by so many of the pilots in the wing. Harry Blake, Blue Section's leader, had 489 hours, and was considered one of the more experienced squadron pilots, but this had been only his eighth combat. Both of these men were virtually founder members of the squadron and core members of the group. Blake had outlived his friend Joe Gifford (killed on 2 May) by less than four weeks.

Anomalously, Beale and Blake had been the only pilots who had worked together throughout the action, and yet it was these two who were surprised and killed. Ironically, the other five pilots, all perilously operating as singletons, had not been bounced, and all had survived. However, the reasons for the tragic double loss are clear. Firstly, the thick haze of this day greatly increased the chances of Japanese fighters closing in unseen at lower levels. It was thick enough below 10 000 feet for Spitfires that had taken off together to disappear from each other's vision; and for shot-down bombers to disappear from sight before they hit the sea. Beale and Blake had descended into this altitude band of the poorest horizontal visibility after making their attacks on the bombers, as shown by the fact that one pilot was able to see the other's Spitfire hit the water so soon after the unseen attack was made.

Also, having conducted a sequence of attacks without fighter interference, the two pilots had fixated upon the bombers rather than maintaining their visual scanning for unseen fighters. After all, they had arrived in the fight when there were no Zeros present, at a time when the Spitfires were taking runs at the bombers at will. They were not the only ones to do this: White had been busy repositioning for his third attack when he belatedly saw the four Zeros fly past to the side – he had not observed them as they approached from behind him, and was lucky that they had been too preoccupied to give him their attention. Jenkins and Turner had also manoeuvred to reattack the bombers in a manner that suggests a reduced level of caution about the possibility of fighter attack.

There was a further contributing factor, namely 1 Fighter Wing's systemically poor combat formation. When Blake reported the Spitfire splashing into the water, he was unaware that it was his partner's aircraft that had crashed, for he reported it generically as 'a Spit'. This shows that, although working the same area of sky, the two pilots had not been flying as a line abreast combat pair, but rather in a loose line astern which placed the No. 2 right out of his No. 1's sight. As the leader, Blake would have come off his firing run first, and had thus been ahead of Beale as they pulled out of their dives and turned for home. The four Zeros had approached from behind them through the murk to get an easy no-deflection shot on Beale from his blind spot. Blake, meanwhile, continuing his descending turn back towards base, had looked back and down in the direction of his turn, to suddenly see the other Spitfire dive into the water with a great splash. Shocked to see it, he was too stunned to be aware of its identity or significance, and made his radio call, but it was already too late, for there was now a Zero behind him as well. Neither pilot made an R/T call to report the height and position of the Zeros, for both had been taken completely unawares by their re-arrival. The Zero pilots had pulled off a perfect bounce, firing from close range and directly astern, and as a result of these very favourable gunnery parameters they had hit their targets so hard with 20 mm explosive ammunition that neither pilot survived.

Harry Blake in happier times, strapping into Spitfire BR543, assisted by Rex Watson (left) and Clive Briggs, at Livingstone in February. Note the parachute harness over Blake's shoulder, while Watson holds one end of the four-point Sutton seat harness. AWM Negative NWA0128

Despite the Zeros' success in shooting down these two Spitfires, the Japanese fighters had not performed well as a bomber escort. Chasing individual Spitfires far away from the bombers was a luxury that a small force of five fighters could ill afford: one element should have stayed with the bombers at all times while the other element did the chasing. Instead, the Zero pilots had overcommitted themselves against individual Spitfire attacks and had moreover failed to score kills thereby, while leaving the bombers unprotected. Given the wide time envelope during which the bombers remained unattended, it is disappointing that the Spitfire attacks had not been more effective than they were. Poor gunnery technique was the main culprit.

The deaths of two men rather took the gloss off the day's results, which had otherwise been gratifying – three bombers were claimed shot down. For once, the Spitfire pilots' claims were right on the money, for Japanese records confirm that three bombers failed to get home to Babo airfield. Two were shot down over the target while a third bomber had limped back on one engine, but the 1100 kilometre flight had been too much for an aircraft in this condition, so the crew had taken it down for a forced landing before reaching base. The big machine had been wrecked in the landing attempt. Given that White's and Jenkins's kills were seen to go into the water, this last aircraft must have been Clark's kill – it had evidently pulled out of the steep dive and limped back at low-level. It is noteworthy that neither of the stricken bombers had suffered fires in their wing fuel tanks. Once again, the supposedly highly flammable G4M's had failed to flame up when hit by 20 mm and .303 inch incendiary rounds, as per previous experience on 15 March and 2 May. These machines had proven once again to be disappointingly hard to shoot down, irritatingly contrary to US experience.

Nonetheless, 457 had achieved the destruction of three bombers and killed 18 aircrew. The code of honour of the Imperial Japanese Navy militated against bailing out over enemy territory when one's aircraft was doomed; rather it was considered good form to go down with one's aircraft and thus avoid the shame of capture. In this context, it was unsurprising that no parachutes at all were seen on this day, this being confirmed by the negative result of the air searches around the island that day and the day after.

Gunnery problems

In order to obtain their results, the pilots had made no fewer than 15 gunnery passes at the bombers – of which only three had been on target. Significantly, every one of the three successful pilots had aimed at individual targets, rather than spraying the whole formation as others had done. Ten out of 15 attacks had been high-closure, high-deflection shots from the beam, but only one of these had obtained decisive hits – White's. This gunnery inefficiency was consistent with the similarly poor results from such attacks on 2 March, 15 March and 10 May. No. 1 Fighter Wing's gunnery was simply not good enough to reliably get results from this type of attack, and this fact would condemn the wing to further gunnery disappointments. By comparison, two out of five of the low-deflection attacks had been successful – four times the efficiency of the beam attacks.

A tactical preference for difficult beam attacks was forced upon the wing by the strong defensive armament of the Mitsubishi G4M in the rear hemisphere. The detailed intelligence collected in 1942 had been so poorly disseminated that both the pilots and intelligence officers remained confused about where the G4M's 20 mm cannon was mounted (it was mounted in the extreme tail, not in the dorsal position). The pilots were nonetheless very aware of the cannon's existence – somewhere – and tried to keep away from it. As Clark, Jenkins and White had found, the Japanese gunners could hit, and in Jenkins's case, hit close enough to cause potentially fatal damage. The high explosive 20 mm ammunition was particularly dangerous, and thus the Spitfire pilots almost invariably tried to avoid attacking from the rear. This can be seen in White's refusal to accept a rear-quarter attack, preferring to go around again and reattack from the beam. The good sense of self-preservation that underlay this decision is shown by the experience of the four pilots who did attack from the bombers' rear sectors: Jenkins, White and Clark all had their aircraft hit by return fire, while Turner saw the tracers and muzzle flashes of the gunners firing at him but broke away before he was hit.

In telling contrast to 1 Fighter Wing's problems with high-deflection shots, US Navy and Marine Corps pilots had achieved excellent results in the Guadalcanal campaign against this same bomber type while employing very similar high-deflection diving attacks. The vastly superior USN/USMC results against similar Japanese raids lay in two significant differences: firstly, the US Navy trained and practised its pilots in these high-deflection attacks much more thoroughly than did the RAF. Secondly, the US Navy was able to staff its squadrons with a strong cadre of prewar professional aviators, greatly boosting the technical proficiency of their units. For example, of the 209 US Navy pilots who flew in the Guadalcanal campaign from August to October 1942, 84 of them were long-service men, trained in the 1920s and 1930s.

By comparison, there were only two prewar aviators in 1 Fighter Wing – Squadron Leader Gibbs and Group Captain Walters – while all the rest were wartime-trained. However, even Walters and Gibbs lacked anything approaching the level of experience of the Americans' senior pilots, for both men had only entered fighter aviation in 1941–42, having spent their previous careers in patrol bombers. Within 1 Fighter Wing, every squadron CO, every flight commander, and even the wing leader himself had received only truncated wartime training, having therefore only a fraction of the flying experience of their US Navy equivalents. In view of such disparities in experience level, it is hardly surprising that 1 Fighter Wing pilots struggled to come close to the gunnery standards set by their allies in the Pacific War. Indeed, within the US Navy, officers like Clive Caldwell, Ken James, Ron MacDonald, Ted Hall, Bob Foster, Rob Norwood, Don Maclean, Paul Makin and Pete Watson would all have been junior grade lieutenants, not squadron COs or flight commanders. Although the fighter units of the more rapidly expanded USAAF of 1942–43 did not enjoy the same depth of experienced airmen as their USN equivalents, their leadership cadres too had much deeper professional experience than their wartime RAF/RAAF contemporaries. For example, Colonel Paul Wurtsmith, CO of Darwin's 49th Fighter Group in 1942, had 4800 hours of fighter time, while his executive officer, Major Donald R Hutchinson, had 2600. Prewar airmen with this level of experience simply did not exist in Commonwealth flying squadrons by 1942. The wartime RAAF's shallow pool of experience is hardly surprising given that the entire service had fewer than 100 officers in 1930, only passing the 300 mark in 1939 and that in 1937, there were only 19 officers of squadron leader rank.

It follows that although the Spitfire wing's preference for high-speed beam attacks was tactically correct, the pilots simply lacked the skill to get results from this technique. Indeed, poor gunnery was a systemic problem among RAF Fighter Command's burgeoning crop of wartime-trained pilots. The experience of Evan Mackie, the future RNZAF ace, suggests the reason for the undeveloped state of gunnery proficiency within 1 Fighter Wing – poor training. He received his fighter training at 58 OTU – one of the two UK-based OTUs that trained most of 1 Fighter Wing's pilots. Mackie found that only a small part of the two-month syllabus was concerned with gunnery, with only three out of 40 flying hours devoted to live firing. Although cine-film exercises (simulated air-to-air gunnery using cameras) were included in the program, he found these to be of 'doubtful value in pointing up aiming faults'. After this very patchy training, pilots were posted to front-line units with as little as 170 hours, only to find that gunnery training was just as neglected there. Mackie joined the New Zealand 485 Squadron (which operated alongside first 452 and then 457 as part of the Kenley Wing), conducting only two live firing exercises from January to March 1942.

High-deflection shooting was so difficult that even the 'crack' fighter units in the US 8th Air Force had difficulty with it. The famous ace pilot, Colonel 'Hub' Zemke, CO of the formidably successful 56th Fighter Group, advised his men not to attempt any shot at more than a 30 degree deflection angle. 'Johnnie' Johnson, the RAF's top ace, agreed with this pessimistic view of pilot gunnery standards: he concluded that because of the poor gunnery training at OTU, the average pilot 'failed' the 'test' of deflection shooting, and could only expect to shoot his opponent down when firing from directly astern at close range. There is no doubt whatsoever that Johnson's summation applied to the pilots of 1 Fighter Wing in 1943. The wing leadership team agreed, having already realised the seriousness of the gunnery problem after the poor shooting on 2 May: tactical instructions were issued to the squadrons on 26 May, recommending that 'no or small deflection' shots be used.

Another dimension of the gunnery problem was the fighter pilot's typical tendency to underestimate the firing range. RAF trials showed that pilots typically opened fire at up to

1 kilometre range, thinking it was the required 260 metres (300 yards). This error was crucial, because to fire from too far out was to miss the shot. Squadron Leader Rod Smith RCAF, an experienced Spitfire combat pilot from the defence of Malta in 1942 who received his OTU training concurrently with the pilots of 1 Fighter Wing, ruled that 260 metres was the maximum practical range (with cannons). The poorer the pilot's marksmanship, the closer he needed to get to have any chance of getting a hit, and Smith considered that 'most pilots were poor shots in the early years of the war'. Despite this, throughout the Darwin campaign, pilots often reported firing from 600 metres or more. Given the underestimation problem, the real ranges must often have been over 1 kilometre.

A compounding factor in the high proportion of missed shots on this day was the Spitfire pilots' use of spraying fire against the whole formation, rather than aimed fire at one target only – as also seen on 2 May. Although as a flight commander he should have known better, Pete Watson repeatedly employed spraying fire, as did Clark in his first attack and probably other pilots as well. Watson openly reported on his use of spraying fire, which shows that within the wing it was considered as unexceptionable or even common. NWA RAAF HQ, however, took a different view, and correctly identified this as one reason for the relative 'ineffectiveness' of the pilots' gunnery on this day. Accordingly, all squadrons were reminded that the poor result bore out the 'necessity for selecting a target and demonstrates [the] futility of spraying a formation. This fact has been long recognised.' Squadron COs were instructed to take 'rectifying action', directing their pilots to select individual targets in future. No. 457 Squadron was aware of the bad deflection shooting of its pilots this day, and requested that squadrons be issued with projectors to enable pilots to be coached in correct angles by watching and critiquing each other's cine-film.

Flight Lieutenant John Cock DFC, an Australian member of the RAF and a Battle of Britain ace, had recently been attached to the wing as an 'RAF Air Gunnery Instructor'. He flew with each squadron to observe their gunnery exercises, the live firing component of which consisted of 'shadow shooting' over the wide expanse of Shoal Bay. Conducted in pairs, this exercise involved one aircraft flying low and casting its shadow on the water, while the other aircraft conducted live shoots at the speeding shadow. This permitted the pilots to practise deflection shooting, with the splash of bullets astern of the fleeting shadow serving as real-time feedback as to how far in front to aim. However, for safety reasons only 30 degree deflection attacks were practised – in other words, rear-quarter attacks, not the 90 degree beam attacks that were so often conducted in combat. Also because of safety concerns, the pilots made these practice attacks at only shallow diving angles, whereas in combat they all too often used very steep dives. Caldwell was credited with inventing the shadow shooting exercise while with the RAF in Egypt, and had introduced it to the Spitfire wing as part of the predeployment training program (using the sheltered waters of Broken Bay as the firing range). John Cock concluded in the end that the standard of gunnery was 'high'. It is not sure how this result should be interpreted, either with respect to 1 Fighter Wing or with respect to his parent organisation in England.

For once, the poor gunnery on 28 May could not be blamed on Spitfire cannon failures. So soon after the wholesale cannon failures of 2 May, it must have been gratifying for the wing to hear that the guns fired reliably. However, this was hollow consolation, for the pleasing gun reliability was the product of the low altitude of the engagement: when high-altitude combat resumed in the next Darwin raid, the cannon problems would return with a vengeance. Similarly, although only one aircraft out of seven had suffered a propeller failure, this too was attributable to the moderate height of the engagement.

A factor not so well realised by the wing hierarchy was that the disorganised individual attacks upon the bombers on 28 May had shown up the Japanese vulnerability to multi-pronged attacks. By unintentionally arriving at different times and attacking from different directions, 457 had exploited the elements of surprise and uncertainty, sending the escorting fighters off in one direction while another attack came in from elsewhere. The next raid would confirm the effectiveness of this tactic of decentralised but coordinated attacks, but would still not alter the doctrinal adherence to the big wing.

The final combat at Milingimbi

Service with the Milingimbi detachment remained unpopular with the pilots because of the discomfort, drudgery and hard labour that operations at that ill-equipped airfield entailed. When 452's Flight Lieutenant Ted Hall returned from there on 18 June at the end of an eight-day detachment, he expressed himself 'joyously' upon his arrival back at the comparative comfort and normality of Strauss. Ironically, although the men perceived Milingimbi as an especially boring backwater in the war, the small-scale untidy air fighting that had gone on there during May had in fact provided the best scoring yet from any of the wing's combats – and the Spitfires had finally shot down some bombers.

From the Japanese perspective, 28 May was the last raid they would make on Milingimbi. In three intercepted raids, they had suffered the admitted loss of three bombers and two fighters, in return destroying three Spitfires and one Beaufighter. The Japanese had demonstrated that they had the capacity to shoot down some Spitfires in air combat, but that was all. Taken together with the inability of the bombers to inflict damage to the ground facilities, the Japanese attacks had had no impact upon the RAAF's operational capabilities.

Decisively rebuffed in their attempt to shut down Milingimbi, the Japanese had to content themselves with a scaled-back program of stealthy air patrols around the area, the ongoing presence of Spitfire detachments forcing them to fly circumspectly nearer the coast. Reccos continued to snoop along the inshore waters at low-level on the lookout for shipping movements and 'easy meat' patrol planes like Hudsons. This ongoing effort achieved success on 6 August, when two floatplanes sank the steamer *Macumba* east of Croker Island en route to Darwin (with the deaths of three of her men). Her loss was keenly felt by the messes and wet canteens through the NWA, for 23 000 cases of beer went down with her – at a time when the presence of beer at a celebration was considered an 'unusual feature'. Similar incidents had also been occurring off Darwin: on 2 July a coastal supply convoy was attacked by an E13A, and again on the 3rd by two A6M2-N floatplane fighters.

However, 308 Radar Station at Milingimbi was plotting the Japanese patrols, identifying a repetitive pattern of courses and turn points. Armed with this analysis, on 10 August a section of Spitfires from 452 was scrambled to intercept and vectored offshore. The Japanese intruders moved along the predicted track and were duly intercepted 50 kilometres out to sea by Flying Officer Fred Young and Pilot Officer Bill Coombes. The Spitfire pilots were flying line abreast at 6500 feet when they spotted two floatplanes in line astern, 3 kilometres ahead and about 3000 feet above, flying away from them. The Spitfires chased, climbing at maximum revs and boost, and caught up. When they got 100 feet above, they dived from the floatplanes' starboard rear quarter. Young moved to attack the leader and ordered Coombes to attack the No. 2 on the left. It was Young's first combat, but he had seniority, so was assigned the lead.

The Spitfire pilots identified both Japanese machines as Mitsubishi F1M2 two-seat reconnaissance floatplanes, but a gun camera photo conclusively identifies at least one of them as a Nakajima A6M2-N – the floatplane version of the Zero fighter. The misidentification is to some extent understandable, given that both types featured a large central float. However, the Spitfire pilots had overlooked the glaring fact that the observation type was a biplane, while the floatplane fighter was a monoplane! Although the A6M2-N was slower than the land-based Zero, it retained much of the agility of the original land-based variant, and these aircraft had already surprised Beaufighter pilots with their Zero-like vertical manoeuvres and rapid turns. Exploiting this performance, both Japanese pilots broke left when the Spitfires dived in, Coombes's target turning so tightly that it disappeared out of his gunsight. He abandoned his attack, rolled out and pulled up. As he zoomed he saw the other floatplane diving away, so moved over to the right to join Young in attacking it, but in so doing he abandoned visual contact with the left-hand floatplane fighter.

Young had been able to track his target in the turn and had fired a deflection shot at it, but meanwhile the now-unmarked Japanese No. 2 came around so quickly that it got onto Young's tail unseen, once it had shaken Coombes off. Tracers suddenly shot past Young's aircraft, so he broke downwards out of the line of fire. A deep bank of cloud sat a little further out to sea, and having counter-attacked convincingly, both Japanese pilots now headed for it at full revs and boost. Young chased again, using his Spitfire's superior speed to overhaul the enemy leader. Approaching in a shallow climb from behind, this time he showed the patience to withhold his fire until he was close enough to kill. He was just about to open fire when the other Spitfire suddenly appeared in front of him, only 20 metres away, diving in from his left and firing at the same target. Both pilots had luckily avoided a midair collision (their squadron mate, Sergeant Eric Hutchinson, had been killed in similar circumstances on 27 January, in a midair collision during practice gunnery attacks on a B-24). Despite Coombes fouling the range, Young still had a clear field of fire at the floatplane only 100 metres ahead, and so he now opened fire, his rounds passing not far from Coombes's starboard wingtip. After only one second of firing, Young's windscreen and canopy were suddenly enveloped in a great gout of flame, oil and molten debris spewing out of the floatplane. He pulled up to the right to avoid contact with larger pieces of wreckage, and then opened his soot-blackened hood to regain some visibility. Looking to his left, he saw the flaming floatplane plunge into the sea. Coombes had been far enough out to the side to avoid the plume of debris, so got a good view of the burning machine disintegrating and falling into the water in pieces. Each pilot claimed one half of this victory.

Looking up from this fiery funeral pyre, Coombes saw the second Japanese machine, higher up and still diving for the cloud. Young's canopy was still too obscured for him to re-engage, so Coombes climbed after it alone. He waited until he got in close before firing, and again the Japanese pilot did not manoeuvre. Firing from 200 metres, he hit the large petrol tank in the Japanese fighter's central float. As the float flamed up, the Japanese pilot belatedly sought to evade by pulling up into a stall turn, then dived away in a different direction, his curving course marked by a thick trail of dark smoke. By the time Coombes had pulled his Spitfire around after it, the manoeuvrable floatplane fighter had got 500 metres ahead. However, the Spitfire overhauled it quickly, and Coombes got right in to 30 metres before he opened fire again, in a long burst with machine guns only (one cannon had jammed and the other had fired off all its ammunition). He saw strikes on the enemy machine, debris fell away from it, and its under-fuselage started smoking. Once his ammunition ran out, Coombes pulled out to the side, hoping that Young was behind him, able to deliver the final blow – but he was not.

As he flew along out to the side, Coombes saw that the fire had burnt away the central float – he could see in one side and out the other through the fire blackened framework. The Japanese pilot was going to get wet no matter what happened. Still smoking, but still flying, the floatplane disappeared into cloud, flying straight, impotently watched by Coombes and, further back, by Young. The former justifiably claimed this machine as a probable. In spite of the low altitude of the engagement, both Spitfires had suffered cannon failures – although the failure to definitely shoot the second machine down must be attributable to the usual marksmanship problems as well. Despite such imperfections, it had been a fair fighting performance from a pair of inexperienced pilots.

The air defence encountered over Milingimbi had been effective enough to discourage further inshore or overland incursions. Japanese air activity off Milingimbi dropped away to the extent that NWA HQ soon reduced the fighter detachment to token strength only – first to only three aircraft, then to two.

28 May pilot table

Sqn	Section	No.	Pilot	Remarks
		1	F/L P Watson	
		2	F/O Turner	
		3	F/O Clark	Spitfire damaged by bomber return fire
	Red	4	F/Sgt Jenkins	CSU failure; Spitfire damaged by bomber return fire
		1	F/O Blake	shot down by fighters & killed, BR526 ZP-V lost
		2	F/O Beale	shot down by fighters & killed, BR493 ZP-A lost
457	Blue	3	F/Sgt White	Spitfire damaged by bomber return fire

NOTE BR462 and BR527 ZP-W received an engine change at Milingimbi starting 1 June, performed by a detachment from 7 RSU. These aircraft were probably those of Jenkins and White, as Clark's machine was not hit in the engine, whereas White's engine had malfunctioned badly at the end of the action. Therefore only two machines remained serviceable after the action.

7
The army raid

After a long six-week hiatus in the enemy's on-again off-again campaign of Darwin raids, the Japanese resumed their high-flying reconnaissance flights on 17 June. Two incoming tracks were plotted by radar, one going over Darwin and the other going further south to photograph the cluster of airfields around Hughes. Sixteen Spitfires were scrambled by 54 Squadron, but the interception proved abortive, purportedly because of 'ionized clouds' over the sea that produced false radar returns and spoiled the plotting. The gunners of the 2/1st LAA Battery at Hughes airfield fired a line of Bofors bursts to give the Spitfires a vector. However, only a single pilot obtained a fleeting sighting, and so both of the Ki-46s got away unscathed to take their photos back to Timor.

20 June

This renewed reconnaissance activity was taken to be 'the usual forerunner of an air raid'. In corroboration, RAAF signals intelligence revealed a sudden increase in Japanese radio traffic, indicating the arrival of a large force of enemy aircraft on Timor. At 9.45 am on 20 June, 38 Radar Station at Cape Fourcroy detected incoming aircraft, and soon after, several inbound plots were detected at 290 kilometres to the north-west of Darwin: this would be Darwin Raid No. 55. At 9.50, control ordered all available aircraft to scramble, and the three squadrons laid on a maximum effort. A total of 46 Spitfires was airborne by about 9.55, showing that the RAAF had been able to replace the heavy losses of 2 May.

No. 1 Fighter Wing went into this next combat with a number of lessons learnt from the previous bombing raids, and with some important tactical principles clearly articulated. The 2 May disaster had produced an intense round of conferencing across all three levels of operational command in the NWA: Bladin's RAAF HQ, the wing leadership team of Walters and Caldwell, and the squadron COs. This was distilled as a memo on 'Spitfire Tactics', which was promulgated to all pilots on 27 May, and which in effect constituted an admission of the wing's poor tactics thus far:

- Low-deflection gunnery attacks were to be used in place of the high-deflection gunnery used hitherto.
- Manoeuvring with Zeros was not to be persisted with after the initial turn, as Zeros had manoeuvring superiority at lower speeds.
- Dive and zoom tactics were prescribed, defined as separate and deliberate attacks, to be launched only once altitude advantage was regained.

- Pilots could engage confidently even at a numerical disadvantage because Spitfires had the speed to disengage safely from any situation.
- Squadrons needed to get in and get out when making the interception, for Spitfires' limited endurance required short-range engagements.
- Line abreast fours were prescribed as battle formation for all squadrons, with the 'loose pair' as the basic tactical element.

Except for the last point, the 20 June combat would show that all of these tactical principles were now well understood by the pilots and formation leaders.

A sequence of aborts

However, Caldwell's intention yet again to lead the three squadrons into action as a big wing would be thwarted by circumstances and by his subordinate leaders' impatience to get at the enemy without the laborious wing climb. A spate of mechanical failures disrupted the wing's command arrangements, causing the wing leadership to change hands several times. Caldwell himself was first to go while orbiting with 457 Squadron at 18 000 feet over the rendezvous point. His R/T failed, so he handed the wing over to 457's Flight Lieutenant Pete Watson, flying up alongside him and indicating this by hand signal. Watson informed control of Caldwell's radio failure, whereupon control instructed 54's Bill Gibbs to take over the wing instead, then providing a vector towards the incoming raid.

Although at this point the three squadrons had not yet achieved a rendezvous, Gibbs had the other squadrons in sight and considered that that was close enough. He headed off on the northward vector, ordering the two Australian squadrons to follow. As the wing headed north it was therefore widely separated: 54 was in the centre, with 452 Squadron 25 kilometres away to the right; 457 had been late to the rendezvous, and although Watson tried to chase after 54, he could not close the gap, so his squadron straggled 10 kilometres behind and below.

As Gibbs climbed away at the head of this ragged column, his CSU failed. Gibbs aborted at once, handing the wing over to his senior flight commander, Bob Foster. Once again, however, control had other ideas, ordering Pete Watson to take over again. Significantly, Gibbs, Caldwell and control had consistently placed flight lieutenants over the very inexperienced Squadron Leader MacDonald.

However, from the moment Gibbs set off on the interception before the rendezvous was effected, the wing lead had become hypothetical only, for in effect all three squadrons were now climbing northward independently. As delegated wing leader, Watson now weighed up the options and decided to back Gibbs's earlier decision to abandon centralised control: a proper wing rendezvous was now quite impracticable, taking into consideration the fact that his own squadron was furthest back in the column of squadrons and thousands of feet lower than the others. Control advised that the raid was already nearing the Roman Catholic Mission on Bathurst Island, inbound and only 80 kilometres from Darwin. Hearing this, Watson announced that to save time, the three squadrons would attack independently. Watson turned his squadron left to get further height overhead Darwin, while the other two squadrons moved northward on a collision course with the incoming raid, with 54 to port and 452 to starboard, just within visual distance of one another.

Both Gibbs and Watson had made good decisions in abandoning big wing tactics for the day, for this would mean relatively rapid climbs in comparison with the wing climb on 2 May. For the first time, the Spitfires would have height superiority upon the first sighting of the enemy, and this would enable an early interception, well before the bombers hit the target – another first. A further benefit would be a combat close to base, permitting the Spitfires to disengage with plenty of fuel in their tanks, thus avoiding any repetition of 2 May's non-combat losses. In spite of these tactical advantages, the depth of Caldwell's doctrinal commitment to the big wing is shown in his after-action report, in which he explained disapprovingly that 'due to some obscurity in the leadership of the Wing at this stage F/Lt Watson suggested that the Squadrons attack independently'.

54's strung-out approach to battle

After Gibbs aborted, two further 54 Squadron pilots suffered CSU failures during the high-altitude climb: Gibbs's No. 4, Sergeant Sid Laundy, and Foster's No. 2, Pilot Officer J Garden. Laundy found that even with a malfunctioning propeller mechanism, he was just able to maintain his position in the formation by using the pitch control lever to make his power adjustments, rather than the throttle. By this means he at first managed to press on and stay with the group, but eventually it became too difficult and so he dropped out and headed back to base. Meanwhile, Garden could not stop his engine rpm from surging erratically, so he also turned back. Another of Foster's men, Flight Sergeant JM 'Wicky' Wickman, suffered a severe coolant leak from his aircraft's glycol header tank, which likewise caused him to abort the climb and head home by the quickest route. Group Captain Walters was also lagging behind: he had started out as Gibbs's wingman, but was drifting backwards through the formation as his engine would not deliver its power.

No. 54 Squadron's formation arrangements were disrupted by this series of mechanically induced drop-outs. As the defective machines aborted one by one, the survivors of Red and Blue Sections drew together and closed up the gaps. These remnants formed into a composite section behind Foster, and thus Flight Sergeant David Wheeler and his very inexperienced wingman, Sergeant Lambert, joined Flight Sergeant Huggard on Foster's wing. This rearrangement was an ongoing process throughout the climb, with the last formation change only occurring as they climbed through 28 000 feet – just before the first sighting of the bombers. By this time, Group Captain Walters had dropped out: he had fallen so far behind the others that he gave up and turned back before the attack started.

That was not the end of it, however, for as 54 continued its climb to the north, tracking towards the Mission Station on the south-east corner of Bathurst Island, the whole of White Section started to drift behind, slowed down by Flying Officer Tony Tuckson's engine failing to deliver its power. As the rest of the squadron drew away in front, Tuckson's three wingmen throttled back to stay with their leader, and thus White Section lagged behind as a separate formation. Flying Officer 'Tony' Hughes's Black Section also failed to keep up with Foster's fast climb, and so 54 became split up into three separate formations, each composed of four aircraft. As 54 advanced to contact, therefore, it did so in the following order: Foster's composite Blue Section, Hughes's Black Section, and even further behind, Tuckson's White Section. Mechanical problems had hit 54 Squadron particularly hard this day, splintering its formation and spreading it out into a ragged column of sections.

The Imperial Army's debut over Darwin

The enemy on this day were taking an unusual route to Darwin compared with those of the previous 1943 daylight raids, which had approached from the west. This time, the raiders took a similar route to those taken by the original Japanese raiders on the 19 February 1942 raid, namely crossing the landmass of Bathurst and Melville Islands and coming in from the north. This fresh approach route was attributable to the fact that this raid was conducted by the Imperial Navy's rival organisation – the Imperial Army. If the navy did it one way, the army had all the motivation it needed to do it the other way.

Recent photographic missions by the 70th Reconnaissance Squadron had reported the stockpiling of equipment at Winnellie camp on the outskirts of the RAAF base, and the 23rd Air Flotilla staff had taken this as evidence of a build-up of Allied airpower in the Darwin area. This intelligence interpretation was correct, for these stores were in fact part of the deployment of the USAAF's 380th Bomb Group to the NWA: men, vehicles and stores were arriving in Darwin through early June and being trucked south to Fenton airfield. However, the Imperial Navy's air units had meanwhile been scattered by the usual Japanese 'fire brigade' commitments further east, and thus 1 Fighter Wing's regular opponents, 202 and 753 Air Groups, were unable to provide the raiding force needed to wreck these Allied preparations.

In an unusual display of inter-service coordination, the Imperial Army's 7th Air Division stepped in to provide the forces needed to resume the air offensive against Darwin. The main bomber formation was thus composed of 18 Nakajima Ki-49 Donryu heavy bombers from the 61st Air Regiment, while the escort consisted of 22 Nakajima Ki-43 Hayabusa fighters from

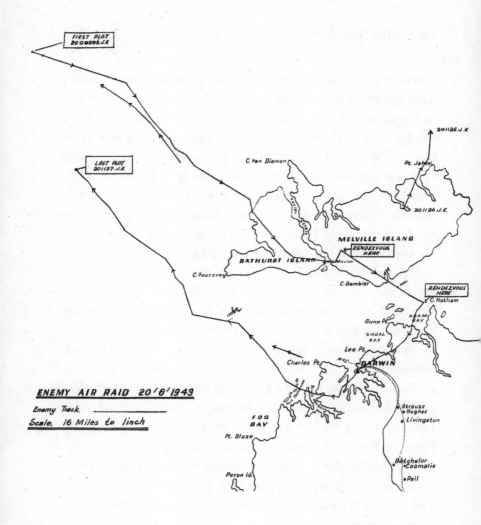

Plot of the 20 June army raid. Note the overland approach over
Bathurst and Melville Islands, the area of the initial combat
over Adam Bay, the position of the first sightings near Cape
Gambier and of the final sighting off Cape Fourcroy; note too
the departing track of the low-level raid off Charles Point.
NAA: A11231, 5/73/INT

the 59th Air Regiment. The latter was a fine prewar outfit that had come through those early months of combat with few losses and so far had had an easy war; after the unit's Darwin raids, the American 5th Air Force in New Guinea would find the 59th to be a noticeably superior fighter unit.

This fighter regiment had only recently re-equipped with the new Ki-43-II Hayabusa. The underwing drop tanks of this improved variant provided sufficient range for the army fighters to reach north-west Australia, and it was this innovation that made practicable this first (and only) Imperial Army bombing raid on Darwin.

The interception

No. 38 Radar Station at Cape Fourcroy was well positioned to track the raid as it approached to cross the northern coastline of Bathurst Island. As the Japanese came further south, the radar stations along the mainland coast obtained contact, enabling 5 Fighter Sector's radar plotters to observe the rendezvous of the fighters and bombers over Melville Island, and to project the flight path of the combined formation on a south-east course towards Cape Hotham (and thereafter south-west towards the obvious target, Darwin). Accordingly, 54 and 452 were vectored towards the Roman Catholic Mission on the south-east corner of Bathurst Island. The two forces were thus flying head-on at one another for a collision over the Clarence Strait. Although it was hazy at lower altitudes, the visibility was good higher up, with some scattered cirrus above 30 000 feet and some altostratus at 15 000.

Foster's Blue Section arrived just south of Cape Gambier (on the southern tip of Melville Island), and commenced a gentle orbiting turn to the right, waiting for the bombers to arrive and scanning the sky anxiously to spot them before they came past.

As the four pilots climbed in line astern through 28000 feet, the enemy were sighted off to starboard in the layer of clear air between the cloud layers. Heading south-south-east, the enemy had almost got past them, and were now directly east of Foster's small force of Spitfires. Foster turned his small formation around at once onto almost a parallel course to the bombers. As the two formations converged, 54's pilots were able to count five vees of bombers heading south in a shallow dive from 25000 feet. Foster also saw 452 far in the distance, out on the other side of the bombers, heading north and seemingly also getting into position to attack. No. 54 was thus on the bombers' starboard side and 452 on their port. The unintentionally dispersed wing had set itself up for an advantageous 'pincer' attack, splitting the defence and creating maximum uncertainty for the escorting fighters. Unfortunately, the potential of this went unrealised for the moment, because 452 had failed to see the Japanese, instead sailing on northward without turning in. Over the R/T, Foster told Ron MacDonald where the bombers were, and 452 turned around.

Once he reached 30000 feet, Foster turned left and moved Blue Section over to the same side as 452. He got his pilots formed up in line abreast and led them right over the top of the enemy formation, moving out beyond the bombers' left flank in order to gain an 'admirable' up sun attacking position off the bombers' front port quarter. The four Spitfires slowly overhauled the bombers, which were now placed to starboard and about 4000 feet below.

Meanwhile, Sid Laundy, having earlier dropped out from Foster's section with a CSU failure, had headed for base. On the way back he saw another group of three Spitfires approaching head-on. As they went past he read their code letters and recognised them as Tony Hughes's Black Section. In spite of his unresolved propeller problem, Laundy turned around again and joined up with them, fitting himself in alongside Flight Sergeant G Horkin and having himself reassigned as Black 4. His propeller CSU was still playing up, however, and as soon as he increased his revs to keep up with the others, he found that the problem recurred, having to repeatedly reduce revs and cycle the propeller pitch controls to clear the fault. Horkin stayed with him through this, but the result was that these two drifted further and further behind Hughes and Flight Sergeant G Ashurst, thereby fracturing Black Section into two separated pairs.

In spite of Black Section's lagging, Foster's elaborate repositioning of Blue Section overhead the bombers meant that it was Tony Hughes, coming along behind, who actually became the first to strike the enemy. He and Ashurst suddenly saw the bombers appear out of nowhere a mere 5 kilometres away, coming towards them nearly head-on and at a 450 knot closing speed, below and just to the right.

As the bombers loomed up at him, Hughes counted 18–19 of them, with the vees arranged almost line abreast, plus six escorting fighters 1 mile behind them and another nine on the bombers' port side. These latter fighters were a long way out on the flank, and were out of formation, looping and rolling around the sky in mock dogfights. This bizarre behaviour was typical of Japanese fighter pilots, evidently intended as a ritual challenge to battle, and would be observed repeatedly in the Darwin air raids, practised by navy pilots as well. It did serve a rational purpose, even if this was rarely fulfilled – namely to draw the defending fighters away from the bombers.

Hughes rightly ignored the stunting fighters, turning right to get up sun of them, and then reversing the turn to dive in and commence his attack on the bombers. He and Ashurst dived straight through the fighters, which had meanwhile seen them coming and pulled up into steep climbs. Hughes got a snap deflection shot on a slow-moving Hayabusa climbing up at him, seeing strikes on its tail before he went past at speed. Continuing his dive at the bombers, Hughes sprayed the whole formation in a long-range burst, in a rather optimistic attempt to 'break up' the bomber group.

Having delivered his first burst so ineffectively from such long range, Hughes turned to the right, dived behind and below the bombers, and then reversed left to come up underneath the leader of the port vee. Zooming up behind it, he fired a no-deflection burst while overhauling it rapidly with the speed he had gained in the dive. Opening fire at 500 metres, he only broke off at 50. The bomber started streaming flame from the centre fuselage and made a gentle dive out of formation, 'burning fiercely'.

Hugely encouraged, Hughes trod hard on his left rudder pedal and skidded over to attack the stricken bomber's wingman, who was now isolated out on the left-hand extremity of the vee. Sliding in behind this bomber, he fired a two-second burst. This one too caught fire, with flames streaming from the port engine as well as the fuselage. Hughes broke off into a diving turn, and when he looked back saw that this bomber was also going down burning. Pulling out 3000 feet below the formation, a fighter came in at him from the side, but Hughes saw it in time to turn into its attack. The Japanese pilot saw that the Spitfire was ready for him, so broke off the head-on pass early without firing, giving Hughes a distant deflection shot as it passed by. He saw no result from this firing, but would claim both of his bombers as destroyed.

However, Hughes's aircraft had been hit by the bombers' defensive fire: 30 seconds after breaking away, his engine lost its coolant and overheated. By attacking both bombers from directly astern, he had lined himself up behind their tail turrets and the gunners had exploited the easy shot. Too busy manoeuvring against the Hayabusa to watch his gauges, he was surprised when his engine suddenly seized and the propeller stopped dead. With the din of engine roar suddenly replaced by howling airstream, Hughes shoved the stick forward and dived steeply away. He only just managed to stretch his glide far enough to avoid going into the water, instead landing wheels-up on the beach at Lee Point. Predictably, the aircraft was then extensively damaged by sea water when the tide came in.

Tony Hughes had fought his highly effective action against the bombers completely alone, because behind him his No. 2 had been fighting for his life under fighter attack – also completely alone. Ashurst had followed Hughes down through the fighters, but one of the Hayabusas got on his tail before he got near the bombers. He broke left into a hard turn and pushed the nose down to accelerate away from the fight. He pulled out far below and zoomed up into a clearing turn, looking behind to find that he had shaken the fighters off.

Meanwhile, Foster's Blue Section had completed its wide orbit onto the up sun side of the bombers, and was now in position off the bombers' port bow. Foster turned right to come in on the bombers' left flank – from the same direction as Hughes. All the manoeuvring had disordered Blue Section's line abreast battle formation and turned it into a loose three-aircraft echelon, with the No. 4, Sergeant Lambert, straggling 600 metres behind the others. Upon Foster's command, all four aircraft jettisoned their drop tanks. Foster now counted 18 bombers in three vees of six – an accurate tally. He also saw seven enemy fighters flying astern of the bombers as close escort, but could not see the top-cover. However, his No. 3, Flight Sergeant Huggard, reported a further nine enemy fighters 4 kilometres off the bombers' port bow (on the up sun side) – the same as seen by Black Section. The raid was by now over Shoal Bay, about 30 kilometres north-north-east of Darwin.

No. 7 RSU's salvage of Spitfire JG795 attracts a crowd of onlookers off Lee Point. F/O Tony Hughes force-landed on 20 June after his engine was hit by bomber return fire. Like many other Spitfires safely belly-landed on the beach, it was swamped by the tide. AWM Negative 152509

From his position up above, Foster saw Hughes make his run at the near-side of the formation and then led Blue Section down to back up Black Section's attack. His pilots peeled off after him in the usual line astern 'string formation', with Sergeant Lambert still dangling behind as arse-end Charlie. Lambert was a raw pilot just out of OTU, and had only been with the squadron three days after a long sea voyage from Britain, but the others just left him behind as they pressed on with their own attacks. As Foster dived towards the port forward quarter of the bombers, he only now spotted the nine escorting fighters – 4 kilometres out from the bombers and in his path. He also saw that Hughes's attack had been successful, for the left-most bomber fell out of formation, pouring smoke and descending. To avoid the fighters, Foster shifted his aiming point to the far end of the formation, on the side opposite to Hughes's attack. This enabled him to pass right over the top of the Hayabusas, and also helped avoid a too-steep diving angle and too-fast dive, as had happened on 2 May. Foster picked out the leader of the right-most bomber vee and fired at it from the beam, ceasing fire at only 75 metres. Breaking steeply downwards, he looked back up to see that the bomber was going down in flames.

David Wheeler, Foster's No. 2, had followed Foster down and made a rear-quarter attack with modest deflection upon a bomber in the same right-hand vee as Foster attacked. Firing in one long burst from 400 metres, he swung in to line astern before ceasing fire. Breaking downwards the moment he took his finger off the firing button, Wheeler rolled into violent evasive turns just in case there was a fighter behind him. He had seen no return fire from the bombers, but as he broke away he heard an explosion just behind his head: his seat armour had been hit by two rounds of 7.7 mm from the rear gunners. His own guns had worked well, with no stoppages for once, and he had seen hits on his target, with smoke streaming from its starboard engine. Sergeant Lambert, coming along behind, saw the engine of this bomber catch fire, and on the strength of this observation Wheeler afterwards claimed it as shot down. It seems that only one bomber actually went down from this end of the formation, and it was likely that Wheeler was primarily responsible rather than Foster, as he had made a more practicable gunnery attack from astern. Both pilots nonetheless claimed a separate bomber shot down.

As Wheeler dived into his attack, he had seen smoke pouring from a bomber on the opposite (port) side of the formation, and after breaking away from his own attack he saw this machine burst into flames and go into the sea in Adam Bay. This was Hughes's kill – no one else had fired at the bombers on the left flank. At that time, Group Captain Walters was further out to the west, heading back towards Darwin; and from that vantage point he saw a tall column of dense black smoke rising from the sea in Adam Bay, 15 kilometres south-west of Cape Hotham.

Having made a damaging attack and evaded the fighters, Wheeler got out while the going was good and dived away for home. As he descended, he saw a parachute above Adam Bay, but upon approaching more closely to ascertain who it was, saw that there was no pilot attached to it. The same eerie scene was observed by Ashurst as he dived out of the fight.

Behind Wheeler, Huggard was descending so fast on his firing run that he only had time for a short burst before continuing down below. As he dived away, he saw Hughes's bomber on the port side of the formation break away 'obviously on fire', plunging down to crash into the sea in Adam Bay. He also saw another burning bomber dropping out of the middle of the formation, continuing on its course but falling steadily below until it too went into the water.

Sergeant Lambert, Foster's badly straggling No. 4, followed the other three aircraft of Blue Section as they dived at the bombers 5000 feet below, but due to the steepness of his own dive, the time delay, and his own inexperience, he did not see his colleagues deliver their attacks. As he lined up for his own gunnery run, he too saw Hughes's bomber on the port side of the enemy formation fall away burning brightly. As he dived in towards the same extreme right-hand vee as Foster and the others had attacked, he saw that a bomber on that side was now also burning very fiercely from its starboard engine – the one hit by Wheeler and Foster. Lambert fired at a bomber to the right of this burning machine, diving from dead astern, but he was moving so fast that he only had time for a snap burst. He saw no result before diving away underneath. Like Wheeler, Lambert applied tactical discretion, continuing on down after his attack and turning for home. He got away safely, which completed a good combat debut for this very green pilot.

Meanwhile, the straggling second element of Black Section, Horkin and Laundy, ran straight into the bombers as the latter headed inbound for Darwin. They found the bombers approaching them from 2 o'clock and thus up sun. Horkin now observed scattered enemy fighters, trailing 3 kilometres behind the bombers and about 2000 feet above them. He ordered the jettisoning of drop tanks and replicated Hughes's approach path – turning right to get up sun then reversing the turn and diving at the bombers' port side. Horkin chose to flatten out the dive angle by leading Laundy towards the far, right-hand end of the bomber formation – just as Foster had done.

Unfortunately, there was a penalty for making an attacking run later rather than earlier: the escorting fighters had woken up and were now ready for them. Horkin and Laundy tried to duck between two vees of enemy fighters that hovered above and out to the side, but unsurprisingly could not sneak past them without a counter-reaction. Laundy saw four enemy fighters coming in from the side just as Horkin was about to fire at the bombers. Laundy warned his leader over the R/T, permitting Horkin to look up just in time to see one of them diving at him. Using a typically Japanese attack profile, the Hayabusa zoomed up overhead, stood on its tail, did a stall turn, and dived neatly down onto his tail. The Japanese pilot had deftly executed this manoeuvre as a means of killing excess diving speed and getting into a firing position without overshooting. Horkin watched it go through the manoeuvre, and then at the last moment pulled up into a steep climbing turn to force the Japanese pilot into an overshoot.

Laundy, coming down behind his leader, found himself in position to attack the counter-attacking enemy fighters from behind, above, and up sun. The Japanese pilots had not seen him, as they had all ganged up on Horkin. Laundy fired upon the left-most aircraft and saw incendiary strikes on its wing and smoke streaming out of its engine cowling. The Hayabusa broke left, flicked over to the right, and then dived away vertically with thick smoke streaming out. As it plunged away into the flat layer of cloud below, Laundy could not get around quickly enough to follow, pulling up to clear his own tail and resume the aborted attack on the bombers. Although he did not see the Hayabusa crash, he claimed it as destroyed nonetheless.

The quick tussle with the fighters had taken Horkin and Laundy below the height of the bomber formation, but the latter was able to climb up beside them to reattack. Having got out in front, Laundy then rolled in, firing upon the bomber on the embattled extreme left end of the formation (where Hughes had attacked). He saw tracer coming up at him from the machine gun in the bomber's side window, and his own guns functioned perfectly for once when he fired back. However, he had not applied enough deflection, for he saw only one incendiary round strike its tail. Then he broke downwards and headed back to base: 54's pilots had been well briefed to avoid exposing themselves to extended dogfights. There would be no repeat of 2 May – they had 'got in', hit hard, and then they had 'got out'.

452's attack

Prompted by Bob Foster's running commentary, Ron MacDonald had realised that the Japanese had got past him and were already somewhere to the south, so had turned the squadron around and pursued them, ordering his men to jettison their drop tanks and to get into battle formation. He finally saw the bombers in the distance on his port bow, counting 20 or so bombers arranged in a broad crescent, with the enemy fighters trailing about 5 kilometres behind, with the highest of them at 27000 feet. This was a poor escorting position, easy to sidestep given that 452 had already reached 29500 feet. While Foster was moving his men over to the eastern flank, MacDonald's squadron moved over onto the western side of the bomber formation – oddly, both squadrons thus swapped places before making their attacks.

MacDonald's Red Section was accompanied by Flying Officer John Bisley's Blue Section, which followed closely behind just off to port. However, White Section was lagging behind by about 3 kilometres, and 2000 feet lower, held up by the engine trouble experienced by its leader, Flight Lieutenant Ted Hall. Hall tried to follow the others into an attacking position high on the bombers' starboard bow, but had to advise the CO that he could not get there – his engine was performing so badly that he could scarcely overtake the bombers. MacDonald flexibly exploited White Section's retarded position by ordering Hall to stay above as top-cover. He pointed out to him the position of the enemy fighters aft of the bombers, and gave him the task of countering these fighters while he himself took the other two sections down on the bombers. No one seems to have seen the fighters further forward.

When Red and Blue Sections were far enough ahead, MacDonald rolled to the left and dived in, with the other three aircraft of his own Red Section peeling off into line astern behind him. These four were followed in by the five aircraft of John Bisley's Blue Section. Like Goldsmith, Bisley was a Malta ace with a DFC (one of only four decorated pilots within the wing), but he had frustratingly missed the action in all the previous raids, and so now he needed to make up for lost time. MacDonald also had a lot to prove: having been appointed to replace Thorold-Smith after the latter's disastrous loss on 15 March, he was new to Spitfires, new to the wing, and had missed the fight on 2 May because of gun failure. This was his second air combat and his first action in command of his squadron.

No. 452 Squadron dived from the beam at the vee of bombers on the near end of the formation – against the enemy's right flank, the same side as Foster attacked, but diving from the opposite side. As the spearhead of his squadron, MacDonald found himself rolling progressively to the right as he lined up on his target, thereby sliding from a beam attack to a rear-quarter attack as he held the bomber in his gunsight. He noticed the muzzle flashes from the bombers' guns. The gunners had opened fire from the very long range of 1000 metres, hoping to deter the Spitfire pilot and induce him to break off early. As MacDonald came in closer, swinging in behind his target, he then entered the field of fire of the bombers' dorsal 20 mm guns. He noticed the bright muzzle flashes of these cannon, but he held his line and opened fire with his own guns at 400 metres.

The bombers were flying such tight formation that MacDonald was able to pause his firing on his initial target and then to tighten the turn to put his sights onto the bomber next to it. He fired a snap burst at this one, ceased fire at 150 metres, and then broke hard downwards in case there was a fighter behind him. MacDonald had seen no strikes on either of his targets.

As he followed MacDonald in, Flying Officer Hal Whillans noticed intensive return fire coming from the bombers, but saw that most of it was directed at MacDonald's aircraft ahead of him. Flight Lieutenant Dave Evans made a rear-quarter attack and fired upon the bomber next to MacDonald's target. Like his CO, he flew through a blizzard of tracer from the bombers' rear gunners, and noticed in particular the bright muzzle flashes from their dorsal 20 mm cannons. Ceasing fire at 200 metres, he pulled up and flashed over the top of the bombers. As he rolled and dived away, he saw his bomber falling away out of formation, leaving a 'white streaky trail', and then it went down vertically out of control. Having to maintain his scan for enemy fighters, he missed seeing it hit the water, but upon looking back saw a dense plume of smoke rising from the impact point on the sea, so claimed it as destroyed. As Evans dived away, a Hayabusa dived from the side and fired a deflection shot at him as he went past. Evans's elevator was hit and he lost the use of the trim tab, but he continued his dive and got away.

Red Section had dived from 29 000 feet to the bombers' height of 22 000 – almost as great a dive as that on 2 May, producing a similarly great attacking speed. Coming down behind the bombers at 380 knots IAS, Whillans lined up on the second-last bomber of the trailing right-hand vee. Opening fire at long-range, he fired a three-second burst, then skidded his gun-sight onto the next bomber in front of it. Unfortunately, both cannons had frozen: the squadron was still out of gun heater pipes, and without them, the high-altitude cold had seized the breech mechanisms. Despite this, Whillans observed .303 inch incendiary strikes on the fuselage of his first target, between the starboard waist gunner and the wing. He broke to the right into the clear air beyond the bombers' wingtips, using his speed to put height and distance between himself and possible enemy fighters. He did not pull out of the dive until he was down below 10 000 feet.

Flying Officer Dave Downes also followed his CO into a rear-quarter attack, finding the return fire from the bombers' dorsal 20 mm guns to be 'particularly intense'. Unfortunately, he had run the gauntlet of the rear gunners in vain, for when he pressed his firing button both cannons and one of his .303 machine guns failed to function. With only three machine guns firing, he saw no results before diving away.

MacDonald's Red Section was irrevocably split up after first contact, leaving the CO to re-climb and continue the fight by himself; none of the others followed his example. Evans, Downes and Whillans had flown with discretion, each making only a single pass at the bombers, clearly aware of their vulnerability as isolated individuals in a large air combat.

John Bisley now led his five Spitfires into the fight, following close behind Red Section. As they dived from 29 000 feet, they spotted two enemy fighters about 4000 feet below. These two had gone unmarked up till now, suggesting that it may have been another such unmarked pair that had bounced Hughes and Ashurst a minute or so earlier. Flying Officer Al Mawer, possessed of an unusual talent for engaging enemy fighters, requested permission to attack them. Bisley gave approval, and so Mawer peeled off after the fighters, taking with him Sergeant Ross Richardson and Flying Officer Keith 'Blue' Colyer. This diversion left only two aircraft to attack the bombers.

Bisley and his No. 2, Flight Sergeant Tony Ruskin-Rowe, came in at the same extreme right-hand vee of bombers as already attacked by Foster, Wheeler and Evans. Before Bisley aimed at his target he looked around, seeing Ruskin-Rowe off to his left making his own firing run at the bombers. Bisley looked back to the front, aimed, and opened fire, pulling in directly astern and firing right in to 50 metres. In spite of both cannons jamming, he saw that the starboard engine of his target was burning. Then tracers passed over the top of his cockpit – he had been bounced! The escort fighters had caught up with 452's attack. Ceasing fire, Bisley broke violently away at once.

Turning sharply, he looked back but could see no sign of Rowe. However, he did witness the awesome end of one of the bombers: it spun down burning with both outer wing panels snapped off outboard of the engine nacelles, splashing into Adam Bay 8 kilometres offshore. Bisley's violent evasion had shaken off the attacking fighters just in time, but his wingman, Tony Rowe, suffered the fate of so many arse-end Charlies – bounced at the end of his firing run. A Spitfire was seen crashing into the sea 8 kilometres north-west of Cape Hotham and this was presumed to have been Rowe. The squadron afterwards conducted extensive searches of the coral reefs, islands and coastlines off the Cape, but without result.

However, the Spitfire that had fallen into the sea was not Rowe's. On 11 July, 452's intelligence officer, Flying Officer JCH Pollard RAF, was led by a party of Aboriginal people to the wreckage of Spitfire BS174, 16 kilometres north of Koolpinyah station, a few kilometres inland of Hope Inlet at the southern end of Adam Bay. Rowe's body was recovered for burial in the Adelaide River Cemetery. His aircraft's gun film was removed and developed, proving that Rowe had made a good attack on a bomber – and on this film evidence, 452 made a posthumous claim for one bomber 'probably destroyed' (but rejected by wing). Rowe had only joined the squadron in April but had 420 hours' flying time, having previously gained operational experience in England. He had been bounced because Mawer's attack on the two enemy fighters had left all the others unsuppressed and free to counter-attack; moreover, Bisley had not seen all the fighters that were actually in the area. As a result, Rowe was hit in the head by 12.7 mm fire as he came off his firing run; his dying hands had put the aircraft in a descending turn and his engine had kept running.

The Spitfire's stability had done the rest, maintaining a gentle turning descent until hitting the ground.

Despite Rowe's loss, Blue Section's attack on the bombers was effective, helped by the fact that, like MacDonald and Hughes, Bisley had attacked from close range and dead astern of his target, ignoring the cone of defensive fire to ensure that he got hits. Dave Downes from Red Section was diving away as Bisley attacked, and he saw one of the bombers fall out of formation straight after, turning south over Cape Hotham and descending to crash west of Koolpinyah station on the mainland. Downes was low enough to orbit overhead the crash site, watching to see if the crew escaped from the burning wreck. They did not, for the fire was intense enough for him to conclude that 'their case is ... hopeless'. He headed back to Darwin, seeing a Spitfire spin into Adam Bay.

While Bisley and Rowe went in at the bombers, Al Mawer had led the attack on the two fighters they had seen at 25 000 feet. It was the first time either of his wingmen had been in combat. Blue Colyer was able to stay on Mawer's wing as they went down, but the inexperienced Ross Richardson was already lagging when his two colleagues peeled off into the dive. He followed after them, but was about 1000 metres behind. From this rearward position, Richardson now noticed an additional 12 enemy fighters further behind the two in front, flying in twos and fours. The two Japanese pilots out in front saw Mawer and Colyer coming down behind them and spoiled the attack with a well-timed break.

Mawer was an experienced combat pilot and an aggressive dogfighter, as he had previously proved on 15 March. Not in the least deterred by the Japanese reputation for dogfighting invincibility, nor unduly influenced by his commanders' stern injunction not to dogfight, he followed the left-hand Hayabusa around in a steep turn. However, he was going too fast to stay with it and so could not get a shot. Rolling out, he reversed his turn in time to see the Japanese wingman coming in at him from the other side. Mawer shoved the stick forward and bunted violently out of the Japanese pilot's gunsight, forcing it to overshoot. Its first attack foiled, this Hayabusa pulled straight up into a stall turn in order to come back down on top of him. However, Mawer reversed into a climbing turn quickly enough to get a shot from below at the enemy fighter's port quarter. He fired a long burst from 200 metres, and saw strikes on its wings and fuselage.

As it zoomed straight up, the Hayabusa rolled rapidly from wings level to a vertical bank. Then the port wing-spar snapped, and the suddenly stricken machine plunged away into a spin with the wing folded up and lying across the top of the fuselage. Nakajima's engineers had concentrated so hard on producing a fine and light airframe for the Ki-43 that the resultant structure had an inadequate safety factor – the type had been plagued with this type of structural failure ever since its introduction into service, and the weakness remained in spite of modifications.

As Mawer was holding his sights on his victim and firing, his own aircraft was hit in the cockpit area by an unseen Japanese fighter – the larger group of escorting fighters behind him had now caught up unseen. He bunted violently then reefed coarsely back on the stick to induce a spin. Upon recovering, he saw the Hayabusa hit the sea near Northwest Island (in the Vernon Islands group, at the open end of Adam Bay), and his gun film later confirmed the enemy fighter's destruction by showing images of its collapsed wing. As Mawer dived away from the combat, he saw two further crashes into the sea – one of them was a Spitfire, victim of the dogfight with the enemy fighters.

A single machine-gun round had gone right through Mawer's cockpit – in one side and out the other. It had thankfully missed his knees and hands, but on the way through it had with unerring precision hit the undercarriage selector on one side and the throttle quadrant on the other. With the hydraulic system thereby rendered inoperative, he now had no means of extending his undercarriage, while his engine throttle was now jammed at 2850 rpm. He took his damaged aircraft back to base.

Blue Colyer had followed Mawer in to the initial attack and lined up to fire upon the right-hand Hayabusa, which was slower to break than the other one. Colyer got on its tail and fired a long burst inside 300 metres. He saw flashes around its cockpit (later confirmed by his gun film) and then it broke away downwards. Colyer followed, but upon looking around saw yet another fighter behind him, already firing – he was under attack from the same newly arriving group as had attacked Mawer. He broke violently and dived away.

Ross Richardson meanwhile was coming along behind, still way out of range as he saw the other two making their attacks on the two Hayabusas. He was trying to follow after Mawer, but lost sight of him as the latter manoeuvred erratically, and thus he found himself alone in an ominously empty sky. Having previously spotted the squadron of enemy fighters following along behind the others, he chose to keep going straight down at high speed, prudently removing himself from the combat.

The Japanese fighter reinforcements had got in among Mawer's group because White Section had failed to suppress them – thanks to Ted Hall's malfunctioning engine, it was still too low to do so. Having been lagging badly behind and below the other aircraft in his section, Hall had handed over to Flying Officer Ken Fox. This left Fox no higher than the enemy fighters – 25 000 feet – so he was not able to make an attack in time to assist the others as planned. Instead, he continued the climb, leaving Hall behind to orbit cautiously (and perilously) by himself at a lower level, hoping for a straggler to pounce upon. None turned up, so Hall took his aircraft back to base.

As he climbed, Fox saw in the distance MacDonald's and Bisley's sections making their attacks on the bombers. Finally getting to 27000 feet, he took White section down upon the enemy fighters 2000 feet below. Fox made a good start to the action by achieving a bounce in the initial attack, and because he was at the head of the queue of diving Spitfires, he got the advantage of taking the first shot as well: as he dived upon the enemy fighters' rear quarter, his target flew straight and level, still unaware of the attack. However, Fox then opened fire from the long range of 400 metres, with moreover a high closure rate and with some deflection – not an easy shot. Therefore he missed, permitting the enemy pilot to realise what was happening and to break into a hard turn. Having missed his chance, Fox rolled onto his back and dived away. White Section had been split up in the dive, and the pilots remained leaderless and perilously separated thereafter.

Pilot Officer Paul Tully came down behind Fox, lining up to bounce a lone enemy fighter 3000 feet below. Easing out of the dive, he approached from its rear quarter and opened fire in a low-deflection shot at the very long range of 500 metres. Going at 350 knots IAS, the range closed so rapidly that he was able to get right in to 50 metres, still firing, by now from directly astern. However, both cannons jammed due to ammunition feed stoppages. Bunting under the target at the end of his run, he rolled onto his back and broke violently downwards, pulling so much G that he blacked out. He continued on down, intent upon putting distance between himself and the fighters. Pulling out well below, he saw what he thought was a Japanese fighter going into the water (although it was just as likely to have been a Spitfire, as we shall see).

The Japanese fighters were distributed about in twos and fours, and this had the effect of spreading White Section out into a scatter of individual Spitfires heading off against their separated targets. Flying Officer Ross Williams had also picked out his target as he dived: it was circling to the right at 22 000 feet, clearly unaware of his approach. He followed it around in the turn, able to stay with it in spite of his speed because of the Japanese pilot's use of only a moderate bank angle. He made a very similar shot to Tully's, using some deflection to open fire from its rear quarter at 400 metres, rolling in to dead astern and firing right in to 75 metres. Like Tully, he missed, and the Japanese aircraft then rolled on its back and pulled around in a half-loop – this was a 'split S', a standard counter-move, enabling the Japanese pilot to exploit his fighter's extreme low-speed manoeuvrability to reverse direction. As Williams overshot he looked behind, seeing that the Hayabusa had got around so rapidly that it was already behind him. Recognising the danger, he rolled onto his back and went straight down to 10 000 feet, thereafter heading back to base.

Flying Officer Bill Lloyd was the third of White Section's three element leaders, leading Sergeant Bill Nichterlein. He followed Fox down, but things started to deteriorate when his aircraft suffered a CSU failure in the dive, leaving him with an overrevving engine in the middle of the combat. While trying to deal with this, he saw an enemy fighter up ahead, but only had time to take a rushed shot at it on the way past. He then saw another one up above, rolling off the top of a stall turn to come down on top of him. At this point, his engine cut – he had managed to reduce the revs all right! Lloyd pointed the nose straight down and rolled into an engine-less spiral dive. Restarting his engine, he obtained normal revs, so pulled out at 5000 feet and climbed away up sun, turning frequently and looking behind.

Of Bill Nichterlein, there was no further sign. Even if he had managed to stay with Lloyd, that would have been no help, preoccupied as he was with escaping from the enemy and simultaneously managing his in-flight emergency. Lloyd's R/T had also failed, cutting off contact with his wingman, who was the arse-end Charlie in a line of diving Spitfires. The first two aircraft of Ken Fox's section had gone through their attacking runs too quickly to experience any Japanese counter-moves, but the three behind them had flown into a disturbed hornet's nest, with alerted fighters now diving in after them. Nichterlein was the most inexperienced pilot in the section, the last man in the line, and out of everyone else's vision. Unlike Williams and Lloyd, he failed to see his attacker before it fired, and so was sent spinning into the water by a close-range burst of heavy machine-gun fire. It was his aircraft that Tully saw splashing into the sea, and other pilots had also seen his Spitfire going into the water in the outer reaches of Adam Bay, near the Vernon Islands.

Unaware of any of this, MacDonald had meanwhile completed a breaking turn after his attack and then zoomed up sun to get on the other side of the bombers. When he had climbed 3000 feet above them and drawn far enough ahead, he rolled into another attack, again from the beam. This time, he fired at the leader of the left-most vee, the same part of the formation as had been attacked by Hughes. Ceasing fire at 100 metres, he bunted underneath and then pulled round into a tight left-hand turn, now noticing the untidy gaps in this end of the bomber formation due to the effects of Hughes's earlier firing. Exploiting the wide gap that had opened up between the disordered outside vee and the centre of the formation, MacDonald was able to pull hard enough in the turn to get behind the left-most bomber of the centre vee. The turn slowed his aircraft, producing an overtaking speed that was modest enough to give him time to concentrate on his gunnery. Firing a two- to three-second burst from within 100 metres range in an easy no-deflection shot, he saw his rounds passing right through the engine and starboard wing of his target. As he broke downwards and dived away, he saw this bomber drop out of formation burning brightly. It descended to crash into Shoal Bay near the mouth of the Howard River, seen by his own No. 2, Evans, by Blue Section's Bisley and Mawer, and by Huggard from 54. MacDonald's final firing pass, from behind at close range, proved once again that this was the most reliable way for a Spitfire pilot to get a bomber kill.

However, his gunnery effectiveness had been at the cost of exposing himself to heavy return fire from the bomber gunners. As MacDonald was firing, the bomber on the opposite side of the vee was only 50 metres away, giving its port side-gunner an easy no-deflection shot. He noticed that he was under 'heavy return fire' before he broke away downwards, and indeed his aircraft was perforated by 7.7 mm rounds, with hits through both wings, around the cockpit area, and through both fuel tanks. Petrol leaked back over the floor of the cockpit, while his sudden violent dive caused the propeller CSU to fail and the engine to overspeed. Upon pulling out, MacDonald climbed up sun, intent upon resuming his attack, but his engine had been running poorly since the overspeed, and with petrol continuing to slosh about on the floor, he sensibly decided to take his aircraft home.

MacDonald had observed two other bombers going down: one went into Adam Bay 15 kilometres east of Escape Cliff (Hughes's kill), while another one crashed on land 3 kilometres west of Koolpinyah station (Bisley's) – thus he witnessed the destruction of three separate bombers, in three separate locations. Unaware of 54's attacks, he assumed all three had been shot down by his own squadron. No. 54 thought much the same. MacDonald saw an additional unidentified aircraft crash into the sea north-west of Cape Vernon. He hoped it might have been an enemy fighter, and it probably was – Mawer's kill.

Meanwhile, Mawer was in his damaged aircraft, with his throttle stuck at combat revs, making a very fast transit back to Strauss to set himself up for a belly landing (with a wrecked undercarriage selector, he could not lower the gear). Overhead the field, he cut the ignition, turned off the fuel, opened the hood, tightened his seat harness, and lowered the seat – to reduce the chance of head injuries if the aircraft flipped over. With the propeller slowly ticking over in the slipstream, he spiralled down for a dead-stick landing. Without the ability to adjust his descent rate by the use of engine power, and with almost certain death if he undershot the runway and went into the trees, Mawer made sure he maintained an extra margin of gliding speed. Lowering the flaps, he cleared the tree line and rolled wings level over the runway. However, with the extra speed that he had put on 'for safety', his aircraft was still above its 60 knot stalling speed, so it just kept floating along only a few feet above the oil-stained dirt of the runway. Mawer eased the stick back, the long nose in front blocking his view of the rapidly approaching tree line at the other end of the strip.

After an interminable wait, the tail wheel touched. Losing flying speed at last, the aircraft sagged towards the ground then suddenly lurched forward onto its belly, careering along through the dirt in a great cloud of dust. Mawer's shoulders were shoved violently into the shoulder straps of his seat harness as the aircraft slid rapidly to a halt. It stopped only 100 metres from the end of the runway – he had run things a little close. The squadron nonetheless thought he had done an 'excellent job' on his belly landing. Spitfire BR548 had bent a couple of its propeller blades and suffered damage to its air intake and underwing radiators.

457's attack

The last of the three squadrons to attack was 457, having initially been in the lowest starting position because of its late arrival at the rendezvous. Once he attained 28 000 feet overhead Darwin, Watson took the squadron out to the north on the lookout for the enemy but saw nothing, and so started worrying that the bombers had got past him. The first 457 pilot to see the bombers was Flight Sergeant Evan Batchelor, Watson's wingman – even before the other two squadrons had commenced their attacks. He spotted them at some distance to the east as they passed over a cloud bank, with the dark bombers silhouetted against the light background. Watson looked in the indicated direction but could not see them. He turned the squadron around anyway, but having come out of the turn, Batchelor now lost sight of the enemy too. Watson took 457 blindly south towards Darwin, anxiously scanning the sky to his left while listening to 54's and 452's attacks over the R/T. He was then guided by position reports from 452's John Bisley, who was following behind the bombers after making his own attack.

Arriving back over Darwin, Watson saw some low-flying aircraft down below over the harbour. Thinking that these were low-level Japanese raiders sneaking in under the radar, Watson ordered Flight Lieutenant Don Maclean to take Blue Section down after them. Maclean obliged, but having descended to 19 000 feet, he recognised them as Catalina flying boats. Blue Section had now lost its height and so had to watch in frustration as the bombers went straight past overhead on their bomb run. As he re-climbed, Maclean saw flaming wreckage burning in the south-west corner of Chambers Bay – the Koolpinyah bomber crash.

Pete Watson's own Red Section was reduced to four aircraft when Flying Officer Bill Gregory experienced a CSU failure on the climb. With his engine racing to 4000 rpm, he aborted, dropped out of formation, and performed the prescribed drill by pulling back both boost and propeller pitch levers. The revs did not drop until he had descended to 7000 feet, but the engine held together to permit a normal landing.

Warrant Officer Clive Briggs was next to spot the enemy – 15 kilometres away, heading straight for them. Pete Watson turned his men left to set up for an immediate head-on attack. By then the bomber formation was coming in from the east to bomb 54's base at RAAF Darwin from 22000 feet; only 3 kilometres out from the target, it was already accompanied by the black airbursts of the AA guns. John Bisley, still climbing up behind the bombers at a distance, saw that the AA fire was initially very inaccurate but that it improved rapidly: the first salvo had exploded fully 10000 feet below the bombers' height, while the second salvo burst 500 feet above them and behind.

As the two formations loomed up at one another, Watson counted only 15 bombers, also seeing a group of escorting fighters both ahead and astern of them. He thought there was something odd about the appearance of the bombers: having assumed that they would once again be navy G4Ms, now he noticed that they had the 'unexpected appearance' of the army Ki-48. In fact this was wrong too, for they were in fact army Ki-49s – the Spitfire pilots' aircraft recognition skills remained poor throughout the campaign, not helped by the configurational similarity of Japanese bomber types, whether navy or army. The same thing applied to the Japanese fighters, with the army Ki-43s on this day confused with navy Zeros. The Ki-49 was such an unknown type to RAAF intelligence that the Koolpinyah wreck was picked over and pronounced to be an 'advanced type' of Ki-21.

At a combined closing speed of 500 knots, 457 closed rapidly with the approaching bombers, but did not lose height until the last moment, causing a repeat of the too-steep dives that had ruined gunnery on 2 May. When almost overhead, Pete Watson half-rolled and pulled, diving down very steeply upon the bombers and leading Red and White Sections down after him. He lined up on the outermost bomber on the right-hand end of the formation and fired from 500 metres in a high-deflection front-quarter attack. Both cannons froze, so he fired ineffectually from long range with machine guns only before bunting underneath at the end of his run and then skidding violently to port in case of fighters. Looking behind, he saw one Hayabusa diving after him, so broke downwards and dived away.

Flight Lieutenant John 'Snapper' Newton followed Watson into the attack, holding position on his right ('snapper' was the RAF reporting term for German fighters, and was thus a satirical reference, an in-joke within the squadron). Newton found the dive very steep, and thus was doing 350 knots IAS by the time he opened fire at the leader of the left-hand vee, also firing a difficult high-deflection shot. At such a closing speed, he only had time for a two-second burst, and did not see any strikes. Ceasing fire at 70 metres, he pulled hard, flashed over the top of the bombers, then rolled over and dived underneath them once he was clear. Following Watson in a long evasive dive far to the east, he pulled out over Adam Bay at 15 000 feet.

In position behind Watson's right wing, Evan Batchelor fired at the leading bomber in the starboard vee and then broke away downwards. As he pushed the stick over to roll his aircraft into the turn, his gloved hand caught the seat harness buckle and dislodged the securing pin. Under the negative G force of the bunt, he was thrown violently out of his seat, banging his head on the canopy and then slumping forward onto the stick. With the stick suddenly forced forwards by his weight, the aircraft pitched down violently completely out of control, with Batchelor pinned underneath the windscreen by the negative G. Needing to sit back down to regain control, he grabbed the stick to steady himself, but the resultant backward pressure on the stick now slammed him back into his seat – so hard under the sudden positive G that he blacked out. Regaining consciousness, he found his face pressed against the canopy while the aircraft flew along upside down at 25 000 feet. Rolling his aircraft drunkenly right way up, he flopped thankfully back into his seat, but try as he might Batchelor could not get his hands on all four ends of the harness to strap himself back in.

Pilot Officer 'Darky' McDowell had tried to stay with his leader, Newton, but as he followed him down in a steep dive, his windscreen de-icer started to leak and the viscous fluid oozed out all over the windscreen, obscuring his vision. McDowell tried to go through with his attack, but he could only line up on his target by craning his head sideways to peer through the windscreen quarter panels. It was no good; he could not see through his gunsight, so he dived past the bombers without firing.

Flying Officer Doug Edwards led White Section down behind Watson, so preoccupied with getting into position and staying there that he only saw nine or ten bombers (rather than the correct figure of 15). He made a head-on attack against the port side vee, fired in to very close range and saw puffs of smoke from his bullet strikes. Bunting violently underneath, he only just avoided collision with adjacent bombers before diving away over Darwin Harbour. By the time he pulled out at 13 000 feet, the bombers were heading away to the south-west.

Edwards's wingman, Clive Briggs, found that in order to keep the bombers in his windscreen he had to dive almost vertically. He had earlier loosened his shoulder harness to assist in looking behind him for fighters, and now found his aircraft descending so precipitously that he fell forward against the gunsight. Bracing his arm against it, he levered himself back into position and tightened his straps. Upon looking up he saw that the bombers had disappeared out of his sight line, but he adjusted his dive angle to line up on them again and opened fire at 600 metres. Keeping his finger on the trigger as they loomed rapidly in his windscreen, he saw no strikes but saw plenty of muzzle flashes from the gunners. Diving straight through, he started to pull out, but found he was going so fast that he could barely move the stick, and lost a lot of height before he could recover to level flight far below.

Flying Officer Jack Smithson had initially followed Pete Watson, but his instincts as an experienced combat pilot told him that the angle was too steep for effective gunnery, so he pulled out to the left to come in from the bombers' other side. From there he made a more practicable front-quarter attack against the outermost starboard bomber, and obtained good hits: his wingman, Flying Officer Bill Halse, saw his leader's cannon shells exploding over the bomber's cockpit glasshouse. In spite of the relative moderation of Smithson's diving angle, the inexperienced Halse still found the dive too steep and the closure rate too rapid, and he was past the bombers before he had time to fire. After firing, Smithson looked behind in time to see a group of enemy fighters coming down after them. He broke hard left, followed by Halse, who was still concentrating hard on staying with his leader. Both pilots then zoomed up together into a climbing turn, levelling out up above the bombers at 26 000 feet.

Smithson scanned the sky again, and saw two enemy fighters flying line abreast 1500 feet below. He got into position and dived in behind them, firing at one of Hayabusas from 300 metres in a relatively easy low-deflection shot. He saw strikes behind its cockpit and then its undercarriage dropped down. As Smithson overshot, going past only 70 metres away on its port side, the Hayabusa rolled steeply away from him to the right, and then fell away into a dive. Smithson got around his turn and back onto its tail as it dived away, but the fighter's dive steepened up so much that he could not follow, and it disappeared under his nose.

Bill Halse meanwhile was almost shot off Smithson's tail, but fortunately this very inexperienced pilot remembered to 'keep his head out of his cockpit'. Still concentrating on following along behind his No. 1, Halse looked up to the right just in time to see an enemy fighter diving at him with its undercarriage extended (this was to kill its speed and prevent an overshoot – Hayabusa pilots dropped the undercarriage in combat as a form of airbrake). Looking around further to the rear, he saw that another one was already arcing around in a horizontal turn onto his tail. He and Smithson had almost been caught in a coordinated bounce, with the leading pair evidently serving as bait. Halse broke violently downwards, losing contact with Smithson and diving away without having fired his guns.

No. 457 had acquired two 'hangers-on' during its approach to attack: Flight Sergeant Keith Cross from 452 and Wing Commander Caldwell (with a dead R/T set). Cross's aircraft had gone unserviceable during the scramble, but the fitters had put it right quickly enough for him to follow the others into the air about 12 minutes later – but all alone. Unable to find his own squadron, at 28 000 feet he had joined onto the rear of 457 just as they got into position to attack. He then dived down after Watson's Red Section, setting up for a head-on attack and opening fire from 600 metres at the leading bomber in the centre of the formation. Ceasing fire at 150 metres, he bunted violently underneath the onrushing bombers and then broke left to give any attacking fighter a deflection shot. Like so many others, Cross's cannons had frozen up, so he had made his attack with machine guns only. He saw incendiary strikes on the bomber's wings and on top of its fuselage, but it did not shift from its position at the head of the formation.

Ever since the failure of his R/T, Caldwell had been tagging along at the rear of the 457 formation. Unable to hear either the vectors from control or the R/T chatter, Caldwell had not been able to follow the tactical situation, but had simply followed the squadron through a series of turns without comprehension. He had still not spotted the bombers by the time the Spitfires ahead of him started peeling off to the left and diving in to attack. Following them down in the unaccustomed role as arse-end Charlie, he still did not sight the bombers until late in the diving turn. By then, he was too low to make an attack, so he just continued straight past them without firing, maintaining his left turn and zooming back up sun for another go, but all alone.

The attacks on the way out

After diving away from their initial attack, 11 pilots (most from 457) re-climbed, heading west again after the bombers, but all separated from each other. Among them was the wing CO, Group Captain Walters, still flying alone. After dropping out of 54's formation, he had headed back to Darwin by himself and then shadowed the bombers through their bomb run from 3000 feet above. He watched the AA bursting off to his left and got within 3 kilometres of the bombers' starboard rear quarter by the time they turned right towards Bynoe Harbour. Noticing a bomber lagging 50 feet below and 50 metres behind the formation, Walters delivered two beam attacks in a row upon this damaged straggler, zooming up into a climbing turn into the sun after each attack – but he saw no strikes. By the time he was back in position for a third attack, the bombers had dived down to 16000 feet and were 15 miles north-west of Bynoe Harbour, holding a noticeably looser formation than before.

McDowell was somewhere nearby, climbing up beside the bombers, also alone. Once he got 2000 feet above them, he turned in and made a diving beam attack. Because of his speed, he only had time for a one-second burst, but fired from very close, seeing strikes all over the centre fuselage and wing centre section of his target. Black smoke poured from an engine, and the bomber dropped 1000 feet below the formation, losing height rapidly and descending towards Port Patterson. McDowell zoomed up in a climbing turn to reattack, but as he did so he spotted an aircraft diving towards him from out of the sun. Breaking violently downwards and diving away over Darwin Harbour, his propeller CSU failed and the engine revs went up to 3800 rpm, but for once the engine responded to his corrective action, and he joined up with Clive Briggs and headed home.

Having recovered from his loss of control but with his seat harness still not secured, Evan Batchelor also followed the bombers out, and as he got close he heard McDowell's R/T call asking 'someone' to watch the bomber he had just 'shot down' (to confirm his kill). Batchelor looked and saw that a bomber was indeed peeling away from the formation, trailing heavy black smoke, followed by a Spitfire. Setting up for his own attack, he shadowed the bombers as they flew up the Cox Peninsula in a shallow dive at 220 knots. Getting up sun of them before they crossed the coast at Point Charles, he dived in for a head-on attack at the centre bomber of the starboard vee. However, neither cannon functioned, so he attacked with machine guns only. His target 'wobbled and broke under and away' from its formation, but Batchelor did not see it again to ascertain its fate. As he broke away in an evasive bunt, he once again banged his head on the canopy because of the negative G – he had forgotten that he was still not strapped into his seat.

Don Maclean's frustrated Blue Section had meanwhile been climbing after the bombers, but the retiring Japanese were going fast. He got to 26 000 feet but fell behind when he moved out to the right to get up sun, finding that the bombers were now drawing away. Maclean's caution stemmed from his awareness of the enemy fighters still flying high on the flanks of the bombers: he was not prepared to risk getting his section bounced, so he did not attack. He watched the bombers retiring out to sea and saw one of their number straggling behind. From his vantage point overhead, Maclean saw one bomber burning on the ground on the Cox Peninsula. His wingman, Flight Sergeant Freddie White, saw a bomber going down over the Cox Peninsula, and then saw a wreck burning on the ground there. These pilots had thus confirmed McDowell's kill.

Flight Sergeant Huggard of 54 had witnessed 457's attack. After the initial combat over Adam Bay he resumed the chase, climbing after the bombers by himself. Following from a distance, he saw another bomber dive away in flames – the time interval suggesting that this was McDowell's victim. Pursuing them out to sea, he saw three patches of oil and wreckage in the sea between Cape Fourcroy and Darwin, far to the west of 54's and 452's initial combat over Adam Bay. The army AA gunners had also witnessed 457's attack, seeing the Spitfires dive through the heavy AA fire to make their attack, with two bombers dropping away afterwards.

Doug Edwards climbed north-west into an up sun position over Point Charles, ready to intercept the outgoing bombers as they crossed the coast. He was distracted from this plan when four Spitfires crossed his nose, 1000 feet higher and flying west. He turned in behind them and followed, now spotting an additional four even further ahead. When he had closed the gap to 400 metres behind them and 500 feet below, he identified them as enemy fighters! At that very moment the four rearward Hayabusas broke in unison and came around after him. Two turned about very rapidly and came at him head-on, while the other two turned right to arc around behind him as he went after the other two – a classic Japanese set-piece counter-attacking move. Edwards recognised his impossible situation and half-rolled at once, diving away in a series of violent spirals. Pulling out at 13 000 feet, he looked behind, confirmed that the fighters were gone, and headed back to Livingstone.

Newton was also re-climbing after the bombers, but he fell into the same trap as Edwards. He saw four Spitfires in line abreast, climbing on the same course at 11 o'clock above. Climbing to join them, upon getting closer he recognised with a start that they were Japanese! In a show of admirable determination he continued the climb, trying to get into position to dive in from their rear quarter – having committed himself to a one-versus-four engagement. Then the centre Hayabusa suddenly stood on its tail and looped up to come down on top of him. Newton pushed his nose down to get some speed then looked up – to see that the looping Hayabusa was already on its way down, poised directly above and inverted. Looking left, he saw that there was another one flying parallel to him. He broke towards it, but this enemy fighter rolled onto its back and disappeared underneath him. Continuing the turn, Newton looked around in time to see it reappear on his tail, already firing. Comprehensively out-flown, out-thought and out-fought, Newton half-rolled and pulled. After a series of rolls, he pulled out at 13 000 feet over RAAF Darwin to find himself alone.

Another detached pilot who followed the enemy out to sea all by himself was 54's Bob Foster. Back at height off their starboard flank by the time they were 15 kilometres north-west of Darwin, he saw a dogfight ahead of him between three enemy fighters and two Spitfires – probably Edwards and Newton from 457. As he approached the melee, one of the Hayabusas detached itself to make a head-on pass at him. He fired at it as it flew directly at him but it broke off early. Firing again with a high-deflection shot as it turned in front of him, he saw strikes on its wing. However, Foster was unable to hold it in the turn despite pulling so much G that he blacked out. Easing the pressure on the stick so that his sight returned, he was alarmed to discover that he could no longer see the enemy fighter – it must be behind him! Breaking violently downwards, he then headed back to base feeling rather chastened by this brush with the manoeuvring power of the 'Zero'.

As Pete Watson climbed back to 25 000 feet, he heard R/T reports warning of enemy fighters. Pulling into a turn to look behind, he saw four of them 5000 feet lower than him, following him out to sea. Fortunately, the Spitfire could out-climb them, so he evaded them by simply maintaining his climb at high IAS. Upon reaching a position in front and above the bombers, he turned in, hoping to get another firing run. He looked behind again as he did so, but could no longer see the Japanese fighters. Refocusing on the bombers, he made another high-speed front-quarter attack, this time upon the leader in the centre of the whole formation. He fired from 500 metres, but again with machine guns only. Breaking off very close, he bunted underneath and dived all the way to 3000 feet to ensure safe separation from the fighters.

Another 54 Squadron pilot, F/Sgt Horkin, had also sought to resume his attack on the bombers and also climbed after them alone. He followed them as they came off their bomb run and as they flew out to the west over Port Patterson. Flying parallel about 3 kilometres out to the side, he gradually closed in as the bombers turned right to assume a more northerly heading for home. He counted only 12 bombers left and saw that their formation had deteriorated greatly – they had abandoned their vees and were now flying in a most un-Japanese disordered gaggle.

When he finally dived at the starboard end of their formation, Horkin found himself going too fast and thus only had time for a rushed snap shot, which he duly missed. Pulling up and looking around him, he now noticed that there was in fact one enemy fighter out on either flank, behind the bombers. Horkin re-climbed, keeping an eye on these fighters, and then dived again on the same extreme right-hand bomber, opening fire with a deflection shot from its rear quarter and then swinging in directly astern. He saw strikes on its wing, there was a puff of black smoke, and debris fell off behind. As he broke away, Horkin looked around in time to see a Hayabusa poised right above him with its undercarriage extended as an airbrake. He watched it as it rolled onto its back and came down at him, but then evaded its attentions by breaking sharply to the right and descending in a series of evasive rolls. Looking back again, he saw that the enemy fighter was still following, but with its undercarriage now retracted. He shook it off in further steep diving turns and then headed for home.

John Bisley had meanwhile been following the bombers out to sea, and counted a reduced formation of only 13 bombers, with only three escorting fighters evident at 20 000 feet, 'well scattered' and 'considerably behind'. Bisley climbed beside the bombers to make an attack, but he fell unconscious due to having exhausted his oxygen. Recovering his senses in time to find his aircraft spinning down through 10 000 feet, he pulled out, thoroughly alarmed by this close shave. Without oxygen, he abandoned the idea of any further attack and went home.

After his earlier abortive attack, Caldwell re-climbed and made it back to 21 000 feet as he chased after the bombers. He was east of Bynoe Bay and getting ready to make his attack when he suddenly noticed that he was accompanied by two enemy fighters – Caldwell's lookout was letting him down today. Climbing up sun to evade them, he then turned around to come back down at them. He hoped to catch them unawares but they saw him coming, and he found himself scissoring desperately with three enemy fighters. Each time he lined up on one, he would see another one turning in on the other side – very similar to his experience on 2 March and 2 May. These army pilots were working as well together as the navy pilots did, executing a team combat drill well beyond the capacity of 1 Fighter Wing's pilots. Caldwell was pushing his luck in fighting one-versus-three against obviously skilled opponents, so he sensibly used his speed to break off and then climbed away again up sun.

Having recovered his height advantage, he turned around once more to come back down. Caldwell looked again for an unwary victim to pick off, and this time found him: as he dived from out of the sun's glare, he caught a Hayabusa unawares and got off a good burst from very close range before zooming back up out of harm's way. Although both his cannons froze up, he claimed hitting the enemy fighter with his machine guns and that it hit the sea 40 kilometres west-north-west of Cape Fourcroy. Caldwell's diving and zooming fight had paralleled the progress of the bombers as they headed away from the coast; and he counted only ten bombers left in formation before they disappeared from sight.

Meanwhile, Group Captain Walters was likewise pursuing a solo fight, gamely maintaining contact with the enemy after his earlier unsuccessful attack on a straggling bomber. As he followed the bombers out to sea, he saw a Spitfire following behind them and so moved over to join up. The Spitfire turned straight towards him, and now he saw its pug-nosed radial engine looming rapidly in his windscreen – a Japanese fighter! Walters found himself in a head-on pass before he had time to aim; white tracer flashed past 3 metres overhead, and then the Hayabusa roared past only 6 metres beneath. He turned hard to spoil its next attack and then climbed up sun at full boost and revs, maintaining a high IAS for safety. Looking back, he saw that the Japanese pilot had given up the chase and was turning to follow the bombers – very conscious of his fuel state so far from home.

Walters turned about, got some more height, then dived down from out of the sun. Pulling out underneath, he approached through the blind spot under its tail, waited patiently until he was very close, aimed and fired. From only 50 metres away he saw strikes on its wing root, but broke off into another climbing turn up sun before he himself was bounced. Thus he did not see the result of his attack, but nonetheless claimed this Hayabusa as shot down 25 kilometres west of Cape Fourcroy. When Caldwell was on his way back from his own combat further out to sea, he saw two large patches of oil on the surface of the sea about 3 kilometres apart, and in the location indicated by Walters. With the 'Wingco' backing up the 'Groupie', Walters's claim was confirmed by this circumstantial evidence. During his final climb up sun, Walters had obtained a good look at the bombers, counting 11–12 of them at 11 000 feet, going north-west about 50 kilometres south-west of Cape Fourcroy. One of them was lagging 200 feet below and 500 metres behind, while another had dropped directly underneath the formation, flying about 1000 feet lower. It is clear that the enemy bomber unit had suffered rough treatment from Spitfire attack.

As usual, however, wholesale cannon failures had hindered the effect of the Spitfire gunnery. Of the pilots known to have fired their guns, in only seven cases had both cannons functioned correctly. In every other case, pilots had had to complete their attacks with one cannon only at best, often with none. No. 457 Squadron's diarist complained of the stoppages, both of cannons and machine guns, 'thus again reducing the strength of this squadron's powers'.

The low-level raid

At 10.43 am, the high-level bombers had dropped a stick of about 60 bombs in a line extending from the RAAF camp on the fringes of RAAF Darwin, across the railway and highway and across the Australian and US Army camps at Winnellie. From Darwin Harbour, the crew of the RAN's ML814 had looked north across the intervening expanse of mudflats and mangroves to see the bombs bursting on the airfield in 'red balls of fire with clouds of smoke and dust'. The anti-personnel bombs had their effect in the congested working area alongside the road and railway, and two men were killed and 13 wounded – all from the Australian Army. Half a dozen buildings were hit, powerlines, telephone lines, railway and water mains were cut, and an American 3 tonne truck destroyed. Most spectacularly, the bombs fell across a railway carriage loaded with POL, and 60 drums of oil went up in flames. The Japanese had caught the ground echelon of the newly arriving 380th Bomb Group in the process of unloading in Darwin Harbour, with the road and railway clogged with trucks and carriages moving east past the southern boundary of the RAAF base. The new American bomber unit, fresh from the United States, had received a rude welcome to the NWA air war.

Soon after, Bill Gibbs had taken his misbehaving aircraft home, landing at RAAF Darwin at about 10.55. Before he had time to climb out of the cockpit, nine light bombers suddenly appeared out of the haze, popping up over the eastern tree line in a neat 'vee of vees' formation and sweeping across the airfield at 100 feet and at the brisk speed of 220 knots. As they thundered past they were closely observed by Gibbs, still sitting in his cockpit; he stayed there, using his R/T to provide a running commentary for control on the movements of these new raiders. The bombers dropped eight 250 kg HE bombs and

A crowd of onlookers by the bomb-burst water pipeline at Winnellie on 20 June. This pipeline, running into town beside the highway past the southern fringes of RAAF Darwin, was routinely broken by the bombing. AWM Negative 052640

twenty 60 kg 'daisy-cutters', the larger bombs fitted with delayed action fuses to prevent the explosions blowing up the bombers as they went by close overhead; as it turned out, only three of these went off, leaving the other five to be dealt with later by the bomb disposal teams.

Pilot Officer Garden had also landed his malfunctioning aircraft just before the strafing attack, but neither Spitfire was hit, thanks to the camouflaged tree-lined dispersals around the perimeter of the airstrip, and the poor visibility from the fast-moving low-flying bombers. Jim Grant of 457 maintained that the morale of the squadrons' ground staff was greatly stiffened by the experience of the air raids. This was easy for him to say, as the two Australian squadrons had never been bombed,

The squadron of Ki-48 light bombers making its first run over RAAF Darwin on 20 June. Note the impeccable formation, and the lowered ventral gun positions, from which the rear gunners sprayed the field with 7.7 mm machine-gun fire. NAA: A11231, 5/73/INT

safely ensconced as they were on their more southerly airfields. No. 54's base at Darwin on the other hand featured very high on the Japanese targeting list. Many of the British ground staff were veterans of airfield attacks during the Battle of Britain, when the squadron had been based at Hornchurch, a forward airfield. According to these experienced men, this low-level attack at Darwin was the most alarming they had ever experienced. Luckily, none of 54's men were hit, although the squadron's photographic and parachute sections were extensively damaged.

After dropping their bombs, the nine bombers disappeared to the south as quickly as they had come, staying low and giving the impression they were going to make a second bomb run on the ships in the harbour. Aboard ML814, Sub Lieutenant Marsden Hordern was estimating the firing range for his 20 mm Oerlikon gunner when the oncoming bombers suddenly wheeled into a starboard turn and reversed their course. With their lower wingtips only 100 feet above the mudflats of Frances Bay, they continued the turn over the depots, tents and dumps that ran along the railway line on the edge of the harbour. Soldiers looked up from their trenches to see the gaggle of bombers roar past, the red circles on their fuselage sides emphasised in the bright sunlight. Rolling out, the bombers headed north-east low down over the mangroves for a second thunderous run across the RAAF base, preceded by a hail of machine-gun fire from the gunners lying prone in their plexiglass nosecones. Gibbs watched them go past again, in a looser formation this time to permit the gunners to freely strafe anything they saw.

An exchange of machine-gun tracers between the bomber gunners and the airfield machine-gun posts criss-crossed the field as the bombers swept over. Flying Officer O'Brien, 54 Squadron's defence officer, manned one of the machine guns and claimed to have hit one of the bombers during the second pass. Indeed, Gibbs saw one of the Japanese machines hit by ground fire: its port engine smoked and it pulled out to the left away from the formation before the pilot got things under control and got it back into position. Flying Officer 'Cecil' Beaton, 54's Engineering Officer, correctly identified the bombers as army Kawasaki Ki-48s, whereas other observers maintained that they were Mitsubishi Ki-46s (the recon aircraft that had been regularly met with in the air from February onwards). That this errant identification was seriously entertained was testimony to the poor level of intelligence on enemy aircraft types (the Ki-46 was almost unarmed, with only a single rearward 7.7 mm).

According to the Japanese plan, the low-level bombers were to have made their bombing run just after the high-level bombers in a tightly coordinated attack, but in fact they had been more than five minutes late. This slippage in the schedule made little difference, however, as the only aircraft that was available for interception duties in the area was that of 54's Flight Sergeant Joh Kelman, who single-handedly constituted the Yellow Section base patrol. However, at the time of the raid he was patrolling between Darwin and Point Blaze in the bumpy air at 200 feet. Hearing over the R/T Gibbs's reports of a strafing attack, he opened his throttle and headed for Darwin, but by then the bombers had disappeared into the haze.

The low-level attack had achieved almost complete surprise, the realisation of 5 Fighter Sector's long-held fears. Nine unescorted light bombers had avoided radar detection by flying below 1000 feet when approaching over the sea, and had descended even lower on approach to Bathurst Island: Father John McGrath reported that they flew past the RC Mission at 'tree-top level'. They came in so low over the sea that the observation post of the Northern Australia Observer Unit at Lee Point only spotted the bombers 3 kilometres out. By then the bombers were only a couple of minutes out from the target, too late for control to effect an interception. The controllers at

5 Fighter Sector then received a personal update on the position of the low-level raid when the bombers roared right over their heads at the Berrimah ops room, strafing as they went. Turning right onto a westerly course, the bombers then followed the railway track to the RAAF base. Heading back out after the airfield attacks, the bombers strafed the gunners of the 14th AA Battery at McMillans (just north of the RAAF base), crossing the coast between there and 54's camp at Nightcliff, and then headed out over the water at 'dot feet'. They were not intercepted, because the whole fighter wing was still at high altitude engaging the main raid.

Thus a force of more than 40 defending fighters had been caught flat-footed, showing the tactical benefits that were obtainable by splitting the defence between two raids. Ever since the 2 March strafing attack on the Beaufighter base at Coomalie Creek, NWA RAAF HQ had been worried about the possibility of further low-level raids, and the 75th Air Regiment's well-planned and well-flown low-level attack upon RAAF Darwin was the realisation of this fear, justifying the measures that had been taken on 15 March and 2 May to retain a force of Spitfires as an airborne reserve over the airfields. However, as this had been so much wasted effort on those days, by 20 June only a token force of three single aircraft was kept back as the 'Yellow Section' base patrol, one over each squadron base.

Individual pilots found themselves nearby but unable to make attacks. Dave Downs was returning to land at Darwin after attacking the high-level bombers when he saw the nine low-level bombers run in across the airfield. However, with only three of his machine guns operating he declined to attack. While he was re-climbing after his pass at the high-level bombers, control provided Hal Whillans with a vector to cut off the retreating low-level raiders, but he saw nothing. John Bisley was above, listening in frustration to the R/T jammed with

RAAF ground crew dig Japanese 7.7 mm machine-gun bullets out of the runway at RAAF Darwin on 20 June. This illustrates the less-than-overwhelming effect of the Japanese bombers' airfield attacks. Left to right: front row – LAC Flinn, Beyass and Talbot; back row – LAC Carstairs and Wiseman, and AC1 Williamson. AWM Negative 052647

chatter about the low-level raid, and because of this he could not get the position of the retiring raiders and had to resort to a fruitless visual search. Ross Williams saw the raid occurring in the distance while he was returning to Darwin after his earlier combat. He was vectored 340 degrees after them and chased at 250 knots IAS, but he too failed to spot them. Clive Briggs and Darky McDowell were out over the Cox Peninsula, re-climbing after the retiring high-level bombers when they heard about the low-level raid through the R/T chatter. They headed towards Cape Fourcroy to intercept, but like so many others saw nothing. The bombers were hard to spot against the sea from above.

Bob Foster had also headed for base after the high-level combat and was approaching to land when he saw the nine enemy machines coming in over the trees on their second, northbound run. Tucking his undercarriage away, he retracted his flaps and continued his turn to come round after them as they disappeared to the north. He overtook them out to sea and dived in for a beam attack – his third attack upon the enemy for the day. Unfortunately, his guns fired only a few rounds and then stopped, so he zoomed away in disgust for home.

Because of Tony Tuckson's engine problems, 54's White Section, however, found itself in the right place at the right time. His men had stayed with him while the rest of the squadron had disappeared into the distance to launch the initial attack over Shoal Bay. Tuckson had lagged so far behind that he had abandoned the chase, deciding instead to await the arrival of the raid over Darwin. As he orbited with his section at 26 000 feet, the low-level attack was reported over the R/T. Thus alerted, the pilots looked down, Tuckson's No. 2, Sergeant Bill Holmes, making the first sighting behind and to the left; peering through the layer of haze down below, he saw the Ki-48s racing north, low down over the surface of the sea. Tuckson led his men into a left turn to go after them, but his engine was producing so little power that as soon as he pulled into the turn, his aircraft stalled and flicked into a spin. The other three Spitfires, now led by Holmes, continued the turn and commenced their diving approach to intercept the low-flying bombers.

By now these three 54 Squadron aircraft had a hanger-on: 452's Ross Richardson. Having disengaged from the combat with the enemy fighters, he had re-climbed and joined up behind Tuckson's section. He and the three 54 pilots were probably the most inexperienced flight of airmen to go into combat on this day – every one of them was a green new graduate. Like several other of 54's pilots on this day, Pilot Officer WH Appleton was so new that he had only joined the squadron three days before. Richardson found that the three British pilots made the error of getting right overhead the retiring low-level bombers, thus placing the enemy vertically below and therefore in an awkward position to attack – much like on 2 May. As he followed the others down in a series of steep turns, Richardson found his aircraft accelerating to 420 knots IAS, losing sight of the others and finding himself isolated. Looking around, he noticed two enemy fighters behind the bombers and gave a warning about these over the R/T.

Recognising his own peril as the arse-end Charlie, Richardson decided to stay above as top-cover and so pulled out of his dive, keeping a wary eye on the enemy fighters and watching the progress of the British pilots' attacks down below. By now his 452 colleague, Ken Fox, had arrived back over Darwin in time to see the low-level attack. He shadowed them out to sea, but upon hearing Richardson's warnings about enemy fighters, decided to avoid the perils of lone combat. The irony is that Richardson had seen Spitfires (probably Fox and Newton) and misreported them as enemy fighters; and this misidentification kept the two 452 Squadron pilots out of the fight.

Meanwhile, the three 54 Squadron Spitfires were diving

into their attacks, but too steeply for good gunnery, not helped by the bomber pilots' impressive display of tight formation at only 100 feet above the waves. This forced the Spitfires to make diving attacks from above, which was hazardous as there was no room to pull out beneath. Even worse, the Spitfire pilots had to dive into the layer of haze below 3000 feet, which hindered their visual perception of altitude above the water. Holmes was first into the attack: he lined up on a bomber but was going so fast at the bottom of his dive that he had to pull out before he could even open fire. As Holmes went through this abortive pass, the other pilots saw the web of tracers coming out to greet him from the Japanese rear gunners. Flying Officer Harold Leonard was next, and he managed things better. He made a rear-quarter attack, but when he pressed the firing button one cannon failed at once, while the other one failed to fire until a couple of seconds had elapsed. Despite this he saw strikes on the bomber: it belched smoke and pulled out of formation. Leonard's wingman, Appleton, confirmed this: he saw Leonard's shells striking its 'greenhouse' and debris falling away. Appleton himself, coming in last, managed to open fire momentarily, but like Holmes had to break away violently to avoid hitting the sea, and saw no result from his snap burst.

A little alarmed at his own close call, Holmes had zoomed up and away, climbing all the way back to 10 000 feet as he calmed himself, tailing the bombers cautiously. Throughout his extended observation of the enemy formation as he climbed up beside them, he saw that Leonard's victim did not crash. No other Japanese machine showed any sign of trouble, so it seemed White Section's attack had failed. Having watched and waited awhile, Holmes then tried again by himself. Diving from the bombers' starboard rear quarter, he opened fire from far out of range, pulling his sights across the whole formation. In spite of the wing CO's strictures against spraying fire, Holmes did just that, and unsurprisingly saw no results from his wild shooting. To make matters worse, his finger slipped off the cannon button by mistake, and so he conducted this long-range fire with short-range machine guns only. His errors were understandable, however, for he had been discomfited by the presence of the sea so close below his bomber targets, and had given himself a scare in his previous attack, so had applied long-range spraying fire as a means of avoiding hitting the sea before pulling out. The 75th Air Regiment's choice of an ultra low-level flight profile on this mission had thus rendered the Spitfire attacks ineffective. Watching from above, Ross Richardson considered that 54's attack had had no effect at all on the speeding bombers.

The inexperienced British pilots now received reinforcement in the shape of 457's Flight Lieutenant Jack Newton, who had luckily emerged alive from his hazardous encounter with enemy fighters a little earlier. He too had followed the R/T chatter in pursuit of the low-level bombers, guided towards them by the sight of one of the 54 Squadron aircraft flying along at 5000 feet – Bill Holmes. Newton attempted to organise a coordinated attack with Holmes but got no answer over the R/T through the chatter-jammed frequency, so then proceeded with his own solo attack. Holmes had not even seen him. Newton showed greater self-confidence by diving from out of the sun upon the bombers' front quarter. Opening fire from 500 metres at the right-most bomber, he saw hits on its fuselage and wing, then pulled up and passed right over the top of the Japanese formation. As he did so, he was taken under fire by all nine of the Japanese rear gunners from close range, and felt the impact of a bullet strike in his aircraft: one round of 7.7 mm struck just underneath his seat, fortunately without hitting either Newton or the aircraft's glycol plumbing. Zooming up and away, Newton rolled over and dived back to sea level in order to regain speed and to give the gunners a difficult deflection shot before moving out of range. In among all the water splashes from the spraying of machine-gun fire at sea level, this manoeuvre was construed by the ever-optimistic rear gunners as a sure sign of his having dived into the sea. The Japanese gunners had fired at him from only 40 metres away as he went over the top, and claimed him as shot down.

Five pilots had fired at the light bombers, but with very little observable result. Bill Gibbs was still sitting in his aircraft back at Darwin listening to all this over the R/T, and he found it all a bit too much to bear. Having monitored the frustratingly slow and inconclusive progress of this interception, he overheard for a second time the same pilot reporting that he was 'closing in' on the bombers. Gibbs could stand it no longer, shouting over the R/T, 'For Christ sake open fire!' The CO's frustration was well justified, but his squadron was unfortunately populated at that moment with some very green pilots, circumstances conspiring on this day to deprive them of experienced airborne leadership.

Tony Tuckson was an example of such a sidelined leader. Having spun out in his misbehaving aircraft, he had ceded his place at the head of his section and had, like Bill Gibbs, been forced to listen to the abortive intercept over the R/T. He orbited alone over the harbour, waiting for the main high-level raid to come past. It did, and he found himself on the right-hand side above a group of six enemy fighters, which were weaving about in a rough line abreast, arranged in three pairs. Tuckson dived on these, aiming for one of the centre pair. He fired a short burst but saw no strikes, for the Hayabusa broke downwards into a diving turn, forcing Tuckson to apply full deflection and thereby ruining his shooting. The enemy fighter then pulled up into a steep climb, proving once again the superior vertical manoeuvrability of the light Japanese fighters. Tony Tuckson pulled up after it but could not follow, so he bunted away into a violent downwards break and dived out of the fight. He had boldly accepted a one-versus-six engagement and had luckily got away with it; if he had pursued the engagement any longer, he would almost certainly have been jumped from behind and shot down.

Sergeant Lambert from 54, after breaking off the initial action over Adam Bay, had subsequently tried to re-engage by following the R/T reports and climbing. Heading off on an interception heading, he joined up with a 452 aircraft and chased all the way to Cape Fourcroy, moving fast in a gradual dive to 5000 feet. However, he saw nothing, so gave up and went home. Flight Sergeant Ashurst from 54 likewise re-climbed, looking for an opportunity to re-engage. Guided by the pilots' R/T chatter, he followed the low-level fight out towards Cape Fourcroy, but also without reacquiring the enemy: the low-level bombers had got away. It had been a bravura performance by the airmen of the 75th Air Regiment.

As usual, Bladin ordered immediate retaliation, and so 2 and 18 Squadrons raided Koepang that night, albeit with the usual questionable results of night-bombing. In addition, standing patrols of nine Spitfires were henceforth mounted every morning over Bathurst Island to guard against any repetition. These became a standard part of the daily flying program, with the aircraft weighed down by large 90 gallon drop tanks to provide a bottom-numbing endurance of nearly three hours. Ironically, however, it was so much wasted effort, for never again would the Japanese employ coordinated multiple raids.

Enemy losses

The fighter pilots of the 59th Air Regiment had shot down two Spitfires, and caused another to belly-land back at base with some damage. In reply, the Spitfires had claimed hits on seven enemy fighters, five of them 'confirmed' as destroyed, three of which were corroborated by gun-film footage. Mawer's victim, with its snapped-off wing, cine-film confirmation, and observed crash into the sea, was the most conclusive. Laundy's victim's smoke was corroborated by witnesses, Colyer's gun strikes were confirmed by cine-film, as was Smithson's victim's undercarriage-drop. However, none of these damaged fighters were seen to actually crash. Walters's claim was supported only by weak circumstantial evidence, while Caldwell's claim lacked corroboration from third-party witnesses. Japanese records apparently attest to one fighter pilot fatality only, that of Lieutenant Kawata Shigeto, but as will be seen, there is little reason for confidence in the reliability of the army's account of this action. According to an ex-75th Air Regiment prisoner of war whose name was recorded as Mizuno (and whose testimony has otherwise been shown to be reliable), three to four Ki-43s were shot down, while another suffered engine failure on the way to the target and went into the sea. The Japanese pilots returned home to claim 15 Spitfires shot down – they had chalked up the Spitfires' downward full-throttle breaks as proof of 'confirmed destroyed'.

The 59th Regiment's pilots had certainly shown themselves to be skilful dogfighters, but they had got carried away 'piling up kills' rather than in fulfilling their assigned role as bomber escorts. They had permitted the Spitfires to make 33 firing passes on the bombers – an unprecedented firing opportunity for the defenders. The result was mayhem within the bomber formation, but to their credit, the men of the 61st Regiment had held on, closed up their ranks, and gone through their bomb run. Nonetheless, they had been very closely attacked indeed, with many aircraft badly hit.

The determination with which the Spitfire pilots had pressed home their attacks on the bombers is shown by the number of Spitfires hit by the rear gunners: one Spitfire was shot down and three others damaged. It was also shown in the effectiveness of the Spitfire gunnery: as was typical, the bombers that were hit hardest had been fired upon from directly astern at close range. The good firing opportunities obtained are evident in the fact that nine pilots claimed to have shot down a bomber. However, none of these claims can be taken at face value, given the more or less simultaneous attacks from different directions and consequent double and triple claiming.

Despite this, it is possible to validate several of these bomber claims by isolating them spatially and chronologically: during 54's and 452's attacks, the pilots saw at least one bomber descend burning into the water of Adam Bay from the extreme left-hand vee (attacked by Hughes from 54), one from the centre vee (MacDonald from 452), and at least one from the extreme right-hand vee (Foster and Wheeler from 54 and Bisley and Evans from 452). The latter crashed near Koolpinyah Station, and the bodies of the eight crewmen were recovered by the RAAF and buried. Although the other two cases are not so definitive, having fallen into the sea, separate bombers were observed to successively drop out of formation, from different parts of the formation, with multiple witnesses attesting to their hitting the water. There was also McDowell's kill, much later and far to the west of these others, and corroborated by Maclean and White.

Thus, at least three of the bomber claims are well supported by evidence. In each of these cases, the successful pilots fired long bursts from short range and close astern – ideal gunnery parameters – and therefore the probability of a kill was unusually high. Tony Hughes fired right in to 50 metres from behind, observing his victim to drop out of formation trailing fierce flames, corroborated by Foster, Wheeler, Huggard and Lambert – all of whom saw a bomber drop away from Hughes's attack and go down burning, and two of them saw it hit the sea. Ron MacDonald too made a close-range astern attack, seeing his bomber drop away burning brightly, to crash in a different location – in Shoal Bay off the mouth of the Howard River. This was his fourth firing pass, having followed a re-climb and repositioning, and thus this crash was later and further westward than the other two, corroborated by Huggard, Bisley, Mawer and Evans. The third case is the machine on the right, which may have been attacked by four separate pilots from both 54 and 452, including by John Bisley, who made the final close-range attack from astern. This bomber fell away burning from the right-hand vee, on the opposite side from Hughes's victim. Downes closely observed a burning bomber descend from that end of the formation after Bisley's attack to crash on land, and therefore Bisley's claim over the Koolpinyah wreck seems established – although it is probable that some combination of Foster, Wheeler and Evans had also contributed to this kill. No. 452 Squadron nonetheless claimed the kill as all its own, and removed the aircraft's mangled tail to Strauss as a grisly trophy of its victory.

Thus there are corroborated accounts of three quite separate bomber crashes. These three kills can be clearly distinguished from one another, eliminating the possibility of conflation. Bisley, an experienced fighter pilot and combat veteran, saw three separate bombers hit the water, as did MacDonald, so it cannot all have been the one bomber. On the basis outlined above, it can be concluded that three Ki-49s went down under attack from 54 and 452. Moreover, there was strong physical evidence of one of the two watery crashes: after the raid, during the air searches for the missing Spitfire pilots, one of 6 CU's Walrus amphibians found the oil slick of a Japanese bomber in Adam Bay, at 330 degrees and 3 miles from Point Stephens. The crew landed in the field of floating debris and picked up two Japanese Mae West life preservers and other pieces of floating wreckage – proof of the destruction of a bomber. Hughes had counted 18–19 bombers before his attack, but after 54's and 452's attacks,

Watson counted only 15, which accords with the three-bomber loss assessment made above. After 457's attack, Bisley counted only 13 bombers left, while Horkin and Walters counted only 12 when they were even further out to sea.

Japanese records show that two Ki-49s were shot down, with one other forced landing on a beach on the southern shore of Timor, while Japanese official war history records *at least* two bombers shot down with the loss of all aboard. According to this account, the aircraft of one of the squadron commanders, Lieutenant Ohta Katsuhiro, was hit and set afire at the start of the engagement. It was recorded that both his aircraft and that of Lieutenant Matsuhara were hit over the target and that in the best Japanese officer tradition both of the doomed aircraft made kamikaze attacks upon AA gun positions. Once the vainglorious rhetoric about the suicide attacks is set aside, this account proves that *at least* two bombers are admitted as shot down over the target, in addition to the one that crash-landed afterwards on Timor. Moreover, the account's details also clearly imply that the bomber losses totalled more than just the aircraft of these two prominent officers mentioned by name. Indeed, the squadron commander's aircraft is said to be 'amongst the first' to be hit and set aflame, implying several losses. A loss assessment of at least three bombers is therefore fully supported by the Japanese official war history.

In contrast to the strong evidence of losses from the high-level bomber formation, there was little evidence to support claims against the low-level raiders. Leonard optimistically claimed one of these shot down, and had it 'confirmed' by 54's intelligence officer, Pilot Officer CD 'Jimmy' Councer – in spite of the fact that every witness agreed that all nine bombers had remained airborne and in formation. Flying Officer Quinn, the wing's intelligence officer, did not downgrade this claim to 'damaged' as would be appropriate on the evidence, suggesting that the wing's intelligence community had permitted wishful thinking to outweigh objective evaluation. Despite this discrepancy, it seems that Leonard and Newton had in fact got some good hits after all, for Japanese records are quoted as indicating that three of the 75th Air Regiment's Ki-48s crash-landed before making their base. The earlier-quoted prisoner of war from the 75th Air Regiment attested that one bomber crash-landed at Lautem airfield, having flown back on one engine; the undercarriage would not extend because of damage from the 'intense AA' over the target, so the pilot had belly-landed his aircraft. Thus the 75th wrecked a third of its aircraft on its hands as a result of the raid, and had been very lucky to escape severe personnel loss.

None of the unit war diaries for the three Japanese army units survived the war, so the usually quoted loss figures stem from incomplete records – which must cast doubt on their authoritativeness. Moreover, Lex McAulay has shown in his studies of the SWPA air war that there were often major inconsistencies and understatements in Japanese army loss reports from this period. Until detailed research into such records is undertaken, and the results published in accessible form, the question of Japanese losses on 20 June cannot be settled conclusively. Until then, an assessment of the evidence suggests that on this day, the 61st Air Regiment lost three crews and four aircraft, the 75th Air Regiment wrote off one to three airframes, and the 59th Air Regiment lost a minimum of two aircraft and one pilot. It had certainly not been the 'milk run' that the 7th Air Division had expected, or that the usually quoted Japanese loss figures suggest. Such relatively favourable combat results for 1 Fighter Wing reflect the outstanding success of the Spitfires in obtaining 33 firing passes upon the bombers. This can be compared with the previous Darwin raids on 15 March and 2 May, when the entire wing had achieved only five gunnery passes on the bombers each time.

The 22 June fighter sweep

The Imperial Army's air offensive was resumed two days later, when radar picked up two large plots, suggesting a bomber force and fighter force proceeding separately for an underway rendezvous – the normal Japanese practice. All three Spitfire squadrons were scrambled at 9.54 am and climbed northward in expectation of a repeat performance of 20 June. For the first time, control deliberately split the wing: Bill Gibbs was appointed wing leader and ordered to rendezvous 54 and 457 over Sattler, and then to climb for height to block the high-level raid; while at the same time, control vectored 452 independently, sending it north to Darwin, where it orbited overhead at 5000 feet on the lookout for a repeat low-level raid. By 10.25, half an hour after take-off, Gibbs's wing was overhead Batchelor climbing through 27 000 feet, but still too low to engage – the slow multi-squadron climbs continued to dog the wing's tactical performance. It was not until the Spitfires finally reached the safe height of 30 000 feet that control vectored them north towards the raid.

By then it was too late. In fact the Japanese had only sent a fighter sweep; and unencumbered by bombers, the Hayabusas of the 59th Air Regiment moved fast, tracked by radar cruising at 225 knots. They described an arc right around Darwin, approaching from the north-west, circling around to the east, and then heading back out to the north over Bathurst Island. Darwin's AA gunners tracked the squadron of enemy fighters as it circumnavigated Darwin at about 30 000 feet, but they stayed just far enough away to keep out of gun range. When the radar plot skirted Darwin, control had interpreted this to mean that the 'raid' was coming south to bomb the airfields, and had positioned the wing over Batchelor to block this. The result was that once the Japanese reversed course and flew away northward on the far side of Darwin, the planned interception was ruined. Still unsure of Japanese moves, and now informed by AA that the existing plot was composed only of harmless fighters, control kept the wing orbiting over Hughes in case there was a follow-up bombing attack. There was none, except for a couple of Ki-46 reccos that once again exploited the tracking confusion to break away from the fighter formation and get their photos. They remained unplotted by radar until they were safely on their way out.

As the enemy fighters retired offshore, control belatedly moved the wing forward to orbit over Point Charles and await developments there. Still suspicious of a follow-up Japanese raid, control then ordered one squadron at a time to land for refuelling, in order to avoid the disastrous situation of meeting a sudden 'sneak attack' with all fighters on the ground. Eventually, however, it was realised that nothing else was going to happen, and so the last squadron was ordered to land, thus ending a very inconclusive operation. RAF doctrine held that enemy fighters could safely be ignored, and control had held everything back in expectation of the second-phase bomber strike that never came.

So ended the short-lived confrontation between the Imperial Army Air Force and 1 Fighter Wing. After this, the Imperial Navy would resume control over the campaign while the 7th Air Division decamped for New Guinea, transferred there as part of the 4th Air Army – the Imperial Army's major reinforcement of that theatre of operations. The move was ill-fated, for the 59th Regiment would be destroyed by attacks upon its base by the US 5th Air Force. The Americans did to the Japanese Army Air Force exactly what the combined Japanese air services had been utterly unable to do to the RAAF at Darwin – to grind its air units into the ground by sustained large-scale raids upon air bases.

20 June pilot table

Sqn	Section	No.	Pilot engaging	Pilots not engaging	Remarks
Wing Co		1	W/C Caldwell		R/T failed, joined on behind 457; both cannons failed
54	Red	1		S/L Gibbs RAF	CSU failure, aborted
		2	G/C Walters		underperforming engine, dropped out, attacked alone
	Blue	1	F/L Foster RAF		both cannons failed
				P/O Garden RAF	initially Blue 2, CSU failure, aborted
		2	F/Sgt Wheeler RAF		initially Red 3; BR484 hit by bomber return fire, 2 rounds 7.7 mm in fuselage, serviceable
				F/Sgt Wickman RAF	initially Blue 3, glycol leak, aborted
		3	F/Sgt Huggard RAF		initially Blue 4
		4	Sgt Lambert RAF		initially Red 5
	White	1	F/O Tuckson RAF		underperforming engine, dropped out
		2	Sgt Holmes RAF		
		3	F/O Leonard RAF		1 cannon failed
		4	P/O Appleton RAF		both cannons failed

	Black	1	F/O Hughes RAF	JG795 hit by bomber return fire, engine stopped, force-landed Lee Point, repaired by 14 ARD
		2	F/Sgt Ashurst RAF	
		3	F/Sgt Horkin RAF	
		4	Sgt Laundy RAF	initially Red 4, CSU failure, aborted, rejoined
452	Red	1	S/L MacDonald	CSU failure; BR574 hit by bomber return fire in wings, fuselage, & fuel tank; repaired on unit
		2	F/L Evans	hit by fighter gunfire in elevator trim tab, BR240 repaired on unit
		3	F/O Downes	both cannons failed
		4	F/O Whillans	both cannons failed
	Blue	1	F/O Bisley	both cannons failed
		2	F/Sgt Ruskin-Rowe	shot down & killed; BS174 QY-W destroyed
		3	F/O Mawer	BR548 QY-M hit by 1 round fighter gunfire through cockpit; belly-landed at base; repaired by 7 RSU, returned to service 4 September
		4	Sgt Richardson	
		5	F/O Colyer	
		6	F/Sgt Cross	scrambled late, joined 457, both cannons failed

	White	1		F/L Hall	underperforming engine, dropped out
		2	P/O Tully		both cannons failed
		3	F/O K Fox		
		4	F/O Williams		both cannons failed
		5	F/O Lloyd		CSU failure
		6	Sgt Nichterlein		shot down & killed; EE607 QY-A lost
	Yellow	1		F/O Watkin	base patrol
457	Red	1	F/L P Watson		both cannons failed
		2	F/Sgt Batchelor		both cannons failed
		3	F/L Newton		hit by bomber return fire, 1 round 7.7 mm in fuselage, aircraft serviceable (serial unknown)
		4	P/O McDowell		CSU failure
		5		F/O Gregory	CSU failure, aborted
	White	1	F/O Edwards		
		2	W/O Briggs		
		3	F/O Smithson		
		4	F/O Halse		
	Blue	1		F/L Maclean	Blue Section detached to intercept spurious low-level contact, section failed to engage
		2		F/Sgt White	
		3		F/O Hamilton	oxygen failure, aborted
		4		F/Sgt R Watson	
	Yellow			P/O Reilly	low-level early warning patrol Gunn Point
		37		11	

Summary:
Spitfires airborne: 48
Spitfires in main wing formation: 46
Mechanical aborts: 6
Spitfires engaged: 37
Spitfires shot down: 3
Spitfires damaged: 5
Pilots killed: 2

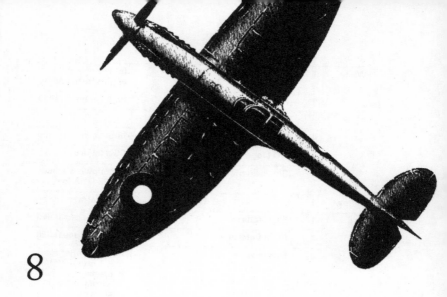

8

A missed opportunity

While the Japanese army airmen packed up for their ill-fated move to New Guinea, the Imperial Navy resumed its responsibility for the offensive against Darwin. However, 753 Air Group was still overcommitted elsewhere and was thus able to provide only a single squadron of bombers for the next raid, rather than the normal three-squadron group. Nonetheless, the escorting fighter force would be very strong – 27 Zeros from 1 Fighter Wing's old opponents, 202 Air Group. Despite 5 Fighter Sector's ongoing worry about further low-level attacks, the 23rd Air Flotilla returned to its usual tactics: it would be sending another high-level raiding force in from the north-west. Indeed, this was the only tactic the navy knew, determined by the characteristics of the only long-range strike aircraft in its inventory: the Mitsubishi G4M. This aircraft type was used as a 'jack-of-all-trades' by the Imperial Navy's land-based units, fulfilling a range of roles that in Allied air forces were performed by a diverse array of types. Japanese naval commanders had been shocked by how vulnerable their prized G4M strike force was in low-level attacks, as proven by some distressing losses against the Americans in 1942. Their Darwin raiding strategy required the minimisation of losses, and this could only be achieved if the G4Ms came in at extreme altitude surrounded by fighters.

On 26 June, signs of a repeat raid came via the RAAF's monitoring of Japanese signals traffic. That evening the Spitfire squadrons were warned that there had been a reconcentration of aircraft upon Timor airfields, and were ordered to be at early readiness the next day. That morning produced unusual overcast conditions for the season, which the Japanese weather reconnaissance sortie noted in time to postpone the raid. However, good weather prevailed the day after, and an inbound raid was detected 240 kilometres north-west of Darwin at 10.23 am on the 28th. It was 45 minutes' flight time away, tracking further east than normal, to come in over Cape Fourcroy on the south-west tip of Bathurst Island. Darwin Raid No. 56 was on its way.

The 28 June raid

Control scrambled all three squadrons, and 42 Spitfires got airborne, ordered to rendezvous over Sattler airfield and then to climb to 30 000 feet. Sattler was a newly instituted rendezvous point, 16 kilometres closer to Darwin than the previous one at Hughes, the change having been made in response to complaints about 54's waste of time and petrol in going so far south to join up with the others. The new rendezvous location was an improvement, but it shows that big wing tactics still held sway,

Pilots at 452 Squadron's 'B' Flight dispersals, waiting for something to happen. Left to right: F/O Kenny Bassett, F/L Paul Makin ('B' Flight commander) and F/O John Bisley DFC.
AWM Negative NWA0254

and this would continue to slow down the wing's advance to battle. It is clear that the successful squadron attacks of 20 June were a mere aberration forced upon the wing by circumstances, rather than the starting point for a new, more flexible and more effective interception tactic.

Caldwell himself was delayed in taking off, so control ordered 54's CO, Squadron Leader Bill Gibbs, to take over the wing. The three squadrons made a 'perfect rendezvous' over Sattler and were then vectored north to Cape Gambier, on the south-west tip of Melville Island. Gibbs got to the Cape at 22 500 feet, still climbing, before control turned the wing about and vectored it back south towards the bombers, which were coming in towards Darwin from the north-west, crossing the Spitfires' flight path from right to left. No. 452 had been late to the rendezvous and so was lagging behind at only 17 000 feet – much lower than the others.

Soon after the turn to the south, 452 suffered a mechanical casualty while climbing through 18 000 feet. After the sustained high boost and revs in trying to close the gap on the other squadrons, Flying Officer Gerald Cowell's engine developed an internal glycol leak. Having burst a gasket, the glycol forced its way into the combustion chambers in the right-hand bank of cylinders and white smoke started streaming out of the exhausts on that side. Cowell reported over the R/T that he was aborting and then pulled out of formation. He cut the engine's magneto switches, turned off the petrol cock, and trimmed his aircraft for a dead-stick glide approach to a forced landing. He landed wheels-up on the beach between Gunn Point and Tree Point, on the coast of Shoal Bay to the north of Darwin. Following SAR procedure, he waited by his aircraft, watching it get swamped by the incoming tide before a boat arrived to fetch him at 5 pm. No. 7 RSU dispatched an expedition to recover the aircraft, but EE608 was written off because of water damage and salvaged for spares. Cowell had only 316 hours in his logbook, 158 of those on Spitfires, despite having been with the squadron for a year – showing once again how brief had been the training for many of 1 Fighter Wing's pilots, and how scanty their operational experience since joining a squadron. No. 54 also suffered an early mechanical incident: Flight Sergeant Joh Kelman, Gibbs's wingman, aborted at the rendezvous because of engine trouble.

Prior to the wing's turnaround to head south, Caldwell had chased it, accompanied by his new wingman, 457's Pilot Officer Darky McDowell. Group Captain Walters, his erstwhile No. 2 and Commanding Officer, had been posted out to command No. 5 Service Flying Training School on 24 June (hardly a plum posting), and Caldwell had taken over as Acting CO. Once the wing turned about, Caldwell was able to cut the corner and join on, taking over from Gibbs as wing leader. He took Winco Section ahead of 54 in the centre, making himself visible in front of the three squadrons. From here, 54 was commanded by Gibbs, 452 by Ron MacDonald, and 457 by its 'B' Flight commander, Flight Lieutenant Don Maclean (whose CO, Squadron Leader Ken James, was on leave 'down south').

The wing's turnabout overhead Cape Gambier from a course of 350 degrees to 170 degrees had been done by wheeling each squadron left. As the three squadrons came out of the turn and headed back south, 54 was in the middle and at the highest altitude of the three; 457 was on the right, closest to the enemy but lower; while 452 was the furthest away, out to the left, and moreover considerably lower. These relative positions would affect which squadron would ultimately get to contact the enemy, and which would not. Soon after the turn, while 54 was climbing past 27 000 feet, control advised that the enemy bore at 2 o'clock at 30 kilometres, and that they were 3000 feet higher. Gibbs looked along that bearing and spotted them from 25 kilometres away – just a few glinting spots in the distance.

The enemy fighters were at 30 000 feet while the bombers were at the impressive height of 27 000. Gibbs reported his sighting and confirmed with Caldwell that he had too. Soon after, the bombers were silhouetted against a low cloud bank and so became easy to see.

A 'vee of vees'

As the Spitfires approached from the north, nine bombers were visible, arranged in a vee of vees, with an escort of nine fighters visible in line abreast, above and slightly ahead. In contrast to their army colleagues on 20 June, the navy fighter pilots were well positioned to block the Spitfires' habitual attacks from the bombers' front quarter. As usual, however, there were additional fighters unsighted by the leaders: 54's Tony Hughes saw another seven Zeros in two groups, above and behind at two different heights, while Bob Foster saw only five or six fighters above the bombers. This inconsistency in observed enemy strength was evident throughout the 1943 raids; the product of the Imperial Navy's dispersed deployment of its escorting fighters. The fact that three experienced pilots each saw different numbers and positions for the escorts suggests that no one had seen all the fighters that were there. This puts into context the apparent ability of the Japanese in previous raids to appear 'out of nowhere' and bounce the Spitfires.

Tactical disagreements

As the two forces drew closer together and as the wing continued its climb, Gibbs saw that his squadron now had superior height, with a position far enough forward on the enemy's line of advance to make an attack against their port beam. Of the three squadrons, 54 was in the best position, being at the head of the wing and highest. Although the other squadrons were not yet high enough, Gibbs wanted to exploit his own squadron's superior position by launching an immediate attack, and accordingly requested permission to turn right to do so. Caldwell declined, as he wished to get the wing more height before attacking and to attack with all three squadrons together.

Gibbs was in some respects the most senior airman present: he was a prewar officer, was of a mature age like Caldwell, and was more experienced in NWA combat than either of the other squadron COs. He had shown himself to be a quick learner, had rapidly established his personal proficiency as a fighter pilot, and because of his previous Coastal Command experience had more flying experience in total than any of the others. If Gibbs judged that he had the height and angle to make an attack, then it is very likely that he had. Caldwell could have permitted 54 to peel off and make its attack as Gibbs requested, while waiting a little longer to get the other two squadrons into position. This would have produced a tactically sound multi-phased attack by dispersing and disordering the escort before the other squadrons attacked. By rejecting this option, Caldwell would once again sacrifice a quick attack with the forces available, in favour of a larger but later attack. This was his consistent pattern throughout the campaign. Thus Gibbs had to sit in his aircraft, chafing with frustration, watching out beyond his right wingtip as the Japanese cruised in their usual perfect formation towards the target. His opportunity passed.

This incident reveals a tactical disagreement between Gibbs and Caldwell that continued throughout the campaign. Flight Lieutenant Ernie Weatherhead, 54 Squadron's adjutant, recalled that the wing debriefs after the combats featured frank and robust discussions of tactical problems. These involved Bladin, Walters, Caldwell, the squadron COs and the controllers – led by Wing Commander Tony Primrose, the chief controller and CO of 5 Fighter Sector. The 'heated' exchanges that were reported show that there were serious disagreements over the conduct of the interceptions. In the absence of meeting minutes, an exact reconstruction of the issues under debate is impossible. However, it is certain that one of the issues was the big wing tactic and its slow climbs, late attacks and clumsy centralised control. Bill Gibbs disagreed with this tactical policy, as shown by his complaints about Caldwell's micro-management on 2 May, his decision for an early climb without a wing rendezvous on 20 June and his request for an early attack on 28 June. He was the only squadron CO with enough seniority and clout to challenge Caldwell, and there was moreover some history of antipathy between the two men, as shown by Caldwell's readiness to blame Gibbs personally for the alleged failings of his squadron on 15 March and 2 May: indeed, Caldwell later recalled that he had threatened to court-martial Gibbs if he 'disobeyed' another 'lawful command' in the air. Moreover, it was not just Gibbs who chafed under the big wing doctrine, for after the 2 May disaster, Air Commodore Bladin had shown his frustration with it by advocating more decision-making autonomy for squadron leaders.

Tony Primrose and his successor, Squadron Leader Colin Woodman, evidently supported big wing tactics, judging by 5 Fighter Sector's demonstrated preference for single-formation interceptions by all three squadrons together: from their perspective in the sector ops room, the fewer the plots on the board, the simpler and more reliable the interception. The American fighter controllers of the previous year had merely provided running commentaries of the enemy's position over the R/T, permitting the flight leaders to manoeuvre as they saw fit to achieve an interception. By contrast, RAF fighter controllers imposed close control over the airborne fighters through the provision of precise steering and climb-to-height instructions. This doctrine of centralised control lent itself more easily to Caldwell's big wing approach, so it seems that the debate placed Caldwell and the controllers on one side, and Gibbs and Bladin on the other. The remaining officers – Ken James, Ron MacDonald and Wally Walters – were either so junior in their roles or so low in fighter experience as to be receptive to Caldwell's immense prestige as a great air ace, and so he was able to secure the leadership team's adherence to the big wing.

On this day, Caldwell's strong insistence upon a wing climb and his rejection of Gibbs's suggestion for an early attack meant that the wing failed to achieve an interception before the bombers hit their target. This was unsatisfactory, given that the Cape Fourcroy radar had given the wing a more-than-adequate 45 minutes' warning in which to get to height and make its attack. The squadron take-offs had been efficiently done, with all aircraft airborne inside five minutes of the scramble alarm, and the wing rendezvous was described as 'perfect'. Nonetheless it was only late during their southward vector that the Spitfires achieved bare height superiority over the raiders. With no other source of delay, the reason for the reversion to slow climbing and consequent late interception must be found in Caldwell's insistence upon a full wing climb and a full wing attack.

The missed interception

As the bombers ran in to the target, the Spitfires were only slowly converging from their enemy's left on almost a parallel course. Caldwell was trying to obtain a position forward on the bombers' bow, setting his men up for head-on firing runs against them straight after the bomb run. Meanwhile, the Japanese bombed unmolested except for the usual AA bursts, watched by the huge gaggle of Spitfires shadowing them out past their port wingtips.

The bombers dropped about 40 bombs in a long north–south swath through the outskirts of Darwin, but achieved minimal results. Nine 60 kg and two 250 kg bombs fell into the army camp area behind the East Point 9.2 inch (233 mm) gun battery (destroying a storeroom), while nine other bombs dropped short into the sea. The line of bomb bursts then continued south-east, scattered waywardly across the area inland from the coast: four 60 kg 'daisy-cutters' fell in the Public Works Department camp, while thirteen 60 kg and three 250 kg bombs landed long, bursting on the mudflats south of Vestey's camp. Damage in the camp areas was light: six huts were destroyed, three huts and one truck were damaged, and powerlines were broken; there were no human casualties. The intended target was unclear: despite its use as a barracks and AA ammunition store, the defunct Vestey's meatworks was nonetheless an odd choice of target for a Japanese force that was aiming to suppress Allied air activity against Timor. The same was true of the East Point gun battery – the army anti-ship guns would have made good targets had the Japanese been softening Darwin up for an amphibious landing, but they certainly were not. In spite of their superior photo-reconnaissance capability, such poor use of intelligence was often a feature of the Japanese raids. As on 15 March, some of the Zeros detached themselves from the escort and came in low to strafe targets along the waterfront, also with very little effect.

The wasted bombs on the 28 June raid show that the Japanese were more committed to preserving their bomber fleet than they were to doing real damage to their targets. Their tactic of seeking the relative safety of extreme altitude contrasts strongly with German practice in the comparable Malta raids of 1942. The objectives in both these Axis bombing campaigns were similar, namely to neutralise a base area by smashing its port and airfield facilities. In pursuit of this goal, Sicily-based German bomber units had pressed their attacks to low altitudes well below 10 000 feet, abandoning the relative safety of formation to dive their Ju88s individually through Malta's formidable AA defence. This low-level diving approach enabled them to place their bombs accurately across airfield dispersal areas and runways, thus doing real damage to the defending fighter force. In so doing, the Luftwaffe had to hazard its poorly armed bombers to both AA fire and opportunistic fighter attack, and took losses as a result. Lacking the Luftwaffe's relative logistical depth, the Imperial Navy by contrast prioritised the preservation of its finite force of bombers over fundamental tactical considerations like bombing effectiveness.

Darwin's AA batteries fired a total of 115 rounds at the enemy as the bombers went past overhead in their usual perfect formation. The guns did not hit anything, but they had once again spoiled the bombing by keeping the bombers at extreme altitude. After the enemy completed their bomb run, Caldwell finally ordered the much-anticipated right turn, to bring the Spitfire wing onto a south-south-west course to cut the bombers off. He gave orders for 457 to go for the fighters while 452 went after the bombers; 54 was to go in last, as a second-wave assault upon the bombers. This tactical deployment is surprising, considering that these dispositions no longer corresponded with the actual positions of the three squadrons, relative either to one another or to the enemy. Once they turned right to close with the enemy, the Spitfire squadrons were now arranged into a rough echelon, with 457 in the front, closest to the bombers, then 54, and finally 452. As the latter squadron was furthest away from the bombers, and lowest, it was simply too far away to lead the attack on them as ordered. Caldwell thus forced the two squadrons that were relatively well positioned to wait for the most poorly positioned to get into its predetermined place – just like on 2 May.

To make matters worse, this plan of attack was thrown into disarray when the bombers made a right turn straight after their bombing run. The Japanese squadron commander could see what was going to happen ahead and had pre-empted the fighter attack by ordering an immediate turn. His formation wheeled about onto a westerly heading, and the bombers put their noses down, advanced their throttles, and retired from the scene at a good speed – the big Mitsubishis had gone into their bomb run at 190 knots IAS, and now they accelerated away at 220 knots in a shallow dive. Having turned away so neatly, the Japanese not only dodged the interception, but placed the Spitfires into an awkward stern chase situation. Confronted by the bombers' untimely evasion, Caldwell turned the wing further right, onto a course of about 300 degrees, and gave chase. This was the second occasion (the first was on 2 May) on which the bombers' customary right turn after bombing threw out Caldwell's positioning of his wing for the interception.

However, just as the wing set off in pursuit, four fighters were reported half a mile away on 54's starboard rear quarter – above and in the sun, clearly getting into position to make an attack. At once Caldwell turned about to the right to deal with them, ordering 54 to follow. He wheeled around straight into a head-on attack against the partly sun-obscured oncoming shapes, and was just about to open fire when McDowell belatedly recognised the 'enemy' as Spitfires. Recognising their silhouettes, McDowell gave a warning on the R/T, thus narrowly averting a friendly-fire incident. The offending Spitfires were probably Tony Hughes's White Section from 54, as is shown by what happened to the same squadron's Flight Sergeant Huggard: with his engine losing oil pressure and failing to deliver its power, he had earlier dropped out of 54's formation, throttled back and levelled off. Once the engine had been given a chance to cool down and the instrument readings returned to normal, Hughes had come past him with White Section in tow, so Huggard had joined on. Evidently, Hughes's section had been unable to keep up with the rest of the squadron, had lagged behind, cut the corner, and been mistaken for Zeros.

This untimely excursion threw the Balbo into further disarray: 457 was now at the front of the column, then there was an empty interval left by the detoured 54, then there was 452 flying at a lower level and finally 54 even further behind and off to the right. Caldwell's attack plan was now irrevocably spoiled, for even the two Australian squadrons were now quite unable to coordinate their attacks. No. 452 was supposed to wait for 457 to attack the fighter escort and then to pounce upon the bombers. However, MacDonald found that as a consequence of his squadron's poor starting position, he was now 25 kilometres behind the bombers. He nonetheless led 452 to the north of the enemy track to try to cut them off once they made their turn onto a north-west heading for home. Following 457, he saw the latter making its attack in the far distance. Many of the aircraft in MacDonald's formation had worn engines that would not deliver their full power, and during the chase these machines now started dropping out of formation and lagging behind. MacDonald had to throttle back to let these laggards catch up, but then his own aircraft suffered an R/T failure, which forced him to hand over command to Flight Lieutenant Paul Makin. The squadron failed to overhaul the diving bombers, and finally Makin made an assessment of the squadron's fuel state and decided to return to base. Throughout 452's abortive chase, a lone Zero had shadowed them, flying alongside at 31 000 feet. It may have been using R/T to report the Spitfires' progress to its leader; and once it became clear that the Spitfires were no threat, it headed off to rejoin its colleagues.

Caldwell meanwhile, having lost visual contact with the bombers because of the excursion after the errant Spitfires, called for vectors from control and for enemy position reports. Following these leads, Caldwell led 54 off to the north-west, in expectation that the enemy would soon turn right to head for home. However, the Japanese kept extending to the west, and so 54's course diverged both from the enemy and from 457. Caldwell led the British squadron further and further out beyond the bombers' starboard flank, unwittingly opening the distance to the bombers. By the time Bill Gibbs finally reacquired the enemy aircraft, they were at his 8 o'clock – almost directly behind him – and 50 kilometres away! All he saw were some pinpricks of light – perspex glinting in the sun. For Caldwell and 54 Squadron, the interception geometry was now utterly ruined.

The British squadron had meanwhile been reduced to just seven aircraft because of mechanical failures and communication failures. When the squadron dived after Caldwell in pursuit of the retreating bombers, Bob Foster's aircraft had suffered a propeller CSU failure, with the usual overrevving engine. He broke sharply out of formation into a diving turn, so abruptly that he did not even make a radio transmission. His wingmen, Sergeant Laundy and Flight Sergeant Wheeler, saw their leader's violent breakaway and thought they were being bounced, so they broke away too and went down after him. Upon descending to

20 000 feet they discovered it had been a false alarm – faced with his overrevving engine, Foster had been so anxious about the possibility of a catastrophic glycol leak that he had headed for the coastline with some urgency. But his failure to use the R/T had unintentionally misled his section and removed it from the engagement. Once they had sorted things out over the R/T, Foster continued on home, leaving Laundy and Wheeler to re-climb, each by themselves, blindly following R/T reports of the enemy going out to sea. They failed to see anything so went home too. Still dealing with a recalcitrant engine, abandoned by the others, and prompted by his fuel gauge, Flight Sergeant Huggard also abandoned the pursuit.

Having finally reacquired the enemy, the now-reduced 54 Squadron group turned about onto a converging west-south-west course, but the enemy in the far distance disappeared once again from view, lost in the haze. Caldwell requested another bearing from control, was advised that the raiders had turned north-west, and so now turned right to give chase. No. 54 droned further out to sea, finally giving up when 80 kilometres north-west of Cape Fourcroy.

457's attack

While 54 and 452 were losing their way, Don Maclean led 457 in pursuit of the enemy, staying in visual contact with them, completing the climb and overhauling them gradually. By the time the bombers were 20 kilometres west of Point Charles, the whole squadron was able to carry out an attack on the enemy raiders – the only squadron to do so. The bombers were then at 23 000 feet, with only three escorting fighters visible at 29 000 feet, 1 kilometre behind them and to starboard. No. 457 was higher still at 31 000 feet, hidden up sun above the bombers' starboard flank.

However, Flight Lieutenant Jack Newton's Blue Section was badly strung out, with three pilots falling behind with underperforming engines – Pilot Officers Bruce Little and Bob 'Gig' Cunningham, and Sergeant Alex MacPherson. Bill Reilly then reported that he also could no longer keep up, but Newton just pressed on alone, holding position beside Red Section while his men limped along behind him in a ragged string. The Blue leader de-emphasised the need for section integrity, intent above all else upon keeping up with Maclean and attacking the enemy.

Maclean's Red Section was in much better shape, with three aircraft up alongside one another, and only Maclean's No. 2, Flying Officer Tony Brook, lagging behind. Brook was a British pilot recently transferred to the Australian squadron from 54 in order to 'make up the numbers'. He was wrestling with a recalcitrant belly-tank release mechanism, but once the tank finally fell free, could keep up again and start closing the gap.

Don Maclean led Red Section down into a steep left turn. As he dived he saw that Newton was well up beside him, and thus 457 went down in a ragged five-aircraft line abreast. When Maclean got within 3 kilometres of the bombers, he saw that the three Zeros had still not seen the attack, and they made such a tempting target that he swung out to starboard to bounce them instead of attacking the bombers. Red Section followed after Maclean, turning sharply through an S-turn and then diving rapidly from out of the sun upon the Zeros' starboard rear quarter. Thus the four pilots of Red Section plus Newton came down behind these Zeros, arriving so close together that they all fired more or less simultaneously from different levels and angles. Maclean's and Newton's decision to gang up on the fighters meant that nine Spitfires were attacking three Zeros – a gross overkill – while leaving the bombers to White Section only. As Brook dived into the attack behind Maclean, he spotted an additional six Zeros out in front of the bombers, in addition to the three that Maclean and Newton were attacking. By then it was too late to do anything about it.

At the head of the diving Spitfires, Maclean opened fire upon the Zeros while they were still flying straight and level. One of his cannons froze, but Maclean kept his finger on the firing button, seeing cannon strikes on the starboard side of the right-hand Zero. Continuing his turn to the left, he moved his gunsight over the centre Zero, still firing, and then sprayed the left-hand one as well before ceasing fire at 100 metres. Although he saw cannon strikes on the left-hand Zero, it then stood on its tail and went straight up, evidently still full of fight. Maclean saw the danger and broke downwards, dived away to regain speed, then pulled up into a climbing turn to look behind. As he zoomed back up, he saw that one Zero was already going down in flames.

Jack Newton dived in to attack almost simultaneously with Maclean. He saw Maclean fire, and then fired a deflection shot from the starboard quarter at the centre Zero. Ceasing fire, his aircraft bumped violently as he flew through the Zero's slipstream and then he broke left into a diving turn. There was a bright white flash and an ear-piercing explosion; his aircraft shook – one of the Zeros, alerted by Maclean's firing pass only seconds earlier, had looped back upon its attackers and was already firing at him from astern. Newton bunted violently out of its gunsight and, after rolling through a series of diving turns, looked around to see that he had shaken off the Zero – but he also noticed the big cannon hole in his wing. Seeing a Spitfire behind him, he turned to join up with it. Too late, he now saw it was a Zero, and it was already inside his turn, about to open fire! Once again he broke downwards, rolling as rapidly as he could from side to side to prevent the Zero from tracking him in its gunsight.

However, the Zero stayed behind him: while Newton was gyrating about, it held its position by flying straight, waiting for him to pull out. He decided to simply outrun it, so stopped manoeuvring, selected 3000 rpm and emergency boost, shoved the nose down and dived for 'the deck'. He did not know how fast he was going as the ASI was not reading – the shell hit in the wing had severed the air line to the Pitot tube. Pulling out low down, he looked behind again to see that he had drawn ahead, but the Zero was still visible behind. Having run out of height, he had little choice but to hold his Spitfire just above the waves, to maintain maximum revs and boost, and to bank on his aircraft's speed superiority. Looking behind, he was relieved to see that he was now drawing away from the persistent Japanese fighter, and at last he headed back to base unaccompanied. Newton's Spitfire, BS543, had been hit in both wings, in the elevator, wing-root, engine cylinder head, propeller and through the wing spar. It was recovered by 7 RSU, repaired, and returned to the squadron on 8 July.

Newton's section had been so strung out and disordered by his haste to get into action that his wingmen were too far behind to defend their leader. However, the pilots of Red Section were well up. Tony Brook arrived just after Maclean's and Newton's attacks, in time to see the left and right Zeros peeling off in opposite directions. The middle Zero, the Japanese section leader, continued straight on, unaware of the attack (suggesting that even as late as this, 202 AG was still not equipped with functional radios in all its aircraft), and so Brook lined up on this one. He fired a long burst from slightly out of range right in to 50 metres, but both his cannons froze, so his attack was made with machine guns only. He missed, for it flew on undisturbed while he broke away to come round again for another attack. This time, the Japanese pilot saw him coming and broke left, but Brook by now had slowed down enough to follow the Zero round in the turn. He fired again but saw no strikes, although the Zero starting streaming heavy grey smoke. Brook broke away downwards to clear his tail, then zoomed back up into a climbing turn. Now he saw a Zero diving away steeply, belching thick black smoke; and believing it was his own victim, he claimed it as destroyed, although it could just as easily have been Maclean's or Newton's – all three pilots had fired almost simultaneously. Looking up to check the position of the other six Zeros he had seen earlier, Brook could no longer see them – they were already on their way down.

The second element of Red Section, Flying Officers Tommy Clark and Bill Halse, followed so closely behind that they got hits on the same Zeros. Thus every pilot in Red Section, plus Newton from Blue Section, had claimed a hit on one of the three enemy fighters. Clark and Halse saw two of the Zeros go down in flames, so Halse shared one 'kill' with Maclean, while Newton shared the other one with Clark. It is not clear how Brook's kill fitted in with these claims.

Bill Reilly had gone into the fight trying to keep up with his No. 1, Newton, following about 200 metres behind as his leader turned hard to go after the Zeros. As Reilly approached the fight, close behind Maclean's and Newton's attack, he saw one Zero pull up, smoking heavily, then it rolled off the top and went down vertically.

Abandoned by their leader, two men from Newton's disordered section managed to stay together as they lagged behind, trying to stay in visual contact with the others up ahead. Gig Cunningham had throttled back to stay with Alex MacPherson and his underperforming engine, but as soon as the attack started, Cunningham lost sight of Newton and Reilly up ahead: during the turn on to attack heading they simply disappeared in the sun's glare. Having rolled into the dive, Cunningham re-spotted Reilly ahead, and then saw Newton a couple of kilometres further on. Confusingly, both Newton and Reilly then suddenly disappeared again as they turned hard right to attack the Zeros – Cunningham had not seen the enemy fighters, so was not expecting his colleagues' sudden manoeuvres. Unaware of the tactical situation, he decided to attack the bombers, telling MacPherson, 'OK, Blue 4, we'll go in'.

As the pilots of Red Section were manoeuvring to get their shots upon the three Zeros, they had failed to see the other group of six Zeros up above – the forward escort Tony Brook had seen. Maclean and Newton had unwittingly led their men down into an ambush. Bill Reilly at that time was a couple of hundred metres behind, watching Maclean, Newton and Brook making their attacks; just as he approached to join the fight, four Zeros dived across the top of him, coming in from the side, while two more dived in from head-on, approaching over the top of the bombers. At once Reilly broke into a hard turn. A Zero passed 100 metres in front of him and he took a snap deflection shot at it, but he fired too late, and the Zero was gone. Finding himself outnumbered and at a disadvantage, Reilly completed a 180 degree turn and dived away towards base at maximum boost and revs. Even further behind the others, Pilot Officer Bruce Little saw the bounce happen up ahead, broke away and dived to safety.

The sighting was too late for Tommy Clark; the first he knew of it was when his aircraft was hit by both cannon and machine-gun fire, including a 20 mm round that exploded against his tailplane. Then the attacking Zero passed so closely under him with such a thunderclap of sound that he thought they had collided. He shoved the stick forward into an evasive bunt but overdid it, pushing the stick so violently that he 'redded-out' from the negative G and lost control; his aircraft fell into an inverted spin. Clark could not get it out of the spin so tried to bail out. He pulled on the canopy release but it did not budge.

Forced to stay with the gyrating and plunging aircraft, Clark refocused on his spin recovery and pulled out at only 2000 feet. The difference between survival and extinction had been a matter of a few seconds, given the precipitate rate of descent that a spin generated. Clark was truly terrorised by the whole experience – by the bounce, the cannon hit, the sudden appearance of the Zero, the apparent collision, the uncontrolled bunt, the red-out, the inverted spin, being trapped in the doomed aircraft and the last-second recovery from disaster with the ground rushing up. He headed back to base in a trembling daze.

Unlike Clark, Bill Halse saw the Zeros coming in time and broke violently downwards at once. However, the sudden dive caused an immediate propeller CSU failure and engine overspeed; although he pulled back the boost and rpm controls, this failed to clear the fault. Meanwhile, the engine spun itself up to 4000 rpm. Halse cut the switches to prevent it blowing up, but even without the magnetos' sparking, the engine temperatures were now so extreme that the fuel/air mixture in the cylinders combusted spontaneously: it ran at 4000 revs until it seized, fortunately without an explosion. As the propeller suddenly stopped dead in front of him, he just kept going straight down, trying to put distance between his crippled aircraft and the enemy. He glided down and crash-landed in the scrub 30 kilometres north-west of Tumbling Waters on the Cox Peninsula, and was found by the army and fetched back to base by one of 457's vehicles. Spitfire BR462 was so badly knocked about in the belly landing in the scrub that it was written off and salvaged for spare parts – having been fitted with a new engine only four days earlier!

Meanwhile, Cunningham and MacPherson, the dangling rear end of Newton's Blue Section, dived towards the bombers to their left and 5000 feet lower. Suddenly, Cunningham saw a Zero appear out of nowhere ahead of him, turning in a circle, and so decided to bounce it instead. This was one of the second group of Zeros that had just bounced the other Spitfires – but Cunningham had not even seen this happen. Benefiting inadvertently from his belated arrival, he lined up on the Zero and fired an ineffective full deflection shot from long range, but was then able to roll in behind it, firing a second and far more effective burst from dead astern at close range – this Japanese pilot had been caught totally unawares. Flame burst from the side of the fuselage behind the engine and the Zero wobbled, decelerating so rapidly that it 'appeared to stop'. Cunningham was still going fast from his dive, so he overshot and passed right underneath it. As he went past, he saw the Zero roll onto its back and dive away. Cunningham half-rolled and pulled in an attempt to follow it, but he still had his elevator trimmed forward for the dive, having forgotten in his excitement to wind it back for the pull out. This meant that he could not pull his nose around fast enough to dive after the Zero; instead, his aircraft involuntarily bunted in the opposite direction and dived away inverted. Hanging in his seat harness under the negative G, Cunningham hurriedly wound the trim back and recovered to normal flight, but by then the Zero was gone. Finding himself alone, he dived away to return to base, claiming his victim as destroyed.

Despite Cunningham's lucky success, it had not been a good tactical display by Maclean and Newton, and this had somewhat spoiled the effect of 457's patient stalking of the enemy. Given that there had only been three Zeros to attack in the first instance, Newton's Blue Section should have stayed up high to counter the eventuality of further Zeros coming down from above. Instead, Maclean and Newton had put all their eggs in one basket and eight pilots had got in each other's way trying to get three Zeros, neglecting their lookout as they did so.

While Maclean's and Newton's sections were bouncing the Zeros, and being bounced by them, Flying Officer Doug

Edwards's White Section had pursued the original aim of the interception by making an attack upon the bombers. Edwards and his wingman, Flying Officer Ian Mackenzie, dived past Red Section and lined up for attacks upon the bombers' left-hand vee. They set up for a rear-quarter attack, but the bombers were diving so fast that the Spitfires had to roll in behind them for a stern attack. Edwards opened fire at long range, rightly concerned about the bombers' return fire, particularly from the 20 mm cannon in the tail. Therefore, he broke off firing at 300 metres range and pulled away out of the gunners' firing arcs.

Mackenzie had meanwhile fired upon a bomber in the right-hand vee; for once, both Spitfires' cannons functioned perfectly, but because they had fired only at long range, neither pilot saw any evidence of strikes. Edwards zoomed up into a climbing turn and positioned himself to reattack. Diving in from the same bomber's port rear quarter, he fired from a little closer this time, but his earlier caution was justified when tracer from one of the bombers' rear gunners flashed closely past his aircraft's nose. Zooming up again to reattack, he saw that his bomber was now dropping back out of formation, streaming grey-brown smoke from its port engine, and the colour of the smoke was deepening. This damaged bomber dropped down into a position 2000 feet directly underneath the others in an attempt to derive some protection from its squadron mates overhead. Frustrated by his target's refusal to burn, Edwards ignored the gunners in the formation above and dived back in, opening fire from the stricken bomber's port rear quarter at even closer range – 200 metres. By now, however, he was firing with machine guns only as he had already expended all of his cannon ammunition in his earlier long-range firing. As the stream of smoke got thicker, the bomber dropped away in a steep glide, now lagging behind the formation above it. Edwards was re-climbing for a fourth attack when a Zero made an attack on him; he saw it coming in from behind, turned into its attack, then dived away at once for base. As he went, he saw that a second bomber was now dropping out of formation after Mackenzie's attack, also trailing dark smoke.

Down below, Pilot Officer Norm Robinson had meanwhile been flying 457's one-aircraft Yellow Section, patrolling his beat between Cape Fourcroy and Point Charles at low-level on the lookout for unplotted low-altitude attacks like that on 20 June. He saw the bombers go past directly overhead and started climbing up after them. Despite climbing at 210 knots IAS, the bombers drew away easily in their shallow dive. Robinson saw that one of them was lagging behind leaving a thick white smoke trail. He followed the smoke trail for 60 kilometres, but saw it disappear by the time the bomber had descended to 5000 feet: either the engine fire had been put out by the extinguisher or the holed fuel tank had emptied.

By now Don Maclean had regained an altitude of 24 000 feet off the bombers' starboard quarter, noticing as he did so one bomber diving out of formation smoking heavily, victim of White Section's attack. As he approached, he saw a Zero flying along behind the bombers and decided to attack it rather than the bombers. He dived and set up for a full deflection shot from its starboard beam, but only had time for a short burst before the Japanese pilot saw him and pulled straight up into a loop. As the Zero arced overhead, Maclean broke downwards and dived away.

At some distance behind Edwards and Mackenzie, the second element of White Section had meanwhile dived in to make its attack, slowed down as usual by an underperforming engine that caused Flying Officer Ken Barker to drop behind. Flying Officer Brian Hegarty stayed with him, and both pilots got a good view of Edwards's and Mackenzie's attack before their attention was suddenly distracted by the sight of Zeros 'milling about' in front – this was the Zero top-cover arriving in the fight and bouncing Red Section. Barker pulled up into a climbing turn at once, just in time to see that he was under attack by a coordinated section of three Zeros: one came in from nearly head-on while another curved around behind him. Recognising his peril, Barker rolled onto his back and dived away. Pulling out at 15 000 feet, he looked back to see that the Zero was still in sight, so repeated the process. The Zero duly disappeared into the distance, and he continued his dive back to base without having fired a shot.

Brian Hegarty lost Barker as soon as he pulled up, and suddenly found himself alone. Afraid of being bounced, he rolled his aircraft onto its back to have a good look behind and below, immediately spotting two Zeros directly underneath him. He pulled back on the stick to dive upon them, but the Japanese pilots saw him coming and broke, forcing Hegarty to take a high-deflection shot at one of them as he tried to turn in behind it. His cannons froze and he saw no strikes before he had to cease fire and break away downwards. Concerned about the whereabouts of the second Zero – which he could no longer see – he spiralled down to 10 000 feet, recovered from the dive and looked behind. Startled to see another fighter behind him, Hegarty resumed the evasive dive, but upon pulling out at 3000 feet, he saw that the other fighter was actually a Spitfire, and approaching closer he recognised the code letter of his section mate, Bill Hardwick, who had likewise dived away from the fight when the Zeros arrived. Both pilots formed up and flew home together.

Meanwhile, Tommy Clark was heading back to base, so shaken that he forgot to put the undercarriage down and went through with a wheels-up landing in spite of the undercarriage warning horn blaring in his ears. Squadron Leader Des Peate, the squadron medical officer, arrived at the scene with the fire crew and found Clark in a still-dazed condition with haemorrhages to his face and eyes from the extreme negative G. Clark was driven back to the A Flight dispersal, where the squadron intelligence officer, Flying Officer PE Goldin RAF, found him to be in such a state that he was unable to answer debriefing questions, and so the MO sent him straight off to station sick quarters. Clark had almost 400 hours, had flown on operations with the squadron in England, and had been graded as an above-average pilot. Exactly one month previously, during the 28 May Milingimbi raid, he had proven himself to be an effective fighter pilot able to carry through with determined attacks and to shoot straight – in the face of fighter attack and heavy return fire from the bombers' rear gunners. However, the trauma he suffered on 28 June caused such nervous strain that he was hospitalised, never again to fly on operations. Spitfire BR541 was repaired by 7 RSU and reissued to 452 Squadron on 16 July.

An evaluation

Despite Clark's ordeal, 457 was very lucky indeed to have escaped from the bounce without a fatality. Its luck could not be expected to continue if such a bounce was repeated, but the ominous lesson was lost in the squadron's pleasure in having gotten away with it today and having apparently scored four victories to boot. Part of the problem had been the failure to apply the discipline of pairs flying. This can be seen clearly in the choice to operate Blue and White Sections as five-plane formations, rather than the more obvious two fours and one two, and in Newton's readiness to split up his section in his hurry to engage the enemy (just like Watson in the Milingimbi raids). This shows how poor an understanding there was within 457 of the two-plane element, in spite of NWA HQ's recent insistence upon it as the building block of all fighter formations. The 28 May raid had already shown the cost of poor lookout within sections, and the continued failure to emphasise pairs flying would increase the chances of squadron pilots being bounced again.

Drilling the pilots on battle formation was ultimately the CO's responsibility, but 457's Squadron Leader Ken James was far less experienced than the unfortunate Ray Thorold-Smith had been. James had served his entire career since OTU with 457 and had seen only two months of operations and only six air combats prior to his arrival in Australia. During this brief operational experience, the squadron had flown the line astern formation as part of the Kenley Wing, so he had had little coaching in the air drills of modern fighter combat. He had been a flight commander for only two months before being made CO and had gone the last year with only one combat operation (2 May). The CO's limited experience was certainly a contributing factor to 457's undeveloped understanding of, and practice in, the discipline of flying in 'fluid pairs'.

Lacking strong tactical leadership from the top, the squadron was reverting to what it knew best – individual dogfighting – in spite of having introduced the new battle formation in April under instruction from Flying Officer Jack Smithson. In all squadrons, the new technique was poorly supported by the training program, which continued to emphasise one-versus-one tail chases, line astern aerobatics and one-versus-one dogfights, instead of team fighting drills. There had been an inbuilt intellectual poverty to the prewar fighter pilot syllabus, which had emphasised 'show-off' aerobatics and one-versus-one dogfighting. The effect of all this was a reinforcement of the pilots' in-built urge to seek individual combat by manoeuvring independently against any enemy aircraft they saw in front of them. Obviously, this produced a very unsophisticated approach to large-scale air combat.

No. 457 Squadron's gunnery had been plagued by the usual gun failures. The squadron correctly considered that this had 'retarded the efficiency of our aircraft'. Only two pilots had fired on the bombers: Edwards and Mackenzie had made a total of five gunnery passes, and had clearly inflicted serious damage, but neither of their victims was seen to crash. Japanese records show that two bombers were indeed hit: one had a burning engine, but the engine bay fire extinguisher succeeded in putting the fire out so that it limped back to base; another had attempted a forced landing at Lautem airfield in Portuguese Timor, but crash-landed in the attempt. The usual double and triple claiming applies to 457's four Zero kills, Japanese records indicating that none were actually shot down, but that three were damaged. Once again, this is puzzling, considering that two of them had been seen to descend in flames with several pilots as eyewitnesses.

If the quoted figures are correct, 457 had written off one enemy airframe, and had had two of its own aircraft damaged in return. A further Spitfire had been written off due to propeller CSU failure, so it had hardly been a good day out for the Spitfire wing, and must be counted as a very disappointing engagement after the good success of eight days before. The 28 June raid had been a once-in-a-campaign opportunity to punish the raiders severely, but the opportunity was missed because it had taken far too long to get all three squadrons into the one place at the one height at the one time. No. 1 Fighter Wing had missed its opportunity because of its self-imposed focus upon preserving the big wing concentration right up to the point of contact. If Caldwell had taken a lesson from 20 June and permitted his squadrons to climb independently, they would have achieved height superiority earlier, and thus could have mounted attacks at about the time that Gibbs suggested, and probably earlier. When sighted, the enemy force was of limited strength, with only nine bombers and nine fighters. This raid was therefore peculiarly vulnerable to successive attacks by three full squadrons of Spitfires. No. 54 Squadron knew that it had been denied the opportunity to follow its own CO into an early attack, but its diarist was very politic about its subsequent failure to intercept the enemy under Caldwell's leadership, explaining tactfully that 'owing to some miscalculation', 54 and 452 had not engaged. No. 457 was also deliberately vague, attributing the failure of the other squadrons to engage to 'various wing organisational difficulties'.

Worn-out engines

The spate of technical failures on 28 June shows that the technical condition of the wing's Spitfire fleet was deteriorating. To replace the aircraft losses of 2 May, second-hand aircraft had been transferred as replacements from 2 OTU – the Spitfire training unit at Mildura. By 28 June, the Spitfire aircraft in 1 Fighter Wing's inventory had seen on average six months of squadron service, and within 54 and 452 only three aircraft could be considered 'new' – with three months or less in service. Early in the wing's tour of duty, serviceability had been excellent, the only real problem being the 'numerous and sometimes dangerous' propeller CSU failures. Although that problem had still not been cured, the engine fitters' attentions were now pre-empted by problems with the engines themselves.

Jim Grant has suggested that the reason for the Spitfires' recent mechanical problems and performance shortfalls was that their engines were now coming up to their 240 hour overhauls and were therefore in worn condition. This might have applied to ex-OTU 'retreads', but an examination of 54's Operations Record Book shows that the three oldest aircraft on the unit had accumulated only about 100 hours' total flying time by June. It was not until October that some of the oldest aircraft in service started arriving at 7 RSU from the squadrons for their 240 hour overhauls. With about 4000 flying hours in total per squadron, aircraft utilisation in 1943 was not heavy, as the wing rationed out its flying hours in order to maintain high serviceability throughout its aircraft inventory. Although individual aircraft might fly several times a day, on average each machine flew only once every second day, and thus clocked up an average of little more than 15 hours of flying time per month. This effort to economise on flying hours was often sharpened by temporary shortages of vital spares: for example, of spare propellers or spare tyres (Spitfire tyres wore out rapidly on rough bush airfields as they were only two-ply, and in September this high wastage was sharpened by trade union industrial action 'down south', which stopped deliveries from the wharves). The resultant modest rate of effort is borne out by the record of pilot flying hours: 54's figures for July show that pilots were getting about 11 hours per month on average – in other words, flying about once every second day, much like their aircraft. This moderate tempo is confirmed by Squadron Leader Ron MacDonald's experience with 452: he flew only 50 hours in six months – little more than two hours per week on average.

All of the Spitfires had been delivered to the RAAF brand-new, therefore with virtually 'zero-timed' engines and airframes. Despite this, the evidence of deteriorating engine performance was plain to see. Indeed, 452 Squadron reported that aircraft could no longer be considered serviceable after 120 hours' flying in the NWA. No. 54 Squadron agreed, reporting that engines were worn out prematurely after six months of scrambles and battle climbs to 30 000 feet. Indeed, through June–July, both 7 RSU and 14 ARD found themselves dealing with a succession of aircraft sent from the squadrons prematurely for engine changes – engine condition was by now so bad that the squadrons could not wait for the scheduled 240 hourly overhauls.

The high revs and high boost of operational scrambles brought out the worst in the Spitfires' power plant, such that any operational scramble was now likely to produce a tithe of damaged and written-off aircraft. The dusty conditions of the NWA's airfields produced accelerated engine wear because of the carburettors' ingestion of dust into the cylinders during taxiing and take-offs, and so by June the pilots were running as big a risk from simply flying their aircraft in operational conditions as they were from fighting the Japanese – as the next combat would emphatically show.

This dire mechanical peril was summed up by what had happened to Flying Officer Ross Williams when 452 scrambled after an incoming plot on 23 June: flying one of the oldest aircraft in service (AR510 QY-B), his engine suffered an internal glycol leak mid-climb at 10 000 feet, with things deteriorating so rapidly that the engine burst into flames only 30 seconds later. With the fate of Eric Moore on 6 March clearly before him, Williams switched off the engine and tried to bail out without delay. However, in bunting his aircraft to obtain a clean departure from the cockpit, the unpowered Spitfire fell into an inverted spin – with him still in it. With the gyrating ground rushing up, he had the greatest difficulty getting out of the cockpit while upside down, snagged to the cockpit by the centrifugal force of the spin. He wrenched himself free from the aircraft with only a second to spare, pulling the D-ring and then almost immediately crashing through a tree and coming to rest dangling 3 metres off the ground with his parachute canopy snagged in the branches above. His aircraft hit the ground at almost the same time only 100 metres away, striking nose first in its inverted spin and flopping onto its back. It started to burn as Williams struggled free of his entanglement, its guns meanwhile pointing straight at him, with the ammunition starting to cook off in the fire. He got free in a hurry, slid down to earth and moved away from the front of the wreck. The section leader, Flight Lieutenant Dave Evans, circled overhead, reassured to see Williams sitting on the ground and calming his nerves and hands by lighting up a smoke. Of course, the scramble was merely a false alarm – just some wayward B-24s.

28 June pilot table

Sqn	Section	No.	Pilots engaging	Pilot not engaging	Remarks
Wing Co		1		W/C Caldwell	
		2		F/Sgt McDowell	
54	Red	1		S/L Gibbs RAF	
		2		F/Sgt Kelman RAF	aborted, engine trouble (BR532)
		3		F/O Thompson RAF	
		4		F/Sgt Wickman RAF	
	Blue	1		F/L Foster RAF	aborted, CSU failure
		3		F/Sgt Wheeler RAF	
		4		Sgt Laundy RAF	
	White	1		F/O Hughes RAF	
		2		F/Sgt Harker RAF	
		3		P/O Appleton RAF	
		4		F/Sgt Horkin RAF	
		5		F/Sgt Huggard RAF	initially Blue 2, engine problems (BR484), aborted, rejoined
	Yellow	1		Sgt Holmes RAF	low-level contact patrol
452	Red	1		S/L MacDonald	R/T failed in BR574
		2		F/Sgt Cross	
		3		F/O K Fox	
		4		F/O Colyer	
	White	1		F/L Makin	
		2		F/O Whillans	
		3		P/O Tully	

	White	4		F/O Bassett	
	Blue	1		F/L Evans	
		2		F/O Watkin	
		3		F/O Young	
		4		F/O Cowell	force-landed Shoal Bay due glycol leak; EE608 QY-V written off
457	Red	1	F/L Maclean		1 cannon failed
		2	F/O Brook RAF		both cannons failed
		3	F/O Clark		damaged in combat, belly-landed Livingstone; BR241 ZP-F repaired by 7 RSU, returned to service 12 Jul
		4	F/O Halse		CSU failure, force-landed Cox Peninsula; BR462 ZP-U written off
	Blue	1	F/L Newton		damaged in combat; BR543 ZP-T repaired by 7 RSU, returned to service 8 Jul
		2	P/O Little		did not fire
		3	P/O Reilly		
		4	F/Sgt MacPherson		
		5	F/Sgt Cunningham		
	White	1	F/L Edwards		
		2	F/O Barker		did not fire
		3	F/O Mackenzie		
		4	F/O Hegarty		both cannons failed
		5	F/Sgt Hardwick		did not fire
	Yellow	1		F/O Robinson	low-level contact patrol
		14		28	

Summary:
Spitfires scrambled: 42
Spitfires in main wing formation: 40
Spitfires engaged: 14
Spitfires written off due to mechanical failure: 2
Spitfires damaged by enemy: 2

9

The first
Fenton raid

From early June, the 380th Bomb Group of the USAAF had been moving into Fenton airfield 145 kilometres south of Darwin. The group's four squadrons of B-24 heavy bombers represented the greatest upgrade to the striking capacity of the NWA. From the Japanese perspective, this was precisely the eventuality that the Imperial Navy's air raids on Darwin had meant to prevent and would represent the failure of their campaign.

The arrival of the 380th in the NWA symbolised the turning of the tide. In accordance with General Kenney's instructions, Air Commodore Bladin would send the 380th out to strike more deeply into the Japanese-occupied Indonesian archipelago than ever before. The 380th had thereby changed the game in the air war beyond Australia's north-western shore.

30 June

The threat posed by the US bomber group's arrival in the theatre prompted 23rd Air Flotilla to reconcentrate its strike units at Kendari ready for a heavy retaliatory air strike against the American bomber base. After its squadron-strength foray on 28 June, 753 Air Group returned in force on 30 June with a maximum effort – 23 bombers, representing the unit's entire inventory of available serviceable aircraft. The group's inability to produce the default-standard group formation of 27 bombers reflects both the growing shortages facing Japanese naval air units following accumulating operational attrition throughout the theatre, and the recent loss and damage from the 28 June raid. Meanwhile, Japanese photographic sorties resumed, with an unintercepted Ki-46 successfully overflying Fenton on 27 June, confirming the latest targeting information for the planned attack.

At 11.18 am on 30 June, the first contact appeared on radar, and soon after 5 Fighter Sector plotted two separate formations at 250 kilometres west-north-west of Darwin, on a south-east course. Both enemy formations joined up when 110 kilometres north-west of Peron Island – an unusually southerly rendezvous point compared with previous raids. When still 50 kilometres out to sea the raid turned east, heading far to the south of Darwin. As the raid passed over Peron Island, coastwatchers confirmed that it was a formation of bombers, tracking for Batchelor airfield. This was Darwin Raid No. 57, but it would not actually be bombing Darwin – judging by the unusual approach path, the target was one of the airfields along the track to the south.

At 11.20, control scrambled the wing and 39 Spitfires were airborne within five minutes, led by Wing Commander Caldwell, who took his place in the centre at the head of 457 Squadron. Four additional Spitfires were deployed as base patrols, flying the usual defensive beats in search of 'sneak' low-level raiders. The main force formed up as a big wing after an 'excellent' rendezvous over Sattler at 6000 feet, climbing away in the wing's standard arrangement of a broad and flat spread of squadrons in line abreast. No. 54 and 452 were led by their COs, while 457 was led by the 'A' Flight commander, Flight Lieutenant Pete Watson.

One of 452's pilots, Flying Officer Jack Lamerton, did not get much further than the rendezvous. He aborted while climbing through 16 000 feet, having suffered a major internal glycol leak. The engine exhausts streamed large white streaks of smoke, and once the coolant had been burned off, the engine seized immediately. Lamerton had enough height to glide back to base at Strauss and to make an approach for a dead-stick landing. Like his squadron mate Al Mawer, who had done the same thing at the same airfield only ten days before, he made sure he had a bit of extra airspeed for his turn onto final approach over the tree line – for safety. Lamerton overshot his aiming point badly and likewise floated down the runway, bleeding off speed so that he could get his wheels on the ground, but the Spitfire was decelerating all too slowly. In desperation, he drove it onto the runway about three-quarters of the way along the strip, but the pneumatic undercarriage oleos bounced it back up into the air, where it continued to float along just above the dirt, still slowing but running out of runway ahead. Lamerton forcibly shoved it into the ground at the end of the runway, retracting the undercarriage as he did so to achieve positive contact with the ground.

However, the aircraft was still going so fast that it slid on its belly for several hundred metres right off the runway and into the bush. One wing 'mutilated' a sandbagged 40 mm gun post on the way past, and this impact pivoted the aircraft so that it crashed sideways through the trees. The fuselage broke and the fuel tanks ruptured. There was a sickening five-second interval during which Lamerton made no move, stunned in the crash by his head's violent impact with the gunsight. Then the spilling 100 octane ignited. The fire truck and ambulance were still racing down the runway, but nearby drivers from 118 Australian General Transport Company beat the professionals to the scene: they were out of their trucks and all over the burning wreck 'by the time you could click your fingers'. The accident had occurred right in front of a traffic jam alongside the end of the runway, while the trucks were held up waiting for the Spitfire to land. Sergeant Viv Devon and LAC Cunnington from 452 also got there quickly from the nearby squadron dispersals, bringing a fire extinguisher.

As the Spitfire burned, these men got on the wing, doused the fire, released Lamerton from his seat harness and dragged him out of the cockpit. Sadly, in spite of their efforts, he had suffered third-degree burns from the petrol fire, and later that evening he died from severe shock in the care of 1 Medical Receiving Station (1 MRS) at Coomalie. He had joined the squadron in March 1942, had 464 hours of flying time, and had been graded above average in his CO's reports. Jack Lamerton had not been a lucky pilot: in the only combat of his career, on 3 May 1942, he had been shot down over England by the rear gunner of a Ju88 bomber. No pilot likes making dead-stick landings over trees, and he had been so anxious to avoid undershooting that he overshot instead with fatal result.

Unaware of Lamerton's fate, the wing was meanwhile continuing with the interception, vectored by control to the north-east in order to provide a safe climb away from the enemy fighters. When it was abreast of Darwin, control ordered a 180 degree turn to head west towards the enemy, advising that the raid was at 25 000 feet approaching the coast. By now it was clear that the Japanese were tracking towards the southern airfields, so control vectored the wing further south to counter this. As the Balbo of Spitfires arrived overhead Batchelor at 28 000 feet, control reported that the raid was now approaching Peron Island. Things were looking good – the Japanese had yet to cross the coast and were still 130 kilometres from any possible target, yet the wing was nearly at the top of its climb. This interception was working out very favourably: because the Japanese were conducting a deep penetration raid, they were providing enough warning time for the big wing to get to height and into position before the bombers hit the target.

The pre-attack manoeuvring

Control had placed the Spitfires on almost a reciprocal course to the incoming Japanese, but displaced to the north, setting Caldwell up for a beam attack from the bombers' port side – the standard interception profile. When the wing was at 32 000 feet and 60 kilometres west of Batchelor, the Wingco sighted the raiders off his port bow 20 kilometres away: they had already crossed the coast of Anson Bay and were at 25 000 feet. After giving the 'Tally-ho' he turned the wing left to come in towards the enemy. Although he now had plenty of height, Caldwell did not send the squadrons straight in on attack headings towards the bomber formation. Instead, he brought the Spitfires around in a wide arc of about 180 degrees, coming up parallel with the bombers but closer in.

This turn onto a parallel heading abandoned any hope of achieving surprise or uncertainty. The Japanese had watched the Spitfires approach, had watched them wheel ponderously about through their big turn, and now they watched to see how and when the attack would develop. The whole force of three dozen Spitfires was gathered in one place within the view of the Japanese fighter pilots, so the Spitfires' moves, when they came, could now only come from that one direction. The mistake of 15 March was being repeated – utter tactical predictability. Caldwell's delaying of the attack also permitted the Japanese to get 30 kilometres closer to their target without molestation – they were coming in at 210 knots, covering more than 6 kilometres a minute.

As they watched the stately approach of the Spitfires, the Zeros edged themselves over into positions from which they could more advantageously swoop upon them during their firing runs. There was no attempt to disturb the Spitfires as they formed up and got into position: as usual, the Japanese fighter unit confined itself to reactive tactics only. This was an acknowledgment of the superior altitude performance of the Spitfires: unable to challenge them to a climbing duel above 30 000 feet, the best the Zero pilots could do was wait for them to come down. While flying alongside the bombers, Flight Sergeant Wickman saw the rear group of Zeros moving closer to the bombers, getting ready to block the Spitfires' attacks. Other small groups of Zeros moved from their starting positions and started climbing. By splitting up into numerous small groups, the Zeros would be a lot harder to see than the immense gaggle of Spitfires that had collected together in one place.

As they flew along parallel with the enemy, the Spitfire pilots too had time to observe the enemy's dispositions. They counted 27 bombers (a slight overestimate) in their usual tidy, compact formation, while the escorting fighters were positioned above these, the highest at 28 000 feet. Five Zeros were observed ahead of the bombers, nine behind and two above. This made 16 in total – an incomplete count, showing once again the difficulty of tallying all the Zeros, especially when they were split up into hard-to-see groups of two and three. Even formation leaders saw only a portion of the escort in spite of the 'perfect' visibility: Rob Norwood saw only nine Zeros in total, divided forward and aft of the bombers; Bob Foster counted only 12–15 fighters, and saw no top-cover Zeros at all; Ron MacDonald saw only 12 Zeros, deployed both in front and behind. Post-operational debriefs produced estimates of a total fighter escort of 20 – still short of its actual strength. The combat on this day was following an established pattern, whereby the Spitfire pilots would commence their attacks from an altitude advantage, but without having spotted all of the Zeros. Caldwell had advised his pilots of the positions of all the enemy subgroups from 15 kilometres out, but by the time the wing had gone through its 180 degree turn, most pilots had lost visual contact with major sections of the fighter escort.

Caldwell's No. 2, Darky McDowell, had been unable to keep up, so Caldwell led the wing by himself, flying in the van of 457 Squadron. He now gave his squadrons their orders: 54 would attack from the bombers' starboard front quarter (on the opposite side to where they were now), 457 would attack the bombers from their front port quarter (on the near side), and 452 would attack the fighters. Thus the bombers were to be caught in a pincer movement, with simultaneous attacks from port and starboard.

The trouble with this tactical disposition was that it was an awkward fit with the actual relative positions of the three squadrons – 2 May and 28 June repeated. No. 54 had the furthest to go before being able to commence its attack, as its starting position was way out on the left flank of the Balbo. Despite being furthest away from the enemy, it was given the longest attack route, required to undertake a wide detour around the front of the bombers in order to launch a firing run against their far side. Given Caldwell's intention to launch simultaneous coordinated attacks, 54's evolution would require 452 and 457 to simply hold their positions off the bomber formation's port bow, waiting for the British squadron to get into position.

Moreover, 54's evolution was more difficult than it sounded: it had to get far out in front of the bombers before turning right and moving over to attack from the opposite side. Under pressure to cover all this extra distance quickly, Gibbs advanced his throttle and put his nose down to gain speed, with his squadron racing behind him trying to keep up. The pace was too fast for Blue Section at the rear of the squadron column, which fell so far behind that Bob Foster gave up and decided to keep his section on the bombers' port side instead. He retarded his throttle and watched the rest of the squadron move out ahead. They were doing all this at 32 000 feet, an altitude at the upper end of the Spitfire VC's height band and therefore a height at which it had anything but a sparkling performance, with the worn-out engines in so many of the aircraft making this performance even more marginal.

All these high revs at high altitude provoked another spate of engine troubles, with Sergeant Dennis Monger aborting out of Gibbs's Red Section before the action commenced. No. 457 also suffered some aborts: the aircraft of Flying Officer Bill Halse suffered a CSU malfunction while climbing through 31 000 feet. The higher his aircraft climbed, the higher his revs rose, and when the tachometer showed 3400 rpm (3000 was the limit) he retired from the formation and descended into thicker air to let the problem clear itself. Flying Officer Brian Hegarty suffered an air lock in his fuel system when he changed over from the drop tank to the main tank (presumably having forgotten to turn the belly tank fuel cock to 'OFF'); the engine cut out, leaving him to watch the rest of the squadron climb rapidly away while he put his nose down into a glide and tried to clear the air lock in the fuel line by switching to the upper main tank. The air lock cleared itself and the engine spluttered back into life, but he returned to base, unwilling to pursue the engagement alone.

After Lamerton dropped out, 452 stayed together well at first, but was then decimated by a series of mechanical aborts: the first of these was Flight Sergeant Frank Turnbull, with yet another propeller CSU failure. At that point, 452's remaining ten aircraft were deployed in line abreast battle formation, positioned well up on either side of the leader.

While waiting for 54 to get into place, 452 stayed at 31 000 feet, flying along out on the bombers' port bow. While he was waiting, Squadron Leader MacDonald tried to give attack instructions to his squadron over the R/T but received no reply. He repeated again and again with the same negative result – his R/T transmitter had gone unserviceable. This meant that for a third combat in a row he would not be able to lead his squadron, and so he moved over towards his No. 3 and waggled his wings at him – the signal to take over. The squadron would now be led by Flight Lieutenant Paul Makin, the 'B' Flight commander. MacDonald dropped back and reassigned himself as one of Makin's two wingmen.

Caldwell had assigned 452 the task of attacking the Zeros in order to keep them away from the other two squadrons. However, 452's newly delegated leader, Makin, now advised the Wingco that he could no longer see the fighters. This threw the whole plan into disarray and prompted a series of exchanges over the R/T while everyone was waiting for 54 to get into position. Caldwell's responses were ambiguously interpreted by 452's pilots as permission for them to attack the bombers instead.

Meanwhile, another two aircraft from 452's Blue Section dropped behind due to mechanical problems, leaving Flying Officer Hal Whillans, Blue 1, all by himself as a one-man 'Blue Section' out on the squadron's right flank. The laggards were Flight Sergeants Keith Cross and Col Duncan, the former with a malfunctioning propeller CSU and the latter with an engine that failed to deliver its power – despite the use of full throttle, it would not hold its place in formation. These two cripples sensibly formed up as a pair to cover each other, but Cross's aircraft soon after suffered a total CSU failure, with his engine overrevving uncontrollably. He applied the prescribed corrective action, but without effect, and within 30 seconds the engine had vented its glycol, overheated and seized up. Cross spiralled down to make a dead-stick landing on a road running through the scrub that he had picked out while descending overhead. However, as he turned in on final approach he realised it was in fact a 'not very much used road' – Stapleton Road, near Coomalie – and unusable. At that height and with a dead engine, the only option he had left was to bank gently away from the road towards the sparsest patch of scrub he could find off to the side.

Now unavoidably committed to a landing in the small timber, Cross held off as long as possible, trying to lose as much speed as possible to make his arrival as gentle as could be. With the long nose obscuring vision ahead and without clear visual references in the nondescript scrub out to the sides, he tried to hold the aircraft straight with the rudder, simultaneously tensing his buttocks against the inevitable crunching impact underneath. One wing snagged on the larger saplings and the aircraft was flung sideways onto the dirt, ground-looping through the scrub, breaking off the engine and coming to rest in a mess of splintered saplings, torn foliage, hot dirt and black engine oil. Cross had tried to brace himself against the gunsight before final impact, but the violent yawing whiplashed his head into the side of the windscreen. Once the noise had stopped, he dropped the side door, unpinned his harness, and removed himself from the wreck as quickly as he could for fear of fire. However, getting out of the cockpit proved more difficult than he had expected, for his ankle was sprained. Hobbling away, he weakly sat down on the dirt track and pressed his glove to his head to staunch the bleeding. He had survived a very rough landing but the aircraft had not – it was laboriously retrieved by 7 RSU and salvaged for parts. Cross was a thoroughly average wing pilot, with 400 hours, of which 190 were on Spitfires.

The squadron engineering officer later inspected the wreckage of BR546 and ascertained that the engine had been hit by one round of 7.7 mm, but the aircraft's demise had been self-generated – the CSU failure had occurred well before contact with the enemy. Presumably, Cross's Spitfire was chased and fired at by a Zero as it descended away, but by then the fate of his aircraft was already sealed.

After Cross had dropped away below, Duncan was left all by himself, lagging badly behind and below the rest of 452. His engine coolant temperature was rising, which forced him to throttle back, but even so, white vapour started coming from his engine's starboard exhausts – indicating an internal coolant leak. The situation was most unpromising: his coolant temperature was already above 140°F (the maximum permissible), he was 80 kilometres away from base, he was all by himself and there were enemy fighters about. Duncan knew that his engine was doomed, but thought it would hold together long enough to make an attack, calculating that his best chance of both attacking *and* surviving lay in staying as close as he could to the squadron, making one diving pass and then bailing out lower down. He therefore pressed on, dropping further behind the others, nursing his engine with a moderate power setting, and anxiously monitoring his temperatures and pressures. The engine ran increasingly roughly and a haze of oil smoke now filled the cockpit. Breathing pure oxygen through his mask and pulling his goggles down to keep the smoke out of his eyes, Duncan sweated impatiently, jerking his head around to scan the sky for opportunistic Zeros.

As usual, the slow wing climb and high-altitude manoeuvring was costing not only time but fuel. Following so soon after the

20 and 28 June combats, this raid had caught the wing with a shortage of 30 gallon drop tanks. Most aircraft had taken off without them and were thus limited to the aircraft's modest 85 gallon internal fuel capacity. Caldwell's delaying of the interception was eating into the Spitfires' limited airborne endurance, but chastened by the 2 May fuel disaster, the pilots were unlikely to take the same risks as they had that day, and so today they would dive for home as soon as their gauges showed 'bingo fuel' – defined as having 10 gallons left upon landing. The time-consuming pre-attack delays would reduce many of the pilots to one pass and then home.

54's attack

No. 54 Squadron was supposed to be the left hook of a two-pronged wing frontal attack. However, Blue Section's failure to keep up meant that the squadron was split up, with only two of the three sections fulfilling Caldwell's orders to attack from the bombers' right. Although Gibbs led these aircraft out in front of the bombers as ordered, the extravagant manoeuvre prescribed by Caldwell was in fact impracticable given 54's bad starting position and the need to do it in a hurry so that the whole wing attack could get started. With the other two squadrons impatiently waiting upon him to get in place, the best Gibbs was able to achieve was to get into position for an attack upon the centre vee, in the van of the bomber formation rather than upon the starboard side as intended: extending the squadron's shallow dive to attack from the far flank would have lost too much height. Therefore, once he was in a reasonable position right out in front, Gibbs announced over the R/T that he was ready, and Caldwell finally gave the 'attack' order, instructing all squadrons to attack in fours and sixes with the aircraft well up, line abreast of each other so that everyone could fire simultaneously. After firing, they were to break right and zoom back up sun to reattack.

Upon hearing the word, 54 now finally dived in at the bombers' front while 452 simultaneously dived in upon the bombers' front port quarter. Leading his seven aircraft down, Gibbs lined up for a beam attack on the left-hand aircraft in the centre vee, rolling into a stern-quarter attack and firing right in to 25 metres. He saw strikes on its port engine, cockpit and front fuselage before bunting underneath and diving over to the far side of the bomber formation. Upon looking back, what he saw was not reassuring: 'a fleeting glimpse on passing through showed enemy fighters closing in'. Gibbs rolled on his back, pulled hard and dived out vertically. After that, he pulled out on the port side of the bombers and zoomed up into the sun, ready for another go but all alone.

Gibbs's No. 2, Flight Sergeant Wickman, had been pushed out of position during the pre-attack manoeuvring and was lagging behind when the attack started. Flying Officer I Thompson took his place, and thus Red Section dived in the following order: Gibbs, Thompson, Wickman and Holmes. The three junior pilots followed Gibbs in and made similar beam attacks against the centre vee of nine bombers, but only Wickman saw any strikes from his gunfire. He saw one bomber fall out of formation with its starboard engine afire and afterwards claimed it as 'probably destroyed'. All three of Gibbs's section mates broke downwards after firing, splitting up and fighting individually from there on.

Holmes did not get much further than that, for as soon as he broke away underneath the bombers it became apparent that his aircraft had been hit by the bomber gunners: oil and glycol leaked back along the cockpit floor, his windscreen was covered in a fine spray of oil and smoke arose in the cockpit. With his engine rapidly venting its coolant, Holmes set himself up in a glide, obtained a homing bearing for Darwin and anxiously set course. However, the coolant temperature rose higher and higher, and so he decided it was time to get out. At 10 000 feet, while he still had the height to bail out safely, he rolled his aircraft onto its back, dropped out and descended beneath his parachute in the sudden quiet.

Both Wickman and Thompson independently crossed under the bombers to reposition themselves out on the port, up sun side, just as Gibbs had done. Arriving there, Thompson saw six fighters in a dogfight, 3 kilometres behind the bombers and 4000 feet below. Heading towards them, he dived in to lend a comradely hand, but when he got in to 400 metres he realised that every one of the aircraft was a Zero – the Zeros were engaged in a mock dogfight to lure gullible Spitfire pilots into an ambush. Wing pilots had previously observed this Japanese tactic and had been briefed to just ignore it. Unfortunately, Thompson had not recognised it for what it was and it was now too late to change his mind, so he continued on, diving in behind the nearest enemy fighter. The Zero broke vertically upwards into a loop and Thompson pulled up after it, but the Zero rolled off the top so rapidly that he could not follow. By now, his Spitfire was zooming skyward, standing on its tail and running out of airspeed – in a patch of sky populated by five further Zeros. Looking left, he saw four of them coming in towards him with the front one already firing. Thompson's speed was now so low that the Japanese pilot scarcely needed to apply deflection. Before his aircraft fell back into a tail slide, Thompson thumped his stick forward and kicked his rudder, breaking hard downwards and rolling and turning all the way down to 12 000 feet. Two of the Zeros went down after him.

Gibbs was repositioning himself for another attack on the bombers when he was interrupted by the sight of a Zero on the tail of a diving Spitfire – Thompson's. He dived after it but as he approached saw another Zero rolling over onto its back to come down on him – he had been caught in the same trap as Thompson. Gibbs displayed the same insouciance as he had shown in his first combat on 2 March, continuing after the first Zero and firing from dead astern at close range until his cannons jammed. He saw strikes on the Zero's wing roots and it smoked and spun, and so he later (optimistically) claimed it as destroyed. Meanwhile, his own assailant had overshot, unable to pull out of its steep dive until it was below him. Gibbs spiralled down, trying to keep both the Zeros and the other Spitfire in sight, but he found himself diving so steeply and going so fast that he lost sight of them all.

Doing 300 knots IAS in his rolling evasive dive, Thompson looked behind to see that two of the Zeros were following, so continued the dive down to 8000 feet. Looking behind again as he started to pull out, he saw one of the Zeros had broken off and was heading out to sea, while the other had disappeared (the one shot off his tail by Gibbs). Then he saw a Zero going down smoking badly – Gibbs's victim; and he also saw a parachute going down and landing in a tree – Holmes. Thompson then headed back to base following instructions from control to join 54's Purple Section as an improvised airborne reserve. On the way he saw two Zeros overhead, heading in the opposite direction for the coast. He opportunistically overhauled them in a full-power climb, got within 600 metres and then opened fire somewhat speculatively at extreme range. His aircraft was already going so slowly in the climb that, as he pulled the nose up to fire, it stalled from the gun recoil and spun away. He went with the spin and dived away hoping that the Zeros had not noticed his attack.

Behind Bill Gibbs's Red Section came Rob Norwood's White Section, diving against the same centre group of bombers. As he approached, Norwood saw one bomber catch fire in both engines, confirming the effectiveness of Red Section's attack. He made a beam attack on his own target and saw strikes on the port engine and fuselage, but upon looking behind saw six Zeros coming down from the right. Norwood broke violently downwards, diving all the way to 12 000 feet and losing his section in the process. He pulled out and climbed up sun to reattack, later claiming his bomber victim as 'probably destroyed'.

Flight Sergeant Harker, Norwood's No. 2, followed him in and made a beam attack against the leading bomber vee at the centre of the whole formation. However, he used so little deflection that he missed his target entirely – so much so that he believed he hit the second vee by mistake! It did not help that he was spraying all three bombers rather than aiming at just one selected target, and firing at long range also. Observing no effect from this wild fire, Harker dived out, following behind his No. 1. He had not seen the diving Zeros.

Harker advised Norwood by R/T that he was behind him, and both pilots pulled out and climbed together on the up sun (port) side of the bombers. They were in line astern and so Harker was out of Norwood's vision; as a result, both pilots failed to see the Zeros that dived in behind them. However, Harker suddenly heard and felt them: a series of loud bangs and thumps shook the fuselage from cannon and machine-gun hits behind him. With the cockpit full of the stench and smoke of burnt cordite, he broke violently into a steep turn and dived away, pulling out just above the trees. By then his radiator temperature was climbing up the gauge, for the Zero's gunfire had punctured his coolant system. At 'nought feet' and with his engine about to seize, Harker had nowhere to go but down, so he force-landed in long grass inland from Bynoe Harbour. He used his R/T to advise his position and Thompson and Norwood from his own squadron acknowledged. Then a low-flying 452 Squadron aircraft waggled its wings at him on its way back to base.

Norwood's White Section had been the last part of 54 to make an attack, and had gone through in the following order: Norwood, Harker, Wellsman and Horkin. Norwood himself had attacked the bombers and got safely away, while Harker had also made his attack and got clear (only to be shot off his leader's tail on the re-climb). From his position at the head of the queue, Norwood had seen the fighter escort coming after him, so it was inevitable that his followers would have a harder time getting clear: the further back in the line a pilot was, the greater the chance of being jumped. At the rear end of the queue, Flight Sergeant Horkin saw that things were starting to deteriorate when he spotted four vees of Zeros coming down after them, diving from their position astern of the bombers. Although his pursuers were only 1000 metres behind, Horkin continued with his attack on the bombers and coolly made an effective gunnery pass, firing right in to 100 metres from the rear quarter. He saw flashes on his target's wing root, fuselage and port engine, and saw it start to smoke badly, later claiming it as a 'probable'.

Suddenly tracers hissed past his starboard wing – the pursuing Zeros had caught up. Horkin broke violently downwards and descended in violent turns; looking behind, he saw the Zero was still there, firing while inverted from his rear quarter, so he pulled harder – so hard that he blacked out from the G. When he came to, he found his Spitfire flying upside down at 15000 feet. Rolling right way up, he saw that the Zero had gone, so started re-climbing. Upon seeing a Spitfire manoeuvring with some Zeros, he came over to lend a hand, but three Zeros started manoeuvring against him, so he decided not to press his luck any further and dived away for home.

Horkin's element leader, Pilot Officer Jimmy Wellsman, was not so fortunate, falling victim to the same bounce from behind while diving at the bombers. He was never seen alive again and was officially assumed to be dead on 15 July. It was not until

21 August that the wreckage of his aircraft was discovered on the edge of the Reynolds River wetlands, 50 kilometres west of Batchelor. He was found near the wreck, lying on his back in the swampy ground with his arms outstretched and his parachute unopened – he had tried to get out of his doomed aircraft but too late, too low. Wellsman had been a sergeant pilot with the squadron since April 1942 and had only recently been commissioned. White Section's four aircraft had been jumped by a full squadron of Zeros, many of which had been unsighted, and two of Norwood's men had been shot down.

While re-climbing to resume his attack upon the bombers, Norwood saw a Spitfire shot down by a Zero and crash – this was very probably Jimmy Wellsman from his own White Section. He dived after the Zero, turned and fired at it, but saw yet others coming in at him, already firing – the Zeros were working together, maintaining the integrity of their three-aircraft sections even in the middle of a dogfight. Norwood broke violently downwards once again and dived away, continuing all the way to ground level. On the way down, he saw six petrol fires from burning aircraft. He tried to get a vector on the R/T for a reattack on the bombers, but there was too much radio chatter; he failed to reacquire the enemy and went home.

Foster's Blue Section meanwhile had remained further to the rear and over on the bombers' port side, and was still having problems getting into position when Caldwell's attack order came. Foster found that his section had drifted so far to the rear that their diving angle was now too flat, and so their intended beam attack would turn into a straggling attack on the bombers' stern quarter. He led his two pilots down after the bombers, but to avoid dropping below and behind the Japanese he had to flatten out the dive, slowing down the rate of closure. With his attack playing itself out in excruciating slow motion, Foster then saw five Zeros rolling in behind.

Nervously holding his line and pressing on with the attack, Foster hoped that he would get within gun range of the bombers before he himself came within range of the Zeros. As he excruciatingly drew closer to the bombers, he came under heavy return fire – the rear-quarter attack had given the gunners an easy shot. Upon seeing all the tracers rising up to meet Foster's aircraft, Sergeant Laundy decided not to make a stern attack after all. Instead, he pulled away and flew along beside the bombers, setting himself up to make an attack upon the bombers' less well-defended beam. This was understandable, but he had thereby split his section up and made himself perilously alone in a dangerous sky. He had not seen the Zeros.

Acutely conscious of the enemy fighters closing in behind, Foster opened fire on the bombers while still slightly out of range. Because their poor starting angle had dictated a rear-quarter attack, he and his No. 2, Flight Sergeant Huggard, did not need to fire with much deflection, and were also able to get reasonably close before ceasing fire. Both factors helped their gunnery. Foster got in to 100 metres, spraying all three of the bombers in the left-most vee. He lined up on the outside bomber, held it in the gunsight with two rings of deflection, pressed the firing button and then just held his thumb on the button while all three bombers passed through the gunsight. He saw results: the outside bomber streamed white smoke from both engines, while the inner bomber also trailed smoke from its starboard engine. Foster later claimed one of these as destroyed and the other as a probable. As soon as he ceased fire, he broke downwards as violently as he could. As he did so, however, his engine suddenly started vibrating, the revs and boost indications started fluctuating, and the coolant temperature started climbing. Believing that he had been hit by a fighter, he dived away in a series of tight turns and headed back to base. After landing, he found that his aircraft had not been hit at all, but his engine had suffered yet another internal glycol leak.

Huggard broke off his firing early because of the fighters behind him and then went down in a spiral dive to 20 000 feet. As he started to pull out, his aircraft was at once violently hit – one of the Zeros had followed him down. He broke downwards a second time into a series of diving turns, this time going all the way to 4000 feet before pulling out. His airspeed indicator and pneumatic system had been knocked out and his windscreen was by now becoming badly obscured with leaking oil, but the engine was still going. Justifiably calling it quits, he headed back to base, where he made a flapless landing. His aircraft had seven bullet holes in it and was sent off to be repaired by 7 RSU.

Flying Officer Ian Mackenzie from 457 had meanwhile attached himself to Foster's section, having dropped out of his own squadron because of an underperforming engine. Finding himself isolated, he had looked to the right just in time to see 54's Blue Section diving into its attack, and so had moved over to the right to join them, diving for a beam attack on the same bombers. As he approached them, he saw that no bomber had yet dropped out as a result of 54's attack. Opening fire at 450 metres in a full deflection shot, only his machine guns functioned – under these conditions, he had little chance of getting hits. Upon breaking away and zooming back up to make another attack, Mackenzie's canopy fogged up, so he wound it back to regain rear vision. Just then he heard an R/T warning, 'Lookout Mac!', and rolled at once into a breaking turn. Looking behind, he saw the black engine cowling of a Zero boring in from directly behind, close enough to fire. He broke away downwards, diving away in a series of rolling turns. Tracers whipped over the top of his starboard wing the moment he started to ease out of the dive, so he continued his evasive turns down to 9000 feet. There he finally found himself alone and returned to base.

With his section mates and Mackenzie distracting the Zeros, Sid Laundy had completed his slow-motion solo overtaking of the bombers and was left unmolested to roll into a beam attack against the extreme left-hand bomber. Firing a deflection shot in to 150 metres, he saw the bomber's port engine start to smoke badly before he broke away downwards. Turning around underneath the bombers, he came back out to re-emerge on the same side as he had gone in. As he came out underneath the bombers' port side, he saw the machine he had fired at falling out of formation, so turned right and climbed, getting into position to reattack it. Just then he then heard Caldwell say over the R/T, 'That one's done for. Leave it for now and attack the others'. Believing that this instruction was directed at him, Laundy turned away from the straggler and continued his climb, repositioning himself for a second solo beam attack on the whole formation. Once again, the Zeros left him alone, which permitted him to roll in and line up on the leader of the port vee – the next bomber in line after his previous victim had dropped out. He fired, using a similar full deflection shot, and saw strikes around its cockpit. At once the bomber rolled abruptly left as if to peel out of formation. Laundy bunted violently under it to avoid a collision, but upon looking up saw that it had now straightened up to rejoin the others. The manoeuvres of this bomber would be consistent with casualties on the flight deck, with one of the pilots incapacitated before another pilot took over the controls: Laundy therefore claimed it as damaged.

Caldwell's advice to this low-hours pilot had been unfortunate, for an isolated and damaged straggler was precisely the best target to attack, especially for a single Spitfire. If Laundy or someone else had pressed home an attack upon the lagging bomber at that moment, its destruction might have been assured. Instead, the damaged machine continued to fly on, and may have got all the way back to Timor. Attacking cripples was a standard tactic of fighter warfare, the best way of getting definite results at minimum risk, and it was overconfident of

Caldwell to deflect his pilots from this opportunity when they were having so much trouble shooting bombers out of the main formation. Indeed, the chance was soon lost, for Ted Hall soon after observed Laundy's straggler flying 3 kilometres behind the main formation, but now protected by a personal escort of five Zeros.

Laundy meanwhile dived away to the other side of the formation and then re-climbed to attack the right-most vee, which by now was lagging behind: one of the bombers was damaged, its doughty section mates staying with their struggling comrade to provide protective gunfire support. Once Laundy had obtained a 2000 feet height advantage, he dived back in for his third beam attack, firing in to 150 metres at his chosen target within the lagging vee. This time, he saw definite results: the starboard engine and the leading edge of the wing burst into flames and burned brightly, and on the strength of this he justifiably claimed it as destroyed. This was good shooting, producing the first outright 'flamer' achieved against the navy bombers. However, Laundy had tarried too long. He broke downwards as soon as he had ceased fire, but too late: at once he felt the tail of his aircraft shudder and then his aircraft flicked involuntarily into a spin. He had been bounced from behind, as was almost inevitable after three very brazen and highly visible solo attacks.

Laundy got his Spitfire out of the spin, pulled the nose up to slow it down, and then jerked on the hood release knob to jettison the canopy and bail out. Unfortunately, the jettison knob came out 15 cm and then stuck. He had to manually prise open the canopy with his fingers, and it took all his strength to force it back along its rails. Left unattended during the pilot's desperate struggle to get out, his aircraft meanwhile fell into another spin. As the gyrating earth rose rapidly towards him, Laundy realised he would be too low to bail out, so he stayed in his seat and gave his full attention to spin recovery instead: stick forward, opposite rudder. The aircraft stopped spinning, and then he pulled as hard as he dared to get it out of the dive, levelling out at only 1250 feet. Having recovered to a normal flying attitude, Laundy tried to maintain level flight, but the engine smoked badly and would only produce 1500 rpm. These revs were enough to support a steady descent, so he changed his mind about bailing out and decided to belly-land instead.

Just then, however, flames flared out of the side of the engine cowling, forcing a rapid reconsideration of his previous decision. Laundy no longer had enough height to roll the aircraft safely – the specified method of bailing out. He simply undid the straps and leads, opened the side door, stood up, and dived over the side. Because of this non-recommended exit technique, he hit the tailplane with his arm on the way past, dislocating his shoulder but without suffering a serious impact injury, as had killed Bert Cooper on 15 March. Thus he was able to yank on the D-ring and make a short but safe parachute descent. As he drifted towards the ground, Laundy watched a bomber coming down nearby. However, subsequent searches failed to discover any wreckage, so the Japanese pilot had evidently taken his damaged aircraft out of combat by diving away to 'treetop' level and then 'hedge-hopping' below the radar back to the coast. Upon landing, Laundy walked east until he found a road then followed it out, but he was not found until the next day, when he encountered two RAAF airmen with a party of Americans – a posse out searching for the Japanese airmen (which they never found). He was 6 kilometres from the Adelaide River, to the west of the highway.

Laundy, a very green pilot not long out of OTU, had single-handedly made three attacks on the bombers, in such an exposed and unsupported manner that he was either heedless of danger or unable to recognise it. However, he proved that he was a talented fighter pilot, for his deflection shooting was good: he saw observable results from each pass, most particularly the 'flamer', which he very reasonably claimed as destroyed. Between him and Foster, Blue Section seems to have hit the bombers quite hard, and this is corroborated by other observers: Flight Lieutenant Norwood and Flight Sergeant Horkin from White Section saw Blue Section's attacks on the left-hand end of the bomber formation, observing one bomber roll left smoking heavily with both engines in flames, plus a separate machine from this vee dropping out of formation, descending with one engine smoking.

The pilots of 54 Squadron had carried out 13 gunnery passes upon the bombers in the initial squadron attack, which shows that the escorting fighters had failed to protect their charges. Having ceded the height band above 30 000 feet to the better performing Spitfires, the Zero pilots had not been able to stop the Spitfires in their dives, and had only been able to make their attacks after the Spitfires had already fired at the bombers.

Despite the inadequacy of their escorting performance, the Zeros had exacted their revenge: of the 11 aircraft from 54 Squadron that had engaged the enemy, four had been shot down, three of them by fighters. Because the British had attacked from the beam or rear quarter rather than further forward against the bombers' bow, they had been exposed to attacks from the rearward fighter escort. A full squadron of Zeros had dived on them during and just after their firing runs, when the Spitfire pilots were at their most vulnerable, concentrating upon the bombers. The Zero squadron had strong numerical superiority against the rear section of the squadron (the part that was attacked), and all three of the fighter victims were hit by gunnery fired from astern – the best killing position. All of them had been surprised from behind while diving or climbing; not one had been shot down while dogfighting. Several pilots, including the very green Thompson, had engaged in dogfights with the Zeros and gotten away with it. Air Group 202's tactics give the lie to the clichéd perception that the Japanese pilots achieved their success through dogfighting. In fact, they were a lot more sophisticated than that, reflecting the Japanese navy's tactical emphasis upon German-style 'hit and run tactics': they used height and sun to get in, make the bounce, and then zoom back up for the next go – very conventional tactics well understood by all air forces in World War II.

With so many gunnery passes accomplished, 54 should have hit the bombers harder, except that every one of 54's surviving aircraft except for Foster's had suffered cannon failures. Thompson's cannons had not fired at all, while every other aircraft had had one cannon fail, usually after only a second's firing, and then the second one soon after that. Experience showed that bombers were rarely shot down with a scattering of .303 inch machine-gun hits at long range (not helped by the fact that the .303 Browning was a 'notably inaccurate' weapon, spraying its bullets in ever-widening circles around the gun axis). There can be no doubt that the failure of the cannons greatly reduced the chances of getting kills. As a result, after the squadron's attack, although two bombers left the formation trailing smoke, none was seen to positively crash.

452's attack

As they had waited for 54 to get in position, the nine aircraft remaining with 452 were right out past the bombers' port bow. After Gibbs finally announced that he was ready, Caldwell said 'attack', and down the squadron went into a head-on attack at the bombers. The three sections wheeled right, losing section line abreast formation as they did so. When they came out of the turn, heading for the bombers, each of the sections were now in

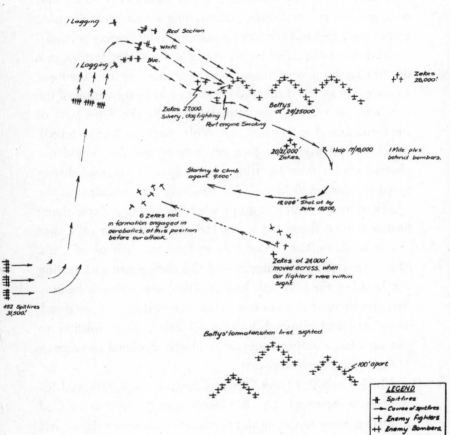

A diagram of the 452 Squadron attack on 30 June. Note the bombers' vee of vees formation, 452's up sun attacking position, the disordering effect of the final turn, the high-closure, high-deflection diving attack, and the stunting Zeros that acted as decoys. NAA: A11231, 5/75/INT untidy line astern, but the sections themselves were still roughly abreast of one another. This gave the squadron a wider attacking front than usual, allowing three aircraft side by side to come in to fire simultaneously. As they rolled out onto attack heading, the Australian pilots saw the effects of 54's attack only 30 seconds or so previously: one bomber was trailing smoke on the outside end of the left-hand vee (the formation hit by Foster's section).

Makin led 452 down from out of the sun, diving fast because of the height gap of more than 6000 feet to the bombers' altitude. He attacked the lead bomber right in the centre of the bombers' great vee of vees (unintentionally the same part of the formation that 54's Red and White Sections had attacked). Makin found that 'though excellently placed [he] could not observe any hit' from his firing – not helped by his great closing speed of about 520 knots TAS. Flashing past underneath the bombers, he was still going fast when he saw two Zeros flying further behind them and lower. He had time to get off a shot at one of them, but too quickly to have much hope of a hit. Makin kept going, banking around in a diving turn and moving out ahead of the bombers, heading like them towards Fenton. Arriving there at low altitude before the raid arrived overhead, he orbited and climbed, looking for other stray Spitfires to join up with. Finding none, he prudently declined to reattack without that mutual support.

Makin's No. 2, Flying Officer Gerald Cowell, followed his leader into the attack dive, but lost him in the turn and ended up further away to the right. He aimed at a bomber on the left end of the enemy formation, but when he fired his guns jammed after only a very short burst: left with only one .303 machine gun still functioning, he saw no strikes. Because of his divergent flight path, when Cowell broke off he found that he had lost his leader. Like Makin, the momentum of his dive took him out far beyond the other side of the bomber formation. There he made an optimistic attack on a group of three Zeros, firing at one of them with his single gun until forced to break away to avoid a rapid counter-attack from one of the others. He then went down into the usual series of diving turns to get away.

Diving behind Makin, Squadron Leader MacDonald too drifted out of position and lost his Red Section partners. Instead, he found himself with White Section, diving in beside them and lining up on a bomber straggling behind the left-hand end of the bomber formation. However, the dive caused his propeller CSU to fail and his engine to overrev. Now he had to anxiously watch the rpm counter and manipulate his propeller and boost levers while simultaneously trying to aim and fire. Although he saw no strikes from his high-deflection beam attack, he did succeed in clearing the propeller fault and stabilising his engine revs. MacDonald used his dive speed to zoom up above the bombers to set up for another attack. He was pleasantly surprised that all his guns had fired.

Leading White Section, Flight Lieutenant Ted Hall's engine cut out on the way down. As Hall went through the engine restart procedure, he drifted back through the gaggle of diving Spitfires, unintentionally putting Sergeant Ross Richardson (the greenest pilot in the squadron) in the van of White Section's attack. Richardson aimed and fired, but both his cannons froze; seeing no results from his fire, he broke downwards and disengaged. Having restarted his engine, Ted Hall then came in and fired, but his port cannon froze. He broke underneath the bombers and zoomed up by himself for a reattack. Flying Officer Bill Lloyd also had armament problems: his starboard cannon jammed after only a second's firing. He nonetheless believed he got hits on his target's front fuselage before zooming back up.

Pilot Officer Paul Tully came in last. Because he came in at the end of the string, the others were in his way, so he swung out wide into a rear-quarter attack. Alone among his White

Section colleagues, he thus found himself under return fire from the bomber gunners. Closing right in to 100 metres, he saw the bright white muzzle flashes of the 20 mm tail guns firing at him. His port cannon jammed, but he saw numerous incendiary strikes on the bomber's port wing. Like the others, he then broke downwards, but as the arse-end Charlie he was unavoidably the last one out. Suddenly he found himself under fire, with tracers flashing past from behind – he had been bounced by a Zero! Luckily, the Japanese pilot missed, and so Tully was able to bunt violently out of its line of fire and dive away in steep turns down to 10 000 feet. Then he re-climbed into the sun (away from the enemy), understandably intent upon avoiding further fighter attack. Hal Whillans, meanwhile, the sole remnant of Blue Section, had dived in by himself, positioned out on the far right of the squadron attack. However, his cannons failed to fire a single shot, and then even his machine guns jammed. He dived away in disgust for home.

Ron MacDonald, having zoomed back up after his first (abortive) attack, was also bounced. He had gained 1000 feet above the bombers when tracers whipped by very close. Savagely pulling the controls back into the 'corner' to spin his aircraft to the left, he looked back to see a Zero 300 metres behind. The sudden spin caused the propeller CSU to fail once more, so he cut his switches in an attempt to stop the engine from overrevving on the way down. Diving vertically with a dead engine, he found that a 'vigorous application of rudder' was needed to maintain the aircraft in a series of dead-stick steep turns. The Zero was still there, following behind and taking snap shots, but MacDonald's maintenance of violent evasive turns meant that the Japanese pilot could not apply enough deflection, so the tracers kept passing behind. Restarting the engine, MacDonald found it overrevving again and now saw that white smoke was streaming out of the exhausts – the usual internal glycol leak. Luckily, at that moment Gerald Cowell was also diving away nearby. He saw a Zero chasing a Spitfire and turned in after the Zero, but the Japanese pilot saw him coming and broke away before he could fire; however, it was enough to have simply chased it off the CO's tail, giving MacDonald the space he needed to deal with his emergency.

By now the CO was going through the bail-out drill. Although he switched off the magnetos, the propeller still spun and white smoke continued to pour out of the exhausts. Opening the hood, he removed his helmet, undid his straps and looked around to have a 'last look' before stepping over the side; but at that moment the engine and the propeller stopped dead. As this meant there was no longer a danger of engine explosion or fire, he now decided to stay with the aircraft. Sitting back down, he trimmed the Spitfire into a glide. After a while he tried restarting the engine, finding that it ran, but very roughly, issuing puffs of black smoke rather than the previous stream of white glycol smoke. However, it kept going long enough to get him back to Strauss, where MacDonald made a normal landing after a luckless and perilous flight.

Ted Hall meanwhile had re-climbed and commenced a second attack against the extreme left-hand bomber. As he rolled into the attack, a Zero suddenly appeared in front and made a head-on attack at him. Unusually, it pressed its attack in to close range. He fired back until it was only 50 metres away and saw strikes, with white and black smoke coming from its engine. The Zero roared past very close just overhead, and then rolled onto its back and dived away smoking. Hall pressed on and resumed his attack on the bomber, but saw no result from his fire. He then dived for home to claim the Zero as destroyed.

Bill Lloyd also re-climbed, but as he came up beside the bombers he observed a group of fighters behind them. The rearward position of these Zeros made them easier to get to than the bombers, so he started climbing up sun, getting into position to bounce them. His engine then developed an oil leak, spraying oil so thickly out over the windscreen that he could not see through his gunsight. He gave up and headed back to base instead, noticing as he dived away that the bombers were now approaching their bomb run to Fenton.

Meanwhile, somewhere behind, Col Duncan was still airborne with his smoking engine. Seeing a straggling bomber that had dropped out from the left-hand end of the formation, he dived to make a firing run at this conveniently placed target. Despite his engine's imminent self-destruction, he concentrated on his attack, firing a deflection shot from the bomber's rear quarter until close range and seeing so many hits that he considered it shot down. Glycol smoke started pouring more thickly from his engine's exhausts, the smoke started getting darker (the engine oil was burning), and the cockpit started getting intensely hot – classic symptoms of a deteriorating internal glycol leak. Executing his predetermined plan, he decided to bail out, but as in Laundy's case, the hood release mechanism did not work: yanking on the black rubber knob to jettison the hood, the knob came away in his hand, leaving him staring in disbelief at the sheared cable dangling uselessly. Dropping the rubber ball, he used both hands to pull back the canopy manually, but it would not budge, held fast in its rails by his aircraft's great speed. Turning off the petrol to stop the engine, he pulled the nose up to slow the aircraft and permit the hood to detach. To provide more leverage as he strained at the canopy, he pushed against the instrument panel with one foot, while with the other foot he steered the aircraft with the rudder bar.

The canopy did not slide back, and gouts of flame and black smoke were now billowing out of the joints in the engine cowling; burnt debris flew back and spattered itself all over the windscreen; and a tongue of flame momentarily flared into the cockpit from underneath the rudder pedals. Duncan knew the petrol tanks right in front of him could go up any moment, so he renewed his attempts to jettison the canopy by brute force: raising his arms above his head, he started belting the sides of the perspex canopy with his elbows. On the fourth blow, the bottom edge on the left-hand side dislodged and, caught by the airflow, the whole perspex moulding was instantly ripped away. Even this apparent salvation brought its own peril, for the wind-suction accelerated the fire, suddenly welling up into the cockpit from under the instrument panel. Duncan pulled out the pin to release his seat harness, but the shoulder straps would not dislodge, as he was inadvertently holding the four-point harness in place by instinctively pushing his body up out of his seat to get away from the fire. Methodically, he sat back down in the bath of flame, the straps then fell away, and he stood up. There was a sudden explosive roar and he found himself tumbling over and over, 'revelling in the icy air'.

Duncan free-fell from 24 000 feet, but sensibly refrained from pulling the parachute D-ring, because he wished to descend as quickly as possible into breathable air and avoid being killed in his parachute by the Zeros. When he had fallen below the altitude band of the combat, he grabbed the D-ring with both hands and pulled, gently drifting down under the canopy from 15 000 feet. At the end of his descent, he fell through the branches of a gum tree, only extricating himself and his parachute from it with some difficulty. Having finally got his feet safely on terra firma, Duncan had a good look at himself, discovering that both knees and his left arm were covered in second-degree burns – which did rather explain the pain. The skin of his entire forearm was hanging loosely from his flesh like a transparent bag, with an egg-sized cup of serum sloshing about within the distended bag of transparent skin. He looked at his watch: it was 12.25 – a lot had happened in that hour since take-off. He laid out his parachute canopy, sat down and applied first aid: he burst the bag of loose skin on his forearm, drained the fluid, applied Mercurochrome from his Mae West first-aid kit, dressed the arm with gauze and safety pins, mounted it in a sling, and sat down to wait for rescue.

Duncan's injuries point to the extreme inadequacy of the RAF flying clothing in hot 'tropical' areas: he had worn the usual shorts and short-sleeved shirt, and had of course only been burned in those resultant areas of uncovered skin. His feet and hands, covered in leather gloves and sheepskin flying boots, had fortunately escaped injury. It was lucky that his face had been high enough above the seat of the fire to escape the worst of the heat, because he had left his eyes unprotected, his goggles pushed uselessly up on his forehead. Duncan was shocked to now see his reflection in the survival kit mirror – the exposed area of his face between helmet and oxygen mask was black with soot, with eyelashes and eyebrows burnt completely off.

Ross Richardson had seen the fiery descent of Duncan's Spitfire and followed him down, circling around his parachute to guard him from attack. A number of pilots observed Duncan's descent and radioed fixes on his position back to control. A ground search party went out after him that afternoon, while Spitfires were sent out looking for him also. The next day, one of the pilots saw a man on the ground; returning to that spot and flying low overhead, Flying Officer John Gould recognised the man as his own missing squadron mate, Col Duncan. No. 452 thereafter maintained a four-day program of supply-dropping sorties – which amounted to little more than making a low and slow pass overhead and lobbing a parcel of rations out of the cockpit. Then Flight Lieutenant Clyde Fenton, the famous prewar 'flying doctor' and CO of 6 CU, got involved: he flew over in an Avro Anson and dropped directions to an army search party. His squadron mates also led a Beaufighter to the spot, which permitted the dropping of larger parcels. These supply drops were limited to the 'essentials' – rations, razors and cigarettes (even though Duncan, unusually for a fighter pilot, was a non-smoker); and as the army ground party drew near, a Beaufighter dropped Verey pistol and cartridges, to permit Duncan to signal his location. Flight Lieutenant Frank Gardiner, the Beaufighter pilot, also dropped the marooned and maimed pilot a note, pointing out that, 'You owe me a bottle of beer for all this'. Duncan was finally rescued by men from the 2/8 Independent Company on 4 July and taken to 1 MRS for overdue medical treatment of his burns. He was a first tour pilot with only 358 flying hours. It is hoped that Gardiner got his beer, for he was killed in a midair collision during a raid on Taberfane on 21 August.

No. 452 Squadron had suffered severely, not from enemy fighters but from its own aircraft: three had been destroyed and one pilot killed, all from glycol leaks. Moreover, 452's attack had been marred by disabling gun problems. Every one of its surviving aircraft had suffered major failures and jams; only in two aircraft had one of the cannons worked long enough to complete a reasonable burst. Unsurprisingly, this meant that 452's gunnery had not produced the results that might have been hoped for from such a well-delivered squadron attack.

No. 452 was blamed afterwards for the losses inflicted by the Zeros, on the basis that it had failed to attack the enemy fighters as ordered, and that as a consequence the Japanese had been free to bounce the attacking Spitfires from above. Although 54 had been the particular victim of this fighter attack, 452's actions had little effect upon 54's losses for a couple of reasons: firstly, the British squadron actually attacked first, hitting the bombers about 30 seconds before 452 did, and secondly, 54 was bounced by the section of the escort that was positioned behind the bombers – furthest away from 452. Given this relative positioning, 54's attackers had unavoidably been left unsuppressed.

Flying Officer Quinn, 1 Fighter Wing's Intelligence Officer, concluded that it was these Zero attacks that had ruined the Spitfire squadrons' section cohesion. However, as all previous combats had shown, the pilots of 1 Fighter Wing rarely retained section or element cohesion after first contact. This was the case from the top down, with many examples of flight commanders, squadron COs and even Caldwell himself splitting from their No. 2s upon first contact and then going off alone to fight. The same was true on this day: the sections lost cohesion not because 452 had failed to suppress the fighters, but because retaining element cohesion in combat was a skill that the wing's pilots had not yet learnt to apply.

457's attack

According to Caldwell's plan of attack, 457 was to be the second wave of the assault on the bombers. He sent it in 30 seconds after 452: Flight Lieutenant Don Maclean's Blue Section and Flying Officer Ken Barker's White Section were to go in first, followed by Pete Watson's Red Section, which Caldwell would lead personally. However, by now mechanical problems had also reduced 457's strength: White Section was now a one-man show – Ken Barker only – and so he attached himself to Maclean's section. Upon the command to go in, Maclean duly peeled off and led his men from out of the sun against the bombers' port bow. Like 452, they had to dive 7000 feet to make their firing runs and were thus moving very fast as they went into their attacks, making similar high-closure gunnery runs from almost head-on.

Caldwell had instructed all squadrons to attack in line abreast to permit entire sections to fire simultaneously. Ken Barker tried to position himself up alongside Maclean, but the steep dive shook out Blue Section into the usual uneven string of Spitfires behind the leader. With Barker in sight out to his right, Maclean conducted a head-on attack, firing in to 75 metres. Upon ceasing fire, he bunted underneath then zoomed back up into the sun. Barker fired at the bomber on the left-hand end of the formation, opening fire at long range, and ceasing fire without result at 300 metres; then he half-rolled and dived underneath.

Flight Lieutenant 'Snapper' Newton, the leader of Blue Section's second element, was initially close up on Maclean as he dived, but moved over to the right to line up on a bomber that was flying by itself out on the enemy's left flank (previously hit by Foster's section from 54). He fired in to 100 metres then pulled up and flashed right over the top. To break away downwards, he rolled onto his back and pulled, his aircraft bumping violently as it dived through the bombers' slipstream.

Newton's wingman, Flying Officer Norm Robinson, was on his leader's port side. He saw other 457 Spitfires making their firing passes up ahead of him, but saw no results from their attacks. Opening fire at long range (600 metres), he found that only three of his machine guns were firing, but he kept his finger on the button right in to 100 metres. Upon ceasing fire, he followed Newton, at first pulling up over the top of the bombers, then half-rolling and breaking away downwards. As his Spitfire's nose dropped into the dive, the propeller CSU failed and the engine overrevved. It did not respond to corrective action and only recovered normal revs once Robinson had descended into the denser air below 10 000 feet.

Maclean's No. 2, Pilot Officer Bruce Little, had diverged from his leader as he dived, lining up on the same machine as Newton was attacking – the bomber flying by itself out on the port side of the enemy formation. Little watched Newton attacking it ahead of him, but Newton seemingly failed to hit, for the bomber flew on without visible ill effect. Little then aimed and fired, but only one of his cannons worked. Seeing no result, he ceased fire and broke away into a steep dive. This caused his propeller CSU to fail and his engine revs screamed up to 4000 rpm. Little chopped the propeller and throttle levers back, and then cycled the propeller lever back and forth, both without any effect on the overrevving. He then closed the throttle, pulled the propeller control right back, maintained the dive, and hoped for the best. Like Robinson, he found that it was only upon reaching the thicker air at 8000 feet that the engine revs dropped back to normal. Unusually, in both cases the engines had not destroyed themselves in the process, so both pilots were able to make it back to base and land normally.

While Maclean's men attacked, Caldwell was still holding 457's White Section up above, watching progress down below. He asked Pete Watson, 'Ready?', and then launched the final phase of the attack, himself leading them down. Thus the last five Spitfires dived in: Watson was to port and Caldwell to starboard, with the others trying to close up beside them. Caldwell made his run against the bombers' port beam. On the way down, he noticed a Zero coming in from the left, but he coolly completed his attack upon his target bomber, opening fire at long range and maintaining the desired deflection in his gunsight by pushing forward on the stick as the range closed. One of his cannons jammed but he kept firing, swinging from the beam onto the bombers' rear quarter and thereby exposing himself to intensive return fire. Caldwell saw the bombers' fuselages speckled with flashes, but was unsure whether these were incendiary strikes from his own gunfire or muzzle flashes from the gunners.

Like many other Spitfire pilots, Caldwell spent too long on his gunnery run for safety, considering that he had already seen a Zero coming for him – indeed, he came very close to being shot down by it. Just as he broke downwards and to starboard after firing, he was attacked from behind by a Zero that he only now saw in his rear-vision mirror: it was close enough for him to clearly perceive the white propeller spinner and the black engine cowling. 'A considerable amount of tracer and fire' passed him, which he evaded by bunting under it.

Watson meanwhile opened fire at the bombers from 400 metres out, but both cannons froze; then he pulled up and broke over the top. He could see Caldwell to his right, now zooming up overhead into a climbing left turn, so pulled up to follow. Looking over his right shoulder, however, he saw Zeros coming down from behind, so broke away downwards into an evasive spiral dive. Watson's No. 2, Flight Sergeant Bill Hardwick, had followed him in, trying to keep up. He opened fire at 500 metres upon a bomber in the left-hand end of the formation, but once again both cannons froze. He kept firing with machine guns only until point-blank range in a high-deflection front-quarter attack. Seeing no strikes, at the last second he pulled up over the top, then rolled and dived as he went past. His aircraft thumped in the bombers' slipstream so violently that he thought he had been hit. Hardwick found himself descending 'at a great rate of knots' inverted but was unable to get the stick back to recover, as the elevator was still trimmed forward for the dive. He only just managed to wind the trim back and recover to normal flight at 2000 feet. By then he was out of the fight.

Flying Officer 'Bush' Hamilton followed Caldwell in, keeping Watson and Hardwick in sight out to his left, and attacking the left-most bomber (the same one attacked by many others). He fired in a high-deflection front-quarter attack right in to point-blank range. Ceasing fire at the last moment, he kicked his left rudder pedal and skidded his aircraft underneath the bombers, then zoomed up on the other side into a climbing turn, pulling so hard that he blacked out. Easing the G, Hamilton recovered his vision just in time to see a Zero diving from ahead firing tracer. Hamilton flew straight at it, pulling up into the sun and seeing the Zero overshoot and pull out 2000 feet below. The Japanese pilot rolled out of his turn and flew along parallel with him, underneath. Hamilton got suspicious of being decoyed and looked around: there were indeed two Zeros behind, 3000 feet higher. He maintained his full-power climb at a high IAS and left them behind.

Hamilton's wingman, Sergeant Bill Basey, had had difficulty keeping up with him and had fallen behind – and thus took on the undesirable role of arse-end Charlie. As he followed his leader into the dive, there was an ear-piercing bang and an incandescent flash on his port wing: he had been hit! Almost simultaneously, a Zero flashed past through his gunsight, 400 metres away, moving from right to left. Basey fired at it instinctively in a speculative full deflection shot, but it was gone, too fast for aiming. He broke away downwards into a series of violent turns, now seeing the big hole that an explosive 20 mm cannon shell had made in his wing. Anxious both about his wing's structural integrity and about the still unseen Zeros, he kept diving, heading for home.

Pete Watson pulled out at 20 000 feet, intending to intercept the bombers on their way out. He was climbing through 23 000 feet over the Mount Litchfield area when a Zero suddenly appeared from out of the sun, directly ahead, coming straight at him. It flashed over the top and pulled up into a steep turn to get onto his tail. Watson broke into the Zero, turned underneath it, half-rolled and dived away in a series of skidding turns.

Jack Newton, meanwhile, having dived away from his initial attack on the bombers, had recovered from the dive down at 2000 feet, and then started re-climbing to investigate a parachute he could see ahead. Fixating too much on this intriguing sight, he missed the Zero that bounced him from out of the sun:

suddenly it flashed past from the left. Fortunately for Newton, the Zero pilot had used a challenging full deflection shot, and so missed. Newton broke left and pulled up into a full-power climb into the sun: for the second combat in a row, he had been dangerously bounced, and had only survived because of the Japanese pilot's poor shooting.

Don Maclean was more successful in re-engaging, regaining a 3000 feet height advantage over the bombers and arriving back in the fight in time to see a bomber dropping out of formation. Diving at it, he made a beam attack on this straggler and saw bullet flashes all over the top of its fuselage, while the port engine started to stream white smoke. However, just then Maclean saw a Zero diving upon him, already firing, so he broke off his attack at once by half-rolling and breaking away downwards. He re-climbed again in time to see the bombs exploding down below on Fenton airfield, but by then his oxygen gauge was in the red, so he returned to base.

Ken Barker had also zoomed back up after his first attack, and was climbing up sun to get into position for another run when he saw a Zero running in behind him. He half-rolled and dived away vertically, but as he did so the fuel-pressure warning-light lit up on the instrument panel, and then the engine cut – there was too little fuel left in the tank he had selected to maintain suction through the fuel pump. Although still worried about the Zero behind him, he started easing out of the dive, pulling the throttle back in order to regain fuel pressure and changing over to the main tank. He had to glide for two minutes, waiting for the air lock in the fuel line to clear, all the while looking anxiously over his shoulders for signs of pursuit. Finally, the fuel warning light went off, then the engine started spluttering, and then fired normally again. He went home.

In 457's attacks, both cannons and machine guns had failed, the incidence of stoppages being so serious that the squadron rightly concluded afterwards that it contributed to its 'lack of score'. Gun mechanisms had frozen and ammunition had jammed in the feed mechanisms. Armament problems had been evident ever since the 15 March combat, but 30 June was the worst day yet: it is likely that the long period spent at high altitude on this day had contributed significantly to this higher rate of failure. The unusually long time spent at extreme altitude is shown by the fact that both Gibbs and Maclean ran out of oxygen during the engagement. Handicapped both by these gun failures and by the pilots' established marksmanship problems in high-closure deflection attacks, 457's gunnery had produced quite disappointing results. Only Don Maclean and Ian Mackenzie had seen evidence of hits, each claiming one bomber damaged. They had attacked the same left-hand end of the same left-hand vee as 452 and 54's Blue Section had attacked, so they may have hit the very same bombers. As he re-climbed up sun out on the port side of the bombers, Gibbs had observed the enemy formation as it headed in procession inbound towards the target. He saw two bombers out of formation, each with one engine smoking – these had dropped out of the left-most vee (attacked by Foster's Blue Section) and the centre vee (attacked by Gibbs's Red Section) respectively. He then watched several groups of Spitfires attack (452 and 457), but with little observable result.

The bombing

Although the GCI radar operators of Fenton's 319 Radar Station were able to plot the bombers coming in from 40 kilometres out, the Japanese went through their bomb run undisturbed by fighter attack. Indeed, throughout the 1943 campaign, in not one instance did 1 Fighter Wing succeed in disturbing the bombers' bomb run. The three big vees came up line abreast of one another, holding their formation on the lead bombardier's aircraft in the centre and putting their noses down in a shallow dive. Down below, the newly arrived Americans of the 380th BG watched from their slit trenches and awaited the greeting from their Japanese opposite numbers. The Australian Army's 133rd Heavy AA Battery fired 46 rounds of 3.7 inch without any discernible effect either upon the neatness of the bomber formation or its bombing accuracy. Down came the pattern of 150 bombs, exploding accurately along the edges of the field, and sending up roiling masses of drifting dust over the 380th's dispersals and technical areas. Three B-24s were destroyed by fire, as were a dozen replacement Pratt and Whitney engines, a petrol tanker, five tractors, and an obsolete CW-22 pursuit plane used as a squadron 'hack'. One RAAF and one USAAF airman were injured, as well as two Bofors gunners from the Australian Army's 149 LAA Battery; but thanks to slit trenches, there were no fatalities.

Never since 19 February 1942 had so many aircraft been hit on the ground in a Darwin bombing raid, which made this the most destructive airfield attack since that day. The 23rd Air Flotilla had successfully struck back at the American unit, the Spitfire wing's interception having had little substantive result in deflecting or diminishing this bombing. The AA crews – seasoned observers and professional critics of bomber opera-tions, and equipped with magnification equipment – counted 21 bombers going overhead at 20 000 feet. Thus only two bombers had been knocked out of formation by the Spitfires' attacks, which corresponds with the pilots' reports. After bombing, the big formation made a 180 degree turn and went out on a north-west heading, the bombers putting their noses down further and accelerating to almost 250 knots as they headed for the coast.

The reattacks on the way out

Climbing up after the bombers, Bill Gibbs saw no Zeros, so took the opportunity to make a succession of solo attacks, diving four times from out of the sun in beam attacks on the bombers. Although he saw strikes on his targets, there was no evidence of definite damage. 'Wicky' Wickman of 54, after diving away from his first attack, had also shadowed the bombers on the up sun side, regaining 30 000 feet in time to see them go through the AA bursts over the target. He waited patiently by himself, staying up sun as the bombers headed back outbound, until he saw his chance: a bomber was straggling 200–300 metres behind the formation. At once he dived in from its port rear quarter and fired a long burst, but saw no results before breaking away.

Gibbs was re-climbing again when he heard Caldwell report that a smoking bomber was dropping back out of formation – the same one as Wickman attacked. Gibbs spotted it and advised Caldwell that he would finish it off, diving at it from dead astern but observing no return fire. Its port engine was already on fire, so he aimed at the starboard one, firing from 50 metres and setting this engine afire too, and so claimed it as destroyed. After this last attack, he counted 19 bombers left in the formation as they headed away out to sea.

As he shadowed the retiring bombers, Gibbs ran out of oxygen, so he descended and requested information from control on any targets at lower altitude. Hearing of none and having refreshed himself by flying at a lower altitude for a while, he permitted himself to be guided by Wickman back to the main bomber formation. Climbing up on the starboard side, Gibbs overhauled the enemy when they were 60 kilometres out to sea beyond Peron Island. He now counted 13 bombers only, again with no fighters, so made a quick attack from dead astern upon the bomber on the extreme right. However, feeling the effects of hypoxia from flying without oxygen at 23 000 feet, his gunnery was ineffective and he saw no results. He finally dived away for home, still looking for low-flying targets as he went. Gibbs had lost his section in the first contact, had fought an individual action thereafter, and was lucky that the Zeros had been engaged elsewhere. Despite the great risks he had taken by flying alone and recklessly continuing the fight without oxygen, it was in some measure due to his moral example that 54 Squadron made a total of 20 gunnery attacks on the bombers before breaking off the action.

Caldwell meanwhile had also climbed into the sun to get back above the bombers. Once he had overhauled them again, he rolled into another firing run. This time, he avoided the return fire by diving underneath and zooming up from underneath. Despite the moderate closing speed of the climbing attack, which permitted him to keep firing to only 10 metres range, both cannons had now frozen, and he saw no results from his .303 inch fire. Re-climbing into the sun, he now saw a Zero in a climbing turn after a Spitfire, so he closed in on the enemy fighter from behind and below. He opened fire at 250 metres, the Zero pulling straight up into a wingover and then diving away. Caldwell pulled around after it and fired again from 300 metres. Breaking off his attack to perform a hard turn to clear his own tail, he then resumed his pursuit of the Zero. He reported afterwards that it continued its dive, leaving a trail of white smoke while passing through 5000 feet, and then dived into the ground and flared into flame. Caldwell re-climbed after the bombers over Cape Ford, but he could not find them again as they flew out to sea.

There had been no special magic about the great ace's fight. He had fought in the same manner as had Gibbs and MacDonald, fighting alone after the first pass, a vulnerable lone Spitfire in a big sky. He had taken his risks as they had done and once again

One of the B-24 bombers destroyed by bombing on Fenton airfield. Its starboard engines were being serviced, as shown by the servicing stand visible by the ruined starboard wing. This aircraft's parking bay at the 380th Bomb Group's newly finished base was completely unprotected. AWM Negative P04330.003

had gotten away with it. By engaging in his solitary combats far from the main engagement, Caldwell was reverting to the 'lone wolf' approach that had defined his fighting style in the desert during his early days with 112 Squadron. Like then, this meant that his claimed victory could not be corroborated – but it was awarded anyway.

Meanwhile, in a grass clearing near Bynoe Harbour, Harker was still standing by his belly-landed aircraft awaiting rescue. He knew that Tiger Moth aircraft were used to pick up stranded pilots from beaches and other remote locations, but could see that the grass in this 'paddock' was too long to permit a Tiger Moth to land. He therefore used his initiative, burning a strip of grass to create an improvised runway. Unfortunately, once the blaze had taken hold the wind changed direction and brought it back towards his Spitfire. Sadly, EE670 took fire and was burnt away to charred wreckage. Ron MacDonald, having survived the combat and landed his damaged aircraft, had meanwhile taken off in another Spitfire, on the lookout for low-level raiders. He spotted Harker's wrecked machine, waved to Harker and radioed control with a fix on the downed pilot's position. A Tiger Moth from 6 CU arrived five hours later and the pilot complimented Harker on the new strip.

Holmes meanwhile had landed by parachute in a wooded area, and had then set out walking towards a river he had seen on the way down, having arranged his parachute canopy in the shape of an arrow pointing in that direction. After a four-hour walk, he reached the river, buzzed reassuringly by a Spitfire on the way, the pilot waggling his wings to indicate that he had seen him. Upon reaching the river, he was picked up after only 15 minutes by a party from the Australian Army.

'Kills' and claims

In spite of its losses when jumped by the fighters, 54 had made the best attack of the day, claiming all four of the bombers that the wing claimed as shot down. The difference is that the two Australian squadrons had come in from higher up and had therefore come in faster and from further ahead, thereby making high-closure passes against the bombers' front quarter – exactly the gunnery parameters most likely to tax the pilots' gunnery skills, as shown in previous combats. By contrast, many of the 54 Squadron pilots had made rear-quarter attacks, although this was quite accidental, merely the result of its awkward attempt to move over to the bombers' far side. It was thus purely fortuitous that 54's attacks had featured the lower closure rates and lower deflection angles which had enhanced their gunnery. On the other hand, this had increased their exposure to bombers' return fire, as Holmes had discovered. Another measure of this set of contrasting gunnery parameters was that in addition to its 'confirmed kills', 54 claimed a further four bombers as 'probably destroyed', whereas once again, the two Australian squadrons were able to claim only a few bombers as damaged – not even a single 'probable' between them. This disparity in claimed results between the British and the Australians shows the basic honesty of the pilots: in spite of the overclaiming problem, pilots' claims were still proportional to observed evidence – if little was observed, little was claimed. The problem lay not in pilots' falsifications but in an overoptimistic readiness on the part of everyone to classify claims as 'confirmed' rather than 'probable' or 'damaged'.

In this case, the evidence used to support 54's claims for 'destroyed' and 'probably destroyed' claims had been observations of bombers with two burning engines; bombers with one burning engine; bombers streaming smoke; bombers falling out of formation; or bombers banking suddenly out of formation. Pilots' claims therefore rested upon quite reasonable evidence, although the usual double and triple claiming obviously applies. The conclusion that a number of bombers were badly hit is supported by 5 Fighter Sector's radar plotting of several separate outbound tracks: these were the direct homeward flights of damaged bombers that had left the formation to limp back to base alone, as observed by Laundy, Wickman and others. However, despite the cumulative impression of badly hit bombers, there was not a single observation of a bomber hitting the ground or going into the sea. Japanese records indicate that one bomber crash-landed on Timor and was written off, while according to a unit history of 202 AG, two others made it back to Penfui but were so damaged that they were never repaired.

Once again, one dimension of the overclaiming problem is the political pressure that Area HQ brought to bear upon intelligence officers in order to confirm the claims of leading pilots. Area had confirmed Squadron Leader Gibbs's claim for one bomber 'probable' as well as two 'damaged'. However, Flying Officer Quinn, the wing intelligence officer, objected that it was only after Foster attacked that the first bomber had descended smoking (as attested by Norwood and Horkin) – that is, subsequent to Gibbs's attack. The conclusion was that Foster had done the damage, not Gibbs. Quinn also disputed the latter's claims for 'damaged' bombers, showing that in these attacks Gibbs had been firing machine guns only (both cannons having jammed), that each attack had been made with only a one-second burst, and that there had been insufficient observed effect to warrant any claim. It is revealing to see how Quinn's principled objections and forensic analysis were stood aside by the higher-up officers: he only held the rank of Flying Officer, after all. The Senior Air Staff Officer at NWA HQ replied curtly by declaring Squadron Leader Gibbs's claims to be 'correct' without any discussion of the specific points raised – hardly a credible response. Intelligence officers at squadron and wing level were simply too junior to exert the 'clout' needed to win such arguments, particularly when the claimant under question was a CO. If Quinn was steamrolled here in his attempt to offer a critical evaluation of Gibbs's claims, what chance did he have with Caldwell's?

Thus the wing's various intelligence officers confirmed the claims despite the lack of crash evidence. Even the admirable Quinn was happy to confirm Gibbs's claim for a 'confirmed' fighter on the basis of its merely spinning away emitting smoke – adequate evidence for a 'probable' claim only. Besides the political pressures, the basic reason for the wing's systemic overclaiming can clearly be seen in the intelligence officers' habitual acceptance of such non-conclusive 'evidence of destruction'. Bailed out bomber crewmen were reported descending in the area between Batchelor and Adelaide River, and 2/6 Cavalry Regiment was ordered to send out vehicles in search of a bomber that was reported as having crashed near Mount Litchfield. However, it turned out that these reports referred to downed Spitfires, and so the searches were called off. The bomber claims were confirmed anyway.

NWA HQ nonetheless remained a little defensive about the published results from the 30 June combat, which suggests some discomfort about their evidential basis. When Area HQ advised 54 Squadron that its pilots' claims had been confirmed, it emphasised that 'all available information' had been 'carefully examined' in order to reach this 'conclusion'. A critic might object that if the analysis had been as forensic as claimed, then someone might have flown over the area of the combat in an Anson or Wirraway to count the Japanese bomber wrecks. So far, there has been no identification of any such specific crash site, which leads to the conclusion that no bomber crashed on land.

No. 1 Fighter Wing's war diary, ultimately sent 'upstairs' to RAAF Command, also protested too much, revealing some sensitivity about the evidence it could adduce in support of its squadrons' claims:

> Although it is known that a number of the enemy aircraft were destroyed, these assessments have been made strictly in accordance with [UK] Air Ministry Orders relating to the assessment of enemy aircraft losses. The assessment has been arrived at from an examination of the combined reports and a further interrogation of the pilots concerned.

Although the Spitfire pilots claimed three Zeros 'confirmed' shot down, in only one case, Caldwell's, was the enemy fighter claimed to have crashed, but even this claim lacked any witnesses or other corroboration, such as a crash site. The other claims were made on the basis of Zeros seen to be leaving trails of smoke and diving or spinning. As previous combats showed, and as many Spitfire pilots could themselves attest, such phenomena did not necessarily indicate destruction. Indeed, Japanese records indicate that not one Zero was lost.

On this reckoning, 1 Fighter Wing had lost the fighter versus fighter combat badly, with three losses to nil victories. Given that all three Spitfires were lost in the bad bounce upon 54, this would not be a surprising result. However, this can be viewed another way: once the Japanese had sprung their ambush, they never again managed to score. In the 'dogfight' proper therefore, they once again found the Spitfires to be very slippery opponents. From the very beginning of this campaign, the Zero pilots had in fact scored their kills by bouncing Spitfire pilots that had become fixated upon the bombers, not by dogfighting with them.

Having begun the combat with a perfect interception and the advantages of height and sun, and having achieved the impressive and unprecedented total of 39 gunnery passes at the bombers, the wing had produced gunnery results that were astonishingly disappointing. The Spitfire pilots' very low gunnery efficiency can be attributed in equal measure to the pilots' inability to make accurate deflection shots, and to the wholesale failure of their aircraft's armament system. Their inability to score produced a feeling of renewed respect for their opponents: in spite of 202 AG's miserable performance in protecting the bombers from fighter attack, 1 Fighter Wing's intelligence officer reported that 'pilots concerned in the engagement were unanimous in their opinion of the high order of airmanship shown by their opponents'. Given that the Zeros were demonstrably impotent at either interfering with the Spitfires forming up above 30 000 feet or in stopping their attack dives, one thing is clear: had the Spitfire cannons worked as advertised and had the pilots been able to perform deflection shooting, the day would have been a disaster for the Japanese.

Mechanical issues

There were three major technical problems with the wing's aircraft: namely the malfunctioning propeller CSU, the leak-prone coolant system and the non-functional armament. The incidence of worn out engines was compounded by an absolute shortage of aircraft, for the mechanical failures in combination with combat losses had produced a higher-than-expected aircraft loss rate under operational conditions. As a result, by the end of June 452 was down to an inventory of only 14 aircraft – a sharp drop from the more normal inventory of 23 that it had had at the end of March – and by 4 July it was down to only 11. No. 457 Squadron too was getting worried:

Replacement difficulties are seriously worrying our engineer officer, as there are rumours that there are few aircraft at southern bases to make good our losses.

The shortage of Spitfires in Australia is shown by the record of Col Duncan's misbehaving aircraft, which had arrived in the wing on 9 May as a replacement for the wholesale losses suffered on 2 May. Jim Grant suggests that it was purportedly a new aircraft, but AR523 was one of the very first Spitfires received by the RAAF (the most recently arriving aircraft had progressed through the alphabet to EE and JG-prefixed serial numbers). This machine had spent its RAAF career thus far at 2 OTU and so was indeed heavily used by the time it joined 452. The appearance of such 'retreads' at front-line units shows that the aircraft supply line was under strain: indeed, the RAAF's entire Spitfire inventory dropped from 147 aircraft at the end of April down to a low of 121 at the end of June.

The supply situation was worse than these figures suggest because of the concurrent creation of a fourth Spitfire unit, No. 79 Squadron, for service in New Guinea. This new unit took the lion's share of the new Spitfire aircraft that were received in March and April, forcing 1 Fighter Wing to soldier on with its existing fleet of older machines. In addition, a ship bringing 11 new Spitfires to Australia, the *Silver Beech*, had been torpedoed and sunk in April, halting Spitfire deliveries at a critical moment. Attrition was really starting to bite into the Spitfire wing, albeit mostly self-inflicted – Jim Grant records that the wing lost 109 Spitfires damaged or destroyed from all causes during its 1943 campaign. One pilot in every two was involved in some sort of non-combat crash or flying accident during that year. No. 7 RSU recovered 79 crashed Spitfires for scrapping or repair up to the end of September. It is therefore clear that combat losses formed only a fraction of the total attrition. These statistics underline the importance to 1 Fighter Wing of the technical services provided by 7 RSU and 14 ARD, which recovered, repaired and recycled most of the Spitfires that were taken out of service and then returned them to the squadrons. Without this deep logistical backup accessed locally within the NWA, the defensive campaign would have stalled.

A fighter aircraft's key characteristics are defined by its power plant and its armament, but both of these systems performed so unreliably in the Spitfire aircraft of 1 Fighter Wing that the type must be considered unsatisfactory for its purpose. In an air force with the luxuries of time and options, the RAAF's Spitfire VC aircraft would have been considered un-combat-worthy, even un-airworthy. No. 54 Squadron had in recent operations suffered more than the other squadrons from these aircraft malfunctions, and made a special mention of it in an intelligence report, warning that 'most of the Squadron's aircraft are rapidly reaching, or have already reached, a condition which makes their continued operational use extremely hazardous, and cannot fail to produce … unfortunate results'.

30 June pilot table

Sqn	Section	No.	Pilots engaging	Pilots not engaging	Remarks
Wing Co		1	W/C Caldwell		both cannons failed
54	Red	1	S/L Gibbs RAF		both cannons failed
		2	F/Sgt Wickman RAF		1 cannon failed
		3		Sgt Monger RAF	aborted, engine trouble (BS218)
		4	F/O Thompson RAF		became Blue 3 when Monger aborted; both cannons failed
		5	Sgt Holmes RAF		shot down by bomber return fire; bailed out near Lucy Mine; BR530 destroyed

	Blue	1	F/L Foster RAF	internal glycol leak (BR495)
		2	F/Sgt Huggard RAF	BR537 damaged by Zeros, repaired by 7 RSU, restored to service 23 Aug; 1 cannon failed
		3	Sgt Laundy RAF	shot down; bailed out 12 km NW Adelaide River; BR490 destroyed
	White	1	F/L Norwood RAF	1 cannon failed
		2	F/Sgt Harker RAF	shot down, force-landed between Bynoe Harbour & Tumbling Waters, due south of Milne Inlet; EE670 written off
		3	P/O Wellsman RAF	shot down & killed, 50 km west of Batchelor near Reynolds River; BR528 destroyed
		4	F/Sgt Horkin RAF	1 cannon failed
452	Red	1	S/L MacDonald	R/T failed; CSU failure; cannon failure; damaged by Zeros, BR574 repaired on unit
		2	F/O Cowell	both cannons failed, plus three .303
		3	F/L Makin	1 cannon failed plus 4 .303
		4	F/O Lamerton	glycol leak, crash-landed & killed; BR241 destroyed
	White	1	F/L Hall	1 cannon failed
		2	P/O Tully	1 cannon failed
		3	F/O Lloyd	1 cannon failed
		4	Sgt Richardson	both cannons failed
	Blue	1	F/O Whillans	all guns failed
		2	F/Sgt Cross	CSU failure before combat; force-landed Stapleton Rd 25 km NW Batchelor; BR546 written off
		3	F/Sgt Duncan	glycol leak before combat; bailed out 30 km SW Batchelor; AR523 QY-A destroyed; both cannons failed
		4	F/Sgt Turnbull	aborted, CSU failure

457	Red	1	F/L P Watson		both cannons failed
		2	F/Sgt Hardwick		both cannons failed
		3	F/O Hamilton		
		4	Sgt Basey		
	Blue	1	F/L Maclean		
		2	P/O Little		1 cannon failed, CSU failure
		3	F/L Newton		
		4	F/O Robinson		CSU failure
	White	1	F/O Barker		
		2		F/O Halse	aborted, CSU failure
		3	F/O Mackenzie		lagged behind due to engine trouble, attacked with 54 Blue Section
		4		F/O Hegarty	aborted, air lock in fuel line
	Purple	1		P/O McDowell	vectored to Point Blaze by control; McDowell was initially Winco 2 but dropped out & joined Purple Section
		2		F/Sgt Batchelor	
		3		F/O Ashby RAF	
	Yellow			P/O Reilly	low-level base patrol
		31		10	

Summary:
Spitfires scrambled: 41
Spitfires in main wing formation: 37
Spitfires engaging: 31
Mechanical aborts: 4
Crashed & written off due to mechanical failure: 3
Shot down: 4
Damaged by enemy action: 2
Pilots killed: 2

10

The second Fenton raid

In spite of the encouraging plumes of black smoke over Fenton seen by the departing Japanese bomber crews on 30 June, one raid would clearly be insufficient to disable the 380th BG's operations. Certainly there was little evidence of their having knocked out the Allied strike capability, for Bladin had made his usual aggressive tit-for-tat response to the Japanese raid, sending B-25s from the Dutch No. 18 Squadron and Hudsons from No. 2 Squadron in night raids against the Timor airfields, and making a return call to the 23rd Air Flotilla at Kendari in the form of a B-24 raid that announced the continued vitality of the Fenton-based bomb group.

Japanese reconnaissance flights resumed on 3 July – generally a sure sign of a raid to come. On the following day, the wing was put on readiness in expectation of a follow-up raid, but it did not eventuate: instead, it was another early-morning Japanese reconnaissance overflight. No. 457 Squadron scrambled against it, but failed to intercept – after some early successes, the wing was now having trouble intercepting the speedy Ki-46s. Meanwhile, the RAAF had used the few days' breathing space after the previous raid to improve 1 Fighter Wing's Spitfire availability – after the low point of only 11 serviceable aircraft on 4 July, 452 Squadron had 15 available by the morning of the 6th. Meanwhile 457's CO, Squadron Leader Ken James, returned from leave on the 4th just in time for the next combat – it would be Darwin raid No. 58.

6 July

The 23rd Air Flotilla had again scraped together all available aircraft for a maximum effort operation. However, its bomber component, 753 Air Group, was only able to put 21 bombers on-line. This reduction in its strength after the preceding raid suggests a declining aircraft inventory within the unit, caused by aircraft written off and damaged in the previous two raids. From the 202 Air Group came an escort force of 25 Zeros, also a reduced strength force, likewise suggesting a unit at full stretch and with some aircraft placed out of service from the previous operations. By conducting three raids in a row at much shorter time intervals than usual, the navy units were suffering the cumulative attrition of operational wear and tear. This is a sign of the narrow margin of resources with which the Japanese maintained their raiding campaign against Darwin, and of the 23rd Air Flotilla's inability to apply the force level and the raiding tempo that would be necessary to seriously degrade the operational capacity of the NWA. It is clear that if 1 Fighter Wing's resources had become a little stretched, then so had those of the enemy; this did not augur well for the ongoing success of the Japanese counter-offensive against the 380th BG.

At 10.37 on the morning of 6 July, radar detected a large raid 260 kilometres from Darwin, and one minute later the controllers at 5 Fighter Sector issued the scramble order. By 10.44 am there were 33 Spitfires airborne heading towards the wing rendezvous at 6000 feet over Sattler. In addition, each squadron provided a one-aircraft Yellow Section: two of these conducted low-level patrols between Darwin and Batchelor on the lookout for surprise low-level penetrations, while the third was vectored at low altitude towards the raid as a 'Jim Crow' patrol, to shadow the raid over land and report its movements to control. The wing rendezvous was accomplished 'without delay' and the wing then climbed away to the east. The three squadrons were ranged in their usual broad and flat 'squadrons in line abreast', with 457 in the centre, 452 to port and 54 to starboard.

Caldwell led 457 personally despite the presence of its CO, Squadron Leader Ken James, who was relegated to flying on Caldwell's wing. Anomalously, this meant that James would lead his squadron into battle on only one occasion – on 2 May. The other two squadrons were led by their COs, but Ron MacDonald's bad run of luck with R/T sets continued: as had happened both on 28 and 30 June, his radio failed soon after the rendezvous, and so for a third combat in a row he had to hand over the leadership of his squadron to Paul Makin, and to drop back in the formation to be led rather than to lead.

As usual, 54 suffered its share of technical malfunctions. Both Flight Lieutenant Rob Norwood and Flight Sergeant C Studley found that their aircraft could not keep up with the others. Studley's propeller CSU malfunctioned, causing his engine rpm to surge, while Norwood's engine would not deliver its revs, and so he found himself lagging further and further behind once the squadron passed through 22 000 feet. He gave up, told the rest of White Section (Spencer and Harker) to go on without him, and joined up with Studley. Control then ordered these two stragglers to orbit overhead Fenton and await the arrival of the Japanese there, reassigning them as an improvised 'Purple Section'. They managed to slowly coax their unwilling machines up to 29 000 feet, but that was the top of their climb: Norwood's worn engine needed 2850 revs just to maintain this height. Flight Sergeant Huggard had a similar problem with an underperforming engine. He too found himself lagging behind, but managed to stay in visual touch with the squadron as they went in to their attack, and then saw the bombers go in to bomb. Despite positioning himself to attack them on the way out, he never caught up and went home without engaging. By this process, 54's 11-aircraft formation was whittled down to only eight aircraft as they approached the enemy.

The Japanese used a similar approach route to the one they had used on the previous raid, crossing the coast over Cape Ford, on an east-north-east course. This approach path was about 30 kilometres further south than it had been on 30 June, easing the controllers' decision-making about what the target might be – obviously Fenton. Control was therefore able to vector the wing more directly to meet the raid without the usual northward detour to protect Darwin. After achieving a rendezvous, the wing was sent east to get some height. Once the raid was reported as nearing the coast and climbing through 20 000 feet, the wing was vectored onto a westerly course towards the enemy and ordered to continue its climb, aiming to obtain an up sun position on the raiders' port bow as in the previous raid. Reaching 32 000 feet when 30 kilometres east of Peron Island, the wing was advised that the enemy were 30 kilometres away at 11 o'clock. Straight after that, control ordered a left turn onto an interception heading of 215 degrees, reporting the enemy as 15 kilometres ahead crossing from right to left. Bill Gibbs once again showed the sharpness of his eyesight by making an early sighting: looking along the search bearing provided by the controllers, he discerned flashes of light – sun glinting on perspex. Calling 'Tally-ho', he estimated their distance at 25 kilometres – showing that visibility was 'unlimited' in the clear air at that height. The achievement of such a neat interception and early 'Tally-ho' was a superb performance by the controllers, showing the proficiency gained since their first uncertain foray on 2 March. It was fortunate that the interception had been efficiently managed, for the wing was still out of belly tanks, and so the endurance of most aircraft would again be limited to that provided by their internal fuel capacity.

Now in visual contact with the enemy, Caldwell led the wing towards the bombers, maintaining a course perpendicular to theirs. As the enemy got closer, now flying at the impressive height of 27000 feet, Gibbs observed the bombers to be in their standard formation – three vees of nine each (although actually only seven). With the great crescent of enemy aircraft only a few kilometres off his starboard bow, Caldwell ordered his Spitfires to turn left onto a parallel course to the enemy. When the Spitfires came out of the turn, they were flying up sun and slightly in front of the bomber formation – much like the position obtained on 30 June. At this point, Caldwell gave his attack instructions: he once again wanted to catch the bombers in a pincer movement – everybody seemed to be repeating their tactics today – and so once again ordered 54 to cross over the enemy and fly out beyond their right flank in order to attack from the other side.

In conformity with this, the British squadron went directly over the top of the wide enemy formation. Some of the pilots had not seen the enemy armada at all while approaching on the long straight intercept heading, one such being Flight Sergeant

George Spencer: the first enemy aircraft he saw were three Zeros that came into view below only as he was banked in his turn right above them. He only saw the bomber formation as he looked further to the left of these Zeros; he had gone over the top of them without noticing! Such late visual acquisitions gave rise to a sense of apprehension among the pilots: having only belatedly noticed a group of four Zeros 4000 feet below them as they crossed overhead, the British pilots now looked nervously about them for more. Someone reported a further group of five Zeros behind the bombers – and this group of Zeros now turned towards the Spitfires and climbed. Other pilots saw yet another group of three Zeros even further back. One of the Australian squadrons reported an additional group of enemy fighters climbing into the sun for an attack on 54, but no one in the British squadron was able to see them: they were visible to the Australians looking down sun from the northern side, but not to the British squinting up sun from the south. The Zeros were hard to see because they were scattered in dispersed groups and superimposed against the landscape below, whereas by contrast the Spitfires were easy to see, concentrated together in a great Balbo and superimposed against the white layers of stratus and altostratus above 30 000 feet.

Ominously, 1 Fighter Wing's usual problem of only partial visual acquisition of the enemy fighter force recurred as the combat loomed. Different pilots saw the number of the two main groups of Zeros differently, with estimates ranging from four to nine in each of these sub-formations. In short, most pilots failed to see all the Zeros; there was generally a further group that remained unspotted as the Spitfire pilots committed themselves to their attacks. The Japanese tactic of splitting the fighter escort into many small formations was as usual making them elusive visual targets. Afterwards, the wing intelligence officers collated all these different counts to assess the strength of the escort at 21 Zeros – a fairly accurate estimation, but not one of the airborne pilots had seen all these at once.

As in the previous raid, 452's pilots had been assigned the role of attacking the fighters and so had a particular need to spot the locations of all the Zeros. They saw more of them than 54 did, spotting one group in front, one out on the left flank, and one behind the bombers, all at 28 000 feet. However, as had happened in the previous combat, confusion soon arose over 452's assigned task. Troublingly, Paul Makin once again lost sight of the fighters just before he was supposed to attack them. He reported his problem to Caldwell, but Ted Hall advised that he could see the rear group of nine Zeros and that he could lead an attack on them instead. Makin agreed to this, but said that as he himself still could not see any fighters, he would lead Red Section in an attack on the bombers – which he could see. Caldwell agreed to this compromise and so the attack could begin. By that stage, Hall's section had got 3 kilometres out to the right of Makin's section and further back – an unusually great separation within a squadron formation. This gave Hall quite a different visual perspective from Makin's, bringing him much closer to the enemy and thus presenting him with this attacking opportunity.

While 452 was trying to visually acquire its assigned targets, it was now 54's turn to do the waiting. The British pilots listened to all this discussion over the R/T with some frustration and anxiety. Gibbs had taken his squadron 8 kilometres out in front of the bombers, ready to turn back in for a head-on pass. Because of the Zeros that he kept hearing about in the R/T chatter, he did not want to wait any longer before attacking. As much as he swivelled his head about, he still could not see them. Gibbs had many times proven the excellence of his vision by getting long-range sightings on the enemy, so his failure to see the enemy in this instance suggests that he was searching in the wrong arcs; his manoeuvring to get 54 into its assigned position had disoriented him. As he searched the sky, Gibbs waited for 452 to sort itself out and announce it was ready. It finally did so, and Caldwell at last gave the word, telling 452, 'Troppo Squadron attack fighters'; and 20 seconds later telling 54, 'Candy Squadron attack bombers'. As these squadrons went in one after the other, he kept 457 up above as a reserve, just as he had done on 30 June.

452's attack

The Australian squadron was to assault the bombers' left front while the British attacked their right front – a repetition of the pincer attack that had been attempted on 30 July. In two separate groups, 452 wheeled about to the right to dive in, with Ted Hall's White section moving upon the rear group of nine Zeros that he had identified earlier, while Makin led Red Section at the bombers further forward. As Hall led his men around behind the rearward Zeros, the Japanese saw them coming and went into a defensive circle, enabling each of the Japanese pilots to cover the tail of the pilot in front.

Hall's four Spitfires dived in, each pilot picking out one of the turning Zeros as his target. However, the speed from the dive meant that Hall was going too fast to be able to turn in behind them, so he was forced into a high-deflection shot – the Japanese defensive tactic was working. Hall fired and missed, then zoomed up away from the Zeros. Pilot Officer Paul Tully moderated his speed by pulling out wider and coming in flatter, and was therefore able to hold the turn tight enough to follow one of the Zeros around for a few seconds. However, before he could fire he had to break away when he spotted another Zero coming in behind him. Flying Officer Bill Lloyd got a good shot at his target and saw some strikes, then zoomed up, as did Sergeant Ross Richardson. White Section had now lost section cohesion, for the four pilots split up as they zoomed in different directions. However, by forcing the Zeros to circle defensively, White Section's attack had succeeded in detaching nine Zeros from the bombers: by circling to spoil the Spitfires' attacks, this squadron of escort fighters was drifting further behind the advancing bomber formation that it was supposed to be defending.

Meanwhile, Makin took Red Section down for a head-on attack on the bombers. Flying Officer Bertie Watkin had dropped out earlier as his underperforming aircraft had been unable to get above 29 000 feet. That left Makin with only four aircraft, but only two of these actually carried through the attack on the bombers. This was because Makin turned aside at the last second to attack a detached section of Zeros that he only now spotted – part of the front group of escorting fighters – taking with him his wingman, Flying Officer Kenny Bassett. Makin had not seen these fighters until he was settled into his attacking dive, and then they suddenly appeared right in front of him. He hurriedly lined up on the left-hand one, while his wingman took the right. Red Section was actually attacking the fighters after all, in fulfilment of Caldwell's original orders. Bassett's target broke left, but Bassett was going too fast to track it and fire, so he overshot at speed, pulling up so hard that he blacked out and lost contact with his leader. Makin fired, but without effect, and also zoomed back up. His bounce had misfired, spoiled like so many others by good Japanese lookout and well-timed breaks.

As the six 452 Squadron Spitfires that had attacked the Zeros zoomed up after their attacks, all separated from one another, there were further Zeros above, which they had so far neither engaged nor seen. This squadron of enemy fighters was the front section of the escort, and now it made its appearance. At the top of his zoom, at 29 000 feet, Lloyd suddenly saw a

Zero coming straight at him, firing in a head-on attack. He fired back, but instead of breaking downwards he kept climbing up sun, and as he did so he found Richardson nearby and so joined up with him. These two tried to climb away, but were bounced from behind by another three Zeros, which used the speed from their dives to easily overhaul the climbing Spitfires. The first thing Richardson knew was when tracers shot close past, fired from behind. He broke away and warned Lloyd, diving away so abruptly that his propeller CSU failed: there was an immediate and severe internal glycol leak, white smoke streamed out of the exhausts, the engine overheated, and then the engine oil started to burn. With the cockpit enveloped in smoke and fire, his legs started to get burnt. Richardson undid his straps and leads and bailed out, pushing hard on the stick to eject himself from the cockpit. This worked, but he bashed his head on the windscreen on the way out and belted his knees on it also. Once clear of his machine, Richardson pulled the D-ring, drifting down under his parachute from the precipitous height of 27 000 feet. Dressed in shorts and cotton short-sleeved shirt, it was a chilly descent out of the sub-zero temperatures of that altitude. Richardson was one of the most inexperienced men in the squadron, and had now been shot down in his third combat. He landed quite close to human habitation, only 10 kilometres south of his own airfield, but was not recovered until two days later by Flight Lieutenant 'Doc' Fenton in his Tiger Moth.

Bill Lloyd meanwhile had broken to the right and successfully evaded the initial attack, but he then stayed too long in the fight. He started turning with a Zero, but as his aircraft slowed, his opponent started getting on his tail. Lloyd belatedly disengaged by deliberately spinning away from the fight; upon recovering from the spin, he continued downwards in a skidding turn. Unfortunately, his engine cut out completely as he shoved the nose down into this violent evasive manoeuvre. Without power, he was forced to reduce the rate of turn, meanwhile kept very busy in the cockpit endeavouring to restart the engine. The resultant lapse of manoeuvring power gave the Japanese pilot his opportunity: the Zero had been spiralling down after him, and Lloyd's aircraft was hit as soon as he relaxed his turn rate. Lloyd rolled back into a diving turn to stay out of the Zero's gunsight, but the damage had been done, and while passing through 10 000 feet the engine caught fire. He bailed out at once, landing in a remote bush location near Murrenja Hill. It was not until 9 July that he was picked up by Doc Fenton's Tiger Moth and returned to Strauss uninjured.

Lloyd was considered an experienced pilot from operations against the Germans, he had been graded above average in his CO's reports, was one of the senior men with 452 Squadron, and had 537 hours in total, including the respectable total of 360 hours on Spitfires. Nonetheless, he had been unlucky in the NWA, for in three combats with the Japanese he had himself been shot down twice and had also lost two wingmen shot down. Certainly, on this day he had contributed to his own downfall by pursuing the engagement under every disadvantage, and his tactical decision-making had been consistently poor – attempting to climb away from the first bounce rather than breaking downwards, and then staying to fight after the second bounce all alone.

As ordered, 452 had attacked its designated enemy fighters and kept many of them occupied, but it had come out second best in this engagement, suffering losses through being bounced by unseen enemy fighters that had remained above. Of the eight 452 Squadron aircraft that had entered the action, only five landed afterwards, with the fate of the three missing pilots worryingly unknown. No. 452's fate on this day was remarkably similar to that of 54 in the previous raid.

While most of the squadron was engaged in these unsatisfying combats with the fighters, the remaining two aircraft of 452 went through with the attack on the bombers. Ron MacDonald and his wingman, Flight Sergeant Jeff King, went down in a head-on attack against the left-hand vee within the great formation. King had become aware he was running out of oxygen as they made their approach, but because he was already so close to the bombers, he pressed on despite the hypoxia; on the way down, he fired head-on at some fighters, but then fell unconscious as he dived past them at the bombers. Hanging unconscious in his harness, he did not fire again, but as an unguided missile his aircraft flew itself through the bombers and out the other side at 450 knots. King woke up to find his aircraft descending through 14000 feet in a high-speed dive. Thoroughly alarmed, and precluded by oxygen failure from further high-altitude flight, he headed back to base, lucky to have survived.

It was the CO himself who thus made his squadron's sole gunnery pass upon the bombers. He made his usual determined and aggressive attack, firing from the front quarter at one of the centre bombers in the vee, but opening fire at the long range of 1000 metres. However, the closure rate was so rapid that he ceased fire at 100 metres only a couple of seconds later. By then he had rolled his aircraft inverted in his efforts to keep his gunsight on target and to keep his finger on the firing button. Tracers flew up at him from the nose gunners and he saw strikes on the bomber's port wing and nose. Then he flashed over the top of it upside down. His Spitfire dropped so closely behind the bomber that he only narrowly missed its tail and bumped violently in its slipstream. MacDonald pulled out underneath and behind the formation, and upon looking back saw his bomber 'dropping back very considerably' from the others with its starboard engine streaming black smoke. At this moment, as Kenny Bassett was diving away after his combat with the fighters, he saw a bomber jettison its bombs, then saw its starboard engine start burning

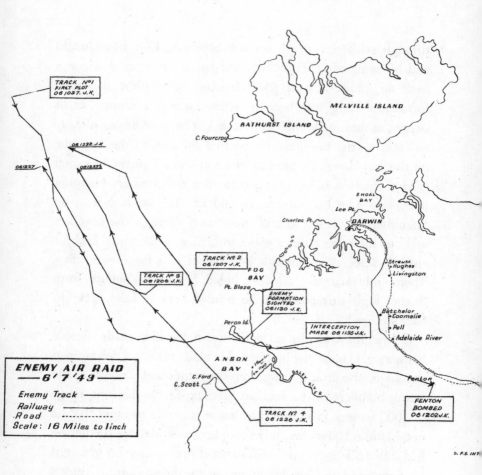

Plot of the 6 July raid on Fenton. The 30 June raid was similar.
Note the early point of interception, the loss of the radar plot
after bombing, then the raid's reappearance on the plot before
crossing the coast outbound; note also the tracks of damaged
bombers heading home early and alone. NAA: A11231, 5/76/INT

before it dived away 'to destruction'. MacDonald claimed this
bomber as destroyed.

Having dived away from his initial firing pass on the fighters,
Paul Makin re-climbed alone, but looked around just in time to
see a Zero coming in behind him. He pulled up and climbed

away from it at maximum power and 250 knots IAS. Although Makin was well behind the bombers, he chased after them in a shallow climb, and would go on to make another attack. His was the only one of 452's aircraft fitted with a belly tank, so after making their initial attacks all the other pilots returned to base at once because of fuel. As usual, of the five surviving aircraft that had fired their guns, every single one had had a stoppage in at least one of its cannons.

54's attack

According to Caldwell's plan, while 452 was engaging the fighter escort, 54 was to make a head-on attack on the bombers. However, as 54 got ready to attack, they suffered the same problem as had 452 – they lost visual contact with the fighters they had seen earlier.

There is already plentiful evidence to show that the pilots' inability to see the enemy was related to poor situational awareness. Subordinate pilots were scanning their allocated search arcs largely unaware of the overall situation, while up front, section leaders and squadron leaders got themselves more confused than was necessary as they tried to get their squadrons into the precise positions that Caldwell had specified for them. They looked in the wrong directions, with their own mental pictures of relative positioning confused by their assigned pre-attack manoeuvres. On this day, all leaders led their men into their attacks without having visually acquired major parts of the fighter escort.

This positional confusion was related to the centralised command of the big wing. Leaders had to attack when and what Caldwell told them to, irrespective of what picture they themselves saw or how or when they saw it. This cut both ways, as Gibbs had found on 28 June: a squadron leader could see a good attacking opportunity but have to forego it because the wing leader did not at that time see that picture in that same way. To make matters worse, the centralised command of the big wing degraded formation lookout, as the section and squadron leaders gave their attention to manoeuvring their formations, holding their assigned positions correctly within the wing, complying with Caldwell's instructions, and trying to see what Caldwell saw. It would have been preferable had they been able to take entire responsibility for their own squadron's place in the sky, to search for the enemy and to manoeuvre thereafter in such a way that their own formation's relative position to the enemy remained in view throughout.

In spite of such positional uncertainties, Caldwell's order committed 54 to start the attack, now. Gibbs ordered Bob Foster, whose Blue Section was to his left (closest to the enemy), to peel off and lead the squadron in. Foster frustratingly replied that he could no longer see the bombers! His inability to see a packed formation of 21 bombers only a couple of kilometres away in a cloudless sky is further evidence of the wing's visual lookout problems – if an experienced pilot like Foster was looking in the wrong direction to see this relatively obvious target, then the Spitfire pilots' repeated tendency to miss small groups of Zeros is placed in context. Nonetheless, 54 turned around blindly to the left to dive on a presumed attack heading. Gibbs sorted out the mess, telling Foster to move Blue Section off to the right, to wait for Red Section to go past, and then to follow him in.

It was during this turn that one of Gibbs's aircraft was seen to break away and dive off trailing white glycol smoke from both exhausts – by now a lamentably familiar sight. Fortunately, they had not been bounced, but rather Flying Officer Bill Hinds's aircraft had suffered a propeller CSU failure. The engine overrevved, produced the usual internal glycol leak and burst its oil seals. Hinds watched the oil pressure dropping, switched off the magnetos, and dived away with a dead propeller – not an unusual predicament for a 1 Fighter Wing pilot in the middle of an action. He glided towards the closest habitation he could see – Port Patterson – and force-landed there in the low coastal vegetation. Spitfire BR495 was so badly damaged that it was written off and salvaged for spare parts.

Gibbs led the small squadron group that remained against the bombers' right front. He was followed by Thompson, Foster, Lenagen, Wickman, Spencer and Harker, in that order – seven Spitfires in total. Gibbs himself fired from long range, spraying his ammunition across the whole left-hand side of the vee. He did this by holding his line and letting the bombers fly through his fire. Keeping his finger on the gun button, he then turned hard left to come in on the lead aircraft, finishing his burst from nearly head-on before bunting violently underneath it. He saw no results from his spraying fire upon the whole formation, but once he started concentrating his aim upon the lead bomber, he saw strikes. By then, however, he was firing with machine guns only as his cannons had stopped after less than two seconds' firing – and thus the powerful cannon ammunition had once again been wasted at long range. His incendiary machine-gun rounds flashed their way in a fiery swath across the bomber's port engine, nose, forward fuselage and wing centre section. Thick black smoke issued from its port engine and it dropped back out of formation. Without cannons, he had failed to deliver immediately fatal damage, but he had still hit it hard with his .303 inch fire. On the strength of the damage and distress visible, Gibbs claimed it as destroyed.

Fiery tracers from the rear gunners chased out after him as he dived away behind the bombers. Once clear of them, Gibbs zoomed up into the sun in a climbing right-hand turn. Looking to the right, he saw that his squadron's attack had had good effect, for three bombers were already dropping down behind the right-hand vee, each with a heavily smoking engine. Suddenly, his attention was diverted by the sight of a Zero on his own tail only 200 metres off – well within firing range. This was the way so many Spitfire pilots were shot down – bounced from behind while re-climbing for their next attack. Gibbs saw his danger just in time and reacted immediately, breaking violently downwards into a series of full-throttle diving turns. Pulling out at 17 000 feet and looking behind, he saw that the Zero was still behind him, so he repeated the process, finally pulling out at 12 000 feet.

Gibbs's No. 2, Flight Lieutenant Thompson, had followed directly behind Gibbs, but his aircraft suffered a propeller CSU failure in the dive, with the engine surging to 4000 revs. Thompson found himself very busy in the cockpit: lining up on the bombers, wrestling with the propeller and engine controls, and scanning the sky around him. He noticed three Zeros climbing towards him from the right, but was going fast enough to get past them, so continued on at the bombers. While still trying to manage his engine problem, he lined up on the extreme outside bomber at the right end of the formation and fired a deflection shot from its front quarter. Seeing no result, but mindful of the Zeros he had seen, he then evaded downwards in a series of diving turns. As he looked back, he saw two bombers trailing streams of smoke. Then the smoke trail from the second one suddenly stopped – the engine bay fire extinguisher had evidently done its job. He also saw two bombers jettisoning their bombs – a sign of a stricken machine and of a crew trying to lighten the load supported by the remaining engine. Thompson's own engine was still overrevving as he dived away, and now he could devote his attention to it. He finally got the revs down, but the recalcitrant engine afterwards kept intermittently spinning itself up to 4000 as he headed back to Darwin, where he was able to land normally.

Behind Gibbs's Red Section came Bob Foster's Blue Section. Foster had previously lost visual contact with the bombers, but once he got in behind Gibbs, he saw them again – ahead and to the left – although he miscounted their number at 27 rather than 21. Troublingly, although he could see the bombers again, he still could not see a single Zero. Pressing on regardless, he lined up behind Gibbs to make a front-quarter attack on the bombers, but upon seeing the volume of tracer coming out at Gibbs from the bomber gunners, Foster moved over to the left to avoid it, setting himself up for a beam attack instead upon the leader of the starboard vee. Rolling in at his selected attack, he fired right in to 50 metres but did not use enough deflection, for his fire fell behind the bomber he aimed at: it appeared to hit the next one in line behind it to the right (closer to Foster). He saw strikes on this machine's starboard engine and fuselage and then bunted underneath it at the last moment. Diving below the bombers, he saw the damaged machine's starboard engine streaming smoke; it then dropped out of formation and moved across to the left, into the 'box' where it would be protected by the others' guns. Foster pulled up when he got past the other side of the formation, using his speed to regain an up sun position out on the bombers' port side for his next attack.

Foster's No. 2, Flying Officer John Lenagen, might have had sharper eyes than his leaders, for he spotted the escorting fighters before the attack started. He saw a group of them nearby, positioned ahead of the bombers and off to his right. These Zeros were at 30 000 feet, and were therefore in position to dive in upon the 54 Squadron Spitfires during their firing runs on the bombers. Because of Foster's unannounced detour to the left to get away from the return fire, Lenagen lost his No. 1 in the dive, inadvertently separating himself further by moving over to the right as he made his own attack. He attacked the centre vee, firing from the beam upon the leading bomber. It smoked heavily and then he broke away downwards, sensible of the presence behind him of the Zeros. On the way down, he saw one bomber with its starboard engine afire, diving steeply away from the right-hand vee that his colleagues had attacked.

George Spencer also moved out to the right, following behind Lenagen and making a front-quarter attack upon the extreme left-hand bomber of the right-hand vee. He saw strikes on its fuselage near the starboard wing-root before ceasing fire at 50 metres, then rolled onto his back and pulled into a diving turn. As he went, he saw one bomber descending away from the formation in a shallow dive. Spencer had not himself seen the top-cover Zeros that Lenagen had seen, and so seemed less concerned about them. He decided to reattack, rolling out of his turn to continue on underneath the bombers to the far end of the formation. Once there he made a rear-quarter attack on the outermost left-hand bomber. He was engaged by tracer fire from the gunners, but saw no evidence of hits from his own fire – not helped by the stoppages he suffered in his port cannon and machine guns. Bunting to pass underneath the bomber, he was almost hit by a string of bombs dropping out of its bomb bay: the crew was jettisoning the bombs as a damage control measure, so he had hit it after all. Spencer had improved his chances of getting hits with his reduced armament by mounting a rear aspect attack.

Spencer's No. 2, Flight Sergeant Harker, came in behind him to attack the right-hand end of the centre vee. He had previously seen the enemy fighters up at 32 000 feet, but nonetheless concentrated on setting up his gunnery attack on the bombers. Trying to reduce the closure rate and deflection angle, he dived beneath the bombers and then pulled up to make a climbing firing run from beneath them. However, this attack profile placed the bombers up sun to him; their big shapes were now silhouetted against the sun's glare as he aimed, and

A still from one of F/Sgt Evan Batchelor's gunnery passes on 6 July. This is a full deflection shot, showing the close range to which pilots often approached while firing. However, few pilots were skilled enough to correctly estimate the 'lead' necessary to get hits from this position. NAA: A11231, 5/76/INT

the sun was so bright he could barely see the sighting ring on his reflector sight, in spite of having set the lamp at maximum brightness. He pulled his aircraft's sunshade up inside the windscreen to reduce the glare and to permit him to see the sighting picture. After this painstaking approach, Harker's gunnery was ruined when his thumb slipped off the cannon button by accident. The resultant .303 inch gunfire produced no visible result before he broke away downwards into a series of evasive rolls. Moreover, his chosen rear-attack profile had brought him into the arc of fire astern of the bombers, and the Japanese gunners had peppered his aircraft with 7.7 mm rounds. Although nothing vital was hit, his aircraft sustained seven hits, four in the starboard wing, one in the port wing, and two in the tailplane and elevator. Pulling around for another attack, Harker saw a Zero flying along behind the bombers, and dived in behind this 'target of opportunity'. Firing speculatively at long range, he was rewarded with the sight of the very much undamaged Zero whipping around in a turn and getting onto his tail. Harker broke violently downwards and spiral-dived all the way down to 3000 feet.

Foster's No. 3, Flight Sergeant 'Wicky' Wickman, had been lagging behind as 54 went into its attack, and so was the arse-end Charlie as they dived. As he went in, he saw that one bomber was already dropping behind the formation on the extreme right, while there was another bomber already on fire in the centre vee. Wickman made a beam attack on the extreme outside bomber, but did not use enough deflection; he saw only a few strikes on its tail, for his fire had mostly passed behind it. Diving underneath the broad bomber formation, he headed for the other side to get into an up sun position for his next attack. Emerging from underneath, he started climbing up beyond the bombers' port side, only 700 metres out from them – just outside machine-gun range. However, his plans suddenly changed when he saw one bomber leave the formation and turn around to head back to the coast, escorted by two fighters.

Wickman decided to target this straggler rather than the whole formation, and so turned around after it. As he approached, the bomber reversed its course as if to rejoin the formation after all. Unfortunately for the bomber crew, this turn took them directly towards Wickman, who was just then diving from out of the sun. He fired a long burst at it from head-on and flashed close overhead. Turning to clear his tail, he saw that the bomber's port engine was now smoking. On the flight deck of the Japanese machine, this event apparently clinched the argument for the 'go-home-now' party, for the bomber now reversed its course again and turned back for the coast. This turn set the unlucky bomber crew up for another attack: Wickman now made a shallow diving attack from dead astern. Running out of 20 mm ammunition, he continued his attack with his .303 inch guns only, ceasing fire at 150 metres. However, he had only seen strikes on its tail, so despite his two low-deflection firing passes the bomber flew sedately on.

Unfortunately for Wickman, he had made one attack too many given the known presence above him of the two escorting Zeros. The first he knew of it was a bullet slamming into the instrument panel. It came from behind him and narrowly missed his body on the way past. At once the cockpit was filled with dense glycol smoke – the Zero had hit his coolant system as well. He turned right to dive for Darwin and the Zeros let him go – presumably, the Japanese pilots were sufficiently convinced by all the white smoke to chalk him up as a kill already. He throttled back and put the aircraft into a glide, but the engine got so hot that he had to bail out at 3000 feet. Despite the late decision and the low height, he got out safely and watched his aircraft hit the ground and explode before he landed in the bush a kilometre away from the blazing wreckage.

After his initial attack on the bomber formation, Foster had repositioned himself 2 kilometres out on their left all by himself. Then he saw a bomber – the same one as Wickman attacked – flying away from the main formation heading north-west for the coast. Without seeing Wickman, he also dived after it in a stern attack, fired a short burst from 300 metres and then broke away, sensibly concerned about fighter attack – even though he had not seen the attendant Zeros (unlike Wickman, who had seen them, but ignored them). The two Zeros were at a lower altitude, having attacked Wickman. Foster dived away to safety, to see that the bomber was now descending abruptly. He continued to look back watching it, and when it was in the far distance, saw it 'crash on land, burning fiercely'. Foster claimed the kill.

457's attack

While 452 and 54 made their more or less simultaneous attacks, Caldwell kept 457 up sun as a reserve, leading it on a parallel course to the bombers while the other squadrons' attacks played themselves out down to his right. When the bombers were 30 kilometres out from Fenton inbound, he ordered 457's Blue and White Sections to attack, while still retaining Red Section in reserve up above.

With Blue Section close behind, Watson now led White Section down in a front-quarter attack against the remnants of the right-hand bomber vee – the same as attacked so effectively by 54 just earlier. He fired but saw no strikes – his port cannon stopped after firing one round – then pulled up to pass close overhead the bombers. As he passed the last bomber, he rolled over and pulled, hitting its slipstream with a violent bump. Spiralling down at 330 knots IAS, he looked behind and saw that Zeros were chasing him – indeed, one of them was already firing at him. He kept on going, all the way down to 15 000 feet before pulling out; he checked his tail then re-climbed after the bombers.

Watson's No. 2, Evan Batchelor, fired at the outside bomber and then turned right around the tail of his target to fly across the open end of the great vee of vees. As he did so, he was exposed to the gunfire of the assembled rear gunners, who blazed away at him as he went past: he could see the gun barrels 'swinging up on to him', the white twinkling flares of their muzzle flashes, and the darting tracers whipping past. Batchelor had intended to set himself up for a stern attack against the left-hand end of the bomber crescent, but the return fire he was experiencing gave him second thoughts, so he broke downwards and dived out the other side to re-climb for another (safer) front-quarter attack.

Watson's second element – Flying Officers Doug Edwards and Brian Hegarty – followed him in, but the latter had become detached from the group, straggling far behind. This was because Hegarty had been unable to detach his belly tank when Watson ordered them released, so had dropped behind the others, held back by the extra drag. Edwards left his wingman behind, following after Watson to attack the right-most bomber. However, when he dived to attack, both his cannons froze up, so he fired with machine guns only. Following Watson out, Edwards pulled up over the top of the bombers and then rolled over and dived away behind them. He lost Watson in the diving turn and pulled out only 3000 feet below the bombers, but was at once bounced by the same group of Zeros that had followed Watson down: one Zero was already firing from his starboard rear quarter at 250 metres. Edwards broke away once again and dived for home.

Meanwhile, Hegarty had been left behind, making a diving attack on the bombers' beam from his detached rearward position. With the much slower closing speed that his poor starting position had delivered, he was a very conspicuous arse-end Charlie, and so was predictably jumped by Zeros before he could open fire. One Zero suddenly appeared from the side and flashed right over the top of him – it had already fired, but the pilot had missed his full deflection shot. Hegarty broke into a hard turn and then looked behind to see another Zero behind him. He continued the roll until he was inverted, then pulled and went down in a series of skidding diving turns. Thinking he was safe, Hegarty started to pull out of the dive, but just then his aircraft was hit by 20 mm explosive shells – one in the port wing tip and another in the starboard wing. One Zero had followed him down, waited until he eased out of the dive, and then fired. Hegarty broke again into another downwards spiral, waiting until 8000 feet before pulling out, this time thankfully finding himself alone. He returned to base, where he found a gaping hole in the aluminium skin under the wing. His aircraft was repaired by the squadron, but the shell had penetrated the spar, so the starboard wing had to be replaced.

Unlike Pete Watson's White Section, the pilots of 457's Blue Section stayed together through their firing runs at the bombers. Pilot Officer Rex Watson had dropped out earlier due to R/T failure, which left only three aircraft under the leadership of Flying Officer 'Bush' Hamilton. Caldwell watched from above as this little string of Spitfires dived through the bombers and then turned right to climb up sun for another attack.

Soon after that, Bush Hamilton and his men were bounced in an eerie repetition of the events on 28 May. All three – Bush Hamilton, Darky McDowell and Norm Robinson – were killed. Caldwell did not see it happen, nor had he seen any of the offending Zeros – the bounce evidently took place in the large blind spot underneath his high-flying aircraft. As with the earlier deaths of their squadron mates Harry Blake and Bruce Beale, the Spitfires were hit so hard that all three pilots died in their aircraft, once again suggesting very close-range cannon fire from directly astern. A stockman on Litchfield Station, Tom Skewes, saw three Spitfires diving away from the bombers chased by Zeros, with two of them crashing at the end of their dives. Both of these aircraft hit the ground nose down at high speed, suggesting that these two pilots had been killed in their aircraft: Hamilton's aircraft smashed into the rocky top of Billabong Ridge, while Robinson's struck the ground 6 kilometres away. McDowell was evidently still conscious as he tried to make a landing 25 kilometres to the north; his aircraft hit the ground near Mt Litchfield at a shallower angle and at lower speed, leaving enough of the aircraft intact to be salvaged later for parts by 7 RSU.

The ill-fated Blue Section had re-climbed for another go, imbued with a degree of self-confidence. This was not entirely ill-founded, for all three had been flying together in the squadron since the UK days, and were considered a 'stout part of the original core of the squadron'. They saw themselves as old hands, and showed themselves to be keen fighter pilots by aggressively seeking out the enemy. The squadron diarist noted afterwards that Darky McDowell had 'possessed a real zeal for combat which may have led to his destruction'. However, all three of them were in fact quite inexperienced: the flight leader, Hamilton, had only had three previous combats.

The deaths of all three men in the one bounce is genuinely shocking. However, the persistent failure of the Spitfire pilots to see the Zeros is already amply established, as is their habit of re-climbing in isolating line astern after making their attacks. There are numerous examples of other pilots being bounced from behind doing just this. Repeated experience proved that if the Spitfire pilot knew the Zero was there, he could make himself a near-impossible target by a violent break followed by downwards rolls. There is therefore no possibility that all three pilots were hit and killed as they dived away from a known attack.

A review of the causes of Spitfire air combat losses in previous combats bears this out: out of a maximum possible 19 Spitfires previously shot down by enemy fighters, no more than five were lost while dogfighting; most were surprised from behind while conducting firing runs or while re-climbing for their next run. The only plausible scenario for Blue Section's loss is that the three Spitfires were hit in the bounce itself before they knew to start evading. If the behaviour of the other pilots during the two Fenton raids is any guide, then they were hit while re-climbing on a course parallel to the bombers.

Moreover, systemic deficiencies in 1 Fighter Wing's use of tactical formation increased the likelihood of being bounced as they climbed. When squadrons or sections dived to attack, they almost invariably ended up as a string of Spitfires in a zigzag line astern, as this was simply the easiest arrangement for the pilots to follow. If a particular section managed to reform after an attack, as Blue Section did on this day, then they reformed in much the same shape – as a string of Spitfires.

---

1 Fighter Wing's line abreast battle formation

± No. 1

± No. 3

± No. 2

± No. 4

An additional factor that increased the pilots' chance of re-climbing in the dangerous line astern formation was 1 Fighter Wing's version of line abreast battle formation. This was 'line abreast' in the sense that each pair flew up alongside the next, but within each pair, the wingman flew nearly line astern to his leader. The resultant four-aircraft formation was surprisingly deep, almost box-shaped, the implications of such a deep

A pair of 452 Squadron Spitfires, showing the deep line abreast combat formation flown by 1 Fighter Wing. This precluded easy observation of the blind spot behind the wingman's tail.
AWM Negative NWA0350

formation being that wingmen became habituated to following along behind their leader rather than flying up alongside him, and that leaders neglected the importance of keeping their wingmen's tails under visual observation – for this was nearly impossible to do within this configuration. On 6 July, Hamilton at the front would have had very little chance of observing any enemy approaching through the blind arc below and behind. He was anxious to regain height for the next attack and in typical 457 Squadron style was not going to slow the climb down by throttling back or weaving to let the others catch up – as per 10 May, 28 May and 28 June. The three pilots died because of poor tactical formation and consequent deficient visual surveillance to the rear.

Meanwhile, control's improvised Purple Section, comprised of 54's Norwood and Studley in their underperforming aircraft, had been orbiting up sun over Fenton at 29 000 feet. They saw dark AA bursts start to appear in the sky, and looking in that direction they saw the bombers coming in on their bombing run at 25 000 feet. Norwood counted 21 bombers plus one straggler coming along behind, surrounded by five Zeros. Studley counted about 18 bombers, noting that the right-hand vee had come apart, with only three bombers left in a ragged and wide formation. This was the vee that 54 had attacked, showing that the British pilots' attacks had been more effective than had been immediately apparent. Studley also reported five Zeros in front of the bombers; and as these were also at 29 000, they were in a good position to pounce if he and Norwood dived.

However, Norwood had not seen these fighters and showed no awareness of their presence, for he dived in right under them for a front-quarter attack on the bombers. It was only as he dived, concentrating on the bombers, that Norwood suddenly noticed two Zeros coming at him from the right. Not having seen any fighters before this, he was startled to see that he was

A typical 1 Fighter Wing Spitfire pilot: 54 Squadron's F/Sgt
CA Studley clambers out of the cockpit of Spitfire AR564 after
a false alarm scramble on 25 July. He has left his flying helmet
draped over the gunsight and his parachute in the seat bucket.
AWM Negative 054794

already 'almost on top of them'. Abandoning the attack on the bombers, Norwood dived away now chased by these same Zeros. Studley, having previously seen the enemy fighters, had followed Norwood down assuming that his leader had been setting up to attack them, and did not realise that his leader had in fact just blundered into them unintentionally. Studley was lining up to fire on one of them when he saw another Zero coming at him from the side, so he too broke downwards and dived away pursued by tracers. Meanwhile, Norwood was being fired upon by two Zeros as he went downwards in a series of steep turns, chased all the way down to 17000 feet, by which time he was doing 420 knots IAS, too fast for a Zero, and so he got away. Studley dived all the way to ground level and then headed home, very aware of his fuel state, landing with only 5 gallons left. Purple Section's attack had been completely spoiled by the attentive escort and by Norwood's poor lookout.

The bombing

After Blue Section attacked, the bombers braved attacks from a succession of further Spitfires that attacked in pairs or as individuals. No. 54 Squadron's detached Yellow Section – Flight Sergeant Horkin – was vectored to Fenton to join Purple Section, but as he climbed to the rendezvous he found himself struggling with yet another malfunctioning propeller CSU. He got up to 30000 feet, but it was a slow climb as he could not get his engine to run at over 2650 rpm without overrevving. Failing to find Purple Section, he got a good view of the bombers coming in over the target, counting 21 of them (which was very close to the real figure of 20) and observing that the left-hand vee was in very bad formation after the savaging it had received in the earlier attacks. Down below, 133 HAA Battery engaged the bombers with 88 rounds of 3.7 inch. Horkin observed that the AA was accurate but did not see any result from it, although the gunners later claimed one bomber shot down. After bombing, the bombers turned right through about 180 degrees and headed back out. Horkin followed, noticing that the whole formation had become very ragged and that five bombers now dropped behind: struggling with damaged engines, the pilots of these aircraft had been able to increase power temporarily to stay with the formation through the bomb run, but it seems they had now had to reduce power to keep the remaining engine's temperatures and pressures within limits.

Once again, the Japanese lead bombardier dropped accurately, for the 1700 metre-wide pattern of 140 bombs fell right across the dispersals and taxiways, cratering the runway, destroying one B-24, damaging three others, and burning 27 000 gallons of petrol when a bomb-sparked bushfire consumed the fuel dump – a visually spectacular bombing result. Also, two 40 mm Bofors guns and one vehicle from 149 LAA Battery were damaged. Fortunately, deep slit trenches again prevented any personnel fatalities.

Horkin now dived in to attack, but his propeller CSU failed again and his engine overrevved; furthermore, as the airspeed built up he had to fight the controls to stop the aircraft from rolling uncontrollably to the right. As the aircraft accelerated in the dive, he could no longer hold the aerodynamic forces with the aileron and so could not physically get his gunsight on to a target. He thus dived past the bombers without firing, no longer in control of his aircraft, and then blacked out as it went into an involuntary high-G pull-out. When Horkin regained consciousness, his Spitfire was descending vertically; but upon looking behind, he saw a Zero pursuing him, so he opted to continue the dive. The engine was still overrevving badly and the oil pressure was rising, so he opened the hood ready to bail out. Easing out of the dive at 15 000 feet, he switched the engine off for half a minute to stop the overrevving. Once he restarted it, the engine ran without surging, so he decided to stay with the aircraft. However, he was not prepared to stay in this rogue aircraft any longer than he had to, so instead of flying back to base at Darwin, he put it down at MacDonald airfield near Fenton. His aircraft had been 'almost unmanageable' and he did well to get it back on the ground safely.

Caldwell meanwhile had been watching the combat from 33 500 feet – the Zeros rarely operated above 30 000, so this was a safe tactical height. He had observed two bombers descend out of formation after the initial attacks by 54 and 452, with one of them turning away and heading north by itself – the aircraft that Wickman and Foster attacked. Then he saw a bomber in the centre streaming white smoke, and he saw two jettison their bombs, with each 'stick' exploding in the bush in separate places. Approaching the target, another bomber started streaming smoke and descending. Caldwell then watched the bombing, considering the AA fire to be neither intense nor accurate (he had experienced German flak). On the other hand, he considered the bombing good, seeing the bursts straddle the dispersals and start fires in three places. As the bombers turned away after the target, he saw yet another bomber lose formation and lag behind. Throughout the bombers' progress in and off the target, he had seen Spitfires make attacks singly and in pairs.

The final attacks

At this point, Caldwell was still accompanied by the two pilots of 457's Red Section – Squadron Leader Ken James and Pilot Officer Bruce Little. After watching the bombing, the three of them turned right and then shadowed the retiring raiders from an up sun perch off to the north. These aircraft were the last reserve, the last formed section from the wing formation yet to attack the enemy. They could have attacked before the bomb run, but Caldwell had held them back. James was getting frustrated, and could see that his fuel state was getting critical, so requested permission to attack. Caldwell had a belly tank on his aircraft while the others did not, so he assented and let these two 457 pilots go, while he himself stayed up high, in the sun, 'observing the results of the engagement and appreciating the tactical situation'. The wing leader's self-isolation was certainly an unwise thing to do in a dangerous sky, on a day when all Spitfire pilots were having trouble seeing the high-cover Zeros. Caldwell was no different in failing to see the enemy, for he had just sent Red Section in underneath some of these same unseen Zeros, which flew lower than Caldwell but remained unseen against the mottled backdrop of the dry land below. As a result, James and Little had now been placed into some peril as they dived into their attack.

This was Ken James's first combat since 2 May, and surprisingly was only his second since his squadron's arrival in the NWA. Because of his fuel state, he led Little straight down for a beam attack at the bombers. When they were still 1000 metres out, Little spotted three Zeros diving upon them from their port side; he warned his CO and himself half-rolled at once and broke away downwards. James broke into one of the Zeros, but because of his dive speed was unable to track the tightly turning enemy fighter, so he too broke away downwards. Pulling out at 15 000 feet, he re-climbed to renew his attack on the bombers. Frustrated by his spoiled attack, distracted by his knowledge of the fighters' proximity, and still worrying about his fuel, he was so impatient to make the earliest attack possible that he made his second run even before regaining height superiority, attacking while still in a climb. As a result, he was again cut off by fighters as he came in from the bombers' beam. Two Zeros attacked, showing the admirable standard of combat teamwork that was characteristic of 202 AG: one Zero made a pass at him while the other stayed above ready to swoop. James turned as tightly as he could when the first Zero came through, pulling so hard that he spun out of the turn (having already been slowed down by his climb). Only recovering at 5000 feet, he was shocked to find that the Zero had followed him down and was coming at him again. He had 'bingo fuel', and could not hang around, so he just dived to 'zero feet' weaving violently. The Zero pilot left him alone and headed for home. James had fought alone, as remained typical of 1 Fighter Wing pilots, and could easily have been shot down.

No. 457 Squadron's detached Green Section was comprised of Flying Officer Ian Mackenzie and Pilot Officer Rex Watson. The latter's R/T had failed during the wing climb, so he had aborted, returned to Livingstone, got in a spare aircraft, taken off again, and headed back to Fenton. There he joined Mackenzie, control designating them as an improvised 'Green Section'. Under the direction of No. 10 Mobile Fighter Sector, they orbited overhead the American base at 20 000 feet – an oddly low height. Mackenzie and Watson were alerted to the imminent arrival of the bombers by the AA bursts, and then by bomb explosions erupting on the airfield below. As the bombers turned about and headed out, these two Spitfires of Green Section climbed up after them in pursuit.

Bill Gibbs, meanwhile, having been chased down to 12 000 feet by a pursuing Zero, had re-climbed and followed the bombers back out. He stayed on the up sun side of them and reached 28 000 feet, high enough to make an attack. As he climbed, he saw several other Spitfires out on the flanks, climbing up for further attacks. Gibbs also saw Zeros loitering up sun, awaiting their opportunity to swoop. He counted 'only' 20 bombers left in formation (having originally miscounted them as 27, not 21). This corroborates other pilots' tallies, suggesting that the bombers had suffered little loss since their run off the target, with only a couple of bombers missing from the formation in total.

Gibbs spotted some Zeros away to his left, but these were still far enough away for him to continue with his attack, so he rolled in for a diving beam attack on the right-most outer bomber, while keeping one eye on the Zeros. Using a full deflection shot, he fired with machine guns only, as his cannons had already suffered stoppages, seeing strikes on its starboard engine and a stream of white smoke (possibly fuel venting from holed wing tanks). The big bomber suddenly pulled so violently out of formation towards him that he had to bunt hard under it to avoid a collision. Checking his oxygen indicator, he saw that the needle was on the red mark, so kept diving to get below 15 000 feet to avoid hypoxia (as he had experienced in the previous raid), and kept going for home.

Evan Batchelor, meanwhile, had been left untroubled by fighters, re-climbing out on the bombers' port side. Paul Makin was also re-climbing nearby, so Batchelor joined him. These two got themselves a good height margin before Makin led them back down for a high-speed beam attack. Makin fired but saw no strikes, then broke away so violently that he blacked out; when he regained consciousness, he found that his propeller CSU had failed because of the dive, and so his engine was overrevving. While he was busy in the cockpit manipulating the engine and propeller control levers and monitoring his engine's revs, pressures and temperatures, tracer hissed past from an unseen Zero behind. Makin broke violently, still trying to deal with his malfunctioning propeller mechanism. He cut the ignition switches and pulled the propeller pitch control right back, but the engine continued to run, screaming at unendurable revs. Fearing a catastrophic engine break-up and fire, he tried to bail out, but his parachute pack got jammed in the open side door as he tried to get out. The ground was coming up so fast that he sat back down abruptly and elected to force-land instead, putting the aircraft down in a swampy clearing in the forest near Surprise Creek, north of Fenton.

Unaware of Makin's plight, Batchelor fired at his target on the left-hand end of the formation, bunted underneath it, then pulled up to attack the right-hand vee on the way out. However, he was going too fast to aim and so failed to fire before bunting underneath these bombers in turn. As he pulled up from this abortive attack, he saw that one bomber had fallen behind from the right end of the formation and that it now flew directly in front of him. He bunted again and tried to line up on this one, but was still closing too fast, once again flashing harmlessly by without having had time to fire a shot. Batchelor dived away after this abortive yo-yoing pass.

Meanwhile, Green Section was chasing along behind the bombers, but Rex Watson's aircraft could not keep up with Mackenzie's – as usual, not all aircraft were performing properly. Mackenzie throttled back to wait for Watson in order to attack together, but was afraid the bombers would get away, so went ahead by himself. As he came up abreast of the enemy formation, he then radioed Watson to ask if he could join him there, but the latter reported that he was still 8 kilometres behind. Mackenzie heard Batchelor making his attack and decided to coordinate with him instead. By this time, he had got right out in front of the bombers and so now turned for a head-on attack. Once again, however, the closing speed was too fast, so he only had time for a snap shot before pulling up and going over the top. Zooming up into a climbing turn to reattack, he then spotted three Zeros above and behind the bombers. They were in a good position to attack him, but showed no sign of having seen him, so he opportunistically pulled around into a beam attack on the bombers. He fired a long burst as he rolled in behind, this time seeing strikes on his target, with a big flash and flames from its port engine – as usual, gunnery results had improved with the slower closing speed and lower deflection of a stern attack.

Pete Watson had regained an up sun position above the bombers by the time they were 25 kilometres west of Fenton heading outbound. As he overhauled them, he saw that the bombers in the centre vee were straggling badly. He got out ahead and then peeled off into a head-on attack, running in at them on the same level and opening fire from 500 metres against the right-hand bomber. Ceasing fire, he pulled on the stick and flashed over the top, then broke into a turn as he passed by. Looking back, he saw that his bomber was now descending with one engine on fire. It had lost 5000 feet by the time he turned away to head back to base, short of fuel.

The controller at 10 Mobile Fighter Sector now broadcast the 'Pancake' order to all pilots (meaning 'head back to base and land'), but Ian Mackenzie was flying one of the few aircraft fitted with a belly tank, so he ignored the order and continued his attacks. Having broken away underneath the bombers after his last attack, he turned to re-climb after them, now seeing that 'his' bomber was lagging behind by itself and trailing smoke. Just as he was about to dive in to deliver the coup de grace, a Zero appeared right in front, turning towards him. He pulled up and put his gunsight on it, finding himself locked into a head-on pass. The Zero loomed up in his windscreen, rolling inverted as it did so; both pilots opened fire at the same time, and Mackenzie too rolled inverted as he fired, getting ready to dive away straight after. Both aircraft roared past each other upside down; the two pilots had ended the combat evenly, neither having got any hits. Mackenzie had no ammunition left, so he now ended an energetic solo combat by pulling hard and diving away to 'zero feet' for base.

Besides Mackenzie, there was another pilot whose aircraft's

drop tank gave him the range to follow the Japanese out to sea – Caldwell. He shadowed the bombers all the way from Fenton to the coast without attacking, still observing the combat from above. He saw that by now there were few enemy fighters left in attendance upon the bombers, most having been scattered by chasing the Spitfires away. As the bombers made their way out, he observed two fires on the ground, plus a trail of smoke as an aircraft descended in flames – but he did not see it actually crash or burn on the ground. In total, Caldwell had observed eight aircraft in difficulties, including three that were trailing smoke; he believed five of these were enemy aircraft, while three were Spitfires. Events would prove that no Spitfires were lost in this phase of the action, so any burning had to be Japanese.

Caldwell finally made his own attack as the enemy crossed the coast of Anson Bay, opposite Cape Ford. He made a high-speed head-on attack upon a bomber that was out in front of the others, then pulled up to clear his tail. It was lucky he had followed this precaution, for upon looking back he saw that he was indeed under attack by a group of three Zeros – this close call emphasised the dangers of flying alone. Following the standard Japanese drill, one of them dived to attack while the other two waited up above for their moment to come down. Caldwell's oxygen had already been exhausted for some time because of his extended flight at 32 000 feet, but he was able to perceive the perils of his situation in spite of the hypoxia, so he broke downwards and got out of there.

The last pilot with a belly tank was Rex Watson, who in his poorly performing aircraft had been left behind by Ian Mackenzie and so had missed the latter's successful individual attack. After an impressively resolute pursuit, he finally overhauled the bombers when they were 30 kilometres out to sea and still at 24 000 feet. He dived from out of the sun for a beam attack upon the starboard vee, turning in behind his bomber target as he fired. His port cannon jammed at once, and the recoil from the starboard cannon pulled the nose downwards off the aiming point. Pushing the left rudder to compensate and to keep the nose from dropping as he fired, he saw some hits. At that point he saw a single Zero coming in towards him, so broke downwards and away. Even though his aircraft had a belly tank, he was now on 'bingo fuel', so he dived away and headed home.

Makin, meanwhile, was on the ground with his pulse returning to normal. He waited by the aircraft until the next day, laying his parachute canopy out next to it as a visual signal. A Beaufighter went past in the late afternoon but failed to see him, because he had by then taken the parachute in to use it as a tent! Believing himself undiscovered, he started walking east, camped overnight, and reached the highway on the afternoon of 8 July, where he was rescued at 3 pm, finding that he was 50 kilometres north of Fenton. Driven to Batchelor for medical observation, he was then received by his unit that evening with some joy, having almost been given up for lost. His aircraft, BS193, had not survived its belly landing in the scrub and was written off and salvaged for parts. No. 452 Squadron's 'B' Flight commander was not having much luck, for he had also force-landed in the 2 May action (that time because of fuel starvation).

After coming down beneath his parachute, 54's 'Wicky' Wickman walked east to a road he had seen from the air, found a nearby clearing in the trees, and set out his parachute as a signal. By that time the action had finished, but all squadrons had meanwhile sent out search aircraft. Just before last light, his parachute sign gained the attention of the hardworking Evan Batchelor of 457, who circled overhead reassuringly. An Anson from 6 CU dropped supplies to him the next day, and then he was recovered by one of the unit's Tiger Moths on the 8th. Wickman's survival was great news for 54 Squadron, but he had annoyingly lost that rare commodity – a new aircraft. Spitfire

JG731 had been one of the latest to arrive in the squadron, a valued item considering the trouble that pilots were experiencing with the older machines.

The postscript to this action was the usual busy program of air and ground searches for the missing pilots, starting that afternoon. The 2/8th Independent Company set out to search for the three shot-down pilots reported in the Brocks Creek area. With three of its men missing, 457 was foremost in the air searches, with the 'B' Flight commander, Don Maclean, taking a leading role in this, as all three men came from his flight. He was out again at dawn the next day, but although he had the satisfaction of locating three pilots in the country to the west of Fenton, and of personally dropping supplies to them, Maclean flew low enough overhead to establish that they were not his own missing men. These searches remained a part of 457's flying program for five days, but it was not until the 20th that McDowell's aircraft was found near Fenton with his body still in the cockpit. His remains were removed to the squadron base at Livingstone and taken for burial the next day in the Adelaide River cemetery. The 300 men of the squadron lined the road as the ambulance drove slowly past, bidding farewell to a much-loved character. Hope was quickly abandoned for Hamilton and Robinson, and indeed their bodies were never recovered. The personal tragedy of this was profound, Hamilton having only just returned from leave in Sydney, where he had been married. Having survived the most dangerous parts of the war, and anticipating the imminent end of his operational tour and a safe posting to a rear area, he had found the confidence to pursue his personal life in preparation for the return of peace. It was not to be. The shattered remains of the two missing Spitfires were only located as a result of searches in the early 1970s, but by then there were no human remains left, and so neither man ever found a burial place.

Results

For this sacrifice, the wing's pilots could console themselves with the thought that they had hit the Japanese hard, claiming five bombers and one fighter 'confirmed' shot down. Of course, the usual double and triple claiming applied: several flights had attacked the same part of the formation in quick succession and therefore had seen the same bombers burning, smoking or falling away. In very few cases were claims for the destruction of a bomber supported by eyewitness testimony of its actual destruction, most claims being made on the basis of bombers merely falling out of formation smoking. Unlike the previous Darwin raids, most of the air combat in the two Fenton raids had occurred over land, so for the first time there was opportunity to correlate claims with crash sites. However, this was not done, and despite the lack of such crash evidence, the intelligence officers confirmed the claims anyway. The observed bomber stragglers, the big gaps in the formation and the observed jettisoning of bombs shows that several bombers had been hit hard, but there was again little concrete evidence of their actually crashing.

Batchelor's bomber 'kill' was said to have crashed near Armawoola Lagoon, Pete Watson's near Mount Hayward, Foster's near Murrinja Hill and MacDonald's 25 kilometres south-west of Batchelor – this last crash observed by two pilots of 452. There were additional observations of aircraft crashing into the sea: an observation post at Redcliffe saw an aircraft descend burning and going into the sea 10 kilometres offshore, while observers at 307 Radar Station at Peron Island saw a burning bomber going into the sea from 2000 feet; in addition, Ian Mackenzie saw a bomber crash in the western reaches of Anson Bay. For only the third time in 1 Fighter Wing's campaign, there was concrete evidence of one of these bomber crashes: Major EC Hennessy of 2/6 Cavalry Regiment recovered documents

A still from F/Sgt Evan Batchelor's gun film, showing his diving front-quarter attack upon the bombers on 6 July. Few 1 Fighter Wing pilots were able to secure hits firing from this position because of the high deflection angle and the rapid rate of closure. Note the typically tight Japanese formation.
NAA: A11231, 5/76/INT

from the wreckage of a crashed bomber near Mount Litchfield. Given the way in which the wild spaces of the Northern Territory swallowed up 457's two Spitfire wreckages, the failure to identify further Japanese crash sites does not exclude the possibility of further unlocated enemy wrecks.

Japanese records indicate that only two bombers were shot down: one on the way into the target, and one on the way out; in addition, two more crash-landed after limping back across the Timor Sea with battle damage. This number broadly agrees with the observed reductions in the strength of the formation as it passed through the sequence of attacks, consistent with the airborne observations and with the lack of crash evidence on land. The evident survival of so many damaged bombers is encapsulated by the story of Superior Flight Petty Officer Torao Maruoka, the observer in one of the bombers of 753 AG's 3rd Squadron: the Spitfires' gunfire tore through the flight deck, killing the pilot and seriously wounding the co-pilot. Maruoka pulled the pilot out of his seat, took his position behind the controls, and successfully flew the aircraft back to base. A total of 13 bombers returned to base damaged, bringing with them five dead men and three wounded: Clearly, the Spitfires had got many hits, but as usual the hits had not been concentrated in vital areas, and although fuel tanks were punctured, they had not burned. Nonetheless, it is clear that 753 AG had had a costly outing.

Against the four Japanese bomber airframes and two bomber crews, the wing had lost the unusually high number of five Spitfires shot down and three pilots killed – ironically, the highest air combat losses of any combat, on this, the final daylight bombing raid.

The Japanese were unable to sustain their raids after 6 July, once again relaxing their pressure on the wing. This was lucky, because with these latest combat losses, the wing had reached a nadir of aircraft availability: 54 complained that it had so few aircraft left that it would be 'flat out raising a flight'. On 6 July, 452's line-up of serviceable aircraft had dropped in one hour from 15 to ten. However, help was already at hand, for at the end of June, Bladin had demanded 22 aircraft and 11 new engines, to be delivered immediately. The RAAF responded, allocating 17 used aircraft at once from existing stocks plus 43 new aircraft which arrived through July and August. Thus the Spitfire fleet was turning the corner: after the delivery of some of these new aircraft in mid-July, 54 noticed a great increase in aircraft availability. By month's end, the squadrons' aircraft inventories returned to healthy levels – for example, by that time 452 Squadron had regained a healthy stock of 23 aircraft.

Bladin ordered his usual symbolic acts of retribution in response to the raid. That night, Hudsons from 2 Squadron raided Koepang town (the port used to supply the Penfui air base), while the next evening, a 'large' seven-aircraft raid bombed what appeared to be grounded aircraft on Penfui airfield. This observation was possible evidence of bombers damaged in the raid and which were yet to be restored to serviceability for the transit flight back to Kendari. On 8 July, the 380th BG announced its continued presence by boldly sending a nine-aircraft raid against Penfui in daylight. The photos they took while over the target showed 13 G4M bombers parked around the perimeter of the airfield, and this show of Japanese strength was taken as a sobering reminder of the limited effectiveness of the Allied bombing – although it might just as easily have indicated the number of damaged Japanese bombers that had yet to be repaired for onward transit to Kendari.

The Japanese had taken a risk in sending an unreinforced raiding force on two deep penetration raids, and they had largely gotten away with it. Indeed, the Fenton raids were the deepest penetrations made into Australian airspace by a full-scale raiding force in the entire 1942–43 bombing campaign. Only one longer raid had been made, by a small force of nine bombers and three fighters against Katherine on 22 March 1942. This target was 140 kilometres further south than Fenton, but that raid had been made in the very early days of the campaign before the establishment of a credible air defence system. On 30 June and 6 July 1943 the Japanese were rewarded for their audacity, and the commanders and airmen of the 23rd Air Flotilla could justly congratulate themselves: for fighting their bombers through to the target against incessant fighter attack, for bombing accurately, and for retiring in good order back to the coast.

The men of the 380th BG had been given some cause to respect their Japanese opposite numbers, and some cause also for being underwhelmed by the effectiveness of their Spitfire defenders. But their own bombing doctrine was built on the interwar doctrinal assumption that 'the bomber will always get through'; success would be determined by the strangling of the opposing air force's ability to operate from its bases, and the Japanese had not even dented this. The prosaic fact was that bombing campaigns were defeated by imposing cumulative attrition that proved unendurable in the long term, and even with their ineffective gunnery, the Spitfires were still writing off bomber airframes and killing bomber crews.

Indeed, 753 AG was slowly running out of aircraft: its raiding strength had progressively dropped from 27 to 21 aircraft, and with 17 bombers lost or damaged on 6 July, the unit would have been down to 'flight strength' for the next raid – had there been one. July 6 showed that the campaign was simply becoming uneconomic for the Imperial Navy's increasingly hard-pressed air force, which could no longer afford the luxury of sustaining the logistical commitment and cumulative attrition that these major set-piece raids represented. The accumulating bomber losses did not affect just the ongoing viability of 23rd Air

Flotilla's strike force, but also threatened the Imperial Navy's ability to conduct maritime patrol and surveillance duties across the broad southern frontage of the Indonesian archipelago: 753 AG had to do double duty in both roles, and thus losses in one role imperilled its capability in the other. Moreover, with Allied offensives gaining momentum along the north coast of New Guinea and up through the Solomon Islands towards Rabaul, the navy's strained resources required the reconcentration of available forces further east. This prioritising of resources made clearer than ever the status of Darwin and the NWA as a subsidiary front to the main game.

6 July pilot table

Sqn		No.	Pilots engaging	Pilots not engaging	Remarks
54	Red	1	S/L Gibbs RAF		both cannons failed
		3	F/L Thompson RAF		CSU failure during combat
		4		F/O Hinds RAF	CSU failure, force-landed near Port Patterson; BR495 written off
	Blue	1	F/L Foster RAF		1 cannon failed
		2		F/Sgt Huggard RAF	BS182 failed to deliver power, dropped out of wing formation
		3	F/O Lenagen RAF		
		4	F/Sgt Wickman RAF		shot down & bailed out; JG731 destroyed
	White	2	F/Sgt Spencer RAF		took over as White 1 when Norwood dropped out; BS305 damaged by bomber return fire, repaired on unit; 1 cannon failed
		3	F/Sgt Harker RAF		both cannons failed

54	Purple	1	F/L Norwood RAF		initially White 1, BR544 failed to deliver power, dropped out and reassigned Purple 1; did not fire
		2	F/Sgt Studley RAF		initially Red 2, BS166 CSU failure dropped out and reassigned; did not fire
	Yellow	1	F/Sgt Horkin RAF		base patrol Darwin-Hughes; CSU failure before combat, did not fire; landed EE636 at MacDonald as un-airworthy
452	Red	1	S/L MacDonald		R/T failed (in BS236); both cannons failed
		2	F/Sgt King		oxygen failed during combat, became unconscious
		3	F/L Makin		CSU failure during combat, force-landed north of Fenton; BS193 QY-V written off
		4		F/O Watkin	BR240 did not deliver power, aborted
		5	F/O Bassett		1 cannon failed
	White	1	F/L Hall		1 cannon failed
		2	Sgt Richardson		CSU failure during combat, bailed out 10 km S Strauss; BS237 destroyed
		3	F/O Lloyd		shot down & bailed out near Murrenja Hill; BR497 QY-C destroyed
		4	P/O Tully		1 cannon failed
	Yellow	1		F/O Colyer	base patrol Hughes-Batchelor

457	Red	1	W/C Caldwell		
		2	S/L James		
		3	P/O Little		
	Blue	1	F/O Hamilton		shot down & killed; BR589 ZP-P destroyed on Billabong Ridge
		3	F/O Robinson		shot down & killed near Mt Litchfield; BS197 ZP-R destroyed
		4	P/O McDowell		shot down & killed near Mt Litchfield; BR499 ZP-V destroyed
	White	1	F/L P Watson		1 cannon failed
		2	F/Sgt Batchelor		both cannons failed
		3	F/L Edwards		both cannons failed
		4	F/O Hegarty		
	Green	1	F/O Mackenzie		
		2	F/Sgt R Watson		aborted as Blue 2 due R/T failure; took off again & reassigned to Green; 1 cannon failed
	Yellow	1		F/Sgt Ashby RAF	Jim Crow' low-level contact patrol
		30		5	

Summary:
Spitfires scrambled: 35
Spitfires in main wing formation: 31
Aborted due to mechanical failure: 3
Spitfires engaging: 30
Spitfires shot down by Zeros: 5
Spitfires damaged by bomber return fire: 1
Spitfires crashed or written off due to mechanicals: 3
Pilots killed: 3

11

The defeat of Japanese reconnaissance

Although 6 July would be the end of the daylight bombing campaign, the 23rd Air Flotilla's continued interest in Darwin was shown by the commencement of a program of large night raids. These would be of significantly greater strength than those conducted during the equivalent period in 1942, for instead of raids of three or six bombers they now sent nine or 18. The target almost always included Fenton, showing that these night raids were a continuation of the tightly focused air offensive against the US bomber unit that had commenced on 20 June. Given that the RAAF did not possess a single radar-equipped night fighter, the Japanese could conduct these raids with the expectation of suffering almost no losses to enemy action.

Japanese sensitivity to losses

Although Japanese losses in the daylight raids had been only a fraction of those claimed by the Spitfire wing, these losses had been significant enough to prompt this reversion to night raids. In less than two months, 753 Air Group had lost a minimum of nine bombers and five crews to the Spitfires. In a logistical context of extreme material parsimony in favour of other battle fronts further east, its strength was declining. In spite of 202 Air Group's ability to shoot down Spitfires, the escorting fighters had largely failed to prevent attacks on the bombers. Indeed, this seemed a deliberate strategy: in practice, the essence of Japanese air fighting tactics was to use the bombers as bait to lure the defending fighters into their firing runs, only then swooping upon them from above. Not once had the Zeros attacked the wing during its climb or interfered with it as it formed up to attack. The Japanese reliance upon the 'bomber bait' strategy for their air combat success is shown by plain statistics: the 202 AG fighter pilots had obtained 80 per cent of their kills in escorted bomber raids, scoring at the good rate of one kill per four fighter sorties. On the other hand, fighter sweeps were quite unsuccessful, requiring more than 20 sorties to secure one kill. These sweeps were grandiloquently designated 'air annihilation' operations, for this was their designed effect according to Japanese offensive doctrine – but they were anything but. The reality behind the big-sounding rhetoric was that without the bombers to draw the 'bees to the honey pot', the Zeros found it very hard to keep the Spitfires at a disadvantage.

It is not clear what the bomber crews thought about their role as 'bait'. Indeed, each of the Japanese units experienced the campaign very differently. From the perspective of 753 Air Group, its bombers had run the gauntlet of sustained and intensive fighter attacks on every raid, and had returned each time to Timor with a harvest of shot-up bombers and crash-landings. It is in this context that the Japanese official war history explains that 'the air defence became very strict and our losses increased greatly. The R.A.A.F. defence fighters and radar system became [*sic*] the highest level in the world'. This is certainly a great overstatement, but it reflects a Japanese perception of the depth of the defence on the other side of the Timor Sea. The Australian air defence radar system guaranteed that every time the bombers went over, they would meet a full-strength Spitfire wing. Although Caldwell's use of the big wing tactic impeded results in the air combats, it was nonetheless powerful propaganda: if nothing else, the sight of a concentrated formation of 30 Spitfires climbing up alongside each time must have made a salutary impression, advertising both the irreducible numerical strength and irrepressible fighting will of the Allies. The Japanese continued to believe they were shooting the Spitfires down in their dozens, yet if they kept reappearing in such numbers, then how many replacements must the Australians have?

The proposition that the daylight raids were temporarily abandoned because of losses is supported by a consideration of the continued operational effort mounted against Darwin by 753 Bomber Group. During the three-month night campaign that followed 6 July, the unit maintained a tempo of two raids per month. This was a reasonable operational intensity by its own standards in the NWA, showing continuing strong interest in Darwin as a target in spite of the tighter operational budgets that now prevailed. Such a raiding program required an operational commitment from 753 AG that was only a little less than that maintained for the preceding series of day raids: the unit put an average of 21 bomber sorties over the Australian coast per month during this program of night raids, little different to the unit's previous daylight raiding output – when an average of 26 bomber sorties had crossed the Australian coast per month.

Even the average raid strength was similar – the daylight raids employed an average force strength of 15 bombers, while the night raids fielded an average of ten.

Given that the bombers' sortie rates and raiding strengths were maintained at a similar level, the only missing element was the provision of fighter escort – and yet 202 AG remained in the area right to the end of the year. It has been argued that it was the 380th BG's deep penetration raids that forced the withdrawal of the 202 AG from offensive operations, redeployed instead to air defence garrison duties at airfields throughout the Indonesian archipelago. This is undoubtedly true, but 202 AG had *always* been deployed in this dispersed manner, reconcentrating itself on Timor only for the mounting of special missions like the Darwin raids. Not much had actually changed in the rhythm of the fighter unit's sporadic forward deployments, as shown by the fact that during September, 202 AG mounted one more maximum effort operation over Darwin, one over Drysdale (as will be seen) and one over Merauke on the southern shore of Dutch New Guinea. In other words, despite the Japanese defensive fighter commitments against the 380th BG raids, 202 AG nonetheless maintained the same scale of commitment to offensive operations as during the June–July 'blitz'.

Moreover, in putatively withdrawing its fighter force from offensive operations, the 23rd Air Flotilla would in effect have conceded the failure of its offensive blitz upon the B-24 base. Despite the good bombing and escorting, the Japanese had thereby conceded their failure to 'annihilate' either the defending fighters or the bombers on the ground – as was the intention.

Given 202 AG's continued offensive commitments, it is clear that the only missing element was the willingness to put 753 Bomber Group back over Darwin targets in daylight. If both the resident bomber unit and its enabling fighter escorts had remained present in strength for service on the northern

Australian battle front until the onset of the wet season, but were not used together in further daylight raids on Darwin after 6 July, then the reason for the abandonment of daylight bombing must lie in a loss of will, and this must have turned upon a consideration of the profit/loss equation.

Therefore, although 1 Fighter Wing had shot down far fewer Japanese aircraft than it claimed, it had hit enough Imperial Navy aircraft to put pressure upon 23rd Air Flotilla's strategic brief to keep losses down and to retain its air units 'in being'. The Japanese operational staffs could see that there had been no weakening of Darwin's air defence, and thus further niggling losses could be projected if the daylight raids were continued. Such losses would quickly reach a point of cumulative unacceptability in a context where the decisive campaign further east took first claim upon available replacements and reinforcements. The switch to inaccurate and ineffective night bombing was a sign of weakness, as it always was – as evidenced by the RAAF's recourse to night operations for its Hudson and Beaufort bomber squadrons through 1942–43, for similar reasons.

Despite their belief that they had scored much better than they had, the Spitfire pilots were modest enough to attribute the cessation of the day raids to other factors. After a three-week hiatus following the 6 July combat, 54 Squadron's diarist concluded that the lack of enemy raiding activity was due not only to some bad weather over Timor in July, but also to 'some depletion of strength in this area as a result of movements eastwards to meet the present Allied Offensive'. No. 457 summarised the situation at the end of July quite accurately, attributing the new 'conservatism' in the Japanese raiding strategy to the enemy air units' deep involvement in the Solomons on top of their recent losses over Darwin. By the end of October, 452 concluded that the Japanese air force was getting such a 'hammering' in New Guinea that they were unable 'to spare pilots and aircraft on the Darwin area'. It is clear that the pilots were receiving good intelligence briefings on the wider war situation, and had no illusions about the fact that theirs was a subordinate battle front.

Indeed, after the opening of MacArthur's offensive in New Guinea at the end of June, there was little prospect of ongoing replacement or reinforcement of the Japanese units on the Darwin front. With Allied amphibious forces progressively pushing north through the Solomon Islands and westward along the northern coast of New Guinea, the Japanese southern defensive perimeter was being levered open. In response, major Imperial Navy air reinforcements were channelled into the Rabaul base to block the Solomons thrust, while the Imperial Army's air force similarly reinforced the Wewak base to oppose the New Guinea thrust. Both of these battle fronts would consume huge quantities of Japanese aircraft, aircrews and ground crews in a remorseless procession of wholesale attrition. From mid-1943, the Americans were forcing the Japanese air forces onto the long downhill pathway of remorseless losses and inevitable defeat.

The challenge of Japanese reconnaissance

Facing a redoubled need to carefully husband its air resources, the 23rd Air Flotilla nonetheless prepared for the resumption of further operations over Darwin by continuing the photographic reconnaissance of its portfolio of bombing targets. This reconnaissance activity presented a considerable challenge to 1 Fighter Wing, as the Spitfires had lately been failing in their attempts to intercept and shoot down the swift and high-flying spy-planes. So far, only twice had the Spitfires succeeded in shooting them down – as long ago as February and March – showing that the Japanese reconnaissance unit had recently been enjoying near immunity to interception. It was one thing for the RAAF's radar operators, plotters and controllers to manage interceptions of large bomber formations, but single fast-moving aircraft targets had proven to be a lot harder to track on radar screens, to place on the plotting board, and to spot in the air. The 70th Reconnaissance Squadron made numerous penetrations of Australian airspace without being intercepted, sometimes without even being detected. No. 452 Squadron alone scrambled aircraft after recco intruders on 25 February, 2 March, 9 April, 29 April, 11 May, 13 May, 24 May, 28 May, 17 June, 22 June, 13 July, 20 July and 7 August – but failed to intercept every single time. Many of these seem to have been weather or shipping reconnaissances that did not cross the coast, but the reconnaissance photographs were getting safely back to base aboard the speedy Ki-46s.

Frustratingly, many times control was able to vector Spitfires into an interception but the pilots would fail to see the intruder. On 4 March, a Ki-46 passed right over the top of a pair of orbiting Spitfires without being seen. On 24 May, an intruder was plotted accurately by GCI radar as it came in from the west to photograph Fenton, but the Spitfires failed to see it despite being vectored by radar to within 3 kilometres of it. Sometimes cloud formations interposed themselves between Spitfires and intruders, but there were many non-sightings on clear days as well. Another problem was unreliable radar plotting: very often control was only able to plot the intruders when they were already outbound, too late to intercept.

The question of Spitfire performance

The Ki-46 was like a scaled-down and slimmed-down G4M, and like other Mitsubishi designs was a very efficient design, featuring the lightest possible airframe for the specified purpose.

Such design efficiency meant that the Ki-46 had the edge on the Spitfire in flight performance, as had been shown on 23 May, when a section of 54 Squadron intercepted one of the Japanese intruders at 25 000 feet over Batchelor. Upon spotting the Spitfires, the Japanese pilot had skilfully turned into the attack and climbed up sun. Rob Norwood found himself climbing after it in a stern chase at 200 knots IAS, with tracers whipping back towards him from the rear gun (relying as they did upon pure speed for safety, not all recco crews used the rear 7.7 mm machine gun, but this one did). He and his wingman, Sergeant P Fox, watched in frustration as the Ki-46 gradually pulled away and disappeared ahead.

Such incidents as this, on top of the complaints coming from the squadrons about their worn-out engines, gave rise to some concern within the RAAF about the performance of its Spitfires. Such perceptions of substandard speed performance were often traced to the Vokes air intake: this protuberant fitting under the aircraft's nose was fitted to 'tropical' Spitfires designated for operation in hot climates and from dusty undeveloped airfields – and was thus standard issue on Spitfires assigned to North Africa, Malta, Burma and Australia. The filter's function was to stop fine dust and sand from being sucked into the carburettor air intake, preventing its ingestion into the combustion chambers and thus avoiding the consequent accelerated engine wear, lowered compression and reduced power output.

Concerned by pilot claims of a 10–15 knot speed loss in Spitfire aircraft due to the bulky Vokes filter, the RAAF's Directorate of Technical Services conducted a series of comparative performance tests. Spitfires fitted with the tropical filter were pitted against Spitfires fitted with a 'temperate' intake like those on UK-based aircraft – intended to restore the original performance. The results came in at the start of September, showing that the adverse effect of the Vokes filter upon Spitfire performance had been grossly overstated: at 21 000 feet, which was not far from a typical fighting height for 1 Fighter Wing, the average maximum speed in level flight for the tropical aircraft was 310 knots TAS – no more than 5 knots slower than the temperate intake aircraft. The RAAF had thus established that the speed performance of its Spitfires was very similar to the figures stated by the testing authorities in Britain. This might have been encouraging, had the RAAF known that the Ki-46 was credited with a top speed of 325 knots TAS at 19 000 feet!

Resumed interceptions of the Ki-46 intruders

On 18 July, nearly two weeks after the last daylight raid, and with the campaign still very much undecided in everyone's minds, the wing was scrambled in response to an incoming radar plot. It soon became apparent that the intruders consisted of only two reconnaissance aircraft rather than a whole raid, and thus 54 and 452 were ordered to 'pancake', leaving only 457 airborne. Following standard procedure, control split the squadron into four sections, placing three of them as 'stops' across likely enemy tracks – over Hughes, Batchelor and Point Charles. The fourth section orbited near the coast ready to be vectored by GCI radar to intercept the Ki-46 as it headed back out to sea. One intruder came in from the west and photographed the cluster of airfields around Batchelor, while the other photographed Fenton – showing that the 380th BG base was still very much on the Japanese agenda. This second Ki-46 was not plotted by radar but was spotted visually going past Darwin inbound; it was not plotted on radar until long after it had taken its photos of Fenton and was already across the coast on the way out – and therefore not intercepted. Mr Wyatt of Mount Bundey Station had observed a twin-engined aircraft circling low over the station, so it seems this machine had avoided radar tracking by flying low across country.

Meanwhile, Squadron Leader Ken James's White Section was vectored into visual contact with the other Ki-46, which by now was heading outbound after photographing Coomalie. James only spotted it when it was 2 kilometres away, heading north at 27 000 feet. He turned after it at once, but the enemy crewmen saw him too, and the Japanese aircraft turned away to the east and accelerated. Despite getting the full 3000 rpm and +9 boost out of his engine, James could not overhaul the recco in the resultant stern chase – because his belly tank would not jettison. However, after a 'fierce struggle' with the D-release next to his seat, the tank finally fell away. Freed of the extra drag, his Spitfire gained 10 knots in speed, enough to let him finally close in on the Japanese machine. James patiently held his fire until he was 250 metres behind the Ki-46, aimed carefully, and fired in a no-deflection shot from dead astern. Pieces of its airframe flew off and then it burst into flames and fell away into a steep dive, the right wing snapping off and gyrating down by itself like a falling leaf. James's section mates – Flight Lieutenant Doug Edwards and Flying Officers Brian Hegarty and Ken Barker – did not get to fire, but witnessed their CO's demonstration of good gunnery. A parachute emerged in the last seconds before the flaming machine struck the ground 30 kilometres south of Point Stuart and 6 kilometres east of the Mary River (100 kilometres east of Darwin), while the detached wing sailed into the ground 2 kilometres away from the main wreckage. The photos of Batchelor and Coomalie were not going anywhere, but the second Japanese machine got away to deliver its Fenton photographs to the Flotilla staffers at Kendari HQ.

After its dreadful day on 6 July, 457 Squadron needed some good news, and the CO had just provided this – in the macabre way inherent to fighter combat. Three officers – Flight Lieutenant Jack Newton, Pilot Officer Ian Morse and the Squadron

Defence Officer, Flying Officer Larry Alderson – set out by jeep to find the wreck. They were guided to the spot by Mr Black, owner of the Point Stuart property, assisted by a party of Aboriginal people who scoured the bush to find the field of debris. Having thereby located the major pieces of wreckage, Newton's team found that the airframe had mostly been burnt and melted beyond recognition: the largest pieces remaining were part of one wing and the fuselage nose cone. Newton was impressed with the immaculately clean condition of the airframe, by the great lightness of its construction, and by the impressive number of fuel cells packed within the wing (eight on each side). He was also intrigued to discover that the observer had been operating an American Fairchild F24 camera.

The bodies of both crewmen were found lying hundreds of metres from the main wreck but in opposite directions, having spilled out of the disintegrating fuselage before it hit the ground. In true Japanese style, neither had attempted to save their lives by resorting to parachutes. The body of the pilot lay on the ground 400 metres from the wreck with his seat parachute burst open by ground impact. The observer had not even attached his parachute pack to his harness, and the canopy had deployed without him, coming to earth 550 metres away: singed by fire and torn open when ejected from the disintegrating wreck, it had floated down by itself. Newton made a grisly inspection of the dead airmen, noting their quilted flying suits and unusual safety equipment, but their faces were too putrefied and crow-pecked to permit the removal of their oxygen masks by the squeamish RAAF officers. Captain Shunji Sasaki and Lieutenant Akira Eguchi were buried the next day by a party of air force intelligence personnel under Flying Officer G Pender. The 70th Reconnaissance Squadron at Lautem had suffered a severe blow after four months of loss-free operations, for Shunji was the unit's CO.

Although the reappearance of the high-flying snoopers usually presaged a raid, three more weeks passed before the next air combat, and this one was yet another reconnaissance. As with the Milingimbi raids, 457 again had the luck to find itself in the role of duty squadron when the scramble alarm came through on 11 August. Ken James led eight aircraft into the air, where they were split up into four sections, vectored to their respective 'stops'. Two Ki-46 intruders again split the defence by taking different inward and outward tracks, one travelling clockwise and the other anti-clockwise as they circumnavigated the great mass of the Tiwi Islands in a great arc. The only contact was made by Flight Sergeant Evan Batchelor, who had become separated from his No. 1, Pete Watson, and been vectored onto the intruder by 10 Mobile Fighter Sector's GCI radar. He spotted the intruder and pursued the interception alone, chasing the slippery Mitsubishi and slowly gaining on it while climbing at 200 knots IAS (310 TAS). At 27 500 feet over Emu Springs, he got within 400 metres of it and made several rear-quarter attacks, but both cannons jammed. Making further attacks, his machine guns started jamming one by one, until only a single weapon was left firing. He exhausted his last gun's ammunition while firing from 150 metres dead astern.

Batchelor admitted frankly that all this firing had been 'without much effect', although he had seen some flashes on the top of the enemy machine's fuselage and a large flash on its port engine. Reduced to impotently tailing the escaping intruder out to sea, he reported its position over the R/T in case other Spitfires could catch up, but they did not and so the Ki-46 headed out over Fog Bay and finally escaped into cloud, leaving Batchelor to return to base without his much sought-after 'scalp'. Upon hearing of the abortive engagement and still crowing about their own recco scalp back on 6 February, 54 chided 457 for its poor marksmanship by dropping a bow and arrow on the airstrip.

Meanwhile, the armourers examined Batchelor's guns, finding that each of the five jams had come from a different cause!

The reversion to night raids

Once the Japanese reconnaissance crews had delivered their target photos, everything was finally set for the next air raid – but disappointingly for the Spitfire pilots, at night. On the evening of 13 August, 18 bombers came over to continue the on-again off-again program of retaliatory strikes against Fenton. The Japanese had chosen a date two nights before the full moon to permit visual navigation as the bombers made their landfall and picked up their waypoints for the run-in to the target. The bright luminescence of a moonlit sky on a cloudless night permitted the enemy pilots to demonstrate the impressive feat of nocturnal formation flying. Approaching the coast in two nine-aircraft waves spaced almost 90 minutes apart, the big Mitsubishis flew in three-aircraft vees to penetrate overland to the target. They used a similar route to the earlier daylight raids by making landfall in the vicinity of Anson Bay.

However, the American bomber base, lying deep inland among the featureless scrub, was much harder to find at night than the coastal landform of Darwin, and one group of bombers got lost, splitting up and meandering about all over the countryside trying to establish its position and that of the target. In the course of this, the inconsiderate bomber crews disturbed the sleep of the men on all the southern airfields, particularly those at Hughes, where the resident AA guns shattered the night's repose. At Livingstone, the Yellow Alert interrupted a big party that was in full swing at 457 Squadron, with the airfield suddenly illuminated by a flare dropped overhead by one of the lost bomber crews. Eventually, most of the Japanese found and bombed Fenton, where they were taken under fire by

150 rounds of 3.7 inch. As usual, the guns did their good work not by hitting anything but by keeping the bombers well above 20 000 feet. The result was the customary ineffectual bombing results: no significant damage was inflicted in this, the third raid upon the 380th BG's base.

No. 54 Squadron scrambled five Spitfires, but control deployed them to defend Darwin rather than Fenton. Four orbited irrelevantly around the edges of Darwin's defensive box, while one was placed under the control of 10 Mobile Fighter Sector's GCI radar to orbit over Hughes. Even with radar vectors, however, a radarless fighter had little chance of obtaining visual contact, so no interception was made. In the Ops Room at Berrimah, Air Commodore Bladin got so frustrated with the misdeployment of the Spitfires that he overrode the controller, ordering the fighters to be vectored west to cut off the bombers' escape path over Peron Island. This too was a faint hope, for nothing was seen, and the bombers escaped unmolested, proving that there was no substitute for radar-equipped night fighters.

The triumph of 17 August

After this dubious success, the Japanese pushed on with preparations for a follow-up night raid, requiring updated target information. The 70th Reconnaissance Squadron had recently been seeking to make its aircraft even more elusive through the tactic of penetrating Australian airspace with two or three aircraft simultaneously, each on a different track. On 7 August, 14 Spitfires from 54 and 452 were scrambled after two separate inbound tracks, but failed to obtain visual contact. The next reconnaissance would exploit this successful tactic, but upgraded to five aircraft, each sent on different approach paths to different targets. It would also feature an increased penetration altitude of 30 000 feet instead of the previously used altitudes of around

25 000; a mark of respect for recent demonstrations of the Spitfire's altitude performance. Each aircraft could cover two or more targets, for the observer was able to change the camera's film magazine between runs. This mission therefore had the capability to photograph every airfield of interest in the area south of Darwin.

Quite independently of this army-run operation, the navy had also decided to send out a reconnaissance of its own on this day, and thus two further Ki-46 overflights were laid on by the navy's 202 Air Group. It was exceedingly unusual for the navy to operate an army aircraft type, as this was an open invitation to be publicly 'one-upped' by the old rival. However, such were the Ki-46's qualities that the navy unit was not too proud to borrow a couple of these excellent machines in order to provide the 23rd Air Flotilla with a long-range reconnaissance capability of its own. The wilful independence of the two services was reflected in the completely separate timing and routing of the 202 AG's recco – there were limits to how far the navy and army were prepared to coordinate their operations. The result was that on this day the five army sorties and the two navy sorties failed to support one another.

On the morning of 17 August, 457 yet again had the fabulous luck to be the duty squadron, and at 10.40 am control sent the first of its sections into the air to intercept the radar-plotted intruders. After the recent raids, control was able to make a confident prediction about at least one of the likely photographic targets, and so vectored Ken James's Red Section southward to Fenton, presciently ordering a climb to the unusually high altitude of 32 000 feet. Arriving over-head the US base at 31 000 feet, James and his No. 2, Bruce Little, were advised by 10 Mobile Fighter Sector that the recco was approaching from behind them, having inadvertently followed them in. They orbited overhead and waited for it.

Five minutes later, they spotted the incoming reconnaissance machine, and they only just had enough height, as the Ki-46 was coming in only 500 feet lower than they were. Jettisoning his drop tank, James ran in for a beam attack, but the Japanese machine was going so fast that he was almost left behind by its speedy progress, forced to swing in astern before he could fire. As on 18 July, James concentrated carefully on his firing, and in spite of one frozen-up cannon he got hits. He was assisted by the failure of the Japanese crew to evade – the pilot was setting up for the photo run, and the observer was bending over his camera, and so the unfortunate men were too busy to spot him before he fired. The Ki-46 was hit, streaming out a billow of flame from its fuselage fuel tank, then plummeting in a vertical dive to explode on the ground. Little did not get close enough to fire and had to content himself with witnessing the CO's kill. It was good propaganda for the wing, as the Japanese machine went to its fiery end in full view of the much-bombed Americans below. The remains of the crew, Lieutenant Shin-Ichi Matsuura and his observer, were removed from the wreckage and buried by men of the Australian Army's 133rd HAA Battery.

Meanwhile, 457's Blue Section were vectored northward: Rex Watson and Bill Gregory were ordered to climb to 30 000 feet to orbit over Cape Gambier, while 'Snapper' Newton and Rod Jenkins were to make 32 000 over Cape Fourcroy – respectively over the south-east and south-west corners of Bathurst Island. The controller had positioned them there to cut off two of the usual Japanese withdrawal routes, but both caught the same enemy machine. Newton could not coax his engine to go above 30 000 feet, so told Jenkins to go ahead without him. Gregory saw the enemy first, at 31 000 feet just to the south of him, heading outbound. He and Rex Watson closed slowly in from the side, flying at 190 knots IAS (307 TAS) on a course that was almost parallel with that of the enemy machine. Watson, in contrast to Newton, found that his aircraft was performing well, for he kept up with the Japanese machine even with his drop tank on. Once he got out ahead of it, he turned in for a beam attack, but the Ki-46 was going so fast that he quickly found himself having to reverse his turn and roll in behind it. From there he fired deliberately three times, repositioning himself before each burst. Despite the failure of one of his cannons, he saw hits: puffs of smoke came from its port engine and there were strikes all over its fuselage and rear glasshouse. Watson then pulled out to one side to let his No. 2 attack, and from this broader viewing angle he could see that he had 'riddled' the enemy machine with his gunfire. Although his own wingman, Bill Gregory, could not catch up, Rod Jenkins had meanwhile seen the Ki-46 go past, and joined the pursuit. He now came in from directly astern with a good overtaking speed, and kept firing right in to 50 metres, when the enemy machine suddenly blew up right in front of him, spraying oil all over his windscreen. The flaming aircraft disintegrated, its broken wreckage plunging away vertically to crash on Bathurst Island, 16 kilometres north-west of the RC Mission. This confirmed kill was shared between Jenkins and Rex Watson. Jack Newton, held back by his poorly performing engine, had to content himself with firing from extreme range and watching the others get the kill. It was turning out to be an awful day for the 70th Reconnaissance Squadron.

White Section meanwhile had been vectored to Batchelor airfield, there to climb to 30000 feet and to report to 10 Mobile Fighter Sector for vectors. Once again, it was the section leader who found himself unable to keep up because of an underperforming engine. Pete Watson had to drop out and level off at 24000 feet to let his engine cool down, as his coolant temperature was red-lining because of the hard climb. Ironically, however, Watson's mechanical misfortune turned out to be a stroke of luck, for as he orbited, carefully watching his temperature gauge, he spotted a Ki-46 coming in from the west. Unfortunately, it was 4000 feet higher as it headed back to the coast with its photographs. Watson turned after it and gave chase, thankful for the breathing space he had been able to give his engine but still keeping an eye on the temperature gauge. Staying in the intruder's blind spot below and behind, he gained height not by climbing but by putting his nose down slightly to gain speed, then pulling the stick back to zoom up a few hundred feet. By this means, in a series of steps, he edged up closer to its height but without closing the horizontal distance. It was therefore a lucky break for Watson when the Japanese pilot throttled back his engines as he neared the coast – presumably thinking that he had made it out safely and needing to conserve fuel for the long flight back to Timor. This enabled Watson to close right in, still unseen in the blind spot under the Japanese machine's tail.

He fired from below and astern from the killing distance of 150 metres. Both engines smoked, then the Ki-46 blew up – so suddenly that Watson's Spitfire was covered in a spray of engine oil. He pulled up to get clear of the flying debris and then spiral-dived in pursuit of the plummeting wreckage to watch the crash. The airframe disintegrated after a second explosion at 5000 feet, the smoking pieces falling into the mudflats off Channel Point near Anson Bay. A parachute opened and floated to earth, but Watson saw that there was no one underneath it: once again, the observer's detached parachute pack had been ejected by the explosion and torn open. The bodies of Lieutenants Kyuiti Okamoto and Yasuo Yamamoto were not recovered from their remote and glutinous crash site. As was always the way in fighter aviation, the 70th Reconnaissance Squadron's tragedy was 457's joy, and so the squadron deservedly celebrated its triple victory, in some measure avenging its losses on 6 July. Deservedly revelling in 'the best day the squadron has yet had', the pilots had a 'slight celebration' that night. After suffering 54 Squadron's little jibe for Batchelor's previous failure to shoot down his recco, 457 now took the opportunity to rub it in: the offending bow and arrow were dropped onto the field at Darwin with a note saying they had proven to be very useful.

At 3.30 that afternoon, control ordered another scramble against two additional inbound recco plots, and four aircraft each from 457 and 452 were ordered off, split up into four pairs which were vectored respectively to Gunn Point, Point Blaze, the RC Mission and Fenton. A 457 section missed the Ki-46 that photographed the US base and then failed to catch it on its way out to sea over Perron Island in spite of radar vectors from 10 Mobile Fighter Sector. Although 457 now considered themselves specialists in shooting down the reccos, this time they missed the interception.

Caldwell was also aloft, paired with Flight Sergeant PA 'Paddy' Padula from 452 as Winco Section. He had taken off to intercept the morning reccos but missed the action, so here he was again, determined to get on the scoreboard. They climbed to 32 000 feet, arriving at that height over Gunn Point, 30 kilometres north-east of Darwin. Warned of the approach of a reconnaissance machine from the west, they headed towards Point Charles in time to see the second reconnaissance machine 20 kilometres away, going through its photographic run overhead Darwin accompanied by a trail of AA bursts. It then headed outbound at 26 000 feet doing only 160 knots IAS (243 TAS). This moderate speed, together with the moderate height, suggests the crew thought there was little risk of interception – 202 AG was less experienced in reconnaissance operations over defended targets than their rivals in the army unit. The navy crew had also tempted fate by tarrying long over the defended area, making four separate photo runs as it worked its way northward along the track from Fenton to Coomalie, Hughes and Darwin.

Assisted by the enemy machine's predictable movements and steady pace, Caldwell and Padula achieved an easy interception. They overhauled it quite easily, using their height superiority to gain speed in a shallow dive. The Ki-46 was still doing only 260 knots TAS at 26 000 feet when they caught up with it 30 kilometres off the coast, giving the Spitfires such a good overtaking speed that they had to weave back and forth behind it to decelerate and avoid overshooting. The Wingco made the first attack and then gallantly pulled out to the side to let Padula have a go, in an effort to let his No. 2 get on the scoreboard. However, the new pilot fired from too far out (600 metres) and so Caldwell took another turn. One of his cannons jammed, but Caldwell got hits, showing his experience by firing right in to 50 metres range. The enemy machine started burning, and after another burst it steepened its dive, descending so precipitously that Caldwell had to lose height at 7000 feet per minute in order to keep up with it. Accelerating to more than 300 knots, the stricken machine smashed into the water with a great splash, 40 kilometres west of Cape Fourcroy. Circling overhead, Caldwell saw three bodies floating in the water, along with two parachutes partially opened by the water impact, and a partially inflated dinghy. One of the airmen, in a black flying suit, lay floating face upwards with all four limbs spreadeagled, and Caldwell received the strange impression that he was still alive. He radioed control to get a fix on the crash position and requested a vessel come out to collect the bodies, but none did.

Naval Air Crewmen 1st Class Tomihiko Tanaka, Shinji Kawahara and Susumu Ito of 202 AG thus died, making nine recco fatalities for the day – a startling and unprecedented disaster. Seven of the best reconnaissance aircraft in the world had been sent out, flying at hitherto difficult-to-intercept heights and intelligently routed on multiple tracks and evasive headings to confuse the defence – but only three of them got back to base.

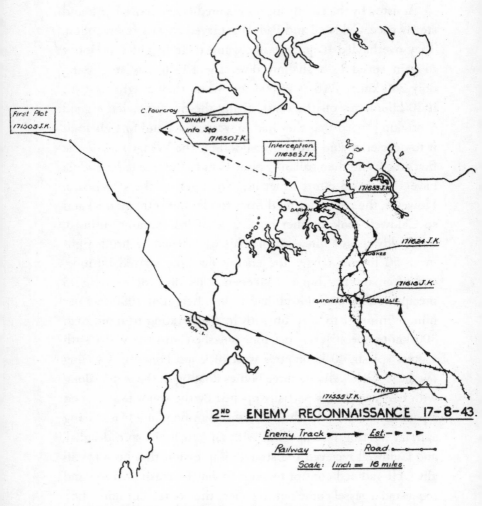

First Plot
171505 J.K.

C. Fourcroy

"DINAH" Crashed
into Sea
171650 J.K.

Interception
171638½ J.K.

171653 J.K.

DARWIN

171624 J.K.

HUGHES

171616 J.K.

BATCHELOR   COOMALIE.

PERON I.

171555 J.K.   FENTON

2ᴺᴰ ENEMY RECONNAISSANCE 17-8-43.

Enemy Track ●————►   Est.— ►- - ►
Railway ————   Road ●—○—○—○
Scale: 1 inch = 16 miles.

The plot of Caldwell's afternoon recco kill on 17 August.
Note the provocative overflights of Fenton, Coomalie,
Hughes and Darwin, and the unbroken radar tracking that
enabled a successful interception. NAA: A11231, 5/61/INT

This was an astonishing coup for 1 Fighter Wing. The Japanese planning staffs had suddenly been almost blinded, for these grievous losses meant that they could no longer hazard their reconnaissance aircraft and crews on unescorted photographic sorties over Darwin's well-defended airfields. In one stroke, 1 Fighter Wing had emphatically gained the upper hand in the battle for air superiority over the NWA, for there could be no resumption of daylight raids without regular and reliable target intelligence.

The triumph of 17 August was gratifying for the pilots, providing some psychological compensation for their earlier losses and a very public validation of their existence as a defensive force. However, the day was primarily a victory for the controllers and the whole ground-based air defence system that had been so painstakingly and incrementally built up over the previous year and a half. From the uncertain beginnings on 2 March, the Australian air defence system was now working smoothly enough to place concurrently three sections of fighters in the right places to intercept three separately routed high-speed intruders. The successful triple interception, and the quadruple kill, demonstrated the maturity of the apparatus that the RAAF had built up with such speed from such a low base.

Despite claims that the 17 August losses had no effect upon the ongoing Japanese reconnaissance program, the evidence shows otherwise – the quadruple interception unsurprisingly caused a reversion to very cautious tactics. RAAF radar continued to detect and plot airspace intrusions after 17 August, with Spitfires scrambled after these contacts six times during the balance of August and September. Given past instances of unplotted recco overflights, some other missions may have reached their photographic targets without detection by the radar operators, but such cases must have been few, given the improvement in the radar coverage that had been achieved during the year – the radar belt had been thickened through the addition of new stations both along the coast and inland, while the long-range Air Warning radars had been supplemented by shorter-range but finer discrimination GCI equipment.

The plotted intruders confined themselves to shallow penetrations and shipping reconnaissances, thereby staying frustratingly out of the Spitfires' reach. For example, on 19 September, the recco turned back before reaching Bathurst Island; on 29 September, it came no closer than 110 kilometres away; on 4 October, it ran from west to east 60 kilometres north of Melville Island; on 15 October, it turned back before Peron Island. Indeed, by the second half of September, the enemy was behaving so circumspectly that 5 Fighter Sector downgraded the strength of the standard intercepting force from the previous two-squadron strength to only flight strength; while by the end of September, the intrusions were so tentative and unthreatening that 5 Fighter Sector ceased scrambling aircraft after them, confining its response to keeping one squadron on ground alert, ready to scramble if the intruder actually came further in. By 23 October, 54 was lamenting that 'the enemy has shown no sign of activity lately, and no enemy have come within our range'. No. 457 also bemoaned the 'standstill' in enemy activity, except for 'a few shy shipping reconnaissances out to sea'. It is very clear that the 17 August disaster had spoiled the game for Japanese recco operations over Darwin.

The Spitfire as a night fighter

In spite of the missing target photos, the 23rd Air Flotilla needed to strike its next blow in the vendetta campaign against the 380th Bomb Group, and so sent out 18 bombers in the early hours of 21 August. The moon was waning, but it was still a bright enough night to make visual navigation practicable.

Although by now the navigators must have known the waypoints to Fenton quite well, the bomber crews nonetheless had a lot of trouble navigating over the darkened countryside: some of the small formations wandered all about the area in search of their target, their warlike effect confined to inflicting sleep-disturbance upon the airmen on the airfields below. Most of the bombers succeeded in finding and bombing Fenton, while others dropped their bombloads on the Beaufighter base at Coomalie. The bombing was typical night bombing – wayward. With bombers meandering about overhead for 20 minutes, Fenton's AA gunners had plenty of opportunity to fire, and got off an impressive 301 rounds of 3.7 inch. No. 452 sent up five Spitfires, four of them patrolling along each side of the defensive box around Darwin, with the fifth sent further south over Batchelor under the control of 10 Mobile Fighter Sector. The first four were in the wrong place to block a Fenton raid, while even with the aid of radar vectors from GCI radar, the fifth failed to contact the enemy.

Although 1 Fighter Wing was a day fighter outfit, it was far from inactive during these night raids. Indeed, ever since their arrival in the NWA the squadrons had been training in night flying, as NWA HQ was preparing them for precisely this eventuality. Unfortunately for the pilots, the Spitfire was an atrocious aircraft for night flying. As William Rolls, a UK Fighter Command veteran, said, 'night-flying a Spit was about the most dangerous thing you could do in an aircraft'. The pilot's forward visibility was obscured by the long nose even in daylight, but at night the glare from the exhausts blinded the pilot so badly that it was 'almost blind flying', with no horizon at all visible at take-off and landing. This made it very hard for the pilot to judge height above the ground on final approach, and also very hard to recognise a swing on take-off or landing. Unsurprisingly, the wing's night-flying program produced a regular harvest of accidents, with much damage to aircraft but fortunately without fatalities.

A good example of these perils was provided by Flying Officer John Gould of 452 during night-flying practice from Batchelor airfield on 16 February: blinded by the glare, he misjudged his height on approach and undershot the field by 800 metres. Suddenly seeing treetops below, he pushed the throttle forward for full power and selected undercarriage 'up'; but too late – the Spitfire descended into the trees. Both wings and the tail unit were torn off and the fuselage rump crashed to earth intact, fortunately without burning. A very lucky man, Gould got himself out of the cockpit in the sudden gloom and was found by a search party sent out from the nearby dispersals – he was wandering around in a daze carrying his parachute, but suffering only from abrasions and shock. Tim Goldsmith had had such a positive view of the Spitfire's handling characteristics that he had declared to his squadron mates that it 'lands itself', even at night; but 'after one trial decided that a Spitfire needed more practice'. In the United Kingdom, Spitfires were usually excluded from night-flying duties in favour of more suitable types, but there was no alternative in the NWA, so training continued in spite of the niggling accidents. The result was that by September, 26 of 54 Squadron's pilots were 'light night qualified' (in other words, in clear moonlit conditions), with 12 of them proficient enough to be rostered on as part of the night-flying team. Supported by this training program, a daily six-aircraft night readiness section at RAAF Darwin was rotated between the squadrons.

Although visibility of 30 kilometres was possible during cloudless moonlit nights, achieving contact with the enemy still entailed a huge helping of good luck and good timing. The previous nocturnal experience of 76 and 77 Squadrons in the night raids from September 1942 to January 1943 showed that visual sightings of bombers in the night sky were possible: they could be detected by the glint of moonlight on perspex; by being silhouetted against cloudbanks; by the flaring of their engines' exhausts; and even by the red glow of the cockpit instrument lighting. Such sightings were just possible in a Kittyhawk, but in a Spitfire there was little prospect of the pilot seeing anything at all outside the cockpit at night because of the blinding exhaust flares on each side of the aircraft's nose, right in his line of sight. The only realistic possibility was to orbit at intervals around Darwin's searchlight belt and to hope for one of the bombers to be picked up by the searchlights. Twenty-one of these were operated by the army's No. 65 and No. 70 AA Searchlight Batteries, guided onto their unseen targets by 'old technology' sound locaters (not radar). Searchlight acquisition of the nocturnal raiders was a prerequisite both for engaging them with AA gunfire and for achieving an interception by Spitfires.

Deprived of action by the Japanese reversion to night operations, the men of 1 Fighter Wing, both pilots and ground crew, were meanwhile 'dying' of boredom, but there may have been some consolation for the more thoughtful of them in the fact that they had obviously won the campaign. The dry season would soon end, closing off the possibility of any resumption of large daylight raids in the towering cumulus and solid overcasts of the monsoon. Signs of the changing season would be evident by October, with increased humidity and rain and thunder almost daily, and 'close calls' in the air from lightning strikes. If the Japanese wanted to raid in daylight again in 1943, they would need to do so soon.

7 September – the last great air battle

The 23rd Air Flotilla was waiting until the September full moon before sending the next raid, but needed to prepare the way for the bombers by obtaining current target intelligence. The scene was thus set for the final large-scale air combat of the campaign. At 8.37 am on 7 September, radar detected an inbound plot 280 kilometres to the north-west of Darwin, heading inbound on a south-east course. Thinking on the basis of recent experience that this would be a reconnaissance mission, control scrambled 457 only. At the squadron, the scramble alarm was rung inconveniently early, before the readiness staff had time to chalk up the pilots' names on the blackboard. Normally, pilots would read their names, call signs and aircraft code letters off the readiness board and then run to their assigned aircraft. Today, with a blank blackboard, they just got in the nearest Spitfire, took off, and sorted themselves out behind leaders once they were in the air. Control then vectored each section independently to the standard 'stops' against reccos.

After 15 minutes, however, the radar return was thickening and had split up into several separate tracks – it now looked like a raid. The other two squadrons were therefore scrambled and ordered to rendezvous as a wing at 6000 feet over Sattler. No. 457's scattered sections were recalled to Sattler, ordered to reassemble as a squadron at 25 000 feet and then to join up with the wing en route to the interception. No. 54 and 457 Squadrons fielded 13 aircraft each, while 452 contributed ten. In addition, each unit sent up extra aircraft on an ancillary program of base patrols and blocking patrols over likely exit points – the controllers were unsure of the exact nature of the raid, and were still concerned to 'stop' any reccos that separated from the main plot. These extra sorties totalled 12, but none of these would engage the enemy. With 48 aircraft airborne, it is clear that after the low point of June–July the wing was now on top of its aircraft availability problems. The low incidence of aborts and technical failures also suggests an improvement in aircraft and engine condition since those 'bad old days'.

The approaching Japanese formation was indeed large, but it was in fact no raid. It was instead an escorted reconnaissance mission, consisting of three Ki-46 photo-planes of the army's 70th Reconnaissance Squadron escorted by 36 Zeros of the navy's 202 AG. The events of 17 August had shown that circumspection was required if Ki-46 aircraft were to survive in Australian skies, checkmated as they were by the Spitfires' good high-altitude performance and by efficient RAAF radar direction – hence this departure from the previous standard procedure (namely, of sending the reccos out unescorted and relying on their performance alone to escape interception). If the campaign was to continue, up-to-date photos were needed, and these would now be obtained by sending the reconnaissance machines over under cover of a strong escort of Zeros – clearly an extravagant, inauspicious and unsustainable expedient.

Because Caldwell was about to be posted out to 2 OTU, the leadership of the wing was delegated to one of the senior pilots – 4's Flight Lieutenant Bob Foster. He was one of the most experienced pilots in the wing – far more so than 452's CO, Ron MacDonald, who was the most highly ranked officer airborne that day other than Caldwell. The Wingco himself saw out the day in a subsidiary role in order to avoid the temptation of 'back-seat driving'. He flew as 452's Green Section leader, sent out on a stopping patrol to Port Patterson, but Green Section failed to rendezvous and the pilots would see no action.

Under Foster's leadership, 54 and 452 rendezvoused and climbed as ordered, but soon after setting off to the west towards Port Patterson, the R/T net was jammed by a loud and continuous high-pitched whistling or screaming noise in the pilots' headphones. This was caused by one of the R/T sets being left on 'transmit', rendering transmissions unreadable. The selected radio frequency was thereby jammed, cutting communication between the wing and control, as well as within the wing. Some pilots switched their R/T sets to 107.10, but most stayed on the jammed frequency, 114.30.

The jamming meant that pilots could no longer receive target information or vectors from control. Moreover, 54 and 452 were at that time on a dangerous vector, climbing up right underneath the incoming Japanese and therefore placing themselves in an ideal position to be bounced. In previous raids, control had demonstrated great care to avoid this, and had no doubt intended to turn the wing off this vector in order to continue its climb safely out to one side. However, now that the communication link was gone, the two squadrons continued their climb straight towards the enemy. The last target information the pilots had received was that the raid was north-west of Port Charles inbound towards Darwin, following a similar approach path to the Darwin raids of 15 March and 2 May. Judging by this, the Japanese would be dead ahead, coming head-on straight for the wing. John Bisley, leading 452's Blue Section at the rear of the Spitfire column, was not happy with being led straight towards the enemy and at an inferior height, and in his combat report he did not spare his criticism of Foster's 'poor leadership' in permitting this to happen.

Deprived of vectors by the jammed frequency, the scattered components of 457 could no longer be vectored into a flying rendezvous with the other squadrons as intended. However, two sections were able to get themselves into good positions to intercept. Having heard control vector the other squadrons towards Port Patterson before the R/T became unreadable, Pete Watson departed with his section in that direction, climbing through 27 000 feet. He found that he and Don Maclean, leading the other nearby section, could just comprehend each other's transmissions through the howling R/T interference, but could not understand any transmissions from the main wing formation. Assisted by this rudimentary coordination, Maclean led his section towards the incoming Japanese, following after Watson. No. 457 had the advantage of height because of its earlier take-off and was thus unlikely to be bounced, but this did not apply to the others.

The R/T jamming had handed the advantage over to the inbound enemy – the expert pilots of 202 AG. This sudden loss of the Spitfire wing's communication lifeline to ground control exposed some of its systemic tactical weaknesses – dependency upon orders from control and from the Wingco, poor lookout, and lack of initiative and flexibility while assembled in the wing Balbo. By contrast, the Japanese pilots had fought their whole campaign largely without radio and had a well-polished set of drills and standardised routines that allowed them to function well without it. Squadron and section leaders were drilled to use their initiative, to manoeuvre for advantage according to the situation as they saw it, to respond flexibly and rapidly to enemy moves, and to reform above the fight in a coherent manner ready for the next attack. Fighting on the enemy's side of the water, they had never had the benefit of ground control for search bearings and target information, and so had not become dependent upon this external help as the Spitfire pilots had. The Japanese style of flying was ideally suited to a disorganised encounter battle where the advantage would go to whoever saw the other side first.

By the time the two-squadron column of Spitfires crossed over the highway on climb to the west through 20 000 feet, there were only 21 Spitfires left in the formation, for two of 54's pilots had aborted with malfunctioning engines. No. 54 was in front, led by Foster, while 452 was behind and 3000 feet lower, led by MacDonald. Flying at the rear of the Australian squadron's formation, Flying Officer Ken Fox was starting to get concerned, thinking they were getting themselves into 'a perfect position to be bounced', and noticing that their formation was deteriorating as they climbed, with the sections straggling behind Foster. Neither squadron was yet in battle formation when they climbed through 23 000 feet, and this was a dangerous height, as the Japanese top-cover generally flew at 28 000 or above. No. 54's sections were flying in old-fashioned vees, while 452's were in line astern – neither was a good formation in which to meet the enemy.

Higher up and further ahead because of 457's earlier start, Pete Watson was the first to see the raiders, observing about a dozen Zeros 6000 feet lower heading inbound between the Berry Springs Rest Camp and the West Arm of Darwin Harbour. He noticed that they were escorting a Ki-46 for a photo run over Darwin. Shadowing them, he called their position over the R/T, but no one in 54 or 452 heard any of his calls due to the radio interference. The main wing formation was out of Watson's view; he had neither contact with it over the R/T, nor any information on its position, so was powerless to influence the coming combat.

The bounce

Foster, at the head of that main formation, now saw the enemy suddenly and 'unexpectedly' – 25 Zeros were coming straight for the wing, only 1 mile away and almost dead ahead, 2000 feet higher. This late sighting was a disastrous way to start the engagement and was a very poor lookout performance on a day with clear visibility out to 40 kilometres. Ron MacDonald, flying further back in the train of Spitfires at the head of 452, had seen the Zeros earlier than Foster, noticing also that they were accompanied by one Ki-46 recco. However, his R/T warnings were not heard by 54 because of the jamming. The R/T jamming affected the pilots in the main formation most severely, for the offending transmitter was in the 54/452 Squadron formation.

Labouring under this handicap, these two squadrons would finish the campaign in the same way as they had started it – by getting bounced.

Having belatedly seen the Zeros, Foster watched the Japanese formation fly right over the top of his squadron and turn right to come in behind him from up sun. Having inadvertently permitted the Zeros to get this close, he had few options left. He could have rolled onto his back at once and dived away for safety, abandoning the sky to the enemy, but if he did this his arse-end Charlies would probably have been caught before they could get away. Foster seemed to be perturbed by the need to get his squadron into battle formation before the fight started, and kept going straight ahead to provide some space and time to do this.

Foster finally acted: after 30 seconds of flying straight, he led 54 in a turn to the right. MacDonald saw this and conformed, leading his squadron into a right turn as well. The R/T was intermittently readable, permitting some pilots to hear Foster's calls – some pilots blamed the bad R/T reception on their own radio sets, reporting 'extremely poor' R/T communication when they got back to base, little realising the actual source of the problem; Flight Sergeant Len Utber from 452 reported the radio reception to be 'so distorted that I hardly heard anything', while squadron colleague Hal Whillans reported the R/T to be 'loud and hard to understand'.

Having turned, Foster then ordered 54 to climb flat out into the sun, but the Zeros' earlier turn had already taken them up sun of the Spitfires. He then ordered 54 into battle formation, disturbing the squadron at a time when the enemy fighters were only a mile or two away to starboard and on the verge of attacking from out of the sun. Foster could already see seven or eight Zeros climbing into an attack position off his squadron's starboard rear quarter, and some pilots heard Rob Norwood warn that enemy fighters were already coming down behind them. No. 54 continued turning to the right in an attempt to face the enemy, with the pilots simultaneously distracted by their attempt to spread themselves out into line abreast. Now Foster saw the Zeros coming down on them, but it was too late; his pilots had still not sorted themselves out into battle formation. Yelling, 'Break! Break!' over the R/T, he went straight down out of the fight, followed by Red Section. He had been forced to do what he had rejected doing less than a minute earlier.

His inexperienced No. 2 and No. 4, Sergeants Whalley and Powell, managed to stay with him as he dived away. However, No. 3, Flying Officer Bill Hinds, was too slow getting away, hit from behind and shot down. His burnt-out aircraft was discovered next day in the Pioneer Creek area, and on the 10th a party of men removed his remains from the wreck for burial. Hinds had only been with the squadron since April after earlier operational service in Britain. He had not been lucky, having crashed his aircraft after a technical failure in the previous raid. Now he died in only his second combat in the NWA.

Foster's late sighting of the Zeros had been disastrous, but no one else had seen them much earlier: once again, the pilots' lookout had let them down. This was not helped by the scrambling climb in wing formation, with leaders and pilots increasingly anxious about keeping up with the other aircraft as the straggling began and the formation deteriorated. The Japanese had made their initial approach not from behind and out of the sun – always hard to see – but from the front, a comparatively obvious approach path that should have been hard to miss. For so many eyes to have missed this sight through a clear sky, things must have deteriorated to the point that leaders were looking in the wrong direction, while followers fixated upon the tails of the aircraft they were trying to keep up with. The pilots' habitual dependency upon control for search bearings was another factor that had weighed against effective lookout. Accustomed to being told in which direction to expect the enemy, on this day the pilots had evidently been looking in the wrong direction – left instead of right. Leaders had displayed poor airmanship, failing to scan the sky to their front in the ingrained expectation that their wing leader would bring them into action correctly.

Ron MacDonald had also failed to obtain an early sighting of the enemy. Once he saw them, he knew that the wing had been caught in a bad position, his immediate instinct being to break downwards and take his squadron out of danger. However, once he saw 54 turn right and climb, he felt morally obliged to conform to what the wing leader was doing. MacDonald had subordinated his judgment to that of the designated wing leader, taking his squadron into an untenable tactical situation even though he recognised it as such. John Bisley, at the head of Blue Section behind him, also saw the Zeros too late – after the wing's right turn – only then noticing three of them to starboard and up sun. He gave a warning, and Pilot Officer Bill Coombes heard this warning through the R/T interference and looked around to see these Zeros above and in the sun. Just then MacDonald ordered his men to get into battle formation and to drop their tanks. Like Foster, he had given the order too late, as the Zeros were already on the way down. Bisley now saw 12 Zeros coming down from the left. He called the break over the R/T but nobody heard, so he started to barrel-roll his aircraft to get the attention of the other pilots. As he pulled up into the roll, he saw Paul Tully's Spitfire to his left already getting hit by enemy fire, with pieces falling off it.

Tully, the CO's wingman, had heard nothing over the R/T because of the 'great distortion' and so remained unaware of the proximity of the enemy. He was flying alongside MacDonald, climbing steeply, when he looked further to the left – to see with a shock a Zero firing at Kenny Bassett's aircraft from directly astern. Tully shouted 'break!' on the R/T and started to roll into his own breaking turn, but even as he did so, the cockpit was suddenly filled by deafening detonations, bright red flashes and acrid cordite smoke: his aircraft also had been hit from behind by an unseen Zero. The Japanese pilot was close enough to be right on target with his 20 mm fire. Tully's aircraft was struck in the engine and cockpit, but he himself was lucky enough not to be hit. He bailed out uninjured, landing in the bush near Tumbling Waters about 25 kilometres west of his base at Strauss. He was picked up later the same day by a truck and returned to his squadron.

Ken Fox also realised too late that they were under attack. He had missed the R/T command because of the interference, but suddenly saw the belly tanks tumbling down from the aircraft ahead of him, and then saw John Bisley, his section leader, break violently left. Fox broke away and 'weaved' violently, followed by his uncomprehending wingman, Flight Sergeant Jeff King. Looking up as he turned, Fox saw four Zeros above him in a good position to attack. He continued the roll and dived steeply away, in his rush to get out leaving his No. 2 behind. Diving vertically at full throttle, Fox's aircraft went beyond its VNE (390 knots IAS), and because of the great speed of this full-throttle descent, he pulled out too low for comfort; indeed, he pulled so hard that he overstressed his wings and twisted the fuselage, and then went home without firing his guns – not a successful outing. Ron MacDonald, having conformed to Foster's movements by turning up sun and climbing flat out, was luckily left alone by the Zeros, and so simply climbed up sun away from the fight. Jeff King saw a Zero higher up being chased by a Spitfire, and pulled up to fire at it as well; he saw strikes, but then stalled and fell away into a spin.

Meanwhile, Flight Sergeant Len Utber had been lagging behind Blue Section, nursing an overheating and rough-running engine. Thus distracted, he did not see the bounce happen: all he knew was that he suddenly lost sight of his leader, Bisley, then his engine cut out, and then he saw King's aircraft spinning away. He shoved the stick forward into a glide, and went through the engine restart. He looked around for someone to join up with, but there was nobody. Looking ahead, he realised he was 2 kilometres behind the other Spitfires, and looking up, saw four Zeros above. Not wishing to be another victim of the arse-end Charlie syndrome, Utber 'broke smartly downwards and returned to base'.

Bill Coombes broke left upon hearing John Bisley's call, but the squadron had been caught in a pincer, for the three Zeros that had been up sun to the right came down too, and so the squadron's left break placed these right behind – in 452's '6 o'clock'. Coombes was bounced by one of these – tracers suddenly flashed past underneath him. He broke violently downwards into a spiral dive, then pulled out and climbed up sun. Coombes's wingman, Flight Sergeant George Benson, also heard the break and turned hard left, to find himself in a head-on pass with a diving Zero. Neither of them got hits. He then saw another Zero on the tail of a Spitfire and dived after it, firing without result. Upon looking back, he saw yet another Zero closing in behind him, so again broke violently away into a spiral dive. As he did so, he saw a pilot under a parachute (Tully), then a Spitfire went vertically past him streaming smoke. Benson disengaged by climbing up sun at high IAS, reached 30 000 feet unmolested and went home by himself.

Tim Goldsmith, despite his relatively great experience as a Malta ace, had also failed to see the Zeros and had also heard nothing through the R/T. It is probable that his eyesight was still damaged from the perspex lacerations suffered when he was shot down on 2 May. In any case, he was bounced in this, his first combat since that day: the first he knew of what was happening was when he found himself being attacked from above. He only just escaped being shot down again, for just as he rolled into a downwards break, tracers shot past him. Looking back, he spotted the Zero that was firing them, so pulled through into a split S, intending to zoom back up at it. As his nose pitched downwards, he saw another Zero coming straight towards him from lower down, so he dived straight at it in a head-on pass, holding fire until it was only 200 metres away. He fired a short burst right in to 50 metres, and the Zero flashed past below. Pulling up into a hard turn, Goldsmith looked back to see the Zero falling away and 'disintegrating'.

Like Goldsmith, Flying Officer Gerald Cowell was completely oblivious to the bounce, having heard nothing and seen nothing. Suddenly, aircraft were manoeuvring everywhere in front of him. Seeing a Zero chasing a Spitfire, he half-rolled, pulled around onto its tail and fired from 300 metres. He saw strikes on the rear of its cockpit, but then it pulled up into a loop. Cowell pulled hard and went up behind it, but he stalled off the top and spun away. As he recovered and dived away, he saw the Zero exiting the scene, 'smoking profusely' from both sides of the engine cowling. Throughout the whole fight, Cowell saw only two enemy fighters.

Flying Officer Kenny Bassett was likewise caught unawares, and similarly only saw three Zeros in total. Comprehensively bounced, he admitted that he only broke away once the Zeros had 'finished firing': Paul Tully had seen a Zero on his tail firing, but the Japanese pilot had missed and Bassett had remained blissfully unaware of its existence. Having belatedly broken into a turn, he zoomed back up, turned in behind a Zero and fired two deflection shots at it before he passed through its slipstream. He saw some strikes on its wing, but was then attacked by the Zero's wingman and so broke away a second time and dived for home.

MacDonald meanwhile had climbed above the fight, but when he came back down to rejoin, found himself manoeuvring against three Zeros, alone. As usual, one of them would come down to make a pass at him while the others stayed up above and bided their time. MacDonald gamely persisted with this in spite of the disadvantageous terms, each time trying to get into firing range of the one making the pass. He could never get within 400 metres of it before having to break away downwards once more, to evade the next one coming through (making exactly the same error as Caldwell had done in the very first engagement of the season on 2 March). Finally giving up, MacDonald dived away, putting the Zeros off their gunnery by skidding his aircraft violently from side to side, stamping hard upon each rudder pedal in turn. However, this violent yawing produced massive drag and prevented his aircraft from accelerating away. So violent was the yawing that each time MacDonald kicked the rudder, his shoulder was flung against the cockpit side and his head bashed against the perspex canopy. Finally he 'got sick of this' self-harm and straightened up to go into a spiral dive instead.

This gave the Japanese pilot behind him the fleeting opportunity he was waiting for, and in that moment the aircraft was shoved about by an unseen hand, there was an incandescent flash, a piercingly sharp explosion, and the cockpit filled with the smell of cordite. Cannon shells had hit MacDonald's aircraft, one of them exploding in the cockpit. His legs were hit by shell fragments, and then his legs were burnt by tongues of fire that started licking out from underneath the instrument panel – the fuel tank in front of his knees had ignited. He pulled the hood release knob at the top of the windscreen, jettisoned the canopy, pulled out his harness pin, opened the side door, pulled off his helmet, and stood up in the cockpit to go over the side. As he did so, he realised that the gunfire had damaged his parachute pack: the canvas casing of the seat-pack parachute was torn and the silk canopy started to stream out and flap around his face even before he had exited the aircraft. Standing there like a statue in the buffeting airflow, he wrapped his hands around the billowing fabric, kicked the stick forward, and toppled out of cockpit like a felled tree.

Aware of the danger of being fired upon while under the parachute, MacDonald held tightly onto the shaking and roaring ball of silk in front of his face, performing an impromptu free-fall descent to 12 000 feet. Then he let go of the escaping canopy, pulled the D-ring, and the parachute opened normally. As he floated down, he saw a Zero diving ominously straight for him. As he got ready to pull on the shrouds to spill air out of one side of his canopy – hoping to spoil its aim – the Zero suddenly stood on its tail and went straight up into a stall turn, for the pilot had noticed a Spitfire approaching to intervene. The Zero thus headed off and MacDonald got down safely – it would have been a bad way to finish the campaign by having the CO killed beneath his parachute. Lest it be thought that shooting parachuting pilots was a Japanese specialty, it was not: even Bluey Truscott had shot a German pilot beneath his parachute; while within the 5th Air Force in New Guinea, it was standard practice to do so if the Japanese pilot had parachuted over his own side of the line and would thus escape capture. Similarly, during the North African campaign, pilots of both RAF and RAAF P-40 squadrons fired as a matter of course at parachutes and at downed pilots on the ground. The days of chivalry in air combat were over, if ever they existed.

MacDonald was at first taken back to his squadron for 'a few beers', and only after that dispatched to 1 MRS for treatment of his injuries. The RAAF medical staff found that his burns were serious, requiring ongoing treatment – he did not resume duty until 27 October after a convalescence 'down south'. MacDonald had been the author of his own defeat on 7 September, having unwisely chosen to manoeuvre alone with three Zeros. His choice of yawing as an evasive manoeuvre was also questionable, given the proven effectiveness of the Spitfires' standard escape manoeuvre of diving turns. MacDonald had not had a lucky time in combat as 452's CO: his guns had failed on 2 May, his R/T had failed in three combats in a row, his propeller CSU had failed midway through his attack on 30 June and now he had been shot down. While MacDonald convalesced, the recently promoted Flight Lieutenant Tim Goldsmith took over as acting CO.

After breaking away from the initial bounce, Bill Coombes re-climbed, arriving back at 24000 feet and then diving from out of the sun at three Zeros he saw circling below. He fired at one but it broke away, so he went straight past, continuing his dive and attacking another one a little lower down. Firing a snap full deflection burst, he saw 'splashes' on its wing, but by this time the other Zero had come around at him, firing a deflection shot at him as he went past. His aircraft was hit in the tail, and Coombes suddenly found that his elevator control had been shot away – he could move the stick forward and aft without any effect. He pulled his aircraft out of its dive by winding the elevator trim, recovered to level flight, and headed for base, where he landed successfully. As he disengaged, he saw a Zero crash at King's Table and burn fiercely.

Despite the muddle and confusion and the dreadful tactical situation, 452 had counter-attacked immediately and convincingly. The Spitfire pilots were reverting to type by accepting a fight even on disadvantageous terms, as they had done earlier on 2 March, 15 March and 10 May. In the absence of bombers to attack, their automatic response was to dogfight with the fighters, in spite of the fact that this contravened the tactical guidelines under which the wing had been fighting since May.

Somehow it went against the pilots' combat ethic to merely dive away without putting up a fight. One dimension of air combat was moral dominance, and 452 was refusing to cede this to the Japanese in the skies over Darwin. No. 452's fightback had been a highly creditable affair: Goldsmith was able to claim one fighter shot down; Cowell claimed another one as probable; while three other pilots – Bassett, Coombes and King – all claimed to have got hits. As the CO ruefully concluded afterwards, given the severity of the bounce and the squadron's bad starting position, it was 'extraordinarily lucky to have sustained so little loss' – thanks to the flying ability and sheer dogged aggressiveness of his pilots.

Some of 54's pilots had also stayed in the fight, and three of them were able to get shots at the enemy. Just before the initial bounce, Sergeant Dennis Monger saw a line of three Zeros coming down towards the tail of 54's formation. When Foster called the break, he turned hard around onto these three and pulled up steeply to attack the leader head-on. Both aircraft fired at each other until point-blank range, and then the Zero pulled up to pass right overhead. The only result Monger saw from his fire was a puff of white smoke. Turning hard after the Zero, his aircraft was still so nose-high from the climbing that it stalled and spun. He held it in the spin until 10 000 feet to evade attack. Like Monger, Flying Officer WH Appleton turned into the initial bounce and fired back, and then continued his climb up sun to gain an attacking position. Diving back to enter 452's dogfight, he saw three Spitfires manoeuvring with seven Zeros, got off a snap deflection shot at one Zero as it crossed his nose, then zoomed up after another, staying behind it as it went straight up, and firing at it from close range. He saw no result from his gunnery before both aircraft fell back into spins from the top of their vertical zooms; they spun down side by side, each of them rotating a different direction as they fell away.

Having initially broken away downwards, Flying Officer Harold Leonard re-climbed. He saw a pilot beneath a parachute (Tully again), then he saw a Zero chasing a Spitfire, pulling up into a climbing turn to go after it. Leonard turned onto its tail and fired from close range, but despite seeing some strikes on its fuselage, the effect of his gunnery was ruined by both cannons jamming after firing only three rounds; then the Zero broke into a hard turn, obviously still well under control. When he saw its wingman sliding in behind him, Leonard rolled onto his back and went straight down. Appleton also re-climbed to follow the retiring Japanese out to sea. Having regained height, he then stalked a group of five Zeros, getting in to 250 metres behind the rearmost of them and opening fire from directly astern. He did not cease fire until he had closed to 100 metres, seeing strikes along the trailing edges of both wings. By then the other four Zeros were breaking away and arcing around to come back at him, so he broke downwards and dived away.

Of the three pilots of 54 Squadron who had fired their guns, every one suffered cannon failures. Evidently there had been little improvement in the functioning of the Spitfire's main armament in spite of constant efforts by the armourers. After Hinds was shot down in the initial bounce, no more of 54's Spitfires were hit, confirming the typical pattern of a convincing fightback after the initial reverse.

The immediate cause of the bounce had been the R/T interference. After the action, 5 Fighter Sector's intelligence officer judged that this had been caused by one aircraft's R/T being jammed on 'transmit'. Spitfire aircraft had a spring-loaded press-to-talk 'teat' button mounted on the joystick, rather than a switch that could be accidentally knocked to the 'transmit' position and left 'on' – and therefore the mechanism was foolproof. Although the wing signals officer made a physical check of every surviving aircraft's 'press to transmit' buttons, and found that they all correctly sprang back to the 'receive' position, this did not prove that one of them had not jammed in flight. Japanese electronic jamming was ruled out, as only one of the Spitfire radio sets' four frequencies was affected and the jamming signal had been so powerful as to indicate very close proximity. The interference suddenly ceased at 9.50 am, around the time stated for the shooting down of Paul Tully and Ron MacDonald. It is therefore possible that one of these aircraft had carried the defective transmit button, which was only turned 'off' when the aircraft hit the ground.

457's attack

While 452 and 54 were fighting back, there was one part of the wing that had obtained both an early sighting of the enemy and had height superiority over them: 457 Squadron. Pete Watson had been tailing one squadron of Zeros towards Darwin. This was a different formation to that which ran into 54 and 452: the Japanese fighter group had split up, with one squadron escorting each of the recco machines as they headed to their respective photographic targets. As Watson was getting into position to attack, he saw the Japanese force split up, with nine Zeros accompanying the Ki-46 through its photo run, leaving only one group of three down below. He exploited his opportunity by taking his section down upon this isolated vee of Zeros. Unfortunately for Watson's hopes of an easy kill, the Zero pilots saw him coming and timed their break perfectly: just as the four Spitfires approached firing range behind, the two wingmen whipped around in startlingly rapid turns. As the Spitfires were going fast from their dives, they overshot, and the Zeros were now on their tails. Watson ordered his men to disengage, and they all broke downwards out of the Zeros' gunsights and away.

Watson's four Spitfires pulled out below and started to re-climb, following the Zeros out to sea and continuing to report their position by R/T. This was one of the few instances in the entire campaign of a four-aircraft section of Spitfires staying together after first contact and retaining cohesion for a subsequent section attack. Clearly, Watson had learnt a lot since the Milingimbi raids in May.

Don Maclean was further behind, also following the raiders out. Guided by Watson's R/T reports, he led his section to an up sun position on another group of Zeros before they crossed the coast near Bynoe Harbour. He then led his men down in a high-speed diving attack from their front quarter, but this was not an ideal attack direction, as it not only presented a difficult deflection shot but was also highly visible to the Japanese pilots. Predictably, the Zeros broke before he got within range, but Maclean took a deflection shot on his target as it turned and saw hits on its fuselage and wing. Flying Officer Bill Gregory and Flight Sergeant Freddie White, however, got good shots from directly astern of another Zero: White came in after Gregory, and got so close behind the Zero during his firing run that he had to pull up violently above its tail to avoid colliding with it. It streamed black smoke and then plunged away, so these two pilots jointly claimed it as destroyed. Maclean re-climbed for another diving pass then dived back in. This time, he succeeded in bouncing a Zero, and saw hits on its fuselage; it started smoking and dived away, steepening its dive and bursting into flames as it fell.

Meanwhile, Pete Watson's section re-climbed, back in position to attack by the time the Japanese were 30 kilometres out to sea. Once again he took his men down, trying to bounce the rearward Zeros from out of the sun. This time, he achieved surprise, for his target did not evade, presenting an easy shot, and so he got hits. Flying Officers Ian Mackenzie and Jack Smithson also made good attacks on their targets, with strikes visible in the cockpit area and centre fuselage, while Smithson also saw an explosion and flames from his target's wing root area. Watson and Smithson claimed their Zeros as destroyed, while Mackenzie claimed his as probably destroyed. Whatever the precise results of their gunnery, it was a well-managed tactical attack, for having got their hits the Spitfires then broke off and used their speed to head home unscathed. This action reflects well upon Pete Watson's leadership: taken together with his creditably judicious leadership on 20 June, 30 June and 6 July, it is clear that Watson had developed as a fighter leader, overcoming the bad start he had made in the Milingimbi raids and vindicating Caldwell's and Walters's faith in him at that time.

Results

No. 457's pilots had seen results from their gunnery attacks and none of their own aircraft were even damaged, partly making up for the bad bounce upon 54 and 452. It is clear that if 1 Fighter Wing's flight commanders had been freed from their rigid subordination to the 'big wing' tactic, they were more than capable of fighting a good tactical fight. Indeed, on this day, if all three squadrons had been free to fight like this, led by leaders empowered to use their discretion, then the day's results would certainly have been a lot more pleasing than they were: at worst, one part of the wing would have been bounced, rather than two whole squadrons.

Some senior pilots in 452, such as Ken Fox and John Bisley, were very frustrated with having been led into the bounce, expressing this in their combat reports. Because Hal Whillans was in Green Section, he had missed getting bounced, but he and the others were frustrated with the R/T communication blackout and their consequent failure to get to grips with the enemy. In addition, in the absence of direction from control, there had almost been a 'friendly fire' incident between Whillans's section and two Spitfires from 457 that had appeared on the scene unannounced – flown by Squadron Leader Ken James and Pilot Officer Bob Cunningham. Whillans vented his squadron's sense of irritation in his combat report, observing that the 457 pilots were 'bloody lucky' not to have been shot down. Once the paperwork had been passed up the chain to RAAF Command, the signal came back from a staff officer in Melbourne requesting NWA HQ 'to ensure F/O Whillans No. 452 Squadron understands that obscenity is not permitted in pilots' reports'.

Considering the appalling tactical situation into which 54 and 452 had been led, the final results looked quite reasonable from 1 Fighter Wing's perspective. Thanks to 457's bounces on the departing Zeros, as well as the effective counter-attacks from some of the 452 and 54 Squadron pilots, the wing was able to claim five Zeros shot down to set against the loss of three Spitfires and one pilot. However, Japanese records indicate one loss only, that of PO1c Yoshio Terai, who was shot down and killed – probably the victim of Don Maclean. Three other Zeroes were recorded as damaged. Given the good firing opportunities that Watson's and Maclean's attacks had generated, this result seems surprisingly poor. Nonetheless, losing three to one would be entirely plausible given the bad bounce upon two of the squadrons.

Watson and MacDonald had each spotted one of the Ki-46 reconnaissance machines, but most pilots had not even seen the Zeros, let alone the reccos that were accompanying them. Thus the elaborate Japanese escorting tactic had worked: the photographic machines were protected, indeed not even attacked. Despite this, the Japanese achievement was hollow, for the very extravagance of the escorting force militated against any repetition – this was clearly a one-off maximum-effort operation. It has been suggested that the purpose of the Ki-46s on this day was not to take photos but merely to lead the fighters to their targets, but this is implausible – the seasoned 202 AG was led by expert long-service naval aviators who had been to Darwin many times, and all previous fighter sweeps had been conducted without any such over-target navigational assistance – including the deep penetration mission to Coomalie (a new target) on 2 March. Clearly, the mission had a dual purpose: as an 'air annihilation' operation against the Spitfires *and* as an opportunistic reconnaissance – as per previous Japanese practice on 2 March, 2 May and 22 June.

The Japanese referred to the whole mission as the 'attack on Brock's Creek' (this being their designation for Fenton), showing that one of the photographic targets was indeed the US bomber base, and that the operation was a continuation of the offensive against the troublesome B-24 unit. The operation was an 'attack' in the sense that the fighter sweep was supposed to 'annihilate' the Spitfires – reflecting the mandatory unreal rhetoric that was characteristic of Japanese commanders' reporting on their operations. The tactical objective of the fighter sweep was clear: once 202 AG finally 'annihilated' the annoyingly persistent Spitfires, 753 AG could then return and 'wipe out' the US bombers (23rd Air Flotilla's intention in all offensive operations from 20 June onwards).

From the perspective of the Japanese photographic recon-naissance unit, the operation seems to have been quite successful, for under cover of the larger operation, the reccos detoured over their targets and took their photos: Pete Watson saw one of the Ki-46s approach from the north-west then turn north over the harbour to make a photo run over Darwin; Foster and MacDonald ran into another Ki-46 with its escort, approaching from the north-west over the Cox Peninsula; while 5 Fighter

Sector plotted the movements of another, accompanied by a squadron of Zeros, which came in across-country from the west then turned left to make an extended run over the airfields along the track, photographing Hughes and Batchelor on a south-to-north run back to Darwin and away. It may be that one of the reconnaissance aircraft detached itself and headed further south for Fenton, but this was neither plotted on radar nor observed by the AA gunners. If such a foray was made, it escaped radar detection and fighter interception.

Despite the frustrating circumstances of the air combat, the wing was encouraged by the reappearance of a large force of Japanese aircraft in daylight, and continued to expect a resumption of the daylight raids. It was called to readiness on 20 September in response to intelligence predictions of such a raid, but the sky remained empty. However, everyone was destined for disappointment, for 7 September had been the 'last hurrah' over Darwin for all Japanese units – fighter, bomber or reconnaissance. After that day, even recco penetrations of Australian airspace declined drastically. This shows that the results of the 7 September combat had been a great disappointment to the Japanese planners, failing to achieve the wider purpose of wiping out the Spitfires. The 70th Reconnaissance Squadron would continue to mount occasional reconnaissances over targets in the NWA until the end of the war, but both their frequency and the depth of their penetrations were sharply curtailed, reduced to the status of a sporadic 'watching brief' only, consistent with the abandonment of offensive operations.

Despite the wing's strategic success in remaining very much 'in being' and failing to be 'annihilated' as the Japanese intended, the 7 September bounce meant that Bob Foster ended his operational career with his reputation under a cloud. Caldwell was scathing about it, considering that Foster had led the wing in a 'disgraceful manner'. It had indeed been a very poor finish for an officer who had been a stalwart fighting leader throughout the campaign. His failure to spot the enemy had been decisive, but this had not been the first such instance of his defective tactical lookout: Foster had had problems visually acquiring the enemy in the previous few raids, but on those occasions he had not been wing leader.

By September, personnel rotations were changing the face of the wing. Air Commodore Frank Bladin had been posted out towards the end of July. His qualities were recognised by a good posting, taking the role of Senior Air Staff Officer of 38 Group RAF in the United Kingdom, where he planned the troop-carrying operations in support of the D-Day airborne assault. He was replaced by Air Commodore Adrian 'King' Cole MC DFC, who had been a World War I fighter ace with the Australian Flying Corps. However, lacking higher command experience in World War II due to a string of second-rate appointments, he could not come close to matching Bladin's knowledge and experience in the role. Balancing this, Caldwell's replacement as wing CO was Wing Commander Peter Jeffrey DSO DFC, a highly experienced fighter pilot with a relevant and substantial World War II CV. Both of 452's flight commanders, Ted Hall and Paul Makin, were posted away, replaced by internal appointees: Dave Evans and the newly promoted John Bisley, while Tim Goldsmith stood in as Acting CO during MacDonald's convalescence.

As they concluded their nine-month tours of duty, the line pilots were also replaced by new graduates from the OTUs. This was not a bad thing, for Bill Gibbs noticed that the new men were much better trained than the originals and needed less continuation training to maintain standards. When Flying Officer Doug Hare and Pilot Officer Rex Sprake arrived at 452 in August – fresh graduates from 2 OTU at Mildura – they were the wing's first 'all Australian' pilots: the first to have received no training in Britain. The wing also benefited from the emerging glut of EATS-trained airmen 'down south' by acquiring some high-hours ex-instructors and ex-staff pilots – men who arrived itching to see some action at last. In August, 452 got Flight Sergeants Patrick Beeston and George Benson, while 457 got Flying Officers Ian Chandler and Neil Ligertwood. However, all these new arrivals had missed the boat, for the battle had already been fought and won.

Some pilots left the wing on sadder terms than this: 452's Flying Officers Al Mawer and Phil Adam died in a midair collision on 26 September while practising air combat manoeuvres. Acting CO Tim Goldsmith had the melancholy duty of officiating at the double funeral held that very afternoon at the Adelaide River cemetery, attended by the whole squadron. Mawer in particular was a great loss to the unit and to the RAAF: his natural gifts as a fighter pilot were shown by his ability to repeatedly manoeuvre himself into Zeros' '6 o'clock' during dogfights: thus in three combats he had made three claims, and unlike most of 1 Fighter Wing's claiming, the evidence suggests that he had actually shot down one Zero and one Hayabusa. Had he seen service under more auspicious circumstances in a bigger campaign, then he might easily have made a big name for himself.

The tight community of 457 Squadron continued to mourn its missing heroes: in late August, when Pete Watson and Bruce Little simultaneously announced in the mess that they had become fathers, the pilots raised their glasses in a 'silent toast' to the memory of Darky McDowell, whose wife had also given birth to a son that very week. Many men were already thinking ahead towards life in a world at peace, but not all of them got there.

7 September pilot table

Sqn	Section	No.	Pilots engaging	Pilots not engaging	Remarks
NOTE Italics indicate deduced flight designations and positions where the records are incomplete					
54	Red	1	F/L Foster RAF		did not fire
		2	Sgt Whalley RAF		
		3	F/O Hinds RAF		shot down and killed near Pioneer Creek, Darwin Harbour; EF558 destroyed
		4	Sgt Powell RAF		did not fire
	Blue	1		F/O Farries RAF	aborted, oxygen failure
		2	Sgt Monger RAF		both cannons failed
		3	F/O Appleton RAF		1 cannon failed
		4	Sgt Holmes RAF		did not fire
		5	F/O Mahoney RAF		
	White	1	F/L Norwood RAF		
		2	F/Sgt Spencer RAF		
		3	F/O Leonard RAF		both cannons failed
		4		F/O Ashby RAF	aborted, CSU failure
	Green	1		F/O Lenagen RAF	scrambled separately, vectored to Bathurst Island as a blocking patrol against reccos
		2		F/Sgt Huggard RAF	
		3		Sgt Allden RAF	
		4		F/Sgt Eldred RAF	
		5		F/Sgt Horkin RAF	

Sqn	Section	No.	Pilots engaging	Pilots not engaging	Remarks
452	Red	1	S/L MacDonald		shot down & bailed out 15 miles W Strauss; LZ884 QY-D destroyed
		2	P/O Tully		shot down & bailed out near Pioneer Creek; BR549 destroyed
		3	F/O Bassett		
		4	F/O Cowell		
	White	1	F/L Goldsmith		
		2	F/O Lloyd		
		3	P/O Coombes		
		4	F/Sgt Benson		
		5	Sgt Richardson		
	Blue	1	F/O Bisley		did not fire
		2	F/Sgt Utber		
		3	F/O Fox		did not fire, overstressed LZ846, repaired by 7 RSU
		4	F/Sgt King		
	Green	1		W/C Caldwell	vectored separately as a blocking patrol over Port Patterson
		2		F/L Evans	
		3		F/O Whillans	
		4		F/O Hare	
		5		F/Sgt Beeston	

NOTE Because of the disorganised scramble, 457's exact flight positions are not clear, and the sections are indicated in Sqn records by name, not colour

457	Maclean's section		F/L Maclean		
			P/O Little		
			F/O Gregory		
			F/Sgt White		
	Watson's section		F/L P Watson		
			P/O Batchelor		
			F/O Smithson		
			F/O Mackenzie		
	Other sections			P/O Jenkins	Initially vectored to anti-recco 'stops', failed to rendezvous with the others due R/T jamming
				P/O Reilly	
				P/O Basey	
				F/O Halse	
				P/O Morse	
	Green	1		S/L James	off-duty pilots who volunteered, got airborne, and were vectored to Port Patterson
		2		P/O Cunningham	
			33	18	

Summary:
Spitfires scrambled: 51
Spitfires engaged: 33
Spitfires shot down: 3
Pilots killed: 1

12

The accounting of battle

Hopes were dashed in the Spitfire wing when the next big daylight raid failed to arrive; instead, the Japanese used the full moon period to continue their night campaign against Fenton. Nine bombers came over in each of two raids, just before midnight on 14 September, and just before dawn five nights later. They headed across country to their favourite target, disturbing men's sleep at the airfields they flew over, and again giving the AA gunners at Fenton good nocturnal firing practice. The night bombing results were, as usual, derisory.

Action at Drysdale

However, it was not just the Japanese bomb aimers that were having trouble hitting their targets. An interception of a Ki-46 over the Drysdale Mission satellite airfield showed that gunnery standards remained an unresolved issue within the Spitfire wing. Drysdale (Operational Base Unit 58) was a bare base airfield much like Milingimbi, but 560 kilometres to the west of Darwin, likewise used as a forward refuelling base for coastal patrols and strike operations. Japanese interest in the place was signalled by a large air raid on 26 September – an unusual combined army/navy raid with 21 army Ki-48 bombers from the 75th Air Regiment escorted by 21 navy Zeros from 202 AG. With no resident Spitfires to defend the place, nor any AA, the Japanese arrogantly bombed unchallenged from only 3000 feet and therefore got away unscathed. The 75th Air Regiment had thus enjoyed tremendous luck with its risky low-level tactics, having mounted two raids on Australia without a single crew lost. Sadly, there were six civilian fatalities from a bomb hit in a slit trench, killing the missionary priest and five Aboriginal children. After this raid, NWA HQ maintained a rotation of fighter detachments at Drysdale to guard against further raids, showing that (as usual) the bombing had had nil effect in shutting down the base – the Japanese planners continued to entertain the fond illusion that a single strike could achieve decisive results, contrary to all accumulated operational experience so far in nearly two years of war.

Area HQ was thus forced to defend Drysdale with Spitfire detachments, in much the same way as at Milingimbi. Although the ongoing Japanese reccos proved elusive, Drysdale's 317 Radar Station was able to plot and correlate their movements to plan a radar-predicted bounce, like in August off Milingimbi. Accordingly, six Spitfires from 457 under Don Maclean were deployed to Drysdale on 3 November, standing by for the next suitable opportunity; and on 6 November they were duly scrambled after a Japanese intruder heading inbound at 20 000 feet. The Ki-46 was successfully intercepted on the way out, becoming the target of gunnery attacks by four Spitfires attacking in turn: these consisted of White Section – composed of the newly arrived Flying Officer Arthur 'Nat' Gould (a veteran of 75 Squadron at the Battle of Milne Bay in August 1942) and Flight Sergeant Bill Basey; and Red Section – composed of Maclean himself and Flight Sergeant Henry Whiting. Blue Section (Warrant Officer Chris Madigan and Pilot Officer Fred Feuerheerdt) was also present, following behind but unable to get into position because the other four aircraft got in the way. The efforts of Gould, Basey, Maclean and Whiting belied their squadron's reputation as specialist recco killers. They lined up to take their shots, conducting a sequence of quarter attacks and then breaking away as if they were attacking bombers with 20 mm tail guns. Despite expending almost 400 rounds of 20 mm and more than 1000 rounds of .303 inch between them, from ranges as close as 50 metres, the enemy machine just climbed away from them in a high-speed chase that ran for 80 kilometres. The Spitfires were climbing at 220 knots IAS (about 310 knots TAS), but the Ki-46 made things difficult by accelerating periodically up to 235 knots IAS. It escaped into a cumulus cloud with its photos, though Maclean and Gould jointly claimed it as damaged on the basis of some unusual engine smoke. For once there were few cannon failures (although both of Basey's jammed), so there was little else to blame but bad gunnery.

The pilots were afterwards condemned for 'extremely poor gunnery' by the new CO of 1 Fighter Wing. Wing Commander Peter Jeffrey was a prewar aviator and an experienced combat fighter pilot, having commanded the first RAF fighter wing in the North African campaign as well as directed the fighter defence of Port Moresby. Jeffrey considered that once a Spitfire got on the tail of a Ki-46, it needed to stay there until the target was destroyed; that gunnery needed to be simplified by firing from dead astern; and that the reccos' negligible return

In front of his aircraft, A58-234 ZP-Y, F/O Jack Smithson tells the story of his night victory of 12 November for the amusement of his fellow 457 Squadron pilots. From left to right: F/Sgt Trevor Russell, F/L Pete Watson, F/O Brian Hegarty, Smithson, F/O Bob Cunningham (with pipe), F/O Gus Haynes, P/O Evan Batchelor, F/Sgt Frank Payne (partly obscured), F/O Phil Goldin RAF, F/L Don Maclean, F/L Doug Edwards. AWM Negative 016411

fire had to be ignored. Clearly, he had no confidence in the pilots' ability to pull off deflection shots. Moreover, as the Ki-46 was faster than the Spitfire, a firing position from dead astern had to be exploited to destroy it in the first attack, otherwise it would outrun its pursuers. Jeffrey was not impressed with his new command: 'The action reflects considerable discredit on the pilots concerned and on the general standard of tactics and gunnery in their squadron'. His response to gunnery results like those on 15 March, 2 May and 30 June would have made interesting reading! Despite the bad shooting, the interception was effective in deterring further inshore reconnaissances: thereafter these sought to avoid contact with Spitfires by staying far enough offshore to keep out of trouble, confining the scope of their probes to shallow penetration shipping patrols.

The final combat

After a two months hiatus in night bombing against Darwin, 753 AG returned in the early morning of 12 November. Nine bombers came to resume the on-again off-again offensive against Fenton. In spite of the full moon, the cloudier conditions of the early wet season made for uncertain navigation, and the bombers meandered about the countryside even more than usual. Many of them got close to Fenton, but they failed to identify the place, instead distributing their bombs across a range of alternative targets from Adelaide River in the south to Darwin in the north. Twenty bombs were dropped on Adelaide River and Batchelor, while another group of bombers dropped 24 bombs upon Parap camp near Darwin, damaging power, phone and railway facilities, and damaging four vehicles. In total, eight men were injured, from both the Civil Construction Corps and the Australian Army. These were the last bombs ever to fall on the Australian mainland.

More significantly, this raid also saw the first nocturnal interception of a bomber by a Spitfire. Flying Officer Jack Smithson of 457 was one of 11 pilots from 54 and 457 Squadrons airborne that night under GCI control; he was vectored to Darwin in time to see the flash of the bomb bursts at Parap. Spotting the dark shapes of three bombers cruising in vee formation at 20 000 feet, he chased them through a cloud and then obtained a clear sighting of one of the bombers when it was illuminated in the beam of a searchlight. Approaching from dead astern, he fired upon the leader in the centre of the vee. The cannons fired perfectly, his high explosive incendiary shells flaring up in the dark 'like neon lights' as they struck the bomber's engine nacelles. Slowing abruptly, the Japanese machine dived steeply away and disappeared from sight. Smithson saw tracers coming out towards him from the bomber on the left before he overshot and pulled up. He waited for the other bombers to pass, then attacked again, rolling in behind his next victim. This one went down unambiguously with flames streaming from its wing, so when he got back he claimed two bombers destroyed.

Japanese records indicate the loss of only one bomber. However, the single loss was bad enough, for in a moment of combat serendipity, Smithson had killed two COs from the Japanese bomber unit. Onboard the shot-down aircraft had been the newly appointed group leader, Commander Michio Horii, and the squadron leader, Lieutenant Takeharu Fujiwara. Both were now dead, along with seven crewmen in the stricken machine. This loss had a 'massive impact on the unit's operations, and further missions over Darwin were immediately cancelled'.

This testimony to the impact of the double loss overlooks a conjunction of parallel factors that had already dictated the abandonment of the campaign: the failure of daytime photo-reconnaissance, the previous inability to sustain daylight raids, the worsening weather of the wet season, and the mounting military crises on other battle fronts as Allied offensives gathered pace. Having shut down its Darwin raids for the duration of the 1943–44 wet season, the only live question for the Imperial Navy was whether it would retain enough resources to resume its bombing of Darwin in the 1944 dry season – and the answer to that was, certainly not.

Thus Smithson had delivered the final death-blow to the two-year bombing campaign on Darwin that had begun with that devastating carrier raid on 19 February 1942. The night bombing had amounted to little more than acts of symbolism: the mere fact of these raids permitted the Imperial Navy to assert that it was continuing its attacks, that it was continuing to put pressure on the Darwin base, and that it was continuing to choke off Allied air operations against its southern defensive perimeter. However, such claims were hollow – pure politics – for the military effects of these raids had been minimal. Worse than that, and for all their spectacular sound and fury, the daylight raids had achieved very little either, in spite of the two well-delivered Fenton raids at the end. Ironically, 753 AG's bombing had finally achieved respectable results just when the day campaign was being abandoned. The admirable work of the Japanese aircrews had been undermined throughout by Japan's flawed war strategy, inadequate resources and immature operational doctrine.

Japanese claims

From the Japanese perspective, all those raids, all those sorties, all those wrecked aircraft (including the inevitable non-combat losses) and the deaths of nearly 100 first-class airmen, had been for very little in terms of their impact in destroying, damaging, deterring or dampening Allied air operations. These had expanded at their own rate, almost unaffected by the raids. The limiting factors to Allied capabilities had never been Japanese attacks on their bases, but political bottlenecks in the provision of matériel. Examples of such limitations include 5th Air Force's refusal to supply the NWA with P-38 long-range fighters, which would have revolutionised Allied offensive operations; and the provision of only a token one-squadron force of B-24s until quite late in the campaign (in June 1943), governed by political decisions in Washington concerning the release of heavy bomber groups for service in the SWPA: the newly raised 380th BG had been slated for the bomber offensive against Germany, but was suddenly reassigned to Kenney's command in the SWPA. If it took the NWA a long time to build up its offensive potential, this had very little to do with Japanese counter-actions, but everything to do with high-level military politics within Allied war councils – and in faraway Washington, not Canberra, Brisbane or Melbourne.

Throughout the raids, not one Spitfire had been destroyed on the ground by bombing or strafing, which provides a measure of the utter ineffectiveness of the Japanese attacks on Allied airfields, standing in stark contrast to earlier campaigns such as Malaya, Sumatra and the Philippines, when most Allied fighters had been lost on the ground. Given the dispersed layout of the NWA airfields, the only way the Japanese could practicably destroy Spitfires was to lure them into the air and destroy them in air combat. From the Japanese perspective, this seemed to have worked very well: a unit history of 202 AG states that 101 Spitfires were claimed shot down, with only three Zeros and two G4M bombers lost in exchange.

The reality was that the Japanese navy fighters had shot down 22 Spitfires at most, not 101. Using the loss figures cited by authors who have gained access to Japanese records, 202 AG in return suffered the loss of five Zeros shot down, while 753 AG lost 11 G4M bombers shot down or written off by Spitfire gunnery. These losses might seem trivial by comparison with the losses in bigger campaigns, but they nonetheless represent an average bomber loss rate per daylight raid of 11 per cent – a difficult figure for any bombing force to sustain over time. Although the losses of bomber crews were less, averaging out at 5 per cent lost per mission, this too was a serious loss rate – it is clear that the bomber unit was facing worrying cumulative attrition. Moreover, the trend was worsening: the more recent raids had been much more damaging to 753 AG than the earlier ones, for the Spitfires were achieving better interceptions, with more aircraft, and getting more hits. The withdrawal of 202 AG to defensive tasks was therefore a convenient way out for a campaign that was going nowhere.

Despite the self-evident failure of the Japanese fighter unit to keep the Spitfires off the bombers, the Zero had nonetheless bested the Spitfire in air-to-air combat, for the navy raids had achieved almost a 2:1 kill ratio (far from the 20:1 claimed). This achievement was not attributable to the aircraft – for the Spitfire had the better flight performance of the two – but rather to the Japanese fighter pilots' far superior battle drills. Their good results had been achieved by using the bombers as bait to lure the Spitfires into attacks, setting up the Zeros for swooping attacks from above as the Spitfires descended and went through their firing passes. The Japanese 'dive and zoom' fighter tactics were very similar to those of the Luftwaffe in the early part of the war, enabling good scoring without undue risk. The Japanese fighter pilots were impressive in their ability to fly and fight in small groups, supporting each other throughout the combats and coordinating their close combat manoeuvres. Japanese teamwork was the decisive factor in their success, offering a stark contrast to the uncoordinated individualism of 1 Fighter Wing. The good results of the navy pilots were helped by the greatly superior reliability of the Zero's Oerlikon cannon compared with the Spitfires' dysfunctional Hispanos. Nonetheless, even with these marked advantages in tactics and hitting power, 202 AG had succeeded in destroying an average of fewer than four Spitfires per month in their 'air annihilation' operations – far too few to have any significant result. The gulf between Japanese doctrine, rhetoric and expectations on the one hand, and actual achievement on the other, gaped wide.

1 Fighter Wing's adverse exchange ratio

There are two sides to 1 Fighter Wing's disappointing score sheet: ineffective gunnery and vulnerability to bounces. Taking the first of these, the severity of the gunnery problems is shown by a striking statistic: Spitfire pilots made a total of 126 gunnery passes at the enemy bombers during seven combats, but they shot down or caused to crash only 15 bombers. On this basis, it took nine gunnery passes to shoot down or write off one bomber. The first reason for this gunnery inefficiency was that the pilots were not adequately trained to perform high-deflection shooting, yet this was the normative attack profile against the bombers. As a result, they generally fired and missed. Secondly, the Hispano 20 mm cannon was so unreliable that the potentially decisive close-range firing was too often done with .303 inch machine guns only. Typically, the cannons would fail in the first couple of seconds of firing, and therefore such cannon rounds as were fired would be wasted at long range. By the time the pilot had closed the range to killing distance, he would be firing with machine guns only. The combination of wayward aiming and almost inevitable cannon failure meant that in the great majority of cases, even when Japanese aircraft were hit, the shots were not concentrated in critical places, but distributed randomly around the airframe. Therefore they were not shot down. In short, the wing got a great many shots at the enemy, but usually failed to convert this to an entry on the credit side of the tally sheet. If, as Caldwell wanted, the wing's Spitfires had been armed with reliable US .5 inch heavy machine guns instead of their mixed 20 mm and .303 inch armament, a greater proportion of kills must have been made (although such a fleet-wide conversion was in fact quite impracticable, given the mid-year Spitfire shortage and resultant urgency to get aircraft from the Melbourne wharves to Darwin).

On the other side of this same tally sheet was the too high number of Spitfires that were lost to Japanese fighters. No. 457's two bad days of 28 May and 6 July alone skewed the figures badly, with five Spitfires and five pilots added to the debit side. Losses were unavoidable if fighter units were to attack bombers as conscientiously as 1 Fighter Wing did, for to make a firing run through the bombers was to knowingly accept the risk of being bounced. The wing's loss rate was, however, magnified by two interrelated factors: the pilots' failure to stick together in pairs, and the deficient lookout that resulted from this. These were systemic deficiencies, the products of inadequate training and undeveloped tactical doctrine. The result was a persistent vulnerability to bounces and a repetitive pattern of 'bad days', right to the end of the campaign: tellingly, 457 Squadron formations were bounced in the combats on 10 May, 28 May, 28 June and 6 July – surprisingly, their lookout procedures did not improve as the campaign progressed. No. 54 and 452 Squadrons were little better, bounced disastrously at the start of the campaign, on 15 March, and at its end, on 7 September. In summary, the credit side of 1 Fighter Wing's tally sheet was thinned out by systemic gunnery problems, while the debit side was swollen by endemic procedural deficiencies.

Although the Spitfires had been bested in the Imperial Navy's major set piece raids, they had done better in the army raid, while the recco kills also boosted their figures significantly.

There is nothing invalid about this accounting: even the redoubtable fighter units of the US 8th Air Force included 'easy meat' training aircraft in their scores. Moreover, the Spitfires' high-altitude recco shoot-downs over Darwin cannot be considered 'soft' kills; indeed, they were respectable feats of organisation and airmanship, for successful interceptions of these machines were otherwise 'very much the exception' in 1943, even by USAAF P-38s. Once all air combats over the NWA are factored in, it can be seen that 1 Fighter Wing had achieved reasonable results in its air combats, writing off about 28 Japanese aircraft (15 bombers, seven reccos and six fighters) for 28 Spitfires written off in return as a result of enemy action. The resultant 1:1 exchange ratio was not unusual by the standards of Allied fighter units in the earlier part of the war, comparable to those achieved by average squadrons in the Battle of Britain, and much better than those of average Spitfire V squadrons in England during 1941–42. Even the overclaiming was not excessive by contemporary RAF standards: the wing had claimed 70 enemy aircraft 'confirmed destroyed', so the overclaiming ratio was less than 3:1.

It has been claimed that only in the defence of Darwin did Spitfire V aircraft 'fail to live up to the high expectations placed on them'. This is an astonishing statement, for the opposite is true: fighter units equipped with the Spitfire V struggled to achieve positive exchange ratios in all theatres of war. The Spitfire V's biggest campaign by far was the fighter offensive against the Luftwaffe over northern France in 1941–42, and there the pattern was set of high losses set against dubious successes. No. 1 Fighter Wing's middling record was typical of Spitfire squadrons in the mid-war period. It was only against the Malta raids of 1942 that the Mark V came close to equalling the Spitfire I's good record in the Battle of Britain (and even there, the Spitfires ended up achieving only a 1:1 exchange ratio).

Despite the fact that the Darwin Spitfires achieved results no worse than those of most of their contemporaries in other theatres, it had certainly not been a brilliant air combat performance by 1 Fighter Wing, always falling short both of its own expectations and of the air combat standard set by the better American units in the theatre.

An unappreciated achievement

Indeed, judging by the record of decorations awarded by the RAAF authorities to participating pilots at the end of the campaign, it appears that the powers-that-be had become somewhat underwhelmed by the Darwin squadrons' performance in combat. In spite of the big raids, sharp combats, respectable losses and claims for heavy losses inflicted upon the raiders – all of which would normally qualify leading pilots for decorations – only three pilots were decorated for their efforts: Clive Caldwell was awarded a DSO, while Bill Gibbs and Bob Foster each got a DFC. The British DFC was exclusive enough to confer enormous credibility because of its connotations of combat leadership in the face of the enemy. Foster was commended for his 'great zeal' in combat, but simple mathematics explains all three awards: Foster and Gibbs had chalked up the five victories that gave them 'ace' status, while Caldwell had also attained the magic five victories which made him an 'ace' in the Pacific theatre. Significantly, two of the three recipients were British officers with 54 Squadron, suggesting also a symbolic act of gratitude towards the British pilots in the Australian theatre.

However, it certainly was not necessary to gain ace status in order to win a DFC, as Pete Watson had proved in England: although he had claimed only two German aircraft damaged in the course of 50 operations and about a dozen combats over

France, he had led the squadron into action several times in the northern spring of 1942, earning his DFC for 'great coolness and courage in action' and for setting an 'inspiring example' to the other pilots. Good form and service precedent would have suggested decorations on similar grounds to at least some of the other Darwin COs and flight commanders, many of whom had shown similar qualities to those of the redoubtable Watson. He himself was the most deserving candidate from the ranks of 1 Fighter Wing, having fought eight combats – an NWA record – having led the wing (as a mere flight lieutenant) and having also successfully led his own squadron on several occasions; indeed, his own squadron considered him a 'distinguished' and 'level headed' leader who had earned another DFC 'many times' while in the NWA. However, Watson had been censured by RAAF Command for his poor combat leadership in the Milingimbi raids, and this was unlikely to have been forgotten in the allocation of decorations.

Other senior pilots in the Australian squadrons were likewise ruled out. No. 452 was particularly handicapped, because none of its leaders had scored well – not the CO, not the flight commanders, not even the 'Malta twins' – which explains why the squadron languished at the bottom of the scoring table. The unit diarist lamented that Paul Makin had been 'never fortunate enough to observe results from his fire' despite leading 'determined attacks'. Moreover, he had twice failed to return with his aircraft. Squadron Leader Ron MacDonald had so failed to impress the new wing CO, Wing Commander Peter Jeffrey, that the latter recommended MacDonald not be given another command until he had passed a CO's course. In the RAAF's eyes, MacDonald's ignorance of air force forms and procedures (and presumably his record of misfortune in combat) outweighed the great moral example he had set for his men, thus precluding the award of a DFC, so he had to content himself with being 'Mentioned in Despatches'. Having been pitched suddenly into the campaign as an unfinished product of EATS, MacDonald had been made to 'sink or swim', and had indeed swum reasonably convincingly, but now he finished without any decoration, confined to desk jobs for the rest of the war.

Even the top-scoring 457 lacked an obvious candidate. Squadron Leader Ken James had failed to distinguish himself because he had missed most of the big combats, leading his squadron into action on only one occasion. Don Maclean had gone through the campaign without blotting his copybook, and had led his men well, but he had had less success than Pete Watson and so was evidently considered similarly undeserving. However, the Australian squadrons belatedly received some recognition when, having distinguished himself by making the wing's first and only nocturnal kill on 12 November, Flying Officer Jack Smithson was awarded a DFC in January 1944 before being posted out as tour-expired.

The RAAF's minimal use of decorations within 1 Fighter Wing could only be interpreted as an official devaluing of the campaign, and implicitly, a slighting of the Spitfire pilots' efforts. This is despite the fact that the 1943 Darwin raids constituted a very significant air combat episode for the RAAF's wartime fighter force, comprising the lion's share of RAAF air combat in the entire Pacific War.

It could not be said that the Spitfire pilots had fought their campaign under a lucky star, and the deaths of 14 pilots in combat is testimony to the adversity that they had faced and of the risks they had run. Out of the 108 pilots who had participated in the actions, 13 per cent had died in action (there were an additional eight non-combat pilot fatalities). Although this figure represents a very significant risk of mortality, this was neither unusual nor excessive by the standards of World War II air campaigns.

A comparison with the UK-based 'Anzac' fighter squadrons confirms that the Darwin squadrons had seen a respectable amount of action, even by comparison with an average Allied fighter unit in the European Theatre of Operations. The average 1943 loss figures for the Australian 453 Squadron and the New Zealand 485 and 486 Squadrons were 12 aircraft shot down and seven pilots killed per squadron – very similar to the average losses for the three squadrons of 1 Fighter Wing in the same year, which shows that the aggregate intensity of combat over the NWA was not dissimilar to that of squadrons operating over German-occupied France.

Despite this, 1 Fighter Wing personnel complained that their 1943 campaign was 'boring', implicitly envying their colleagues who stayed behind with RAF Fighter Command. The pilots had resented being transferred from England to a putatively second-rate defensive air force in a backwater theatre of war. After deployment to the NWA, they struggled to maintain morale in a campaign where 'nothing ever happened'. After the creature comforts and glamorous social life of English airfields and the stimulation of involvement in the biggest war going, this response was understandable in the context of their deprived and uncomfortable life on isolated bush airfields. Despite their superior location near the coast, even the men of 54 Squadron could not wait 'to get away from a place which by no stretch of the imagination could be described as pleasant'.

Contrary to these negative perceptions, the three Darwin Spitfire squadrons saw as much air combat action in total as would have been the case had they stayed in the European theatre – judging by their sister squadrons' experience in England over the same period. Indeed, once the fighter units of the US 8th Air Force started accompanying the bombers into Germany from late 1943 onwards, the European air war increasingly bypassed RAF Fighter Command, permitting the RAF ace 'Johnnie'

Johnson to complain that 'a man could complete a tour of ops and never fire his guns in anger'. Most of the Darwin Spitfire pilots did a whole lot better than that.

The wing's loss rate in the major combats was high – 12 per cent of the Spitfires that engaged enemy fighters were shot down (very similar to that of the 49th FG in 1942, which after the game-changer day of 25 April suffered a combat loss rate of 11 per cent). In turn, they had imposed a loss rate of 5 per cent upon the Japanese in the major daylight raids – again, very similar to that inflicted by the Americans in 1942. This Japanese loss rate was fully comparable with that suffered by the RAF and USAAF in their bombing campaigns over Germany, so was not a bad result for a World War II defensive fighter force. These percentages show that Darwin's defenders showed the fighting qualities necessary to attack escorted bombers: namely, the 'dogged determination' involved in making themselves vulnerable to fighter attack. Moreover, in assessing these relative loss rates, it must be remembered that the Spitfires were typically outnumbered, on average numbering only 60 per cent of the strength of the Japanese raiding force.

Japanese failure

The transfer out of the theatre of 753 AG in November 1943 meant the end of the two-year Darwin bombing campaign. In the same month, the exhausted and understrength 705 AG arrived in Sumatra for rebuilding after a long tour of duty in the Solomons. The Imperial Navy took the opportunity to do a swap, assigning 705 to the defensive patrol duties along the southern defensive perimeter that had hitherto been the task of 753. This rotation freed the latter unit to be redeployed to Tinian in the Central Pacific, where it was immediately destroyed on its airfield by the US Navy. To its cost, this fine bomber unit found that the scale, tempo and intensity of air operations in the US island-hopping offensives was of a different order entirely to that on the Timor front. This was the decisive battle, and the American air forces delivered a brutal tutorial to the Japanese in the application of overwhelming airpower.

However, even before this, and even without facing this massive preponderance of Allied force, the Japanese had already lost the battle for air supremacy across the Timor Sea front. In the end, they could no longer afford to continue their campaign over Australia, because the defence was too strong, and their losses would not be worth the limited results. The air defence of Darwin in 1942–43 therefore can be considered a successful campaign for the RAAF, but the victory was one of superior Allied logistical depth rather than one of outright victory in battle. But this was typical of all successful air campaigns in World War II – over time, the better organised and better resourced side always prevailed, without exemption, and irrespective of kill ratios. The RAF's Desert Air Force emphatically proved this point over North Africa in 1941–43: the Luftwaffe fighters consistently out-scored the RAF fighter squadrons in this campaign, but nonetheless failed to apply airpower effectively and so lost the air battle. Certainly, an air campaign could never be won in the Japanese fashion: by an interrupted program of on-again off-again raids, and the merely sporadic if sometimes sharp losses that these occasioned. Japanese doctrine held that the 'mental strength' of its warriors would overcome material shortages in battle, but in the remorseless arithmetic of an air campaign, there was no substitute for numbers.

Once the bigger campaigns further east started sucking in Japanese resources, there could never be enough left over to do a proper job of the Darwin campaign. Matériel shortcomings meant that only one big push could be fully supported, and after that one single day in February 1942, that push was always somewhere else, never again Darwin.

Postscript

Bypassed by MacArthur's push to the Philippines in 1944, the Japanese retained possession of Timor until the end of the war, and they continued to mount maritime patrol missions across the north-west Australian coast and to send occasional Ki-46 photo-reconnaissance missions to the Darwin area. One of these was intercepted and shot down by 54 Squadron over Truscott, Western Australia, on 20 July 1944, giving 1 Fighter Wing its last kill of the war. The last known penetration of Darwin's airspace was on 2 March 1945, when a Ki-46 arrived overhead in daylight, only belatedly recognised as enemy. By then, 452 and 457 had been moved forward to Morotai to join the RAAF's 1st Tactical Air Force. In a bizarre case of imperial penance, these two Australian squadrons were replaced at Darwin by 548 and 549 Squadrons RAF, thereby leaving three squadrons of bored British fighter pilots to see out the end of the war in a bypassed theatre where truly 'nothing ever happened'. Meanwhile, 452 and 457 joined 79 Squadron to form 80 Fighter Wing, with which on 20 June 1945, RAAF Spitfires scored their final victory, when pilots from 457 Squadron shot down another Ki-46 over Labuan in Borneo. The RAAF's relegated status within MacArthur's Americanised SWPA command is shown clearly in the fact that two entire wings of Spitfires claimed only five kills in total after the conclusion of the 1943 campaign.

Towards the end of 1943, 1 Fighter Wing's pilots began to be posted out as tour-expired. The British pilots of 54 Squadron were repatriated (sometimes after a tour of duty instructing at 2 OTU), while the Australians were distributed throughout

Australia in rear area RAAF establishments. There many of them served out the remainder of the war, left on the shelf by the prodigious output of trained pilots that the RAAF was by now producing, and left behind by a Pacific air war that from 1944 had become virtually an American monopoly. They served as flight instructors, staff officers, fighter controllers, base commanders – and sometimes even as fighter pilots! Even for the lucky ones who got a second tour with 452 or 457, there would be no more air combat, and thus the 1943 campaign would be the climax of their operational flying. The mercy of this was that, with very few exceptions, if they survived Darwin 1943, they survived the war. A snapshot of the pilots' post-NWA careers can be provided by some statistics from 457 Squadron: out of 46 pilots who flew with the unit in the NWA through to late 1943, only ten saw a second operational tour; and out of the 40 pilots who survived their service in 1943, only two failed to survive the war. By 1945, there were so many underemployed Spitfire pilots in the RAAF that several dozen of them transferred to the Royal Navy in a desperate attempt to see some air action with the Seafire squadrons of the British Pacific Fleet.

By 1945, the glut of EATS-trained fighter pilots in the RAAF was matched by a glut of Spitfires: there were so many of them in the inventory that they were coming off the wharves, stored at aircraft depots, and then scrapped postwar unflown. It was this sort of material profligacy, writ large across all Allied air forces, that had secured air supremacy and military victory in World War II.

Acknowledgments

My thanks go to Jane Murphy, Gary Conwell and Bill Tainsh for reading the manuscript, and to the National Archives of Australia and the Australian War Memorial for providing such user-friendly access to a national treasure: our archives. Thanks also to Lex McAulay for his corrections, suggestions and encouragement, to Christopher Shores for his kind provision of those old *Air Classics* articles, and to Trudy Cooper for producing two nice maps.

Without the generosity, respect and love given so unstintingly by Jane, Charlotte and Elizabeth, this book could never have been written.

References

Basic primary sources

Unit diaries and Operational Record Books (ORB) in the National Archives of
   Australia (NAA), Item A9186 (all NAA files used in this book are located in
   Canberra):
1 FW, in Item 662
7 RSU, in Item 371
31 Sqn, in Item 61
54 Sqn, in Item 89
452 Sqn, in Item 137
457 Sqn, in Item 143
5 Fighter Sector ORB, in AWM 54 Item 21/1.
Pilots' combat reports, composite combat reports, ammunition reports and other post-
   action correspondence in NAA A11326 Item 13/INT; A11231 Item 5/71/INT;
   and A9652 Box 30.
Spitfire casualty reports, in NAA A9845 Items 271–74.

Preface

Notes

p. xii   Peter Ingman, *Spitfire VC vs A6M2/3 Zero-Sen*, Osprey, 2019.
p. xii   J.D. Webster, 'Spitfires over Darwin – 1943', *Top Cover Issue 1*, Clash of Arms
         Games, 2013, pp. 18–26.
p. xii   Brian Weston, *A Coming Of Age For Australia And Its Air Force: The Air
         Campaign Over Northern Australia – 1943*, Canberra, Air Power Development
         Centre, 2013.
p. xii   *The Empire Strikes South*, Avonmore Books, 2017.

Introduction

Grant, *Spitfires over Darwin 1943*.
Odgers, *Air war against Japan 1943–1945*.
Shores, 'The Churchill Wing'.
Stephens, *The Royal Australian Air Force*.

Chapter 1   Playing catch-up
Notes

p. 1   For accounts of the 19 February raid, see: Gill, *Royal Australian Navy 1939–1942*, pp. 584–96; Gillison, *Royal Australian Air Force 1939–1942*, pp. 423–32; Grose, *An awkward truth*; Hall, *Darwin 1942*; Lockwood, *Australia's Pearl Harbor*; McCarthy, *South-West Pacific Area – First Year*, pp. 68–72; Mulholland, *Darwin bombed*; Powell, *The shadow's edge*, pp. 75–94; Harry Rayner, *Scherger*; Robert J Rayner, *The army and the defence of the Darwin fortress*; Shores et al., *Bloody shambles, Vol. Two*, pp. 174–83.

p. 2   For Imperial Navy strategy, see Evans & Peattie, *Kaigun*, pp. 406–11, 453–54.

p. 2   For no fighters and the non-air defence of Darwin, see Helson, *The forgotten air force*, pp. 47, 50, 58–60.

p. 2   For 'no real threat' to Australia doctrine, see Coulthard-Clark, *The third brother*, p. 443; and Williams, *These are facts*, pp. 224–25.

p. 2   For the prewar RAAF, see Coulthard-Clark, *The third brother*; Gillison, *Royal Australian Air Force*, pp. 1–57; and Stephens, *The Royal Australian Air Force*, pp. 25–57.

p. 2   For Burnett's preferment of RAF interests, see Hewitt, *Adversity in success*, pp. 5–7.

p. 3   For EATS, see McCarthy (1988) *The last call of empire*; Gillison, *Royal Australian Air Force*, pp. 79–89; and Stephens, *The Royal Australian Air Force*, pp. 59–74.

p. 3   For 1941 RAAF aircrew output, see John Golley, 'Training: a vital command', in Jarrett (ed.), *Aircraft of the Second World War*, p. 297.

p. 3   For the defeat of Allied fighter forces in early 1942, see Shores et al., *Bloody shambles, Vol. One*; Shores et al., *Bloody shambles, Vol. Two*; and Burton, *Fortnight of infamy*.

p. 4   For the 1942 Darwin campaign, see Cooper, 'Warhawks over Darwin', *The Territory at War* (2019), and Lewis, *Eagles over Darwin* (2021).

p. 4   For Japanese losses in 1942 Darwin raids, see Tagaya, *Mitsubishi Type 1* Rikko *'Betty' units of World War 2*, pp. 43–44; and Kawnano Teruaki, 'The Japanese Navy's air-raid against Australia', National Institute for Defence Studies, 29 August 1997, quoted in 'Takao Kokutai', www.j-aircraft.com, accessed 10.9.2009; and Pajdosz & Zbiegniewski, *3/202 Kokutai*, pp. 42–48.

p. 5   For Darwin's place in MacArthur's SWPA strategy, see Helson, *The forgotten air force*, pp. 48, 60.

p. 7   For the Brisbane Line, see Horner, *Crisis of command*, pp. 26–27, 48–50, 69–75, 85; and Burns, *The Brisbane Line controversy*.

p. 7   For radars, see Alexander, Cooper & Porter, 'Radar and the bombing of Darwin', *Historical Records of Australian Science*, 12-4: 429–55; Mellor, *The role of science and industry*, pp. 441–44; Lockwood, *Australia's Pearl Harbor*, pp. 146–47; and '105 Mobile RDF Station', and '39 Radar Station', in home. st.net.au/~dunn, accessed 2009.

p. 8   For radars on the US west coast, see Kenney, *General Kenney reports*, p. 17.

p. 8   For the superior radar ranges of 31 Radar Station over 105 Station, see 5 FS ORB, in AWM 54 Item 21/1.

p. 9   For 'second eleven', see Stephens, *Power plus attitude*, chapter 3.

p. 10   For Evatt and the Spitfire wing, see Freudenberg, *Churchill and Australia*, pp. 416–19.

p. 14   For Gibbs's CV, see Woodgate, *Lions and swans*, p. 79.

p. 15   For Foster's 'no experience' quote, see *Tally-Ho!*, p. 88.

p. 15   For 452 and 457 squadrons' records in the United Kingdom, see 'An account of the work of Australian personnel in single engine squadrons of Fighter Command', in AWM 173 Item 7/4 Folder 5.

p. 16   For 452 Squadron's overclaiming, see Cooper, *'Paddy' Finucane*, pp. 202–203.
p. 20   For the 452 legend, see Southall, *Bluey Truscott*, p. 93.
p. 20   For the Spitfire's media-image, see McKinstey, *Portrait of a legend*.
p. 20   For the squadrons' 1943 scorecard, see Woodgate, *Lions and Swans*, p. 160.
p. 26   For 23rd Air Flotilla strategy, see Odgers, *Air war against Japan*, p. 43
p. 26   For Japanese perimeter strategy and the policy of limited losses, see Rorrison,
         Nor the years contemn, p. 351.
p. 26   For 753 AG's 1942 campaigns and losses, see Tagaya, *'Betty' units*, pp. 63–64.
p. 26   For 3 AG and 753 AG Guadalcanal losses, see Lundstrom, *The first team and the
         Guadalcanal campaign.*
p. 27   For Japanese fighter units' oversupply of pilots and shortage of aircraft, see
         Lundstrom, *The first team: Pacific naval air combat from Pearl Harbor to Midway*,
         p. 45.
p. 27   For 'most redoubtable' fighter unit, see Peattie, *Sunburst*, pp. 259, 262.
p. 27   For 3/202 AG history, see Hata & Izawa, *Japanese naval aces and fighter units in
         World War II*, pp. 123–30, 270, 278, and appendix B.
p. 31   For Japanese reinforcement of Timor, see Gillison, *Royal Australian Air Force*,
         p. 648.

Chapter 2   The raid on Coomalie Creek
Primary sources
Combat reports in NAA A11231 Item 5/61/INT Part 3 and Item 5/70/INT.

Notes
p. 35   For RAAF Signals Intelligence, see Bleakley, *The eavesdroppers.*
p. 40   For RFC/RNAS quote, see Hanson, *First blitz*, p. 13.
p. 40   For Beaufighter operations, see McDonald, *Coomalie Charlie's Commandos*,
         pp. 22ff, 28, 53, 58–59.
p. 42   Regarding Bob Foster's status as the sole Battle of Britain veteran, Robin
         Norwood is stated as a fellow veteran; however, he only joined 65 Squadron
         on 2 September 1940, the month following its withdrawal to Scotland; and
         the unit did not return to southern England until November, following the
         conclusion of the battle – see Rawling, *Fighter Sqns of the RAF & their aircraft*,
         p. 161; and Wynn, *Men of the Battle of Britain*, p. 303.
p. 43   For Ki-46 fatalities, see Alford, *Darwin's air war*, p. 41.
p. 46   For AW radar's characteristics, see Alexander et al., 'Radar and the bombing of
         Darwin', pp. 443, 446.
p. 53   For Frank Gregory, see Rayner, *Darwin and Northern Territory Force*, p. 186.
p. 57   For Japanese decoy bomber tactic, see Lundstrom, *The first team and the
         Guadalcanal campaign*, pp. 261, 271.
p. 63   For evasive bunt, see Oxspring, *Spitfire command*, p. 45.
p. 66   For belly-tank splashes, see McAulay, *Into the dragon's jaws*, p. 69.
p. 66   For Japanese losses, see Shores, 'The Churchill Wing', *Air Classics*, 17-4:
         pp. 12–19; Shores's assessments are repeated more accessibly in Price, *Spitfire
         Mark V aces 1941–45*, pp. 69–76.
p. 68   For Bill Gibbs's appointment, see Foster, *Tally-Ho!*, p. 88.
p. 70   For Bobby Gibbes's opinion of Caldwell, see Alexander, *Clive Caldwell, air ace*,
         p. 85.
p. 71   For 49th FG's impression of RAAF, see Ferguson & Pascalis, *Protect & avenge*,
         pp. 26–27, 41.
p. 72   For Bladin's visit to New Guinea, see Hewitt, *Adversity in success*, p. 101.

Chapter 3   'A sharp reverse'
Primary sources
Combat reports in NAA A11231 Item 5/61/INT PART 3 and Item 5/71/INT.

Notes
p. 74   For Bladin's 'first plot' advice, see Gillison, *Royal Australian Air Force*, p. 559.

p. 76   For Japanese intelligence, see Evans & Peattie, *Kaigun*, pp. 416, 421–23; Kotani, *Japanese intelligence in World War II*, pp. 98–99, 108–109.

p. 76   For Japanese recognition of Spitfire threat, see Hata & Izawa, *Japanese naval aces*, p. 128.

p. 76   For Japanese bombing strategy, see Evans & Peattie, *Kaigun*, pp. 336–43.

p. 80   For Caldwell flying fast, see Alexander, *Clive Caldwell*, p. 85.

p. 89   For glycol leaks, see 'Ethylene glycol inhalation health effects' in akochealth, and 'coolant fluid vapor' in www.pilotfriend.com, accessed January 2010.

p. 89   For Varney's death, see Rayner, *Darwin and Northern Territory Force*, pp. 202, 204.

p. 93   For 2/11th machine gunners, see Rayner, *Darwin and Northern Territory Force*, p. 201.

p. 101   For Thorold-Smith's ditching, see Grant, *Spitfires over Darwin*, p. 68.

p. 102   For Finucane's advice on ditching, see Possé, *Together up there*, p. 61.

p. 105   For Caldwell's criticisms, see Bostock, HQ RAAF Command to HQ NWA, dated 30.3.1943; and Caldwell's 'Tactical Appreciation – Combat Darwin 15.3.43', from 1 FW to HQ NWA, 20.3.1943, in NAA A11231 Item 7/14/AIR.

p. 106   For Japanese inability to expand air forces, see Goldstein & Dillon, *The Pacific War papers*, pp. 23–24.

p. 110   For oxygen hypothesis, see Grant, *Spitfires over Darwin*, pp. 65–68.

p. 110   For Sly's testimony of Thorold-Smith, see *The luck of the draw*, p. 32.

p. 112   For MacDonald's CV, see NAA A9300 Item MACDONALD RS.

p. 114   For spraying fire, see CO 1 FW to all Sqns, dated 2.6.1943, quoting a signal from NWA to 1 FW dated 1.6.1943, in NAA A11231 Item 7/14/AIR.

p. 114   For Malan's rules, see Spick, *Allied fighter aces*, pp. 90–91; and Oxspring, *Spitfire command*, p. 73.

p. 115   For 20 mm ammunition effectiveness, see Gustin & Williams, *Flying guns*, pp. 39–49.

p. 115   For G4M fire extinguishers, see Takaya, *'Betty' units*, p. 68.

p. 119   For RAF confirmed kill criteria, see Stokes, *Paddy Finucane*, appendix C.

p. 120   For Zero's superior alloy, see Peattie, *Sunburst*, pp. 90–91.

p. 121   For Japanese 'turning-in' manoeuvre, see Peattie, *Sunburst*, appendix 9.

p. 122   For RAF view of aerobatics in combat, see Hillary, *The last enemy*, p. 67; and Price, *World War II fighter conflict*, p. 147.

p. 122   For RAF Air Fighting Tactics and 'cross over pairs', see NAA A11326 Item 8/1/INT.

p. 123   For Stan Turner's explanation, see Lucas, *Malta*, p. 29.

p. 123   For Major Johnson's view on lookout, see O'Leary (ed.), *VIII Fighter Command at war 'Long Reach'*, p. 33.

p. 123   For RAF combat formation confusion, see Shores & Ring, *Fighters over the desert*, p. 219.

p. 124   For Bluey Truscott's 'fluid fours' with 452, see AWM 173 Item 7/4 Folder 5, p. 44.

p. 124   For Kenley Wing, see Avery, *Spitfire leader*, pp. 51–53; and Johnson, *Wing leader*, p. 158.

p. 124 For desert air force line astern, see Brown, *Desert warriors*, pp. 15, 29, 43.

p. 124 For 54's vees, see Foster, *Tally-Ho!*, p. 167.

p. 125 For Japanese three-plane tactics, see Lundstrom, *The first team: Pacific naval air combat*, p. 610.

Chapter 4   Failure of the big wing

Primary sources

Report from HQ NWA to HQ RAAF Command, dated 26.5.43, in NAA A11231 Item 7/14/AIR.

Report on first 6 months' service of No. 452 SQN in SWPA (North West Australia) Feb. 6 to July 6, from 452 to NWA, dated 31.7.1943, in NAA A11295 Item 7/12/AIR PART 1.

Combat reports in NAA A11231 Item 5/72/INT.

Notes

p. 130 For Goldsmith's 'beat up', see Grant, *Spitfires over Darwin*, pp. 45–46.

p. 139 For no Spitfires in sight from the ground, see Foster, *Tally-Ho!* pp. 141, 143–48.

p. 146 For propeller failures, see Operational Notes for Pilots on Merlin 46 Engines, in 7/13/AIR; and Henshaw, *Sigh for a Merlin*, pp. 79, 133.

p. 147 For Fox's crash, see Woodgate, *Lions and swans*, p. 136.

p. 163 For MacDonald's recollections, see Morton, 'Spitfires over Darwin', pp. 19–24, 68–72.

p. 171 For 'youthful enthusiasm', see Alexander, 'The day the planes "all fell into the sea"'.

p. 173 For Spitfire drop-tank endurance, see CO 1 FW to NWA HQ dated 29.1.1943, in NAA A11231 Item 7/13/AIR.

p. 173 For Hardwick's story, see 'Pranged by the bloody navy', in Grant, *Spitfires over Darwin*, pp. 171–76.

p. 179 For systemic overclaiming, see F/O Quinn to Staff Intelligence Officer RAAF HQ NWA, 12 May 1943, in NAA A11231 Item 5/72/INT.

p. 180 For Japanese losses, see Lewis, pp. 102, 104.

p. 180 For US Navy damage statistics, see Price, *World War II fighter conflict*, pp. 59–60.

p. 182 For Hispano cannon, see Gustin & Williams, *Flying guns*, p. 27.

p. 182 For Austin Belt Feed Mechanism, see Grant, *Spitfires over Darwin*, p. 75.

p. 183 For wing climb rates, see 54 Sqn to 1 FW HQ dated 10.12.1943; and HQ 1 FW to 54, 452, and 457 Sqns, dated 12.1.44, in NAA A11231 Item 7/13/AIR.

p. 184 For USAAF fighter tactics, see Holmes (ed.) 'Twelve to one'; and O'Leary (ed.), 'Long Reach'.

p. 184 For the Luftwaffe's use of small group tactics and the RAF's slow learning in North Africa, see Shores & Ring, *Fighters over the desert*, chapter 12.

p. 185 For MacDonald's quote on losses and tactics, see NAA A9695 Item 1018.

p. 186 For 2 May Beaufighter raid, see Parnell, *Beaufighters in the Pacific*, p. 91; and McDonald, *Coomalie Charlie's Commandos*, p. 72.

p. 187 For Stagg's survival, see Grant, *Spitfires over Darwin*, p. 82; and Alford, *Darwin's air war*, p. 42.

Chapter 5   Dogfights over Milingimbi

Primary sources

Combat reports and correspondence in NAA A11231 Item 5/79/INT and Item 7/7/AIR.

Notes

p. 192 For Milingimbi base, see NAA A705 Items 7/1/694 and 151/2/752.

p. 192 For Milingimbi's port, see Hordern, *A merciful journey*, p. 95.

p. 193 For 934 AG, see Powell, *The shadow's edge*, p. 140; and McDonald, *Coomalie Charlie's Commandos*, pp. 101–102.

p. 193 For the *Patricia Cam* and Kentish's murder, see Powell, *The shadow's edge*, pp. 139–40.

p. 194 For Beaufighters, see Parnell, *Beaufighters in the Pacific*; and McDonald, *Coomalie Charlie's Commandos*.

p. 201 For Beaufighter VHF R/T, see request from NWA RAAF HQ to RAAF Command, dated 26.5.1943; and the negative reply from RAAF Command, dated 15.6.1943, in NAA A11312 Item 6/10/AIR.

Chapter 6   Success at last

Primary sources

457 Squadron combat reports in NAA A11231 Item 5/80/INT.

452 Squadron Fighter Combat Report, 'Interception enemy aircraft north of Milingimbi', in NAA A11231Item 5/61/INT PART 2.

Notes

p. 226 For Bladin's rebuke of Ken James, see Signal, NWA HQ to 1 Fighter Wing, dated 13.5.1943; and Letter, CO 1 Fighter Wing to 54, 452, and 457 Sqns, dated 14.5.1943, in NAA A11231 Item 7/7/AIR.

p. 241 For no parachuting, see Tagaya, *'Betty' units*, pp. 48–62.

p. 241 For US Navy high-deflection gunnery, see Lundstrom, *The first team: Pacific naval air combat*, pp. 580–87 and between pp. 402–403.

p. 241 For numerous examples of successful deflection gunnery, see Lundstrom, *The first team and the Guadalcanal campaign*.

p. 243 For US Navy pilots' seniority, see Lundstrom, *The first team and the Guadalcanal campaign*, pp. 537–45.

p. 243 For Wurtsmith's hours, see Craven & Cate (eds), *The Army Air Forces in World War II, Vol. One*, p. 412.

p. 243 For only 19 squadron leaders in RAAF, see Wilson, *The eagle and the albatross*, p. 173.

p. 244 For Mackie's view, see Avery, *Spitfire leader*, pp. 34–40.

p. 244 For Zemke's view, see O'Leary (ed.), *'Long Reach'*, p. 19.

p. 244 For Johnson's view, see Johnson, *Wing leader*, p. 126.

p. 245 For RAAF response to May combats, see CO 1 FW to all Sqns, dated 2.6.1943, in NAA A11231 Item 7/14/AIR; and HQ 1FW to 54, 452, and 457 Squadrons, dated 27.5.1943; and 1 FW to NWA HQ, dated 26.5.1943, 'Spitfire versus Zeke tactics', in A11231 Item 7/7/AIR.

p. 245 For underestimation of range, see Gustin & Williams, *Flying guns*, p. 94.

p. 245 For Smith's view, see Smith, *The Spitfire Smiths*, pp. 113, 115.

p. 248 For *Macumba*'s sinking, see Powell, *The shadow's edge*, p. 141.

Chapter 7   The army raid

Primary sources

'Report on enemy air operations – 22nd June 1943' by 5 FS, dated 23 Jun 1943, in NAA A11231 Item 5/61/INT PART 3.

Combat Reports in NAA 11231 Item 5/73/INT.

Notes

p. 254 For tactics, see Memo by G/C Walters, HQ 1 FW to HQ NWA, dated 27.5.1943, re. conference held by AOC NWA on 24.5.1943 and subsequent conference with Squadron COs on 26.5.1943; Memo HQ 1 FW to 54, 452, 457 Sqns on 'Spitfire Tactics', dated 27.5.1943; Memo HQ 1FW to HQ NWA on 'Spitfire versus Zeke-Tactics', dated 26.5.1943; all in NAA A11231 Item 7/7/AIR.

p. 257 For Garden's, Appleton's and Lambert's greenness, see Foster, *Tally-Ho!*, p. 152.

p. 259 For 753 AG inability to provide strike force, see Alford, *Darwin's air war*, p. 44.

p. 261 For 59th Sentai's record in New Guinea, see McAulay, *MacArthur's eagles*, pp. 64, 95–96.

p. 276 For Rowe's crash, see Grant, *Spitfires over Darwin*, p. 122.

p. 299 For 380th BG being caught in the move, see Wright, *The flying circus*, p. 97.

p. 303 For 54 Squadron 'worst raid yet', see Woodgate, *Lions and swans*, p. 145.

p. 303 For ML814's perspective, see Hordern, *A merciful journey*, p. 102.

p. 312 For Gibbs's outburst, see Foster, *Tally-Ho!*, p. 155.

p. 314 For 'Mizuno' POW, see 'ATIS PW Report No. 951' from Group 461 RAAF Darwin to 105 FCU, 23 Oct 1944, dated 12.10.1944, in NAA A11231 Item 5/73/INT.

p. 314 For 59th Sentai claims, see Sakaida, *Imperial Japanese Navy aces 1937–45*, p. 59.

p. 317 For floating bomber debris, see 'Air sea rescue – 20th June 1943', in AWM 64 Item 6/1.

p. 317 For Japanese official history, see Powell, *The shadow's edge*, pp. 184–85.

p. 317 For Japanese losses, see Lewis, p. 111.

p. 318 For incomplete IJAAF records, see Shindo, 'Japanese operations against the Australian mainland in the Second World War', in *Australia-Japan Research Project at the Australian War Memorial*, ajrp.awm.gov.au/ajrp, pp. 3–4, accessed 16.10.2009.

p. 318 For IJAAF loss discrepancies, see McAulay, *MacArthur's eagles*, pp. 58, 73, 91.

Chapter 8 A missed opportunity

Primary sources

Combat reports in NAA A11231 Item 5/74/INT.

Notes

p. 332 For Weatherhead's recollections, see Woodgate, *Lions and swans*, p. 235.

p. 332 For Gibbs's previous experience, see Woodgate, *Lions and swans*, p. 79.

p. 332 For Caldwell's court martial threat, see Grant, *Spitfires over Darwin*, p. 60.

p. 335 For German bombing tactics at Malta, see Brennan & Hesselyn, *Spitfires over Malta*; and Rolls, *Spitfire attack*, chapter. 6.

p. 351 For Ken James's previous experience, see 'Report of enemy raid on Darwin – 2/5/43 Raid No. 54', by 1 FW HQ, in NAA A11231 Item 5/72/INT.

p. 351 For prewar RAAF fighter training, see Coulthard-Clark, *The third brother*, pp. 179, 188, 190.

p. 353 For 240 hourly overhauls, see Grant, *Spitfires over Darwin*, p. 108.

p. 354 For individual aircraft histories, see Morgan & Shacklady, *Spitfire*, pp. 194–207.

p. 354 For 120-hour engine wear figure, see 'Report on first 6 months' service of No. 452 SQN in SWPA (North West Australia) Feb. 6 to July 6 1943', by F/L Maclean, acting CO 452, to SASO NWA, dated 31.7.1943; and 'Report on first six months' operational service of No. 54 Sqn in South West Pacific Area (N.W. Australia), by CO 54 Sqn to SASO NWA, dated 16.7.1943, both in NAA A11295 Item 7/12/AIR PART 1.

p. 354 For 54's flying hours, see Woodgate, *Lions and swans*, p. 153.

p. 354 For MacDonald's flying hours, see NAA A9300 Item MACDONALD RS.

Chapter 9   The first Fenton raid

Primary sources

Combat reports in NAA A11231 Item 5/75/INT.

Notes

p. 358   For 380th BG, see Odgers, *Air war against Japan*, p. 61; Alford, *Darwin's air war*, pp. 48–49; and Williams & Gotham, *We went to war*.

p. 358   For US bomber operations in the NWA, see Helson, *The forgotten air force*, pp. 128–31.

p. 361   For 118 AGT Co drivers, see Rayner, *Darwin and Northern Territory Force*, p. 282.

p. 382   For Luftwaffe-style Japanese tactics, see Lundstrom, *The first team: Pacific naval air combat*, p. 614.

p. 382   For .303 Browning's inaccuracy, see Gustin & Williams, *Flying guns*, p. 54.

p. 388   For Duncan's story, see Duncan, 'Fiery exit', in Grant, *Spitfires over Darwin*, pp. 180–94.

p. 399   For ground losses on 30 June at Fenton, see Williams & Gotham, *We went to war*, Part V and VI; and Alford, *Darwin's air war*, p. 49.

p. 410   For *Silver Beech* loss, see Odgers, *Air war against Japan*, p. 63.

p. 410   For Spitfire losses, see Grant, *Spitfires over Darwin*, appendix 4.

p. 411   For 54 Sqn's complaints re aircraft, see Memo, I.O. 54 to I.O. 1 FW, dated 6.7.1943, in NAA A11326 Item 13/INT.

Chapter 10   The second Fenton raid

Primary sources

Combat reports in NAA A11231 Item 5/76/INT.

Notes

p. 438   For Hamilton and the missing men of Blue Section, see Grant, *Spitfires over Darwin*, pp. 125–27.

p. 439   For the previous experience of Hamilton et al., see 1FW Report of enemy raid on Darwin – 2/5/43 Raid No. 54, in NAA A11231 Item 5/72/INT.

p. 440   For 1 Fighter Wing's deep line abreast formation, see 1 FW to NWA, 'Spitfire versus Zeke – Tactics', dated 26.5.1943, in NAA A11231 Item 7/7/7 Air; this is corroborated in Cotton, *Hurricanes over Burma*, pp. 328–37, and in Sortehaug, *The wild winds*, pp. 81–82, showing this deep formation to be normal in the late war RAF.

p. 458   For the Mt Litchfield bomber crash, see Rayner, *Darwin and Northern Territory Force*, p. 297.

p. 458   For Maruoka's feat, see Tagaya, *'Betty' units*, p. 69.

p. 459   For Bladin and Spitfire supply, see Odgers, *Air war against Japan*, p. 63.

p. 460   For 'the bomber will always get through', see McCarthy, 'Did the bomber always get through?: the control of strategic airspace, 1939–1945', in Stephens (ed.), *The war in the air 1914–1994*, p. 70.

Chapter 11   The defeat of Japanese reconnaissance

Primary sources

Report of Enemy Air Raid No. 59 on Darwin – 13 August 1943, by 5 FS, in NAA A11231 Item 5/77/INT.

Report of Enemy Air Raid No. 61 – 21 August 1943, by 5 FS, in NAA A11231
Item 5/78/INT.
Combat Reports in NAA A11231 Item 5/61/INT PART 2 and 3; and AWM 64
Item 6/1.

Notes

p. 465 For Japanese official history, see Powell, *The shadow's edge*, p. 185.
p. 467 For withdrawal of 202 AG to combat 380th BG raids, see Richard L Dunn,
12 O'Clock High forum, http://forum.12oclockhigh.net, quoted by Edward
Rogers in email dated 5.10.10.
p. 467 For 202 AG movements, see Hata & Izawa, *Japanese naval aces*, p. 130.
p. 471 For Spitfire performance, see Minute by DDTS dated 30.8.1943; and Signal by
DDTS dated 4.9.43; both in NAA A705 Item 9/53/27.
p. 472 For intercept plan for recco's, see HQ 1FW to HQ NWA 27.5.43, in NAA
A11231 Item 7/7/AIR.
p. 474 For Newton's journey, see Grant, *Spitfires over Darwin*, pp. 122–24, and 'Search
for and examination of crashed Japanese reconnaissance aircraft "Dinah"', by
F/O P Goldin, I.O. 457, to 1 FW HQ, dated 24 Jul 1943 in NAA Item 5/61/
INT Part 3.
p. 474 For 70th Squadron fatalities, see Alford, *Darwin's air war*, pp. 45–46; and
'Crash of a Japanese "Dinah" on Opium Creek Station', www.ozatwar.com/
ozcrashes/nt171.htm, accessed 20.10.2010. There are some unresolved
inconsistencies in crew identities.
p. 477 For 17 August recco sorties, see Pajdosz & Zbiegniewski, *3/202 Kokutai*, p. 76.
p. 487 For night-flying Spitfires, see Rolls, *Spitfire attack*, p. 32.
p. 488 For 54's night flying, see Gibbs's CO's report for September, quoted in
Woodgate, *Lions and swans*, p. 158.
p. 489 For Kittyhawk pilots' night sightings, see 5 FS Report, 'Detection of enemy
aeroplanes at night', in AWM 64 Item 6/1.
p. 489 For Spitfire blindness at night, see Wellum, *First light*, pp. 122–23.
p. 501 For MacDonald's combat, see Morton, 'Spitfires over Darwin', pp. 70–72.
p. 502 For shooting at parachutes, see Stokes, *Paddy Finucane*, p. 104; Park, *Angels
twenty*, p. 171, and Brown, *Desert warriors*, pp. 41, 86, 113.
p. 505 For R/T jamming, see 'Escorted Reconnaissance 7th September 1943, Report
by Signals Officer No. 1 Fighter Wing HQ on VHF Channel', in AWM 64
Item 6/1.
p. 509 For Whillans's obscenity, see Signal, RAAF Cmd to NWA HQ dated
26.9.1943, in AWM 64 Item 6/1.
p. 511 For Caldwell's comment on 7 September, see Alexander, *Clive Caldwell*, p. 152.
p. 513 For Mawer's death, see Mawer, *Diary of a Spitfire Pilot*, pp. 199–202.

Chapter 12 The accounting of battle

Primary sources

Combat reports in NAA A11231 Item 5/61/INT Part 2 and 3.

Notes

p. 523 For 12 November fatalities, see Tagaya, *'Betty' units*, p. 69.
p. 523 For Japanese casualties, see Shores, 'The Churchill Wing', pp. 17–18.
p. 526 For 20:1 kill ratio claim, see Hata & Izawa, *Japanese naval aces*, p. 129.
p. 528 For Caldwell's preference for 12.7 mm armament, see Woodgate, *Lions and
swans*, p. 42; and Alexander, *Clive Caldwell*, p. 162.
p. 529 For Ki-46 interceptions as 'exception', see 'Mitsubishi Ki-46', *Air International*
(Nov. 1980) 19-5, p. 231.

p. 529 For Battle of Britain unit statistics, see Alcorn, 'Top guns', p. 27 – out of 50 squadrons engaged, 23 achieved an overall exchange ratio of 1.2:1 or less. Also see Carlquist, 'Top guns analysed', p. 19 – on any given combat day, only seven out of 50 squadrons 'won their battle' by obtaining an exchange ratio of 1:1 or better.

p. 529 For RAF Fighter Command's 1941–42 statistics, see Sims, *The fighter pilots*, pp. 184–88; Franks, *Aircraft versus aircraft*, pp. 96–98; and Terraine, *The right of the line*, p. 285.

p. 529 For Price's statement, see *Spitfire Mark V aces*, p. 6.

p. 529 For Malta air combat statistics, see Shores et al., *Malta*, pp. 645–64.

p. 529 For Spitfire operations over the Western Desert, see Shores & Ring, *Fighters over the desert*, chapters 9–11; for Spitfire air defence of Calcutta, see Shores, *Air war for Burma*, pp. 125–29, 139–43.

p. 531 For MacDonald's report and career, see NAA A9300 Item MACDONALD RS.

p. 533 For 453 Squadron statistics, see Bennett, *Defeat to victory*.

p. 533 For 485 Squadron statistics, see Sortehaug & Listemann, *No. 485 (N.Z.) Squadron 1941–1945*, pp. 48–52.

p. 533 For squadrons' loss statistics, see Franks, *Royal Air Force Fighter Command losses of the Second World War, Vol. 2*.

p. 533 For boredom, see Woodgate, *Lions and swans*, p. 105.

p. 533 For 452's negative attitude to service in Australia, see Southall, *Bluey Truscott*, pp. 140, 142.

p. 534 For Johnson's complaint, see Johnson, *The story of air fighting*, p. 196.

p. 534 For 705 and 753 AG movements, see Tagaya, *'Betty' units*, p. 69.

p. 534 For 'dogged determination' in attacking bombers, see Shores & Ring, *Fighters over the desert*, p. 220.

p. 534 For the fate of 753 AG, see Tagaya, *'Betty' units*, pp. 81–82.

p. 535 For Japanese belief in 'mental strength', see Jisaburo Ozawa, 'Development of the Japanese Navy's operational concept against America', in Goldstein, *The Pacific War papers*, p. 74.

p. 536 For 20 July 1944 kill, see Report in NAA A11326 Item 1/5/INT.

p. 536 For 2 March 1945 recco, see Rayner, *Darwin and Northern Territory Force*, p. 2.

p. 536 For 548 and 549 Sqn in Australia, see Possé, *Together up there*.

p. 536 For 457 pilots' post 1943 statistics, see Grant & Listemann, *No. 457 (R.A.A.F.) Squadron*, pp. 54–88.

Bibliography

Air International, 'Mitsubishi Ki-46: the aesthetic Asian', vol. 19, no. 5 (November 1980), pp. 227–33.

Alcorn, John, 'Battle of Britain top guns', *Aeroplane* (July 2000), pp. 24–29.

Alexander, Bruce, Cooper, Brian & Porter, Hal (1999) 'Radar and the bombing of Darwin', *Historical Records of Australian Science*, 12-4: pp. 429–55.

Alexander, Kristen, 'The day the planes "all fell into the sea": Darwin Raid 54 – 2 May 1943', *Sabretache*, March 2005, in findarticles.com, accessed 17.11.2009.

—— (2006) *Clive Caldwell, air ace*, Allen & Unwin, Sydney.

Alford, Bob (1991) *Darwin's air war 1942–1945: An illustrated history*, Aviation Historical Society of the Northern Territory, Darwin.

Avery, Max with Shores, Christopher (1997) *Spitfire leader: the story of Wing Commander Evan 'Rosie' Mackie, DSO, DFC and bar, DFC (US), top scoring RNZAF fighter ace*, Grub Street, London.

Bennett, John (1994) *Defeat to victory: No. 453 Squadron RAAF*, RAAF Museum, Point Cook, Victoria.

—— (1995) *Highest traditions: the history of No 2 Squadron, RAAF*, Australian Government Printing Service, Canberra.

Bleakley, Jack (1992) *The eavesdroppers*, Australian Government Publishing Service, Canberra.

Brennan, Paul, Hesselyn, Ray & Bateson, Henry (1943) *Spitfires over Malta*, Consolidated Press, Sydney.

Brown, Russell (2000) *Desert warriors: Australian P-40 pilots at war in the Middle East and North Africa 1941–1943*, Banner Books, Maryborough, Queensland.

Bungay, Stephen (2001) *The most dangerous enemy: a history of the Battle of Britain*, Aurum Press, London.

Burns, Paul (1998) *The Brisbane Line controversy: political opportunism versus national security, 1942–45*, Allen & Unwin, Sydney.

Burton, John (2006) *Fortnight of infamy: the collapse of Allied airpower west of Pearl Harbor*, Naval Institute Press, Annapolis.

Carlquist, Tom, 'Top guns analysed – combat efficiency', *Aeroplane* (October 2000), p. 19.

Cooper, Anthony (2016) *'Paddy' Finucane and the legend of the Kenley Wing*, Fonthill, Stroud.

Cooper, Anthony (2019) 'Warhawks over Darwin: The 1942 Campaign', *The Territory at War*, Katherine Historical Society, Katherine, pp. 98–112.

Cotton, MC 'Bush' (1995) *Hurricanes over Burma*, Crawford House Publishing, Bathurst, NSW.

Coulthard-Clark, CD (1991) *The third brother: the Royal Australian Air force 1921–39*, Allen & Unwin, Sydney.

Craven, Wesley Frank & Cate, James Lea (eds) (1948) *The Army Air Forces in World War II, Vol. 1: Plans & early operations, January 1939 to August 1942*, University of Chicago Press, Chicago.

Craven, Wesley Frank & Cate, James Lea (eds) (1950) *The Army Air Forces in World War II, Vol. 4: The Pacific: Guadalcanal to Saipan*, University of Chicago Press, Chicago.

Cross, Robin (1987) *The bombers: the illustrated story of offensive strategy and tactics in the twentieth century*, Bantam Press, London.

Ellis, John (1990) *Brute force: Allied strategy and tactics in the Second World War*, Andre Deutsch, London.

Evans, David C & Peattie, Mark R (1997) *Kaigun: strategy, tactics and technology in the Imperial Japanese Navy, 1887–1941*, Naval Institute Press, Annapolis.

Ewer, Peter (2009) *Wounded eagle: the bombing of Darwin and Australia's air defence scandal*, New Holland Publishers, Sydney.

Ferguson, SW & Pascalis, William K (1996) *Protect and avenge: the 49th Fighter Group in World War II*, Schiffer Publishing, Atglen, Pennsylvania.

Foster, RW with Franks, Norman (2008) *Tally-Ho! From the Battle of Britain to the defence of Darwin*, Grub Street, London.

Francillon, René (1987) *Japanese aircraft of the Pacific War*, Naval Institute Press, Annapolis.

Franks, Norman (1986) *Aircraft versus aircraft: the illustrated story of fighter pilot combat since 1914*, Bantam Press, London.

Franks, Norman LR (1998) *Royal Air Force Fighter Command losses of the Second World War, Vol. 2: Operational losses 1942–1943*, Midland Publishing, Hinckley, Leicestershire.

Freudenberg, Graham (2008) *Churchill and Australia*, Pan Macmillan, Sydney.

Gibbs, EM (1943) 'Scramble!', *RAAF Log*, Australian War Memorial, Canberra.

Gill, G Hermon (1985) *Royal Australian Navy 1939–1942*, Collins, Sydney.

——— (1968) *Royal Australian Navy 1942–1945*, Collins, Sydney.

Gillison, Douglas (1962) *Royal Australian Air Force 1939–1942*, Australian War Memorial, Canberra.

Goldstein, Donald M & Dillon, Katherine V (eds) (2004) *The Pacific War papers: Japanese documents of World War II*, Potomac Books, Washington DC.

Grant, Jim (1996) *Spitfires over Darwin 1943: No. 1 Fighter Wing*, RJ Moore, Melbourne.

Grant, Jim & Listemann, Phil (2007) *No. 457 (R.A.A.F.) Squadron 1941–1945: Spitfire*, Philedition, Boé Cedex, France.

Grose, Peter (2009) *An awkward truth: the bombing of Darwin February 1942*, Allen & Unwin, Sydney.

Gustin, Emmanuel & Williams, Anthony G (2003) *Flying guns – World War II: the development of aircraft guns, ammunition and installations 1933–45*, Airlife Publishing, Shrewsbury.

Hall, Timothy (1980) *Darwin 1942: Australia's darkest hour*, Methuen Australia, Sydney.

Hanson, Neil (2008) *First blitz: the never-before-told story of the German plan to raze London to the ground in 1918*, Doubleday, London.

Hata, Ikuhiko & Izawa, Yasuho (1995) *Japanese naval aces and fighter units in World War II*, Naval Institute Press.

Hata, Ikuhiko, Izawa, Yasuho & Shores, Christopher (2002) *Japanese Army air forces units and their aces 1931–1945*, Grub Street, London.

Helson, Peter (1997) *The forgotten air force: the establishment and employment of Australian air power in the North-Western Area 1941–1945*, MA Thesis, UNSW.

Henshaw, Alex (1990) *Sigh for a Merlin: the testing of the Spitfire*, Arrow Books, London.

Hewitt, JE (1980) *Adversity in success: extracts from Air Vice Marshal Hewitt's diaries 1939–1948*, Langate Publishing, Melbourne.

Higham, Robin & Harris, Stephen J (eds) (2006) *Why air forces fail: the anatomy of defeat*, The University Press of Kentucky, Lexington.

Hillary, Richard (1969) *The last enemy*, Pan Books, London.

Holmes, Tony (ed.) (2004) *'Twelve to one': V Fighter Command aces of the Pacific*, Osprey, Oxford.

Hordern, Marsden (2005) *A merciful journey: recollections of a World War II patrol boat man*, Miegunyah Press, Melbourne.

Horner, David (1982) *High command: Australia's struggle for an independent war strategy, 1939–45*, Allen & Unwin, Sydney.

Horner, DM (1978) *Crisis of command: Australian generalship and the Japanese threat, 1941–1943*, Australian National University Press, Canberra.

Ingman, Peter (2019) *Spitfire VC vs A6M2/3 Zero-Sen: Darwin 1943*, Osprey Publishing, Oxford.

Jackson, Robert (2003) *Combat legend: Mitsubishi Zero*, Airlife Publishing, Marlborough, Wiltshire.

Jarrett, Philip (ed.) (1997) *Aircraft of the Second World War: the development of the warplane 1939–45*, Putnam, London.

Johnson, JE (1956) *Wing leader*, Chatto & Windus, London.

—— (1987) *The story of air fighting*, Arrow Books, London.

Jones, George (1988) *From private to air marshal: the autobiography of Air Marshal Sir George Jones*, Greenhouse Publications, Richmond, Victoria.

Kenney, George (1997) *General Kenney reports: a personal account of the Pacific War*, Office of Air Force History.

Kotani, Ken (2009) *Japanese intelligence in World War II*, Osprey, Oxford.

Lewis, Tom (2017) *The Empire Strikes South: Japan's Air War Against Northern Australia 1942–45*, Avonmore Books, Adelaide.

Lewis, Tom (2021) *Eagles over Darwin: American Airmen Defending Northern Australia in 1942*, Avonmore Books, Adelaide.

Lockwood, Douglas (1988) *Australia's Pearl Harbor: Darwin 1942*, Penguin, Melbourne.

Lucas, Laddie (1992) *Malta – the thorn in Rommel's side: six months that turned the war*, Stanley Paul, London.

Lundstrom, John B (1994) *The first team: Pacific naval air combat from Pearl Harbor to Midway*, Naval Institute Press, Annapolis.

—— (1994) *The first team and the Guadalcanal campaign: naval fighter combat from August to November 1942*, Naval Institute Press, Annapolis.

MacLeod, Roy (1999) 'Revisiting Australia's wartime radar programme', *Historical Records of Australian Science*, 12-4: pp. 411–18.

McAulay, Lex (1986) *Into the dragon's jaws: the Fifth Air Force over Rabaul*, Champlin Fighter Museum Press, Mesa, Arizona.

—— (1989) *Against all odds: RAAF pilots in the Battle for Malta 1942*, Hutchinson Australia, Sydney.

—— (1998) *Four aces: RAAF fighter pilots, Europe and North Africa 1941–44*, Banner Books, Maryborough, Queensland.

—— (2005) *Macarthur's eagles: The U.S. air war over New Guinea, 1943–1944*, Naval Institute Press, Annapolis.

McCarthy, Dudley (1959) *South-West Pacific Area – First Year: Kokoda to Wau*, Australian War Memorial, Canberra.

McCarthy, John (1988) *The last call of empire: Australian aircrew, Britain and the Empire Air Training Scheme*, Australian War Memorial, Canberra.

McDonald, Kenneth Neal (1996) *Coomalie Charlie's Commandos: 31 Squadron RAAF Beaufighters at Darwin 1942–43*, Banner Books, Maryborough, Queensland.

McKinstey, Leo (2007) *Portrait of a legend: Spitfire*, John Murray, London.

Mawer, Allen Granville (2011) *Diary of a Spitfire Pilot over the English Channel and over Darwin*, Rosenberg Publishing, Sydney.

Mellor, DP (1958) *The role of science and industry*, Australian War Memorial, Canberra.

Minnett, Harry (1999) 'Light-Weight Air Warning Radar', *Historical Records of Australian Science*, 12-4: pp. 457–67.

Morgan, Eric B & Schacklady, Edward (2000) *Spitfire: the history*, Key Books, Stamford, Lincolnshire.

Morton, Fred (1980) 'Spitfires over Darwin: the story of the Royal Australian Air force's Churchill Wing and their battle against the Japanese', *Air Classics*, 16-9: pp. 19–24, 68–72.

Mulholland, Jack (2009) *Darwin bombed: an A/A gunner's reflections*, Jack Mulholland, Wyoming, NSW.

Odgers, George (1957) *Air war against Japan 1943–1945*, Australian War Memorial, Canberra.

O'Leary, Michael (ed.) (2000) *VIII Fighter Command at war 'Long Reach': the official training document compiled from the experiences of the fighter escorts of the 'Mighty Eighth'*, Osprey Aviation, Oxford.

Overy, Richard (1996) *Why the allies won*, Pimlico, London.

Overy, RJ (1987) *The air war 1939–1945*, Papermac, London.

Oxspring, Bobby (2004) *Spitfire command*, Cerberus, Bristol.

Pajdosz, Waldemar & Zbiegniewski, Andre R. (2003) *3/202 Kokutai*, Kagero, Lublin, Poland.

Park, Ted (1994) *Angels twenty: a young American flier a long way from home*, University of Queensland Press, Brisbane.

Parnell, NM (2005) *Beaufighters in the Pacific: a history of the RAAF Beaufighter squadrons in the South West Pacific Area*, NM Parnell.

Peattie, Mark R (2001) *Sunburst: the rise of Japanese naval air power, 1909–1941*, Naval Institute Press, Annapolis.

Possé, Victor (2003) *Together up there: the unit history of No. 549 RAF/RAAF fighter squadron in Australia during World War Two*, Australian Military History Publications, Sydney.

Powell, Alan (1992) *The shadow's edge: Australia's northern war*, Melbourne University Press, Melbourne.

Price, Alfred (1975) *World War II fighter conflict*, MacDonald & Jane's, London.

—— (1976) *The bomber in World War II*, MacDonald & Jane's, London.

—— (1989) *The Spitfire story*, Arms and Armour, London.

—— (1992) *Spitfire: a complete fighting history*, PRC, Hong Kong.

—— (1997) *Spitfire Mark V aces 1941–45*, Osprey, London.

—— (1997) 'Myth and legend', Part 1, *Aeroplane Monthly*, October, pp. 20–23.

—— (1997) 'Myth and legend', Part 2, *Aeroplane Monthly*, November, pp. 12–15.

Price, Alfred & Blackah, Paul (2007) *Supermarine Spitfire 1936 onwards (all marks): Owners' Workshop Manual, an insight into owning, restoring, servicing and flying Britain's legendary World War II fighter*, Haynes Publishing, Yeovil, UK.

RAAF Directorate of Public Relations (1943) 'Spits up north', *RAAF Log*, Australian War Memorial, Canberra, pp. 74–79.

Rawling, John DR (1969) *Fighter Sqns of the RAF & their aircraft*, MacDonald, London.

Rayner, Harry (1984) *Scherger: a biography of Air Chief Marshal Sir Frederick Scherger*, Australian War Memorial, Canberra.

Rayner, Robert J (1995) *The army and the defence of the Darwin fortress: exploding the myths of the critical phase, 'til September 1942*, Rudder Press, Plumpton, NSW.

—— (2001) *Darwin and Northern Territory Force*, Southwood Press, Sydney.

Rolls, William T (2004) *Spitfire attack*, Cerberus, Bristol.

Rorrison, James D (1992) *Nor the years contemn: air war on the Australian front 1941–42*, JD Rorrison, Brisbane.

Royal Air Force Museum (1976) *The Spitfire V Manual*, Arms and Armour Press, London.

Sakaida, Henry (1999) *Imperial Japanese Navy aces 1937–45*, Osprey, Oxford.

Sarkar, Dilip (2006) *Bader's Duxford Fighters: the big wing controversy*, Victory Books, Worcester.

Shindo, Hiroyuki (2001) 'Japanese air operations over New Guinea during the Second World War', *Journal of the Australian War Memorial*, June 2001, in findarticles.com, accessed 10.9.2009.

—— 'Japanese operations against the Australian mainland in the Second World War: a survey of Japanese historical sources', *Australia–Japan Research Project at the Australian War Memorial*, ajrp.awm.gov.au/ajrp, pp. 3–4, accessed 16.10.2009.

Shores, Christopher (1981) 'The Churchill Wing: a radical reassessment', *Air Classics*, 17-4: pp. 12–19.

—— (2005) *Air war for Burma: the Allied air forces fight back in South East Asia 1942–1945*, Grub Street, London.

Shores, Christopher & Cull, Brian with Malizia, Nicola (1991) *Malta: the Spitfire year 1942*, Grub Street, London.

Shores, Christopher & Cull, Brian with Izawa, Yasuho (1992) *Bloody shambles, Vol. One: The drift to war to the fall of Singapore*, Grub Street, London.

Shores, Christopher & Cull, Brian with Izawa, Yasuho (2009) *Bloody shambles, Vol. Two: The defence of Sumatra to the fall of Burma*, Grub Street, London.

Shores, Christopher & Ring, Hans (1969) *Fighters over the desert: the air battles in the Western Desert June 1940 to December 1942*, Arco Publishing Co., New York.

Sims, Edward H (1967) *The fighter pilots: a comparative study of the Royal Air Force, the Luftwaffe and the United States Army Air Force in Europe and North Africa 1939–45*, Cassell, London.

Sly, Edward (2003) *The luck of the draw: horses, Spitfires and Kittyhawks*, Publishing Services, Sydney.

Smith, RIA with Shores, Christopher (2008) *The Spitfire Smiths: a unique story of brothers in arms*, Grub Street, London.

Sortehaug, Paul (1998) *The wild winds: the history of Number 486 RNZAF fighter squadron with the RAF*, Paul Sortehaug, Dunedin, NZ.

Sortehaug, Paul & Listemann, Phil (2006) *No. 485 (N.Z.) Squadron 1941–1945*, Philedition.

Southall, Ivan (1958) *Bluey Truscott: Squadron Leader Keith William Truscott, R.A.A.F., D.F.C. and Bar*, Angus & Robertson, Sydney.

Spick, Mike (1997) *Allied fighter aces: the air combat tactics and techniques of World War II*, Greenhill Books, London.

Stanaway, John C & Hickey, Lawrence J (1995) *Attack and conquer: the 8th Fighter Group in World War II*, Schiffer, Atglen, PA.

Stanley, Peter (2008) *Invading Australia: Japan and the battle for Australia, 1942*, Viking, Melbourne.

Stephens, Alan (1992) *Power plus attitude: ideas, strategy and doctrine in the Royal Australian Air Force 1921–1991*, Australian Government Printing Service, Canberra.

—— (2001) *The Royal Australian Air Force: the Australian Centenary History of Defence, Vol. II*, Oxford University Press, Melbourne.

—— (ed.) (2001) *The war in the air 1914–1994*, Air University Press, Maxwell Air Force Base, Alabama.

Stokes, Doug (1983) *Paddy Finucane: fighter ace*, William Kimber, London.

Tagaya, Osamu (2001) *Mitsubishi Type 1 Rikko 'Betty' units of World War 2*, Osprey, Oxford.

Terraine, John (1988) *The right of the line: the Royal Air Force in the European War 1939–1945*, Hodder & Stoughton, Sevenoaks, Kent.

Wellum, Geoffrey (2003) *First light*, Penguin, London.

Williams, Richard (1977) *These are facts: the autobiography of Air Marshal Sir Richard Williams*, Australian War Memorial, Canberra.

Williams, Theodore J & Gotham, Barbara J (2007) *We went to war: 380th Bomb Group – World War II*, Theodore J Williams, West Lafayette.

Wilson, David Joseph (2003) *The eagle and the albatross: Australian aerial maritime operations 1921–1971*, PhD Thesis, University of New South Wales.

Woodgate, Fred (1992) *Lions and swans: the continuing story of No. 54 (Fighter) Squadron, Royal Air Force, with detailed account of Spitfires in Darwin, 1943–1945*, Fred Woodgate, Sydney.

Wright, Jim (2005) *The flying circus: Pacific War 1943 as seen through a bombsight*, The Lyons Press, Guildford, Connecticut.

Wynn, Kenneth G (1989) *Men of the Battle of Britain*, Gliddon books, Norwich.

www.adf-serials.com

Index